A Song for Else

A SONG
for
ELSE

VOLUME II
The Overthrow

BY
CHRISTOPHER J.
ZEHNDER

AROUCA
PRESS

ISBN: 978-1-99918-27-3-1 (pbk)
ISBN: 978-1-990685-28-6 (hardcover)

Arouca Press
PO Box 55003
Bridgeport PO
Waterloo, ON N2J 3G0
Canada
www.aroucapress.com
Send inquiries to info@aroucapress.com

For Katherine

HISTORICAL NOTE

IN THE PREFACE THAT INTRODUCES THE first volume of *A Song for Else* (*The Vow*), I delineated briefly the periods covered by each of the parts of my trilogy. This, the second volume, I wrote, "takes up the story's thread and pulls it through the epoch that is sometimes called 'the heroic period' of the Reformation." This period is perhaps the most interesting in the story of that great religious, cultural, and political revolution. Indeed, it was its most creative time, the period of its youth, when the Reformation movement had not yet passed into the "middle age" of its institutionalization or been coöpted by the cynicism of politics. Like innocence, it did not last long, a mere eight or nine years; but it was so brief a time that established the phenomenon of Protestantism, the seed of our modern and, now, post-modern world.

I invite my readers to rejoin our protagonist, Lorenz List, as he stumbles his way through the confusion of the Reformation's "heroic years." To help readers on this journey—cognizant as I am that the events of the German Reformation are not as well-known to English speakers as the corresponding events in England—I have provided a brief timeline of the major happenings that form the background of my story. The skeletal overview that follows will not provide readers with a thorough account of the time and its events (I hope my novel inspires to further study), but it will help place the story in its historical context.

1516 In October, the bubonic plague (Black Death) strikes Wittenberg.

1517 On October 31, the Eve of All Saints, Martin Luther nails his Ninety-Five Theses on indulgences to the door of the Castle Church in Wittenberg—the opening act of the Reformation. Soon the theses, translated from Latin into German, are distributed by pamphlet form throughout Germany.

1518 Luther, already a celebrated and vilified figure, offers his theses on grace at the chapter of the Augustinian Order in Heidelberg.

In June, the process against Luther initiated in Rome. Luther meets Cardinal Cajetan during the *Reichstag* in Augsburg. Cajetan urges him to recant.

1519 Luther's criticisms of Rome and the Church grow more trenchant and heretical.

In July, Karlstadt and Luther debate Johannes Eck in Leipzig. Luther rejects the authority, not only of the pope, but of ecumenical councils.

1520 In June, Pope Leo X issues a bull, *Exsurge Domine*, condemning Luther's errors and threatening excommunication if he refuses to recant. Luther's old enemy, Johannes Eck, delivers the bull to Germany.

From August to October, Luther issues three great pamphlets that develop his teachings on the authority of the Church, the sacraments, and Christian liberty: *To the Christian Nobility of the German Nation, On the Babylonian Captivity of the Church,* and *On the Freedom of the Christian Man.*

On December 10, Luther publicly burns the pope's bull in Wittenberg.

1521 Luther, before Kaiser Karl V at the *Reichstag* in Worms, refuses to recant.

The Kaiser and *Reichstag* issue the Edict of Worms, condemning and outlawing Luther

Luther goes into hiding at Wartburg Castle.

A radical reformation takes hold in Wittenberg. Luther secretly visits the city and approves the progress of the reform. The "Zwickau Prophets" preach in Wittenberg.

1522 In March, Luther returns to Wittenberg and condemns his radical followers.

1523 Luther marries Katharina von Bora

1524 The Peasants' Revolt begins in the summer.

1525 In March, the city of Nürnberg embraces the Reformation and abolishes the Mass.

In the spring, the Peasants Revolt is crushed.

A SONG
for
ELSE

VOLUME II
The Overthrow

Ach, Else, liebes Elslein mein,
Wie gern wär ich bei dir!
So sein zwei tiefe Wasser
Wohl zwischen dir und mir.

Das bringt mir große Schmerzen,
Herzallerliebster Gsell!
Und ich von ganzem Herzen
Halt's für groß Ungefäll.

Hoff, Zeit wird es wohl enden,
Hoff, Glück wird kommen drein,
Sich in all's Gut verwenden,
Herzliebstes Elselein.

Ach, Else, longed-for Elselein,
How I long to be with thee!
For so the deep mid shorelines
Far sunders thee from me.

Which brings me deepest anguish,
Heart's all beloved friend!
And I, heart's eyes full open,
Behold my fortune's end.

My hope, that time will end well,
That good hap may be mine,
That all will end in love's joy,
My longed-for Elselein.

Es waren zwei Königskinder,
Die haben einander so lieb,
Sie konnten zusammen nicht kommen
Das Wasser war viel so tief . . .

There were two king's children,
Who loved each other so
Each could not come to the other
For the water that was too deep.

INTERLUDE

DARKEST MORNING. THE CANDLE HAD guttered out. The moon had long since set.

How long until sunrise?

He could not see her. If he reached out, he could touch her. But he could see nothing—not her, not the wax-like pallid sheen of her cold, cold skin. Not the picture just above her bed—the image of Flora, depicted by a skilled hand.

How long until sunrise?

Light, only light, he thought, could delineate the lines, restore color to the cheek, enkindle the flesh with warmth. Light, light of sun, not the moon sheen revealing, distorting. He could not see her now; not by candle flame, not by cold moonlight.

How long until sunrise?

Did he want the sunrise? Its light would only show him, however close she lay, how far she was from him. Better the darkness deceiving than the truth-telling light. Now, at least, he could think her as far from him in flesh as she was in spirit.

The deep water sundered them.

* * *

Then it had been different. He had written the letter, sealed it, and sent it to her with the next pack train to Nürnberg. He had thought, "I have severed the tie that bound us, I have bound myself to another. The memory will fade with the passing of time; distance and time will ease the longing. Sight of her will not kindle desire. She will become as a distant memory . . . "

But the memory did not fade, the longing did not ease. It rather grew more distinct, day after day—those days when he and Sebastian were preparing themselves to enter the cloister. Sebastian seemed suffused with quiet joy; "but I, myself, felt nothing." No, rather, he did feel something—desire for Beatrice, whom he had made Else. Why, he thought, "why do I know no peace? I do not ask for joy, only peace and the cessation of desire." But the desire did not abate—and when he thought of the monastery, he felt only a dead hollowness within.

But then he thought—was this a trial to test his resolve? Perhaps God was allowing the test, to see if he would persevere in his vow. The cloister is a battlefield, where demons flocked to defeat the heroes of Christ. When he passed into the monastery, he would be stepping out onto the field of battle. But, he thought, even if I am assailed from without, I shall be strengthened by peace, a peace within.

But what did he feel when he and Sebastian entered the cloister as postulants only a few days past Epiphany? He felt nothing. Even in the peace of the cloister, he felt no peace. He felt no turmoil. It was as if he were dead inside.

* * *

Her body on the bed before him. Had he ever really known peace? He had tasted it in the church at Weissenbrücke; it had teased him when he had embraced her that dark night, under the spreading limbs. And when, after so many years, he had held her again—but, no, he had found no peace then. He had found pleasure, but no peace. The union of their bodies had left their souls wide asunder, though they pretended it was not so.

Fulcite me floribus,
stipite me mala ,
quia amore langueo . . .

6

But love proved naught but dust and ashes.

Was she now at peace? He had given her peace, though by all he thought right, he ought not have. He could not give peace; it was not his to give. But when he had signed her, he believed he was giving what he himself did not possess.

Rest.

Final reconciliation.

Peace.

* * *

It had been the peace of a corpse he had felt as postulant. And nothing changed as closer loomed the day of his profession.

He and Sebastian were received together as novices. And he recalled that, in the months of the novitiate, he was no less intense in his prayers than Sebastian. He fasted and kept vigil. He sought to spark some small feeling in his breast—but he could feel nothing; that is, except for *her*. Sebastian, however, seemed to burn with divine desire. Lorenz would, looking askance, catch a glimpse of his friend—at Mass, praying the Divine Office, even when performing menial tasks—his countenance wore a light of whose source Lorenz knew nothing.

But one day, he found Sebastian despondent. When he inquired the cause, Sebastian turned to him and begged his prayers. "I feel I am not worthy—indeed, I am not worthy. But you—I feel you are very close to God . . ." Lorenz promised to pray for his friend; but, he thought, it could do him no good. And he wondered what Sebastian would think, if he saw the inside of him.

Indeed, what would Sebastian have thought had he read his thoughts the day when the two of them, prostrate before the altar, heard the words, "What do you seek?" He heard Sebastian's voice: "God's grace, and your mercy." And he repeated the words.

Then he could hear the prior raise Sebastian to his feet. Then—

7

"Are you anyone's bondsman?"

"No."

"Have you any secret disease?"

"No"

"Are you married?"

"No."

Are you married? It was then that all became clear to him, and a cold dread seized him. That question would be asked of him, and what would he answer? They had vowed to one another; they had consummated their vows: were they not man and wife? But he had vowed himself to God — to the very life to which this question ("are you married?") like a gate barred the way. He could open the gate, but only with a lie. If he spoke the truth, he would be shut out from God's mercy — but could one buy God's mercy with a lie?

He felt himself being raised. He heard himself answer, "no," to each question. Then the prior asked that question. He hesitated. Doubt confused him. Fear like a million tiny pin thrusts pricked at his mind and heart. He wondered that the prior's countenance did not change — did he not wonder why the answer was so long in coming? When at last he had resolved to answer, he felt he could not command his voice. But the word leaped to life in his mind, and then hesitated on the threshold of the lips: "yes, I am married . . . " he would say. "Yes . . . "

But these were not his words. Only one word, and that word was "no."

"Are you married?"

"No."

He scarcely heard the prior's further questions — about whether he was prepared for the rigors of the life. But he knew what to answer: "I am, with God's help, and as far as human frailty allows." He muttered the words perfunctorily and endured what followed: the tonsure and the vesting with the black habit. Then the prayer: "Accept O Lord this servant of thy grace, and grant that by thy help he may persevere in thy Church and merit eternal life . . ."

*   *   *

He had vowed a vow, that day in the *Domkirche* in Erfurt; he dared not break it. Yet, now that he had perjured himself before God, was he not living a lie, perpetuating a sacrilege, if he kept his vow? But then again—hadn't the vow been a response to an inner prompting? Had not God called him? Was it not clear that only in the cloister he could atone for his sins and preserve *her* from shame and dishonor? Surely, it was God who had called him—circumstances had compelled him.

But in the days following his entrance into the monastery, when he was in the solitude of his cell, another, more terrible conclusion confronted him. God perhaps had called him to the cloister—had willed that all the events should have proceeded as they had, but not so Lorenz List could atone for his sins. No, the utterly other, the inscrutable, swathed in darkness impenetrable, had beckoned him to make the step he did—only that he might stumble. *It* had demanded his obedience, only that he might sin. And when *It* could have hindered his perjury, *It* was silent. Only when he had spoken the words that now implicated him in a lie did *It* reveal *Its* displeasure. Now, if he broke his vow, he sinned. If he kept his vow, he sinned.

This revelation at first had made him indignant—how could *It* toy with him so? But when had he obeyed *Its* law? And who was he, the clay, to question the art of the potter? *Its* wisdom transcended the knowledge of man, infinitely—so many of his teachers said; we know nothing of *It* save *Its* will, whose determinations could not be judged by mere human wisdom. Even had he not transgressed *Its* law, had he the right to contend with his maker and lawgiver?

This revelation filled him with dread and horror. He was transfixed as by the down thrust of the archangel's spear. Claw as he might, tear as he would at the relentless decree, he could not alter it.

Whether it brought salvation or damnation, he had only to follow the course he had chosen, to the end.

*   *   *

How long until sunrise?

No, he did not want to hasten the morning. It would come soon enough.

. . . Those days long past. The terror of them. But, then, they had borne their fruit. . . .

Had they borne fruit?

He had been certain they had.

He had thought he had to pass through the horrors of death, like some new Orpheus, in order to know light and life. He had emerged from the grave to behold — not again, but for the first time — the sun. It had dazzled him with its brilliance. He had wandered, confused. But when, at last, his eyes grew used to the light, he saw and understood. For at his side had walked his Eurydice, hand in his hand, beautiful in the new-found dawn.

But now he wondered — was not even that a deception? A dream of light, from which he awoke into a deeper darkness? She had passed again into the netherworld, her parting words not a sad "farewell." No, not so sweet as a sad farewell. Her words, though spoken of herself, spoke of him and shattered the dream in a thousand particles. It was gone, and she was gone; and he was left alone with himself.

No, the morning could wait. He did not want to see what he had wrought.

THE PLAGUE

CHAPTER 1

THEY HAD CALLED THEM—HIMSELF AND Sebastian—the "two friends." Though particular friendships were discouraged, no one of their superiors took their friendship amiss. Was it because they had entered the monastery together—and that, it was thought, neither would have done so without the other? Perhaps it was that Sebastian was most careful to avoid exclusivity. Or was it, rather—as Lorenz himself thought, with hindsight—that he, without Sebastian, would not have persevered, and his superiors knew it? He would scarce have admitted it at the time, but Lorenz in more mature years recognized that, though Sebastian always claimed that, had it not been for Lorenz, he would never have had the courage to break with the world, without Sebastian Lorenz could not have borne the burden of conscience. Whether Sebastian himself recognized this, Lorenz couldn't say; but that it escaped the keen eyes of his superiors, he doubted.

Of course, Lorenz never once laid bare his sin to Sebastian; he even tried to conceal his inner struggles. To the face, he tried to appear the serene monastic — struggling with sin, yes, but not contending with the giant, Despair. But this struggle could not escape Sebastian, that most attentive of friends, though for long he never let on that he guessed. Such was the man's delicacy.

Yes, Lorenz was certain that Sebastian had surmised the state of his friend's soul — how could he not notice it, he who seemed so serene in the new life, whose inner sight was not obscured by the fumes of conscience? Lorenz knew that Sebastian struggled with sin—that he wept for his sins; but Lorenz was certain, it was not out of fear. It was love that moved Sebastian.

* * *

Then came the day, only a little past a year since his entrance into the monastery, when the prior told him, "You will be ordained a priest."

Lorenz knew this day would come—and he had dreaded it. With horror he contemplated the laying on of hands—but more, the words spoken by which he would change bread to God. Dared he, in his lie, to hold truth in his hands? Would he not defile the mystery? Would he not be accursed, like the sons of the priest Eli, *qui dormiebant cum mulieribus quae observabant ad ostium tabernaculi?*

* * *

"You are terrified of love?"

"Yes, of love, if you call it that. I do not know if it can be so called . . ."

"But what else is he, but love?"

What else? Lorenz could think of other words to describe it: terror, enigma, deceiver, master of disguises, revealer. But he dared utter none of these.

"He is love, certainly. But only to those whose sins do not provoke his wrath."

They were walking in the cloister garden. Lorenz had asked Sebastian the question he had been burning to ask him—had he felt fear that day when he placed his hands in the bishop's hands, when he felt the chrism on his hands, his head, his chest? And when he took in hand the round disk of bread to speak it God—

"Fear—yes, I felt fear. I thought, how could mere flesh and blood approach the mystery and not be unmade?"

"Then how did you have the courage to go forward?"

Sebastian did not answer directly, but pondered. Then—"I remember, once, when I was a child, out of carelessness I broke a tankard that my father loved to drink from. I was terrified of what would happen to me when he found out. I thought of hiding the pieces, but then I thought—*he will discover it, he always does*. So I took the broken cup to him and confessed all. He said, 'You have been slack in your duties. This time, it is just a cup; next time, it will be something bigger. You must be punished.' I wept, fearing his anger and the punishment; but I did not ask for mercy. He thrashed me and sent me directly to bed. The next day, he was to me as he had ever been—as if I have never broken the cup. Really, he was kinder to me than before—and, as I think back on it now, I understand that he did not thrash me as much as he could have—and why? Because he punished me for my own good, not to vent his wrath. His justice was a mercy."

Church bells rang the hour. Lorenz counted them—one, two, three, four. They would soon have to part. Sebastian was quiet as the bells rang—they were a joy to hear, those bells. They rang through all the stretches of Erfurt, recalling men to time, flowing ever onward, like the waters of the Gera. Into and through the city, and then out and onward it ran; to where, Lorenz could not say.

When the last trembling of the air faded into stillness, Sebastian continued. "I have thought much on justice and mercy. Men tend to think them opposed, and mercy merely the setting aside of justice. And, often, for us, it is so; but not always. My father would have failed in mercy had he not been just. Justice was the expression of his mercy. And so it is with God, I think. We learn that all God's ways are justice and mercy—but then we are tempted to think justice the fundament and mercy the concession. God's relenting. But, *frater*, it is not so—no, for joy, it is not so!"

Lorenz wondered at his friend. He seemed suddenly filled with joy. Lorenz wondered whence could come such joy.

"No, *frater*, it is rather this—mercy is the fundamental ground of all being. Justice springs from mercy. Indeed, for God to be just, he must be merciful, for in no way does he more fully return what he owes himself than by being merciful."

Lorenz pondered the words. Then, "I do not understand," he said.

"Think, Lorenz!" (In the vehemence of his joy, he forgot to call him *frater*.) "What is creation but an act of infinite mercy? Did God act justly when he created the universe? Who was his creditor? To whom did he owe anything, except himself? And he himself possessed himself entirely. No, creation was pure mercy; whatever of justice was in it sprang from mercy."

The two friends were silent for some time. Lorenz pondered the words. How to reconcile this picture of God with his own experience of God? If it were so, if God were truly mercy, why had he found himself in impossible straits where, on the one side yawned the chasm of dishonor—for her and him—and on the other, betrayal. He had, he thought, sailed straight through to certain safety, only to discover a worse peril.

"But what of sinners? God has not such mercy for sinners— His punishments . . . "

"Justice," said Sebastian, "is born of mercy—even in its punishments. If there were no mercy, there would be no justice. Justice expresses mercy—for, consider: in mercy, God draws being from non-being; but sin is descent into non-being again. Sin would draw the universe again into chaos. I fear you think God wields his punishments much like the cruel man does; but there is no cruelty, no blood lust in God's justice, for by it he draws back into being what has fallen into nothingness. In mercy, he recapitulates his first creation and even draws it unto new heights of perfection. By his justice, God sets right all that has fallen awry. And is this not a mercy?"

"But what of hell?" Lorenz almost whispered these words.

"Hell?"

But before Sebastian could answer, the church bell struck the half hour. One, clear dulcet trembling of the air. Sebastian glanced upward, as if startled. He seemed to fix his eyes for a moment on the spire, and then smiled. When he turned his eyes again on his friend, "Hell," he said, "is a mercy, for those who would have nothing of mercy. It sets them in right relation to the whole in which they would otherwise have no part. But we will speak of this more later. We must soon to Vespers."

The two men parted and went, each to his cell.

CHAPTER 2

LORENZ FELT NOTHING OF MERCY WHEN he said his first Mass. He trembled when he held the Body in his hands. He feared that, when he took the chalice, he would spill the Blood. His communion was an agony of terror—he was consuming his enemy, eating and drinking damnation to himself. He might have fled had not the prior been at his side.

Could he repeat this, day after day, week after week, year after year? This he wondered that first night as he lay awake in the darkness of his cell. At no time had he felt closer to God, but he had derived no comfort thereby; for he, mere stubble, had touched consuming fire. He repeated over and over again, *miserere mei!* But he knew he prayed into the void. There would be no pardon.

But as the days and weeks passed, it was his despair that provided him some relief. He was accursed, numbered among the damned—but was this not *Its* will? If he committed sacrilege, it was by an arcane decree. There was no question of turning from his sin—for, if he attempted it, he would sin again. He was hedged in by sin. Strangely, such thoughts calmed him. When terrors assailed him—at night, in the darkness, in the early morning when he rose for Matins, when he tried to turn his mind to God, at Mass—he endured until the calm of despair overtook him again.

But despair was an unreliable comforter—more effective was distraction. But what could distract from thoughts of the state of his own soul? His life in the cloister, attending to rounds of prayer, contemplation, *ascecis*—these brought God ever to his mind, and the condition of his soul. He longed to escape what he deemed his prison, but there was no egress from the cloister. He had vowed; there was no turning back.

One cold day, more than four weeks after his ordination, Lorenz was summoned to the prior. When he entered the cell, he knelt before the prior and kissed his hand.

Lorenz knew the prior to be a kindly man, but his demeanor that day was stern. Lorenz felt ill at ease.

"*Frater*, I have consulted with the Father Vicar concerning you, about how you should be disposed for the glory of God and the good of our holy order. Perhaps it reveals the will of God that, without prior discussion between us of the matter, Father Vicar and I had arrived at the same idea—that you, *frater*, should again take up your studies in the university. It is Father Vicar's will, and mine, that, beginning the summer term, you will commence studies in philosophy, with a view to attaining the degree of *magister*."

"May God's will be done."

As he left the prior's cell, Lorenz felt a buoyancy of heart that he had not known for the two years he had been in the cloister. Later that day, Sebastian noticed his friend's demeanor and smiled. "It is long since I have seen you so blithe," he said.

"Am I blithe?" Lorenz replied. "Perhaps it is the unlooked-for that has affected me. Father Prior has told me that I shall again take up my studies in the university."

Sebastian's smile grew brighter. "Well, then, if you are not blithe, I will be," he said. "For I, too, have been told to return to the university. We shall again be students together."

Lorenz, too, smiled. "It seems they don't want to split up the *two friends*, eh?"

"So it seems," Sebastian laughed. "*Ach*, dearest brother! God is good, is he not? He has delivered us from the world, granted us, though unworthy, the dignity of priesthood, and now blesses our hearts' desire—the study of his creation. God, indeed, is good."

"Yes, indeed," Lorenz replied—but he spoke only with his lips, not his heart.

* * *

For Lorenz, philosophy was the distraction he needed from the terror of divinity. For much of his day now he could contemplate the contours of the world, not the condition of his soul. Once again, after almost a year and a half in the cloister, he felt the pleasure of inquiry and thought, of discussion and disputation. And he knew the satisfaction one feels in the praise of his masters.

The nagging fear over the state of his soul only increased the intensity of his application to study. He poured over his books every moment he could spare from his priestly or monastic duties. He turned every conversation he could—with Sebastian, or with others—from God to nature. And on account of his zeal, Lorenz became known as one of the most promising students at Erfurt.

Of course, he knew he did not surpass Sebastian in sheer brilliance or penetration. But Sebastian was a sign of contradiction at Erfurt, for he resolutely opposed the *via moderna* of the Occamists. As ever, Lorenz thought Sebastian made the better case. The way the Occamists trod led nowhere. Still, to oppose the *via moderna* was no way to win approbation or fame at Erfurt. If Sebastian's opponents could not defeat him in disputation, they could disparage him outside the lecture hall.

But over time Lorenz felt himself being drawn into the "modern way." In part this was because of Doctor Jodokus Trotwetter, famous for his great learning not only at Erfurt and her sister university at Wittenberg, but throughout Germany. Doctor Trotwetter taught Occam with a swaggering self-assurance. And he, rare among the scholastics, had a deep regard for the new poetic learning. And this great man had taken the lowly Augustinian monk, Lorenz List, under his tutelage. "*Pater*," Doctor Jodokus said to him one day, "yours is a rare condition—a union of zeal and a marked aptitude for learning. Make me, I pray, your guide, and you shall, I am certain, attain the heights of learning."

Lorenz felt as he did when—now it seemed so long ago—Mutianus had singled him out for praise. Yet, Jodokus' approbation had the more draw, for it met with approval from Lorenz's superiors. There was talk of his standing for *magister* sooner than might be expected for one so young—he was then but one score years and two—and then, of course commencing the course of study in theology. For Lorenz this was a fulfillment of desire. Though he knew the Augustinians had nurtured many scholars, he had, when he entered the cloister, abandoned any thought of pursuing his studies. His was to be simply a life of penance, he had thought.

* * *

It had taken him by surprise. He had not expected it. It was a very cold day in late winter, when the snow lay like a hard crust on the ground, that he was summoned to the new prior. Johann Lang was not an impressive figure; his less than average height was diminished the more by his stoop-shouldered demeanor. His eyes were light blue and watery, and his tonsured hair lay limp over his temples. He was a kind man, however, and greeted Lorenz warmly. "God's blessing on you, *frater*! I hope, with all this cold, that you are in health?"

Yet, whatever unfavorable impression Frater Johann's appearance might make on Lorenz and his brother monks, they knew he was a man to be respected. He was a *magister* and had been a lecturer at Wittenberg; and though he had not yet been made a doctor of theology, but was still only *baccalaureus biblicus*, it was known that the vicar, Frater Martin, reposed great confidence in him. Lorenz's brother Augustinians held Frater Martin in the deepest regard, both for the power of his intellect and the depth of his spiritual penetration.

Lorenz could only wonder, then, why Frater Johann had summoned him. But his wonder increased the more when the prior told him, "the vicar himself has taken a great interest in you, *frater*."

Lorenz learned that his superiors and the *magistri* both had agreed that he was ready to receive the degree of *magister philosophiae*. Lorenz was befuddled at the news. Why he? He could think of others—particularly Sebastian—who were more worthy of the honor. There must have been some confusion, some mistake . . .

"No, *frater*; no mistake. It is you who have been chosen; and it is your part to accept the decisions of your superiors, even if you feel yourself unworthy."

Lorenz learned that he would commence his studies in theology, but not at Erfurt. He would be sent to the Augustinian *conventum* at Wittenberg. As a *magister*, he would lecture in philosophy at the university there while he pursued his own studies. "You will lecture on Aristotle's *Ethics*; so, I would suggest, you begin preparing your lectures before you leave for Wittenberg. You will begin in the summer term."

Lorenz knew it was his part to obey, and he bent forward to kiss the prior's hand. But as Lorenz turned to depart, Frater Johann called him back. "One more matter, *frater*," he said.

"Our decision that you should pursue studies in theology

was based on the gifts of mind Our Lord has bestowed on you. Our decision that you study at Wittenberg was based both on what you could contribute to the young university and for perhaps more weighty reasons." The prior paused and then began to speak more softly, as if he were broaching a delicate subject. "I have learned of your mighty struggles of soul. You have wrestled with the Fiend and, though not defeated, have yet enjoyed no victory. With the vicar's blessing, I send you to Wittenberg, to the care of the vicar himself—a man who has undergone struggles such as your own and still suffers the assaults of our common Enemy. Speak to him, open your soul to him. If any man can, he will show you the way of peace."

It was not until he attained the cloister garden that Lorenz fully understood everything he had been told. And it was not until he reached his cell that he realized that he would soon be leaving for Wittenberg, alone. His friend, Sebastian, would remain behind, in Erfurt.

CHAPTER 3

THE CITY CHURCH REARED ITS UNGAINLY bulk over the *Marktplatz*. It was a monumental structure: two stone towers, rectangular, topped with pyramids of stone. It was stark and blunt. It was brutal.

But the eyes of the young man, tonsured, clad in an Augustinian habit — "simple, very simple," Lorenz thought — shone with admiration. He was from these parts, from a village not far distant. For him, Wittenberg was a grand city, and he was eager to show this newcomer its grandeur.

"It is a wondrous church, isn't it?" he asked in his (to Lorenz's ear) rough, Saxon brogue. "So very different from our cloister church, you know. I must show you the inside — but not right now. And, anyhow, you will see it often enough. But now I want to take you somewhere else." As he said this, the monk's eyes sparkled.

Wondrous is not the word Lorenz would have used to describe this church, or anything else he had yet seen in Wittenberg. *Dreary* came more readily to mind. He had thought the seat of Friedrich, called "the Wise," one of the seven electors of the empire, would possess a splendor befitting its master's rank. But Wittenberg knew neither better days nor, it seemed, was destined for future glory. It was a diminutive town, an overgrown village, distinguished only by a castle, a crudely wrought parish church, and a new, upstart university.

It was but two days since he had halted on the banks of the Elbe and, looking across that water, contemplated what was to be his new home. Images of Nürnberg and Erfurt danced in his imagination—Wittenberg was an ugly *Hausfrau*, a misshapen dwarf, compared to those ladies of renowned beauty. Erfurt, set amid wooded hills and fertile valleys; Nürnberg, a queen, diademed, hill-enthroned, clad in a brocaded gown of rich design and costly fiber. But Wittenberg—merely a congeries of mean houses, spread over sandy, infertile heaths. Not a mountain or a hill in the distance to break the monotony that stretched around it.

Lorenz had seen the cloister church, of course. It was a wood frame structure, of uncertain age but of certain decrepitude. It would not need a strong wind to collapse it, he thought. He had not yet been to the parish church; but from what he had seen of it at a distance, he need not, he thought, hasten an acquaintance. And his host, the young Frater Jürgen, was eager to impress this stranger, not with the town's chief church, but with what he thought Wittenberg's greatest ornament.

Lorenz knew what that was. It could be nothing other than the Castle Church. He had heard of its fame even in Nürnberg. Even so great a city as Nürnberg could not boast of the graces the Elector's chapel could bestow. The relics of the Castle Church, the indulgences attached to them . . .

"It is said, *frater*, that here are some 19,000 sacred bones, as well as other holy relics!" Frater Jürgen's expression was animated. "You cannot see or venerate them now—one has to wait until All Saints, you know, when the Elector displays them. *Then*, you may see bones of our Holy Father, Augustin. There is a tooth of Sankt Hieronymus, and pieces of Sankt Chrysotomus and Sankt Bernhard. But these are not all!" And here Frater Jürgen's voice dropped confidentially. "Our elector has obtained four hairs of Our Lady, a piece of Our Lord's swaddling clothes, a gold coin given him by the Three Kings, one of the nails driven through his hands, and—a strand of his beard!"

Lorenz merely nodded his head. He was not one to discountenance such things; but all this mongering after relics—what did it import? Sebastian had been censorious. "Don't you see, *frater*," he had said to him shortly before his departure from Erfurt—they were discussing this very church—"it is nothing but trafficking in the sacred? One cannot buy God like that!" Lorenz was inclined to this opinion, but he hesitated. After all, this "relics trade," if one wished to call it that, was countenanced by some distinguished theologians and blessed by the pope. Who was he to doubt that if, on All Saints, one venerated the relics and...

"...and offers a small donation"—Frater Jürgen again intruded on Lorenz's consciousness—"he can reduce Purgatory for himself or others by 1,902,202 years and 270 days!" (*This poor monk*, Lorenz thought, *knows the exact figure!*) "What other city in the empire offers such privileges to faithful souls?"

Lorenz did not answer, nor did his companion seem to expect an answer. But as they were returning to the convent, Lorenz contemplated this "privileged town," this ugly heap set on a sand hill, this Wittenberg, seat of the great Elector Friedrich the Wise, straddling the very edge of barbarism; a last, mean outpost of civilization. (As they passed a tavern, a stinking drunkard, stumbling out of the doorway, collided with them; and, then, after giving them an angry look and cursing them, turned and voided his stomach on the pavement.) If the graces here were so abundant, why was the place so degenerate—and ugly?

* * *

...You need not fear, most dear friend, that I could
ever suspect you of forsaking your duty. I know you
to be most conscientious in the fulfillment thereof.

So—though you might have suspected it—I did not think you would have betrayed the charge committed to you as *magister*.

Still, I think you may be over scrupulous. I think it is your primary task to expound the text of Aristotle—but I don't think it untoward of you to challenge your students, even with some of your own questions. After all, Aristotle is not Holy Writ—and, I agree with you, that his *Ethics* are deficient in light of what God demands of Christians. Thus, I don't see why you shouldn't spur your students to think beyond the written word, to view Aristotle in relation to the teachings of Our Lord. Thus, they will deepen their understanding of the *Ethics* and at the same time refer to the teaching of Holy Church.

I would write more, but I have not the leisure at present—nor do you have the time to read long missives. I do have some news for you; I have been told that I shall stand for the degree of *magister* in the autumn and will then proceed to theology. I shall not, it appears, be sent to Wittenberg but shall probably remain here, in Erfurt. But, from what you have written, I don't think I would get along well in Wittenberg. I am interested in hearing your account of Father Vicar's lectures; I have heard much about him here, but I have not been pleased with some of what I've heard. Perhaps you will dispel my doubts—and indeed I hope you do, for I understand he is a very observant son of Our Father Augustin. May God keep you.

Sebastian Engelder, Augustinian

* * *

"You have not yet met Father Vicar, but you will soon. He has gone to Torgau, you know, to check on the mills there. That is one of his duties—he has so many, you know!"

The distance from the Castle Church to the Augustinian cloister was not far, but Frater Jürgen limped of one foot, so they had to halt betimes to allow him to rest.

"Wittenberg, you know, is not as big as Erfurt, so I hear—or as Nürnberg. They tell me you come from Nürnberg?"

"Yes, I lived there two years . . . "

"Well, I've never been, you know, to Nürnberg or Erfurt. But I imagine them as like to Wittenberg, only much larger. *Much* larger." Jürgen glanced over to Lorenz, as if seeking confirmation.

"Yes, they are much larger."

"But neither city has such a treasury of graces as our own Wittenberg! We are like a little Rome, you know?"

Frater Jürgen rose with difficulty—Lorenz hastened to help him, but he waved him away. The small brother limped his way toward the cloister.

"*Ach, frater!* Nor do those cities have such a treasure of grace as our Father Vicar! You should hear his sermons! I, of course, do not attend his lectures, but they draw, you know, so many scholars! So many more than other lectures, I hear. Father Vicar is not so much a scholar—though he is that, a great scholar—but he is inspired, like a prophet or apostle! I have heard him called another St. Paul. Indeed, when I hear Father Vicar preach, I think of the Apostle—though it is said *he* was not a great speaker, while Father Vicar is, you know."

Lorenz had heard something of Frater Martin, in Erfurt. He drew a following among certain brethren. *Magistri* at the university spoke highly of him. He did not know what Sebastian thought of him. Nor did Lorenz himself know what to think of him.

" . . . Indeed, some of the brethren have said they have heard nothing like Father Vicar's teaching. They say that, before they attended his lectures, they thought little of Holy Writ. Oh, being sons of St. Augustin, they have read their share, you know—but they say they had not known what riches lay there. I myself, you know, who do not read, have since begged them to read me something of Scripture. And they have not begrudged me, you know . . . "

They had arrived at the cloister. When they parted, Frater Jürgen bade Lorenz good even, and added: "Father Vicar should return tomorrow—but you may not meet him even then. He is so very busy with the affairs of the Order, you know. Betimes he doesn't even attend common prayer."

And Frater Jürgen turned and limped toward his cell.

*　*　*

Lorenz folded Sebastian's letter, and placed it aside. *I have heard much about him here, but I have not been pleased with some of what I've heard.* What had Sebastian heard? His friend, he feared, was at times too precise. Praise of Frater Martin was universal in Wittenberg. And, since he had been attending his lectures, Lorenz knew why.

That cold winter's day, now six months past, when Frater Jürgen had shown him Wittenberg, had stirred Lorenz's curiosity of Frater Martin. He recalled, in Erfurt, Frater Johann's words about the vicar and his mighty struggles of the soul: "Open your soul to him. If any man can, he will show you the way of peace." Who was this man, he had wondered, whom everyone seemed to regard so highly? He was intrigued. He eagerly awaited meeting him.

But though the vicar returned to Wittenberg the very next day, it was over a week before he called Lorenz to him. What struck Lorenz when first he met him was his appearance. He had not known what he expected Frater Martin to look like, but it was not like *this*. Frater Martin had a peasant's features—a rough angularity, a coarseness. But when Martin looked up at him, Lorenz was startled by the power of the man's eyes. They were small eyes, somewhat deep set, and blue; but one could glimpse in them the burning intensity of the soul that kindled them. The Father Vicar's words to

29

him were few and businesslike; it seemed as if he were pre-occupied with other thoughts. His "God's welcome, *Frater*, to Wittenberg—Father Prior at Erfurt has spoken well of you," was perfunctory, or so it seemed to Lorenz. He would have thought little of the vicar, Martin, had it not been for the power of his eyes.

And this impression was strengthened a hundredfold over the next several weeks. Lorenz attended Frater Martin's lectures on the Epistle to the Galatians. Lorenz, of course, had read the epistle, but Frater Martin's exposition of it was unlike anything he had heard before or he himself had conceived. It was as if Paul were telling a tale of struggle, a mighty struggle—verging on despair—of contending forces of darkness and light. And it was the speaker himself who was being beaten back, beaten back, and stumbling into defeat. But finding in that defeat the victory for which he dared not hope.

"Turn your eyes to the brazen serpent, Christ crucified. Turn your eyes to him, believe with all your heart that he is our righteousness and our life . . . "

" . . . The cross, the cross alone—that is the Christian faith! The struggle with death, the battle against unbelief and despair—these are not dissipated by the resurrection. Paul says that through the law, he is dead to the law that he might live in God. We must die to the law, if we are to be resurrected with Christ . . . But the cross remains! It is only in the cross, in Christ's desolation on the cross, when he cried with the psalmist, 'My God, my God, why hast thou forsaken me,' that we find Christ . . . "

" . . . But he does not seek our works, for we must die, not only to the Law, but to our own works. Our works condemn us, for we do them under the Law. But we are driven into Christ's embrace, if we despair of our own righteousness and believe that he is our righteousness and our life . . . "

"... But still the temptation remains, the temptation to trust in ourselves. This is the cross, the anguish of fear that Christ is false. You will not escape this anguish, this terror—that Christ is the condemning judge, enthroned on the rainbow, with the pit of hell yawning beneath him. You cannot appease this judge by your own works, by fastings, vigils, deeds of almsgiving. If you try, you will find him still the judge. No, it is only by believing that he is your righteousness that he will appear to you, not as judge but as the loving shepherd ..."

"... Do you fear his condemnation? Then receive his forgiveness! Do you fear for your own sins? What sin can be more horrible than to reject the proffered grace and spurn his righteousness? This is God's abundant love, that he offers you his righteousness only if you despise your own ..."

"... *I do not frustrate the grace of God*, Paul says. How does he not? By believing that Christ is his righteousness! If we do not believe this, we reject grace; and if we reject grace, we deny Christ ..."

"... This is the cross, our despair over ourselves and fear that his promises are false. But this very fear is the sure sign that we are his—if we cast ourselves into the arms of his mercy and say, *give me thy righteousness, and take thou my sin* ..."

Lorenz had not heard anyone, among his confreres or his superiors, speak with such unction. He had feared theology—to open again that book of terror. He had found refuge in the study of nature, where he could hide himself from the "presence of the Lord." He had trembled at the thought that he would, again, emerge from the leaves, his nakedness exposed.

And the God of whom Frater Martin spoke was indeed the God of terror and judgment. But, it seemed, God was such only to sinners—those who strove and struggled to win God's favor. Those, however, who denied their own righteousness, who ceased striving—these found judgment as it were transformed into Mercy. Was striving to be good, to fulfill God's commands, then, the only sin?

No one, Lorenz thought, had ever spoken like Frater Martin—except, perhaps, Bruder Heimrad. But there was this difference—one, the significance of which, Lorenz could not yet divine. Frater Martin spoke always of faith and trust, while Heimrad had spoken of love.

* * *

He felt the slam against his side, something hard striking his head. He was almost knocked to the ground. The other tripped on his own feet and fell. Lorenz turned to see him, sprawling, face down, on the street. He glanced over at Frater Jürgen, who appeared startled and afraid. Then he looked down again at the man.

He lay still for a moment, but then slowly rolled onto his back. He was a large man, fat. He wore only breeches and a filthy shirt, untied at the neck. His round head was bald; grey stubble grew thick on his cheeks and chin. He was sweating. (It must have been hot in the tavern, Lorenz thought.) He lay on his back a few moments and then rolled over and laboriously pushed himself up onto his knees, and then onto his feet.

The man's features were coarse. His mouth gaped. (He was missing two front teeth.) He seemed confused. His plump hand, covered with white hair, he ran over his face and his head, and then grasped the back of his neck. His features contorted into a snarl, his small eyes narrowed. He stumbled toward Lorenz, who moved aside. The man stopped, swayed, and, lifting his head, looked full into Lorenz's eyes.

The man's eyes were vacant, like a beast's. They were a pale gray. They flashed with the rage of a beast. His lips moved as if he would speak; but at first they formed no sound. Then the words flowed out of him. Lewd words, filthy words. Later, Lorenz could not remember them, except their import . . .

But he remembered, behind the rage, the vacancy in the man's eyes—was there a human soul there? They were looking full on Lorenz but, it seemed, not at him. Then, a paroxysm shook the thick frame of the man. He grabbed at his belly, bent forward, and voided his stomach on the uneven cobbles.

Lorenz turned, and started walking. Frater Jürgen followed. He could hear the man's retching. The two continued on. Lorenz was angry and disgusted. His head ached.

That night—at Vespers, Compline, and when, at last, he lay himself down on his bed—he could not shake the remembrance of the man's eyes. What lay behind them? Did anything lay behind them? But when, at last, he himself lay upon his bed, to his wonderment, he no longer felt either anger or disgust. What he did feel was pity. Profoundest pity.

CHAPTER 4

THE AIR WAS COOLING INTO FALL. HE had received his latest letter from Sebastian. Their exchanges had not been many—no more than two or three. But the change they wrought in their friendship had been precipitate. Lorenz thought he and Sebastian were swiftly ceasing to understand one another.

Lorenz unfolded the thick paper. Sebastian's fine hand, letters exquisitely formed, lines straight as a rule. A small cross at the head of the paper. He read the first few lines, stopped, and then folded the letter again. He placed it on the table and then leaned back in his chair.

He did not understand Sebastian. The theology students to a man had nothing but the deepest regard for Frater Martin. Even learned doctors regarded him with respect, Lorenz knew. Sebastian was, of course, right—there was something strangely new in what Martin was teaching; but to Lorenz's mind it was redolent of the newness, and freshness, of spring.

Indeed, it seemed as if Frater Martin had done nothing but blow away the layers of dust that for too long had lain thick on the pages of the Gospel. One could now discern the shape of the letters, illuminated in gold most pure and unalloyed. And these letters formed words, and the words were joined into sentences expressive of hope and consolation. The text of Scripture had been given tongue, announcing tidings of great joy.

No, Sebastian, he thought, though a brilliant mind deeply rooting, was nevertheless too much the scholar, too much the logic chopper. He would complain betimes of the too subtle distinctions of the Scotists—but wasn't he, in his own way, very much like them? He could discourse of the branches, the limbs, the twigs; he could delineate the subtle structure of the leaf; but he could not, his friend Sebastian, behold the tree entire. At times, it even seemed that all these—the branches, limbs, twigs, and leaves—were only discrete entities to Sebastian; that he knew not how they emerged from the tree or bore relation to each other. He could only see the parts scattered into non-life, not the ever-burgeoning vibrancy of the tree.

Ever since he had entered the monastery, Lorenz had been reading Scripture. But what had it meant to him? It had been a tale of nightmare—visions of love transforming themselves into terror, a nauseous topsy-turvy torturing him with a sweetness that, tasted, turned to bitterness on his tongue. It was so like the dreams he had in fever, vivid and terrifying, but meaningless to the memory upon awakening. Scripture to him spoke nothing but confusion. He could find no consolation in its words.

He unfolded Sebastian's letter and read again—

> How is it, I pray, if it be true that our acceptance of Christ's righteousness suffices, that Our Lord himself will judge us according to our works? I accept that our righteousness, before our reception of grace, is nothing but dirty rags in God's eyes; but is true righteousness never to be ours—will we never be truly just—by Christ's gift to us? St. James insists that our works justify us—that, indeed, our works are what give life to our faith, not our faith to our works. And even in his Epistle to the Galatians, which, it seems, you cite almost solely, St. Paul says that nothing avails but *faith that works through charity*. I am not entirely

certain what the Father Vicar is actually saying, but
what I think I understand of it does not seem to
square with the whole of Scripture...

The whole of Scripture—it was precisely that united witness
that had so befuddled Lorenz. What did it tell him of God,
except that he is unfathomable? Was that not the burden of
Job's song—that the One who had tortured his servant merely
to score a point against Satan, in the end cast aside even that
mask to uncover a faceless, terrible mystery?

Quis enim resistere potest vultui meo?

And was there, in the end, any face at all?

God the Father. The judge. The healer. The torturer. He
who rides on the wings of the Cherubim and gazes into the
depths of the abyss, who loves those who fear him, but hates
those who despise him.

But does he even love those who fear him? Was it love that
lacerated the soul of Abraham when it demanded the blood
of his only son, the son of the promise? And why? To test
Abraham's faith? Was anything unknown to him who knows
all? Then, why? Why?

*And he said to him, take your only begotten son whom you
love, Isaac, and go into the land of Vision and offer him there, a
holocaust...*

And if he had spared Isaac—what then? He did not have
to spare him, for he was the God who demanded all from a
man, who took from him everything he loved. And then left
him with nothing but terror.

Parce mihi ut rideam antequam vadam et non subsistam.

It was thus he thought of God before he heard Frater Martin.
Frater Martin, it seemed, had found the key to the riddle of
Scripture, the riddle of God. It was as if Lorenz had for the
first time heard the Gospel, and with the joy of this discovery,
he had written to Sebastian. But Sebastian's replies were full of

caution and increasingly censorious. And thus Lorenz, despite the beckoning of his own heart, hesitated fully to embrace the doctrine Frater Martin taught.

* * *

"You feel the terror over your sins—I do not say you shouldn't, for it is a terrible thing to fall into the hands of the living God."

"So it is as they say—he will judge us for every transgression?"

"His law will judge our every transgression—if we strive to live by it."

"But are we not to obey his law?"

The man's eyes were small and deep-fset, but powerful. Most powerful.

"If we strive to live by his law then, yes, we must obey it. We must obey it, but we cannot."

"And the alternative?"

Lorenz knew the answer. He had heard it in Frater Martin's lectures. He had found it in his sermons. But he had come to his father to hear it spoken, not to a multitude, but to himself. Somehow, if it were said to him, alone, it would be true for him as it was for others.

"And the alternative?"

"It is to make him who became sin to save us from sin to become sin for us. Let him take your sin and give you his righteousness."

"I have striven after righteousness. I have sought to drive sin from me, but the more I strive, the more I am conscious of sin." Lorenz knew he did not speak the entire truth. Could one strive against sin while living a lie?

He feared he was saying only what he thought the other wanted him to say.

"I know whereof you speak; but sin cannot be overcome that way. In sooth, dear brother, when one strives against sin, he sins, for he seeks to establish his own righteousness apart from

God's. All our acts, both those we think virtuous and those
we think sinful, are themselves sin, for they are done without
Christ. They equally call down God's wrath on us. Only his
righteousness makes us righteous. Suffer him to clothe you
in his righteousness!"

Frater Martin's words were measured; his manner was calm.
But they seemed to overlay a hidden turmoil. He seemed to
understand whereof he spoke.

"But what must I do?"

"Nothing. You must do nothing, for no act of yours can win
Christ's righteousness. Only believe—believe he has forgiven
you, and he will make your sin his own and his righteousness
your righteousness."

"But what of love?"

"We cannot love God unless we are righteous. If we strive to
love him to win his favor, we sin, for we are seeking to establish
our own righteousness apart from his. Rather, believe, and all
things will be yours."

"But mustn't we seek to love God?"

"Dear brother, do you yet not understand? We must only
believe. In faith we attain all righteousness, for by faith Christ
embraces us and covers our nakedness with himself. He will
grant us love and all good works, but neither love nor good
works make us righteous. Only Christ, through faith. Do you
yet not see?"

CHAPTER 5

A KNOT OF MEN, WITH WOMEN AND children. Some were gesticulating; others stood dumbly, with looks of dismay and confusion.

Frater Jürgen left his side and limped over to where they stood. Lorenz remained alone in the street.

The crowd, standing before the tavern, was growing every moment.

Frater Jürgen pushed his way through. The crowd parted like a yawning mouth.

The boy grabbed the sleeve of the friar's robe.

Jürgen knelt down before a heap on the ground. He leaned forward, turning his head, as if listening.

He rose quickly, and still kneeling, twisted his torso around. Lorenz saw him beckon.

Where Jürgen knelt, a man lay.

I know'd he'd drunk too much — and when he did, look out!
What'd he do?

He jus' struck out. He cursed him roundly, and jus' struck out!

The man was fat. His round head was bald; gray stubble grew thick on his cheeks and chin. He was sweating. But this time he did not rise, he did not curse. He clutched at his chest.

Hans, he weren't goin' to take it, this time. He's patient, Hans is — but he has his limits....

... He slammed him in the gut, Hans did ...

39

. . . He fell backward, 'cross a table. Rolled off it, on to the floor. He got up . . .

The man's eyes were gray—gray as the sky on a cool autumn day. But now, *now*, they weren't vacant. There was a man within.

. . . It was then he started grabbin' his chest. He roared like a beast—'twas horrible. . . .

. . . He rushed out into the street . . .

. . . He roared, jus' like a beast . . .

No, no. "There is no beast here," Lorenz thought. "There is a man." He looked fully into the man's eyes, and he felt pity. Those eyes, those eyes besought him—a sinner.

No, it was not the sinner they sought. It was the priest. Pity, profoundest pity. Lorenz fell on his knees beside Jürgen. He whispered in his ear—"fetch me the holy oils!" Jürgen said nothing. He rose clumsily. "He will not make it in time," the priest thought.

He bent his head over the man's head. He spoke into the man's left ear—"are you sorry for your sins?"

The man gasped. "Forgive . . . forgive . . ."

The priest spoke the words quickly, making the sign of the cross. *Ego te absolvo . . .*

Ego

Te

Absolvo . . .

In nomine Patris, et Filii, et Spiritus Sancti.

Amen.

Vacantly. The gray eyes stared vacantly into the sky. It was blue, cloudless. The hand lay, limp and still on the chest.

It had been none too soon.

* * *

Lorenz straightened himself. The crowd of men, women, and children stood silently around the body. But Lorenz paid them no heed. It was on the boy, standing stock still, his lands hanging at his sides, his eyes — gray, like the dead man's eyes — gazing dumbly on the heap before him, that Lorenz looked. Then suddenly, like an eagle swooping down on his prey, the child fell prone over the body.

"Papa! Papa!"

The shriek tore through Lorenz's breast, like a sudden knife thrust. He remembered another boy, who cried thus, long ago. He reached a hand and placed it on the tousled, blond hair. "Be comforted my child — *Ach!* Be comforted. He is at peace. I was here."

He rose, still looking down at the weeping child. He then glanced up at the crowd. "Does anyone know this man? Where he lives?" No one answered. He turned to see if anyone behind him knew. He saw Frater Jürgen coming toward him.

"I have the oils," he said. "I met Frater Adam. He ran and fetched them. Here they are." And he handed them to Lorenz.

"We do not need them now," Lorenz said. They both looked down at the boy and the body.

"Does anyone know him?"

"I know where he lives," Jürgen said. "His wife begged alms of us. It is only a few streets over."

"You men there," Lorenz commanded three stout fellows, who were staring down at the child. "Take up the body. Follow us."

*　*　*

"But the prince did what the king told him to. Why couldn't he marry her?"

Lorenz smiled, and then laughed. "*Ach*, Jonas, you ask me to tell you this story, but you will not let me go on, for all your questions!"

"It is not fair that he couldn't marry her!"

"No, you are quite right," Lorenz agreed. "But if the prince were allowed just to marry her, then the story would end — and would be as boring as you say my saints' stories are. It is sadness and disappointment that makes stories interesting, isn't it?"

The boy did not answer. He had become pensive.

As on other days, he had found the child, Jonas, playing in the city square. The boy played alone. Frater Jürgen had told him that Jonas had played thus, even before his father's death. Other boys had mocked him for his father's drunkenness; but Jonas, being a tall boy and strong, defended himself well. In time, he was left to himself.

Lorenz wondered at the boy. He had wept unconsolably on his father's corpse, both when it lay on the street and on the straw, in the small room where he lived now only with his mother and his sister. But when it lay buried in its pauper's grave, the boy ceased his weeping. He became—as Jürgen said he had ever been—untimely grave. Playing deliberately in the city square.

Day after day, as he passed from the parish church to the cloister, Lorenz would linger and watch the boy. Until one day, a week since, he spoke to him. He told him a story.

"Sadness and disappointment make a story interesting—but do not fear, it will all end in joy."

The boy said nothing, and Lorenz continued the story—how the princess' father pursued her and the young king's son, but she turned them, herself into a rose and him into a briar. When the queen, her mother, discovered the ruse to the king, he pursued them again, but the princess changed herself into a church and the prince into a preaching friar. The king was again deceived, but not the queen; she found the two fugitives in a forest—her daughter changed to a pond and the prince into a duck on the pond. The queen, seeking to catch the duck, drank all the water in the pond but grew sick and vomited out the water again. She then relented and gave her daughter three walnuts, saying they would help her in time of need.

As he told the story, Lorenz felt himself pulled into it. The sorrow of abandonment the princess felt when the prince, through his mother's enchantment, forgot her and was betrothed to another—he could feel the pang of it, her sense of desolation. She did not know it had not been a callous heart but a befuddled mind that made him forget her. But she would not abandon him. She emptied herself of her glory, served as a miller's servant, until the day of the wedding. Then, breaking open the first walnut, then the second, she found within them beautiful gowns, in which, adorned, she for two days hindered the vows; for the vain bride would not pledge herself until she was clothed more richly than that maiden. And then the plaintive cry, outside the prince's bedroom door at night—"I saved you from my father's wrath—the forest was cut down for you, the pond was cleaned for you, the castle was raised for you. By my arts, you were changed into a briar, to prick my father's grasping hand; by my magic, you were made a preaching friar, to soften my father's hardened heart; by my lore, I was changed to stagnant waters, to sicken a ravenous belly—how, how could you have thus forgotten me?"

And then, at last he heard her, and remembered.

The third walnut she cracked open, and adorning herself in the gown they found therein, the most beautiful gown of all, the prince led her, rejoicing, to the altar.

When he had finished the story, Lorenz wished he could find a meaning in it, as Bruder Heimrad had found in his stories. But he could not.

It was the boy who broke the silence. His eyes, as they looked up into Lorenz's, were thoughtful.

"The princess was faithful to the prince. Why?"

Lorenz hesitated, but then said, "because she loved him."

"But she thought he forgot her."

"Yes, she did," Lorenz said quietly. "But that is the nature of love, my son. It is faithful, even to death."

CHAPTER 6

THE RAIN HAD CEASED. HE SMELLED A freshness in the air as he stepped outside, through the side door of the small stone church. The trees, huddled about the church—beyond them, the open fields, fallow—were red and gold in leaf. The grass, still green under his feet. He looked upward—the clouds were parting, uncovering the pale, blue sky of autumn.

A woman, elderly but stout, her head swathed in a red scarf, begged a blessing. He made the sign of the cross over her, *Benedicat te Omnipotens Deus, Pater, Filius, et Spiritus Sanctus. Amen.* She then reached into a bag, pulled out a loaf. Her work-worn hand held it out to him. He took it with thanks.

When he passed from the enclosing trees, he took a path, toward the west. It was muddy because of the rain, so he thought to walk along the grassy border of it. He stood for a moment, as if hesitant; he remembered that he still held the loaf in his hands. He opened the flap of his satchel, and placed it within.

A little over a quarter of a mile brought him to the main road. When he reached it, he stopped, and looked to the south and west. There, on the far side of the river, rose Wittenberg. He thought the sight of it improved at a distance. He turned a little and looked back over his shoulder; he could see the village church steeple rising through the little grove of trees, bright with fall colors. He smiled faintly, and then turned to continue his journey.

He had come to this little village a little over a week ago. Its curate had died suddenly, and they needed a priest until the new curate should arrive. He had come to bring salvation to the village people—he who himself needed it so sorely. He had said Mass, heard confessions, visited the sick; he had baptized a child. He had come to bring salvation; but, he thought, his salvation lay not here, but in the ungainly little city that sat just across the water.

Or did it?

He had not had much time, these past eight days, to think much about himself. When he was not saying Mass or attending to other spiritual duties, he paid visits to the people of the village. They were a rude bunch, poor and ignorant—they did not compare well to the peasants of the Altmühl, his home. (How strange, he suddenly thought, that he should be comparing peasants, as if he himself were not one!) But it was in performing priestly tasks, he now reflected, that he felt a flickering of hope; that, somehow, in so doing . . .

But as he walked slowly down the road, coming ever closer to the city, he reflected on the vanity of that hope. Wasn't it just self-deception? *This* was not the lesson the Father Vicar had wanted him to learn, he was certain. No, not in doing did one draw nigh to God. Hadn't he, in all his busy bustling over the last ten days, but added more to the weight of sin that so burdened him? In seeking to please God (what else, after all, had he been doing?) hadn't he but offended him all the more?

*   *   *

He had been surprised and a little disappointed that day when the Father Vicar had told him to go and minister to the little village. He was a *magister*, not a curate. But he did not express his misgiving to Frater Martin. He obeyed.

It had only been a few days after he had met with Martin.

"I cannot help but feel," he had said "—dare I say that I am certain that God has damned me?"

Frater Martin looked him full in the eyes. "Is he reading my heart, my soul?" Lorenz wondered. No, he thought; for those eyes, powerfully intense, like two burning coals, seemed rather to look within than out.

"God, my brother, works by contraries. It is when a man feels himself lost—when he feels God bearing down on him in wrath—in that very moment, he is close to salvation."

"I do not understand . . . "

"Nor can you. You must only believe. When God is set to justify a man, he damns him. His love is revealed in his wrath. Why? Because man must be goaded to despair—to be convinced that in himself there is naught but sickness, sin, and death. As long as a man clings to even the smallest crumb of his own righteousness, God will terrify him. He must be driven to a horror of the abyss of sin that is his soul. He must cry out that his righteousness is but dirty rags, that all his virtues are nothing but sin."

Lorenz longed to ask him—"have you, too, suffered such terrors?" But he feared to ask. Instead, he said, "is there ever any peace?"

"The Christian life is continual penance. It is the cross. But in the tumult of crucifixion, salvation begins. You must become as a sheep for the slaughter, for in baptism you were made to die with Christ. This death is the conviction that you are utterly lost—but it is when you are convinced of this that light begins to dawn. Peace comes through Christ's word by faith."

As Lorenz passed from the road onto the bridge crossing the Elbe, he pondered these words. There were moments when he thought he could confess himself sin and abandon himself to Christ, who became sin for him. That all he must do is to cease from striving. But he hesitated, as one hesitates on the edge of an abyss.

Why, why would he not abandon himself to peace?

* * *

It was Sunday afternoon. Lorenz half expected—indeed, he hoped—to find the boy Jonas playing in the city square. He was not there. Remembering the loaf in his satchel, Lorenz thought to seek out the boy's dwelling before returning to the convent.

He reflected on how he had come to feel a fondness for the boy. His first feeling—when the boy in tears embraced his father's body—had been pity. But when he had followed the body to the poor, one-room dwelling that had been its home and witnessed the boy's affection for his dead father and his solicitude for his mother, who had seemed befuddled and confused, Lorenz added admiration to his pity. The sister, some several years older than her brother, appeared aloof and cold. But Jonas, though only a child of ten years, seemed to have forgotten himself in attending to his mother and his father's corpse.

But it was Frater Jürgen's account of Jonas' father that deepened Lorenz's admiration for the boy. The father had come originally from Zwickau to Wittenberg and had been a day laborer. When not in his cups, he was a kindly man; but when he drank—which he did frequently to excess, squandering his family's money—he would become violent. He brawled with men in the tavern, with anyone who (he thought) crossed him as he stumbled home after a carousal. And he behaved, in private, as he did in public—until he slept off the fumes of drink.

Jonas was betimes the object of his father's drunken cruelty. Yet the boy wept inconsolably for his father dead. "Would I have wept so for my father?" Lorenz wondered.

It was the sister who opened the door to Lorenz's knocking. A thin girl, blond, with a peevish expression, she looked dully at him. "I have come," Lorenz said, "with something for—for the family."

The girl said in a tone that matched her demeanor, "Jonas is within. Mother is sick."

"May I enter?"

The girl did not answer.

"Perhaps I can be of assistance...."

Without a word, the girl opened the door wider. Lorenz could see, across the small, squalid room, a bed of straw, and a boy sitting beside it. Jonas glanced toward the door and then bent forward to whisper something in his mother's ear. He then rose and walked to Lorenz. The boy looked worried.

"Mama is very sick," he said.

Lorenz walked over to where the woman lay. She looked up at him, glassy-eyed. He felt her forehead; it was hot. "My daughter," he said to her softly. "Is there aught I can do for you?" She at first didn't seem to hear; but then she slowly shook her head. "But I can give you my blessing?" he said, forcing a smile. Then he signed her.

Jonas followed Lorenz, who motioned the boy to step outside. "Listen," he said. "Your mother is very sick—I tell you this, because I know you are brave. I shall return to the convent and then seek out Lucas Burchard, the physician. He tends to the brothers, and I shall send him here."

The boy frowned and shook his head.

"You needn't worry," Lorenz hastily added. "I shall tell him to do it for Our Lady. He is a good man. Do not fear. The only thing is, I do not know if I shall find him directly. He may not come right away. It all depends on when I find him."

Lorenz turned to go; but then he remembered. He pulled the loaf from his satchel. "Here, take this," he said. "I'll have Bruder Jürgen bring you some more food."

And Lorenz hastened toward the convent.

CHAPTER 7

THE PHYSICIAN'S NEWS CHILLED LORENZ. Lucas Burchard shook his head. "This is not the first case. Just last night, a child died of it. I was called, but it was too late."

"Is it too late for her?" Lorenz knew the question was foolish.

"Some survive. Most die of it. Her case, however, is not promising."

"And the boy?"

"He must be gotten away from there."

"But he won't leave?"

"No."

The previous evening, Lorenz had sought for the physician, Lucas Burchard, but could not find him. It was not until the morning that he at last discovered him. He begged him to go to Jonas' mother; but when he gave directions to the dwelling, Burchard stared at him blankly. Lorenz could guess what he was thinking.

He had just returned. He had told Lorenz simply, in the cold, detached way that the priest so wondered at: "The buboes, it seems, appeared first this morning, under the armpits. Probably elsewhere."

"And how is she?"

"The woman is in great pain." Burchard slowly shook his head. "The daughter—a thin, unpleasant girl—is utterly useless. She just stands there and gapes."

"And the boy?"

Here Burchard's eyes softened a little, though his tone remained taut. "He attends assiduously to his mother."

Lorenz asked what could be done. Burchard again shook his head. The buboes would have to be lanced, he said. She needed to be bled.

"I will fetch the holy oils," Lorenz said. "Wait. I will return with you."

The doctor shot him a queer glance but he said nothing. For some moments the two men stared silently at one another. Then, the priest —

"For the sake of Christ, Burchard! For the sake of Christ!"

Burchard lowered his eyes. He did not speak. Then, he looked irresolutely up at Lorenz. The priest could see uncertainty in the man's eyes.

"For the sake of Christ!"

Burchard nodded. He pulled at his beard. "All right," he said at last. "I will wait for you."

Lorenz turned to go, but the physician stopped him. "The boy, Father," he said. "You must get the boy away from there." Lorenz nodded, and went to fetch the holy oils.

* * *

The small room was a squalor of suffering. The woman had been transformed to a writhing mass of pain. She complained of knife-like thrusts, lacerating her flesh. The buboes had burst into an ooze of pus and blood. A putrid stench pervaded the room and almost made Lorenz retch.

Burchard tied a napkin about his nose and mouth and advised Lorenz to do the same. But Lorenz scarcely heeded the charge. He had never seen such suffering. Before him, on the straw, writhed a human figure, horridly disfigured, moaning. The image of God. *Let us create man in our image and likeness*—the verse that stirred to life in his mind sounded like mockery

Could one call *that* the image of God? Or her husband, who died like a dog in the street? He had seen paintings, depictions of Adam and Eve in the garden. Such, one thinks, are God's image: the flesh, pure and pristine in its nakedness, lovely to behold and soft to the touch. The fragrance of flowers pervading the air. Man and woman in the glory of their innocence.

But this! Where could one see God in that broken and bleeding body? The eyes wide open, staring at nothing; regarding only the pain within. The hands clawing at the floor. The low groans of animal suffering. And the stench of rotting flesh. He breathed it in, and exhaled it. Breathed it in and exhaled it. There is no air but this air, he thought. No sweetness but this stench.

He breathed it in and exhaled it. Breathed it in and exhaled . . .

It was then he recalled Burchard's words. The air, the breathing of it—that brought on the disease.

He could see himself, reduced to the sufferings of this woman—could he endure it? The fingers distended, then closing, crushing the straw; the writhing torso; the eyes wide, staring out in pain—and then death. And judgment. For him, such pain—nay, far worse than such pain—for eternity.

Should he not seek to preserve his own life? Perhaps he could yet be redeemed, make atonement, if he did not die. Did not one have first to consider his own salvation? Not lose his soul for another? If he turned and left this pestilent room, he could yet, perhaps, escape death; but if he approached her? Touched her with blessing?

His eyes fell, then, on the boy, Jonas. He sat on the floor at his mother's side, beside him a bowl of water in which he dipped an old rag to cool her brow.

Lorenz was resolved. He was a priest. He must not flee, like a hireling. He took a step toward the misery before him — and then remembered Burchard's counsel, to cover his nose and mouth. He recalled the napkin the doctor had handed him. It was in his hand. He hesitated, and then dropped it.

He knelt before the woman. He looked into her eyes, but he could see naught but animal suffering in them. Again, doubts rose within him, but he suppressed them. He bent his ear to her lips to hear her contrition, and then, uttering the words of salvation, anointed her.

He rose, and seeing Jonas staring up at him, beckoned the boy to come with him. Jonas hesitated, but then followed the priest.

* * *

The air outside the room was sweet — even in that neighborhood. Lorenz reflected that he had never breathed so sweet an air. He drew it into his lungs, deeply, and exhaled. But then he saw the boy, looking up at him, waiting.

"My son, you must not remain here. Come with me — I will find you safe lodging."

Jonas said nothing. He simply looked up at Lorenz. "What is he thinking?" Lorenz wondered.

"Don't you understand," he said with more vehemence than he had intended. "The sickness — it is deadly! You must not remain here longer!"

The boy still said nothing. He did not change his expression.

"My son, you must hear me!" a panic rising in his breast. The child must be made to understand! "This place is perilous for you! You must come away with me!"

Then the boy spoke, softly, calmly, seemingly without fear. "But I cannot leave mother," he said.

Lorenz felt desperate. "It is dangerous for you, most dangerous!" he said. His voice, he knew, betrayed his fear. "Your mother would not want you . . . "

But Jonas said, "but I cannot leave her."

Lorenz knelt before the boy. He grabbed his arms. His grasp was firm, too firm.

"But don't you see?" he said. "Don't you know what might befall you, if you remain here?"

"I know," the boy said, in the same even tone. "But I will stay," he said.

For several moments Lorenz merely looked into the boy's eyes. There was a depth to them, a depth he had never before seen. With a feeling of wonder, shot through with fear, he merely said, "Why?"

"Because I love her," the boy said, with the same simplicity. "And love is faithful, even to death."

Lorenz rose. He laid his hand on the boy's head, and then nodded. The two, the boy leading the priest, turned and reentered the small, noisome room, where the sick woman lay.

CHAPTER 8

I T WAS AS IF HE HAD FORGOTTEN FEAR OF
death. There had been talk in the convent of sending the
brothers who were students away; but he had asked leave
to stay. The prior would hear nothing of it at first; but Lorenz
would not let up in his appeal.

"If many more grow sick, they will need the ministrations
of a priest."

The prior folded his arms and lowered his head in thought.

"My call—I am a priest. A priest first, not a student."

The prior looked up. He seemed to study Lorenz's face.

"Can we suffer that anyone die unshriven and unatoned?"

"You know, *frater*," the prior at last said wearily, "that whether
you go or stay is not finally in my power to decide. If Frater
Martin thinks you should leave, then I . . ."

"Then you can plead with him for me." Lorenz had interrupted his superior, but he felt no compunction.

The prior paused, but not, it seemed, because of the affront.
At last, he shrugged his shoulders. "I could, indeed," he said.
"But I cannot assure Father Vicar's acquiescence. But I shall try."

"And in the meantime?

"In the meantime—in the meantime, I will give you leave
to do as you will in this matter." And the prior smiled. "Can
I oppose such a headstrong will as yours?" he said.

*   *   *

54

He felt as if he had plunged into the misery of hell. He passed from sickroom to sickroom—in the hovels of the poor, the more commodious houses of craftsmen, the statelier dwellings of well-to-do burghers; but everywhere, the same misery, the same putrid stench, the groans, the writhing, the utter helplessness. Day after day, from morning until sunset, he tended to the ailing souls of the sick. He spoke words to comfort them, absolved them, anointed them. The fear of contagion had caused even close relations to shun their suffering kinfolk, so that, often, he found himself tending to the physical as well as the spiritual needs of the sick. Some of those he visited after a time recovered. But most of them, one after another, passed into silence.

Only a few days after he had anointed her, Jonas' mother died. With Frater Jürgen, who often accompanied him now, Lorenz hurried to the dwelling, to make sure the body was removed. He found the boy there, as he had expected, at his mother's side. The child did not weep; he merely sat on the floor, against the wall, with his legs folded in his arms, pulled against his breast. When Lorenz entered, the boy looked up at him; there was no expression in the eyes, of sorrow or of fear. Lorenz did not know what to say to the boy, so he uttered what he thought merely a pious commonplace—"She is at peace, now, my son." The boy said nothing—he only looked steadily on the priest. But then, like a cat springing on its prey, he jumped to his feet, and throwing himself forward, buried his face in Lorenz's scapular.

"What shall happen to the boy now?" Frater Jürgen asked, when they had left the dwelling. "He cannot subsist, you know, as before—begging, doing odd jobs. And the sister—I shudder to think what she might come to."

Lorenz did not feel like speaking, but he forced himself to reply: "No, the sister shall be cared for. A tradeswoman has agreed to take her in, to help with the housekeeping. And as

55

for the boy—I have spoken to a cobbler in the town—he lost his own son last year and has none to help him. He has agreed to take the boy on as apprentice, without payment at all. I think you know him—Karl Strom, a most Christian man."

"I do know him, and you are right. He has a most Christian heart."

But in the days and weeks that followed, Lorenz could give little thought to Jonas. The plague did not abate, and daily he attended to those struck down by it. Day after day, he met death in the faces of those to whom he gave absolution. But though he often longed to flee from the sights, the sounds, and the stench, something within pricked him on. It was not a goading but the very impetus of his own heart. It was not pity, either—or it did not seem so to him. He could not quite say what it was; all he knew was that it worked against his repulsion and bade it yield—and it was he himself who gave the command.

And, strangely, he felt no fear for himself. Well he knew that he could be the next victim, but he felt no dread of it. Did he long for death? No, he knew he did not—for what waited for him beyond. Yet, somehow, he felt that his own eternal destiny did not matter, not when he possessed the one thing that could decide the destiny of so many. Nor did he comfort himself with the hope that, somehow, what he was doing would at all alleviate the pangs that awaited him. He knew that all his good deeds, added up, could not even begin to fulfill the exactions of him whose comfort he was daily, hourly, offering to suffering souls.

It was as if he himself mattered not at all.

* * *

It happened on a day when he was feeling thoroughly exhausted. He was returning to the convent with Frater Jürgen—they had been saying that it seemed, at long last, the sickness was subsiding—when he was accosted by a servant of Karl Strom. "My master sent me to you, Father," he said. "He bids you to come quickly to his house. It is Jonas . . . "

Lorenz did not stop to inquire. He had guessed. What had seemed to pass so lightly over the boy, striking so many around him, had at long last seized him. He bade Frater Jürgen to fetch Lucas Burchard and then to return to the convent to explain his absence. As he approached the house, he was filled with dread. What would he see there? The young child, his sweet, clear skin erupting in black swellings, his young eyes staring wildly in terror and pain, his groans and, maybe, screams—*Ach!* Could he bear it? Yet though part of him wanted to turn and flee, the inner unction that had urged him into so many sickrooms propelled him toward the house and the sick bed of the child.

He felt he scarcely had the strength to open the door to the room; but he did. There before him, on the bed, covered in blankets, lay the child—but his face was not hideous. It was white and, seemingly, transparent, but beautiful as if it were cut from marble by a deft hand. He approached slowly, for the child seemed to be sleeping. But as he stood over the bed, the boy's eyes opened. He looked steadily up at Lorenz, and then smiled.

"Father!" the boy said, and raised his hand to him. Lorenz took the hand—it was white as snow but very warm—and sat down beside him on the bed. He did not know what to say, but he lifted his free hand and brushed the wisps of blond hair from the boy's forehead. "God's blessings on you, my son," he at last forced himself to say.

The boy replied nothing. He simply looked full into the priest's eyes. What Lorenz saw in the depths of that gaze startled him and then filled him with wonder. It was joy, profoundest joy, overflowing the brim of the child's soul, and running forth as if (Lorenz thought) to water a dry, parched world. Lorenz could feel it moisten his own dry heart.

"You are happy." He meant it be a question, but it came from his lips a simple declaration.

The boy nodded.

"Why?"

The boy appeared to wonder at the question. His eyebrows drew down over his eyes, as if he were trying to scrutinize the priest's face. The boy's expression confused Lorenz. He felt ashamed and embarrassed. It was as if he should know the answer.

"You shall get well," he at last said, because he had to say something. But the boy only shook his head.

"No, Father," he said. "I will die."

The starkness of the words startled Lorenz. He was in the presence of mystery. It was as if Jonas was looking out across the threshold of another room, vast and limitless. He understood that the boy spoke truly. He would die.

But he asked him anyway—"how do you know?"

"I know," the boy replied simply. "I will go to pray. They asked me if I wanted to."

"And what did you answer?" Lorenz feared to ask the question.

"I said I wanted to."

Lorenz felt a profound sense of awe. What could he say to this? Of course, the boy could merely have imagined the whole business—he was certainly feverish, though not too much so. It could all have been just a dream. But in the depths of his heart, Lorenz knew it wasn't a dream. All had happened just as Jonas had said. God was taking his own to himself, gathering him into his reward. And why? "Because he loves much," Lorenz thought.

He knew he should rejoice—Jonas would escape the wretched world, that promises so much of joy but pays out only in grief and misery. The boy was highly favored of heaven;

he would dwell close in to the bosom of God. What more could one ask of life? But Lorenz could not rejoice; he could only feel the misery that was his recompense. And he understood why. He loved Jonas. He loved him like the son he would never have. In the short time of their acquaintance, he felt as if he had been given the merest taste of God's gift to even the most wretched of men—he been given to know something of what it is to be a father. He had loved and been loved in return—he who had been cut off from love by the sternest of vows. And now he would lose that love—and if he were to prove himself worthy of it, he would, like Abraham, have to offer it freely to the stern deity that demanded it of him. "But," he thought, "I am not Abraham."

He rose and blessed the boy. He said he would return the next day—though he knew in his heart he would never see the living boy again. He moved toward the door, and, taking hold of the latch, turned to look at the boy one last time. (He lay on his bed, happy. Happy!) He felt so very sorry—sorry for himself. He could scarcely control his voice, but he managed to say: "for me, Jonas—will you pray for me?"

The boy answered with his smile.

* * *

Lucas Burchard was waiting just outside the door when Lorenz came out. The doctor entered the room and closed the door behind him.

Afterwards, Burchard accompanied Lorenz to the doors of the convent.

"The boy is not afflicted with the plague," the doctor said. "His is just a minor ailment. He is feverish, but not dangerously so. He will recover, for he is young and strong. I have no fears on his account—though, of course, one can never be certain."

Lorenz turned and studied Burchard's face. He could see, by the flickering light of the brand, the physician's expression—impassive and matter-of-fact. He was saying just what he thought. He was not offering false comfort.

One can never be certain—but Lorenz was certain. The boy would die, and for reasons the medical man could not discern by his art. But Lorenz said naught to contradict. He only nodded, offered his thanks, and then turned and took hold of the large knocker by which he would seek admittance, again, into the cloister.

THE
DISPUTATION

CHAPTER 1

A DREAM OF LIGHT—HE COULD VIVIDLY recall the day, the very hour, the moment the luminous orb first peered over the horizon. A year had passed since Jonas' death—a year of darkness and shadows. It had seemed to him that the sun of hope would never rise again; Jonas had taken it with him into the grave.

But to the carnal eye all did not seem so dark. The plague had passed almost as quickly as it had come. He had returned to his studies and his own lectures on Aristotle. He was making great strides as a scholar; there was talk that he would attain the doctor's cap sooner than his fellows. And he had earned the regard of his brothers in the cloister. They thought him most pious and observant; a priest who had risked sickness and a cruel death to bring peace to the stricken.

But he knew it had all been a sham. He was the same old hypocrite. Why had he tended the sick? Why had he risked his health and his life? He examined his heart; he sought to plumb the depths of his intention—but he could come up with no satisfactory answer. And had he not simply done his duty? And was the fulfillment of his duty enough to atone for his sin? No, he thought. The answer was a simple, emphatic no.

And even the small, flickering flame of light that had been granted him but a short time—a boy, bright with love—even that had been taken from him.

So it was that even when that brighter light surprised him after his long, restless night, he could not immediately see it. He was blinded by its brightness.

But, of course, how could he understand its purport? It was like the dawn must have appeared to the man born blind, when first he saw it. An awakening in the east, a dim effervescence of the vast and blinding glory it presaged.

* * *

He had risen before sunrise, for Matins, on that Feast of All Saints. He had joined in the conventual Mass, and said his own Mass. But for meals and the hours he must pray, he spent the day in his cell, lost in study. After Compline, he lay down to sleep.

It was thus he had heard nothing of the event that, but the day before, had set the tongues of Wittenberg's scholars wagging. The next morning, All Souls, he said his three Masses, broke his fast, and then set off for the parish church, where he would hear confessions until the afternoon.

Returning from the church, he met the archdeacon.

Everyone called him — Andreas Bodenstein — "Karlstadt," for he came from Karlstadt-am-Main, a town in Franken, though far from Lorenz's home village. Karlstadt was a well-fed, secular cleric, who had studied under the Dominicans in Köln and in Florence and Rome. He had for years held forth on the *via antiqua* and had been, for a time, openly skeptical of the new theology that was sweeping the university. Then, shortly before Lorenz had come to Wittenberg, Karlstadt turned his back on scholasticism and all its ways. He commenced lectures on Augustin. Since that time, he spoke of nothing but Scripture and the Fathers, and without demur derided the very "logic-chopping" of which he had once been a foremost champion.

He, in his blunt way, accosted Lorenz. "Ah, Frater Laurentius," he said in Latin. "What think you of your vicar, eh? A mighty stroke, a most mighty stroke, wouldn't you say?"

Whatever is he talking about? But before Lorenz could utter a word of inquiry —

"*Ach!*" Karlstadt exclaimed, slapping his hands together, "I told the masters, back in the day when I conferred the doctor's cap on Frater Martin — I told them, *expect great things of this man!* And I have not been disproven — no, by God! He has shaken up this university, that's certain! And, 'tis certain, that he'll next shake up Germany! *Ach!* It was a mighty stroke!"

Karlstadt pursed his lips and shook his large head. Lorenz again tried to ask what this "mighty stroke" could be, but the archdeacon paid him no heed. It seemed as if he had forgotten Lorenz was there.

"You know," Karlstadt said, now in German, nodding his head and shaking a fat finger at Lorenz — "you know, I wondered at his audacity, last year, when he gave that sermon — on the eve of All Saints it was, by God! The very same day! God! I thought — what will the Elector say? Luther is tipping the apple cart, he is, I said. But His Lordship didn't do a damn thing, not a damn thing! And it was the day before the dedication, too! And this wasn't the only time he'd pilloried the cock and bull trade — no, by God! Now, don't get me wrong, *Frater*" — here Karlstadt grabbed Lorenz's shoulder, and shook it a little — "I greatly honor our prince, I do! He is a good Christian — but his relics and their *thousands of years of indulgences* stink in my nostrils. They bring in a goodly bit of gold to him, that's certain — and our university has benefited by that, no doubt. And, to tell you the truth" — here Karlstadt lowered his voice a little — "it is for the competition that His Lordship will not suffer the archbishop's indulgence to be preached in his lands — of that I'm certain! But now — what will the Elector do now? He cannot easily ignore it now, can he?"

"Ignore what?" Lorenz managed to squeeze the words in — but Karlstadt seemed not to hear him.

"Why, all those pilgrims to the *grand display* will see the paper flapping there when they pass through the great doors—though almost none of them will bother to read it, even if they could understand it. But the Elector—God! It's a mighty good thing that Spalatin is Luther's friend—though Friedrich holds your vicar in high regard. By God—hasn't he put his university on the map?"

When Karlstadt at last bade him good day, Lorenz felt as if he had passed from a storm of bluster into a calm. He puzzled over Karlstadt's words. The archdeacon's meaning was not so opaque that Lorenz could not see it. Frater Martin had nailed theses for debate on the Castle Church door—and it was these that had stirred up Karlstadt so. It was, of course, no unusual thing for a *magister* to publicize theses he proposed for debate in this way. It had not been so long ago that Karlstadt himself had posted his own theses against the scholastics. But Frater Martin's theses—on indulgences, it seemed—had whipped up Karlstadt's enthusiasm. But this, Lorenz reflected, was really not too hard to do. Karlstadt was given to enthusiasms.

It was this reflection that determined Lorenz—he would return directly to the cloister, not by way of the Castle Church. He was already familiar with Frater Martin's views on indulgences. He had heard neither of the sermons; but chance conversations with those who had had revealed for him much of their content. And he had been the vicar's student long enough to deduce his basic attitudes on the subject—

Indulgences, though valid in a limited way, encouraged false confidence.

The pope has no power over souls in purgatory, and could only remit penalties he himself, or the Church, laid on men.

Nothing so heretical, or revolutionary, in all that.

Sebastian, of course, could probably pull some subtle heresy (that no one else could find!) from the vicar's words. Sebastian was always so very precise. Too precise.

That evening, during the singing of Vespers, Lorenz's mind strayed to Karlstadt's words. His enthusiasm. Did it mean anything? Lorenz smiled to himself. No. Karlstadt was nothing but an oiled weathercock that pivoted with the faintest hint of every passing breeze.

*   *   *

It was but a few days later that he was given a copy. He had made it a point to avoid the discussions among the brethren. Their enthusiasm annoyed him . . .

But when, at last, he read the words, he felt a deep stirring within. The strafing winds of his long winter of fear and despair had left a dead barrenness in their wake. No life, no hope of spring. Only eternal winter. But now, a burgeoning—no new growth to be seen; no, nothing so certain as that. Just a stirring in the soil; a promise that life lay latent within.

What was it in the words that worked the change? He could not say. They proposed no remedy for his despair, no assuaging of his fears—

> *Our Lord and Master Jesus Christ . . . intended the whole*
> *life of believers should be penitence . . .*
> *. . . inward penitence . . . which is naught, unless it out-*
> *wardly produces various mortifications of the flesh . . .*

But had not his life in the cloister been unremitting penitence? No, no—he laughed at the thought. It had been but a pretense of penitence. He did not repent of his sin; he had hidden his sin, had wallowed in his sin, nurtured and cultivated his sin. It had not been penitence he had felt.

It was not such words, noble though they sounded, nor the clarion phrases that called, as it were, to struggle, that moved him. Nor was it the forays into theological dispute; they allured his intellect but did not touch his heart. No, it was not even so much what the author said, but his turns of phrase that, like a brief tightening of the voice, a quick glance of the eye, or a brushing of rose on the cheek suggested a mood that the literal sense belies.

> *Imperfect soundness or charity . . . brings great fear . . . very near to the horror of despair . . .*
>
> *Hell, purgatory, and heaven seem to differ as despair, near despair, and security differ . . .*
>
> *Who knows if all the souls in purgatory desire to be redeemed . . .*
>
> *True contrition seeks and loves punishments.*

He who wrote these words understood the terrors of the soul alive to the filth of sin. He understood the horror of the inward look. He had tasted despair, which does not seek easy pardon or strive for reward. Its prayer is not for mercy—for it dares not hope for mercy—but punishment. He recalled his wonder (in his days of innocence) that the souls of the condemned should long to cross the river of the dead to the pains of hell. But now he understood their longing.

But their longing was not the author's longing. He spoke not of despair but of true contrition that "loves punishments." Despair lusts for punishment, like the lecherous a woman's body; contrition longs rather to make satisfaction. Thus could the author speak of following Christ "through pains, deaths and hells"; for, though those who thus follow will enter heaven only after many tribulations, they *will* enter heaven.

Not so the souls—like his own—that long for hell.

* * *

"You are not a hair-splitter. God! I was sure you were not—you are a son of Augustin!"

"I am," he replied calmly (as he always did to the archdeacon's vociferations). "It is only . . ."

"*Then*, you *must* see the significance of it all! *Himmel!* He's *striking* at the *root*—your Luther is striking at the root!"

68

Karlstadt's heavy face was flushed. His eyes, distended and round. Flecks of foam stood at the corners of his mouth.

"So you say," Lorenz replied. "But I don't see that he is saying anything so very radical. It seems you would make him a Hussite."

Karlstadt spluttered, "No, no, not at all! I'm not saying he's a heretic—no, by God! But he is striking at the root! Here, look at this"—and the archdeacon thrust a piece of parchment in Lorenz's face. "Read here!" (his thick finger punching at the words). "He says a true Christian has a share in all the benefits of Christ and the Church, even without the pope's pardons! He says, here, that every bishop and, indeed, every curate has the same powers as the pope does over the souls in purgatory! And, what's more, every Christian who feels compunction has full remission of pain and guilt, with or without pardons!"

"But perhaps it is because we often don't feel any compunction that we need pardons," Lorenz said, with a shrug of the shoulders. "If so, then Father Vicar is merely adding a needed distinction. He's not denying the necessity of papal pardons."

"*Ach!* Yes, *distinctions!* Scholastics are always talking of distinctions that cut the fire of the Gospel to a mere flicker. But you"—and here Karlstadt held out his hands in appeal—"you, *Frater*—you are not a logic-chopper!"

"You don't have to be a logic chopper to make distinctions," Lorenz said, standing and wrapping his cloak about him. He was feeling somewhat vexed. "After all, our Holy Father Augustin made distinctions. My point is just this, and only this. The Father Vicar is making some important clarifications—but you and others are exaggerating them and distorting them beyond all measure. You say you don't think he's a heretic—well, you'll make him one, if you do not temper your speech. You'll push him where he has no intention of going!"

* * *

A week passed, and then a half month—and to Lorenz's wonder, interest in Father Vicar's theses did not abate. No, but like a fire leaping first from stubble, their vehemence in short order ignited the small kindling of an ever-widening circle of readers. It was not long before they were biting into more substantial fuel and threatening a general conflagration.

A week passed; then a fortnight. Then another week. Then, a month. Printed again and again, the theses had passed far beyond the confines of Wittenberg, far beyond the borders of Electoral Saxony. They were gone forth into all of Germany, it seemed. Sebastian had read them in Erfurt (and in a letter to Lorenz had censured them). Lorenz learned from Burchard that the humanist sets in Nürnberg and Heidelberg had enthusiastically embraced them—and that some were waving them as a standard for revolt against Roman greed and Roman oppression. And not only the learned were talking about the theses; for he heard that, without Frater Martin's leave, they had been translated into German. Tradesmen were reading the theses, as were the literate peasants. And for those who could not tell an A from an E, the theses were being read aloud in the streets!

He knew why the theses so stirred the hearts of his countrymen—his Folk. They had for too long felt the burden of Rome's exactions. Gold flowed out of Germany like water out of a damaged cistern. And where did it go—all that money paid for benefices, for the privilege of controlling multiple benefices, for a thousand dispensations to do what should not be done? Into Italy. Into the coffers of the curia. Even the princes had voiced their grievances against the Roman she-wolf; but, then, wolves ever snarl over their common prey.

And for too long Rome had been using religion like a whore to seduce the "pious Germans." Indulgences, ever more indulgences, hawked, of course, at bargain prices! Was it not a pious

70

deed to build a fitting temple over the bones of Sankt Peter? To shelter them from the pelting rain and burning sun? And if piety alone could not move, there was *this*—a toss of gold into the coffer bought not only honor for the saint but pardon for souls in purgatory!

Frater Martin was showing all of Germany that they were being played for fools—

> *The treasures of indulgences are nets, with which they now fish for the riches of men.*
>
> *Why doesn't the pope empty purgatory for the sake of most holy charity and of the supreme necessity of souls . . . if he redeems an infinite number of souls for the sake of that most fatal thing, money . . . ?*
>
> *Why doesn't the pope, whose riches are today like those of Croesus, build the Basilica of St. Peter with his own money, rather than with that of poor believers?*

Ach! Frater Martin *could* speak to the hearts of the peasants and common folk! But he was not poking a stick to enrage a caged dog. It was zeal for God's house that moved him. He was crying out, like another Jeremias, against the cynical lassitude of the worshipers of the gold coin "that in the coffer rings." And, still prophet-like, he was directing the people's gaze to what alone truly matters—the Church's *true treasure . . . the Holy Gospel of the glory and grace of God.* Nor would he stoop to offer the wide road of ease to Christians, those *exhorted to strive to follow Christ the Head through pains, deaths, and hells.*

It was this, and this alone, that drew Lorenz again and again to the theses. He heard in them the voice of one who himself had descended through the hell of despair, but had passed from that utter darkness to behold once again the lights of heaven.

Lorenz longed to follow—but, he thought, "Even if I have a Virgil to guide me, I have no Beatrice to plead for me."

* * *

It was the month that promises of spring, but lingers in winter. Lorenz was passing from the doorway of the parish church when he was accosted by a student.

"*Magister,* have you seen this?"

Lorenz turned round. It was Heinrich Wässerig, a first-year philosophy student. The young man's face was flush with excitement.

"What is it?"

Wässerig thrust what looked like a pamphlet into Lorenz's face. "It's Tetzel," he said with agitation in his voice. "Tetzel has published theses against Frater Martin! That peddler in the booth over there is hawking them!"

Before Lorenz could reply, Wässerig, catching sight of a fellow student striding some yards away, bundled against the cold, cried out, "Matthias! Wait!" The other halting, turned to see who was hailing him.

Wässerig, abandoning Lorenz, ran to his friend—it was, Lorenz saw, Matthias Kahl, another philosophy student, though a year ahead of Wässerig. He showed Kahl the pamphlet and then pointed to the peddler. Kahl hesitated, then motioning to Wässerig to follow, walked toward the booth.

Lorenz followed at a distance. He was curious to see what Kahl would do. Kahl, who styled himself something of a poet, was, Lorenz knew, a vociferous critic of Aristotle and an outspoken proponent of the ideas of Karlstadt—and it was thus he had become a leader among the students. But Kahl did nothing but approach the peddler, pick up a pamphlet, and glancing through it briefly, pull out his coin purse. He turned and walked away slowly, reading. Wässerig followed.

Deciding there was nothing more to see, Lorenz returned to the convent.

* * *

Not an hour passed before Lorenz was disturbed from his reading by a knock on his cell door. He opened it to find Frater Jürgen.

"There is quite a stir in the *Marktplatz!*" he said breathlessly. "The students have attacked the booth of a pamphlet seller and are preparing a bonfire!"

Lorenz followed Jürgen from the convent, toward the market. There they found a large group of students standing around what looked like a pyre. Lorenz joined a knot of his confreres who were watching the goings on. "What is happening?" he asked one of them.

"A peddler," the other said, turning to Lorenz, "had the folly to come here hawking Tetzel's theses against Father Vicar. He set up his booth over there — you can still see it, though he has no more wares to sell." The friar said this with a chuckle. "A few students bought pamphlets, and then probably went off to inform the others. Then, a couple dozen students arrived and seized what were left. Some came with faggots and a pole! It seems it was all planned in advance. The man was a fool to bring Tetzel to Wittenberg . . . "

"*Ja*, he deserves what he gets!" chimed in another friar.

Frater Jürgen leaned close in to Lorenz. "Is this right?" he quavered. "It is theft, you know — destruction of property!"

But Lorenz did not answer him. His whole attention was focused on the goings on.

Matthias Kahl stood atop the pile of faggots, with his left arm wrapped around the pole. He was leaning slightly forward, declaiming to the crowd.

" . . . He dares to call our Luther a heretic! Tetzel! The rancid preacher of pardons — the preacher that uttered such vile words about Our Lord's mother — I will not repeat them here. No, by God! You have all heard the report of them. All of Germany revolts at the report of them. And why did he utter them? Why?"

73

Several students cried out in answer, though Lorenz could discern only one voice—

"To fill the coffers of the curia!"

"Indeed!" Kahl continued, shouting over the crowd. "You have it, Götz! God, you have it! *Ja*, to fill the curia's coffers, so the *Lord Cardinals* can pay good German gold to weigh down their tables with the richest viands, get drunk on the best wine, and deck out their lovers with the most sumptuous clothes—whether they be women or boys!"

Loud guffaws from the crowd of students drowned out for a moment Kahl's tirade. Lorenz saw that some of his confreres, too, had joined in the mirth.

Kahl now tried to raise his voice over the clamor. "And we know...The Dominicans...truly dogs they are, but not of the Lord...!"

(Several of the students took to barking and howling.)

" ...The Dominicans, hairsplitters and logic-choppers, *angelic* doctors, clasping fair nymphs to their breasts, cleaving them with the most subtle *distinctiones*..."

"Humph! Humph!"

" ... They get their share of the swag! They devour the scraps that fall from their master's table ...

"But at least they get the scraps!" shouted one of the students

"You couldn't have said anything truer, Klaus!" Kahl chimed. The laughter rose, but Kahl, gesturing silence, continued in a more measured tone. "But let us not disparage these most subtle masters! We cannot wield as finely honed arguments as they—nor can we contend with those who can even work up miracles to disparage the purity of God's mother... "

The crowd again roared. One student cried out, in a shrill, piping voice—"and they have worked an even greater miracle, Matthias! They have made Tetzel doctor of theology!" The voice was Wässerig's.

"*Ach!* You are right, my good Heinrich! I had nearly forgotten it myself! Indeed, this is even a greater offense before God, I deem, than the fakery in Bern!"

"Burn them! Burn them!" The students cried out in mock offense, through their laughter.

"Alas, we cannot!" Kahl declared. "We don't have them here. We don't even have Tetzel—the *dog* who had the effrontery to yap at the heels of our Luther. But we have the next best thing . . . "

"The theses! The theses!"

"Yes, the theses! Shall we proceed to the trial?"

The crowd roared its approval.

"Then be silent, so we can hear their defense!"

Slowly the students subsided into silence. When they were at last quiet, Kahl, with a most solemn mien, held up one of the pamphlets. He shot it a look of deep displeasure, and then, bellowing in a deep baritone, cried out: "Do you recant your errors?"

Silence.

Kahl bellowed again: "I ask you to declare before this most solemn assembly—do you recant?"

Again, silence.

Then Kahl, lowering the hand with the pamphlet, sighed. For a moment he appeared to withdraw into deep thought; but then, rousing himself, and raising his right hand on high (the left grasping the pamphlet) he shouted the verdict—

"Your silence condemns you!" And turning to the crowd, he commanded, "Deliver the guilty one over to execution!"

Several students, their arms full of pamphlets, now came forward. They dumped them on the faggots at Kahl's feet. He leaped from the pile, and taking a flaming brand from the hands of another, raised it on high.

"I declare before God and this solemn assembly," he cried in stentorian tones, "that you stand condemned of errors heretical, near heretical, false, nearly false, ambiguous, none-too-clear, captious, temerarious, and offensive to pious ears! Or, at least, to our ears! I deliver your body to the flames, and your soul to the devil!" And slowly lowering the brand, he touched the flame to the straw at the base of the pile.

Anathema sit! Anathema sit! the students cried, as the pile of faggots and pamphlets roared with flame. Some, even among Lorenz's confreres, were clapping. Lorenz himself turning away from the spectacle, caught Frater Jürgen's eye. The simple brother regarded him beseechingly. Lorenz glanced again at the bonfire, and then, turning his back on the spectacle, walked away, with unsteady step, towards the convent and his cell.

CHAPTER 2

THEY HALTED BEFORE THEY DROVE ONTO the bridge—as if they wanted to savor the moment. It had been so many days, long days of walking, and then riding; and here they finally were, poised to cross the bridge that spanned the wide Neckar and led into beautiful Heidelberg on the far bank.

No, the city was not so grand as Nürnberg—but it was lovely. Lorenz had heard so much of Heidelberg on the journey that, when he first espied the spires of the castle, just peeping above the height of the Friesenberg, he felt its seduction. Like a fair woman, slowly disrobing, it came into view—first the castle, lordly, on the north and westward facing slope of the mountain, and then below it, the town rising on the lap of land between the hills and the river.

The houses of the town did not cascade from the *Berg* like the train of a kingly garment as in Nürnberg; rather, the castle in regal isolation, like a king enthroned, gazed down on the town's humility, nestled at the foot of its protecting eminence. No, Heidelberg was not so grand as Nürnberg; but it was homely. It was a city, but with the air and intimacy of a village.

"I have seen Rome, purported to be the queen of cities; but, to my mind, its ancient piles cannot compare with this German beauty. And it will be seen—God chooses the weak to confound the strong."

77

When Frater Martin said this, Lorenz turned his eyes from the city. His superior's eyes were fixed on the town—and the same admiration shone from them that Lorenz felt brimming in his own heart. But the city held Martin only a moment. With a peremptory, "come, let us go on—they are expecting us," the carriage jerked forward, and then rumbled onto the bridge.

*　*　*

Only three weeks before, Lorenz had not thought he would be attending the general chapter of his order in Heidelberg. Frater Martin was to go, for at the chapter he would surrender his office as district vicar; but it was not certain who, if anyone, would accompany him. The entourage would not be large, for it had to be inconspicuous. In the six months since he had nailed his theses on the Castle Church door, Martin's fame had spread all over Germany; and report of him, it was said, had reached even the curia in Rome. Everywhere, Martin's theses had won adherents and followers but had inspired enemies, too—dangerous enemies. Some feared Martin would set out for Heidelberg, never to return.

Despite the danger, Lorenz had longed to accompany his vicar—partly because he wanted to get out of Wittenberg for a while, but mostly because he sensed that what was to transpire at Heidelberg would have profound significance. For, not only was Martin to lay down his office (a *pro forma* affair), but he was to defend a new set of theses he had composed—this time, not on indulgences but on the doctrine of grace.

Lorenz was surprised, but relieved, that when the travelers left Wittenberg they were accompanied by a small, armed escort, provided by Elector Friedrich. This alone was evidence that Martin's life was in danger, and it witnessed to the profound regard the great elector had for his Wittenberg professor.

The journey had commenced in early April—they traveled by foot, and the weather was still cold and often rainy. Yet,

Martin seemed to reckon little of this—he jested that all the journey's hardships were ample satisfaction for his sins, so that he no longer stood in need of indulgences. At Weissenfels, and then at Coburg, they were well received; but at Würzburg, the bishop himself, Herr Lorenz von Bibra, gave them a warm welcome; the Elector had given Martin a letter of introduction to His Lordship. It was at Würzburg that, to Lorenz's joy, they found Johann Lang, who had just arrived from Erfurt. With Lang and another brother Augustinian, their small group traveled by carriage the rest of the way to Heidelberg.

They arrived in that city only five days before Martin's scheduled disputation on his theses.

* * *

"Most assuredly, you bring a most precious letter of credit!" These words, spoken by Georg Simler, grand chamberlain to the *Pfalzgraf*, Wolfgang von Bayern, deepened Lorenz's wonder. That morning, Frater Martin had, in jest it seemed, asked for Lorenz's company in a visit to the castle of Heidelberg. As they climbed the Jettenbühl, Lorenz looked back over his shoulder at the vista of the city, below—the beautiful Necker, the wooded mountain that loomed on the river's right bank, and into the distance, where, out of eyesight, flowed the mighty Rhine. When at last they had reached the castle gate, Martin turned and lingered over the beauty that lay at their feet. "How fair our land of Germany is, is it not, *Frater*?" he said to Lorenz.

The "letter of credit" won for Martin and those who would accompany him a reception with the Count Palatine, the Elector Wolfgang. That afternoon, Lorenz found himself again ascending the castle mount, but in the company not only of Frater Martin, but of Johann Lang and the Augustinian vicar, Johann Staupitz. Even before he had entered the monastery, Lorenz had heard much of the great Staupitz—indeed, even in Nürnberg, among Herr Auer's learned coterie, the name of Staupitz was a talisman of power. Upon their arrival in Heidelberg, Martin had introduced Lorenz to "my dearest father," as Martin affectionately named Staupitz. The round, full face of Stauptiz was gentle; and, in his soft-spoken way, he greeted Lorenz, saying, "*Frater*, I have heard much about you—much of good."

The Elector showed every honor to the small band of Augustinians. He personally showed them the ornaments of the castle, its lofty and lordly halls. He regaled them with the richest refreshment, as if they too were lords, not lowly monks. And then he bade them dine with him the following night. "I will be entertaining a number of guests, all of whom are eager to meet you." The Elector used the plural "you," but, Lorenz noticed, his eyes were fixed on Martin.

It was in a carriage, provided by the Elector, that they returned to the Augustinian convent in the city; and it was in another carriage that they ventured back to the castle the following night.

* * *

The dining hall of the *Pfalzgraf*, lofty, walls bedecked with tapestries, glowed with the light, it seemed, of a thousand candles. Upon their arrival, Elector Wolfgang himself took them personally in hand—he gestured to the long, oaken tables, weighted with meats of every variety, breads so white that it seemed they would melt at the taste, bottles and pitchers of wine—"from our vineyards on the Necker and the Rhine," he told them. Lorenz had heard of the quality of these wines, and he longed to test their report. It appeared there would be ample opportunity to do so that night.

Already, quite "a number of guests" had arrived; a rather large number, Lorenz thought. But a seemingly never-ending stream of guests continued to flow in, until the great hall was surfeited with feasters. The Elector himself introduced Frater

Martin and his party to various guests—wealthy burgomasters, merchants, clergy, masters and doctors from the university. All seemed eager to make the acquaintance—of course, not of himself or Frater Johann, for that matter—but of Staupitz and, most of all, Frater Martin. It was soon clear that the guests had come that night for no other reason than to see the Wittenberg doctor, whose fame had spread over all Germany.

Lorenz soon wearied of the innumerable introductions ("how trying it all must be for Father Vicar!" he thought) and allowed the meandering crowd to flow between him and his superiors. He was now alone amid the throng—a cacophany of male voices, female voices, of various ages; some refined, others coarse. "I have been too long in the monastery," he thought to himself. "*Ach!* For the quiet of my cell!"

Then he heard the music—it came from the far end of the hall. He made his way through the crowd until he found the musicians—a soprano, alto, and tenor *Blockflöte,* one performing on the viol, and another on a lute. He allowed their music to envelop and cut him off from the noise of the hall.

Servants were wandering the hall. Two approached him, one carrying a tray with glasses, another with an earthen pitcher. The one with the tray bowed, and offered him a glass, while the other filled it with a golden wine. Lorenz noted them as if through a cloud—a cloud of music; he took the glass and lifted it to his lips. It was a sweet wine, and heady—had he ever tasted such wine before? As he sipped the wine, he felt ever more withdrawn from the crowd—it was as if he had been enclosed in a limbeck. Now, there was only the wine and the music.

Then, as though rising through and articulating the flowing harmony, first one voice and then another took up the melody and wove each his strand into a fabric of most exquisite sound. They gave tongue to the sorrow the music, unadorned by voice, spoke to the heart:

Ich stund an einem Morgen
Heimlich an einem Ort
Da hätt ich mich verborgen,
Ich hört ein kläglich' Wort
Von einem Fräulein hübsch und fein,
Das stand bei seinem Buhlen,
Es muss geschieden sein.

"She stood near to her sweetheart, he must from her depart" —
Lorenz turned the words over and over again in his mind as
the voices subsided and the instruments repeated the melody,
varied it, and then repeated it again. He sipped the wine and
contemplated the words . . .

Again the instruments gave way and the voices gave tongue
to their mood:

Herzlieb, ich hab vernommen
Du wolltst von hinnen schier,
Wenn willst du wiederkommen,
Das sollst du sagen mir;
So merk, Feinslieb, was ich dir sag,
Mein' Zukunft tust du fragen,
Ich weiß weder Stund noch Tag.

"When will you come again—that must you say to me";
the words and music, and the influence of the wine, carried
Lorenz back to what now seemed another life—when he
left her and she begged of him, "when will you come again?"
And, then, he could not say—did he ever think he would
return to her, or did he know even then that when he turned
from her that one last time, he turned from her for good
and ever?

In Wittenberg, he rarely heard such music. He joyed in it,
though it was sad and worked sad thoughts in him. But the
music gentled the thoughts. They did not work the fear in
him that they did when in the quiet of his cell or chapel they
came on him unbidden. They did not inspire the longing—not

the same longing—as when they crept upon him in the night. Now, they were sweet, like the wine, and like it, heady.

* * *

"P-p-p-lease accept my apologies, *B-b-ruder,* but I saw you standing here, and I thought I just needed to m-make your acquaintance."

It was a rude jolt—he felt as if someone had shaken him awake; the sweet dream vanished away. The voice was deep and round, somewhat coarse, but with an affectation of refinement. Lorenz wondered if the stammer were real.

He turned to see its source. The man was stout but tall. He wore a coat of costly stuff, lined with ermine. A gold chain hung from his neck, a jewel pendant. His white, pudgy hands gestured as he spoke, and his fingers were heavy with rings. He reeked of scent. One of the wealthy merchants of Heidelberg, Lorenz decided.

"I hope I do not d-disturb you—but when I saw you standing here, I thought you m-might be one of the Augustinians from Witten-b-berg. Do you hie from thence?"

Lorenz wanted nothing more at that moment than to withdraw from the man. But he forced himself to answer: "yes, I come from Wittenberg."

"And d-did you travel in the train of that Great Man, about whom all Germany is a-b-buzz?"

Lorenz thought, "the man is oily and affected." He wished he would go away—

"If you mean our Vicar, Bruder Martin—"

"*Ach!* Yes! It is *precisely* him I mean," the man interrupted. "You must tell me of him—all Germany is in uproar over him, but one can scarcely believe common report. But one who knows him, who has lived with him . . ."

"I know what I can tell you," Lorenz said. "Bruder Martin has been vicar of our district; he is one of the learned doctors of our university, and a most observant monk."

The man now eyed Lorenz doubtfully. He shook his head. "You say you hie from Wittenberg," he said. "But you don't sound like a Saxon . . ."

"That is because I am not a Saxon." Lorenz smiled faintly. "I come from the region of the Altmühl, not far from Nürnberg. I have lived in that city . . ."

"In Nürnberg? *Ach, Gott!* I d-d-deem any man blessed who has lived within its walls! In Nürnberg, you say? Why, there is a contingent from that city, here, at this very feast! I should introduce you to them—perhaps some may b-be your friends . . .

"From Nürnberg are you? How do you find Wittenberg? I have not been to Wittenberg, no, not yet. My business has taken me to Erfurt and Leipzig, but not Wittenberg. But why would I go there? It is but a small town, insignificant; I confess to you, though I share not their opinion, our learned men—our d-doctors and m-m-magisters here in Heidelberg—have not held your university in high regard—no, not at all. But d-do they not f-feel the fools now? The eyes of all Christendom are now turned on Wittenberg . . .

"Where have been our Heidelberg d-doctors, over these many d-decades? Have they spoken for Germany? Have they sounded the clarion call for the f-fatherland? We have been soaked, desp-p-oiled by Rome, to stuff the maw of the curia and, I d-dare say"—here he spoke *sotto voce*—"the p-p-pope as well!

"Where have our *Heidelberg* doctors and magisters been? Arguing nothing but abstruse p-points of doctrine and philosophy, while their people are robbed. To what p-poverty has Germany been reduced?" The man's rings flashed in the light cast by a nearby flambeau. "But upstart Wittenberg, the infant university, rises up to lead Germany, while her betters follow shamefaced, hat in hand. Your Luther has st-truck a blow for liberty . . ."

Lorenz wanted to get away from the man—but the last words stung him. "But it is not for liberty, not that sort of liberty, that Bruder Martin contends," he said. No sooner had he spoken the words than he realized how his voice betrayed annoyance. But, it seemed, his companion did not notice it. Instead, he plowed through Lorenz's resistance—

"Your Luther has given us a voice! *Why doesn't the pope, whose wealth is greater than the richest Crassus, not build this one basilica of St. Peter with his own money rather than with the money of the poor faithful?* The people, the p-people are repeating this again and again! We have thought it, b-but we couldn't p-put it into words. We have thought, but hardly d-dared to say it! Luther has said it for us!"

All the while the man spoke, Lorenz noticed (much to his annoyance) that his round eyes were darting here and there over the crowd. No sooner had he uttered the last words than his eyes fixed themselves on a point, and he exclaimed, "*Ach!* Now are you in luck! Over there [one fat finger pointing across the room] is a kn-not of Nürnb-bergers. Come with me—I will introduce you . . ."

The man grabbed Lorenz by the upper arm. They wove their way through the crowd toward a group of finely dressed men. Two of the men noticed their approach and haled Lorenz's companion. The other three, standing behind the two, were facing away; one of them was gesturing toward the ceiling. Lorenz's companion began to babble to the men—even before they were in earshot.

"M-my friends! Here is one of L-luther's companions—from Wittenberg!"

He then began to explain that Lorenz was not *from* Wittenberg! No, but he came from their very own city—from Nürnberg! The men's eyes betrayed no recognition. Lorenz then interposed to explain that he was not *from* Nürnberg but that he had studied there for a time. He was reluctant, however, to mention Herr Auer to them. But the men seemed little interested in the details of Lorenz's Nürnberg sojourn. They were eager to hear what he could tell them about Frater Martin.

"I understand," said one of them, "that you are a companion of that Luther about whom all the world is talking?"

"Yes, I am," Lorenz replied. "He is my superior and teacher—I am studying for my doctorate in theology under him."

"Indeed? Then you are a *magister*?"

"Yes."

"Then, pray, tell us what we want to know about him . . . "

"But wait," said the other. "Our comrades here may want to hear this"—and he turned and addressed the others.

When the three Nürnbergers turned to see what their companion was talking about, Lorenz felt his heart leap within him; then he felt confused. Two of the men were well into their middle age; but the man between them, wearing a simple scholar's cap, was young—it had been he that had been gesticulating toward the ceiling but a few moments before. It was on this younger man that Lorenz looked.

At first, the younger man beheld Lorenz with that look of complacent benevolence that one assumes when he first meets an agreeable stranger. Then his eyes widened and his mouth opened slightly. For a moment, the two men fixed their eyes on one another, saying nothing. It was the other that at last broke the silence.

"My God! Is it really you, Lorenz?"

Lorenz smiled (he felt) nervously. "Yes, it is really me," he said. "I was wondering if you would recognize me, Veit."

CHAPTER 3

"As YOU CAN SEE, MY FATHER HAS NOT allowed me too much luxury here."

Lorenz looked about him; he almost laughed. The room was not overly large, it was true; but it was comfortable. A recessed window, with a seat, looked out on the city, with a view of the lofty Church of the Holy Spirit. Facing this window was a wide hearth that housed a lively fire. Cushioned chairs stood about a wide oaken table, on which a substantial meal and a flagon of wine had been placed. A built-in bookcase held a number of leather-bound tomes—the envy of students. A doorway to the right of the fireplace issued into an adjoining bed chamber. Compared to this room, Lorenz's own former digs (which he had thought quite comfortable) at the *Georgenburse* in Erfurt seemed like a monastic cell.

Throwing his coat onto a chair by the door, Veit strode over to the table, and taking the flagon, filled two large glasses with golden wine. He offered one to Lorenz.

"My father," Veit continued, "thinks a student should live a spartan life."

"Not that I am discontent—I am not!" He quickly added. "No, I am quite content," he mused, almost sadly.

It was but an hour past noon when Lorenz arrived at the house of one of Heidelberg's substantial merchants, to sup with Veit Scheuerl. He had felt some unease in coming, for he knew not in what direction their conversation would turn. It had been six years since he had seen Veit, and a little less than five since their last communication—a letter he had written to tell Veit of his intent to enter the monastery. He wondered what might be Veit's demeanor toward him. But now that the man he met—for Veit was now a man, fuller in girth and sporting a short but thick beard—displayed the same whimsicality that he remembered of him, Lorenz felt more at ease.

"Are you hungry?" Veit said. "Please, sit down—I have ordered a good supper for you. Don't be bashful—sit down and eat . . ."

The meal was indeed good—Lorenz had grown unused to such fare, the likes of which he had not enjoyed since leaving Nürnberg. He had to remember that he was a monk.

Their conversation at first turned on mere commonplaces. Veit asked after Lorenz's journey and evinced surprise when he learned that it had been mostly on foot. "It is not that we wouldn't have ridden—as, finally, we did," Lorenz said. "It's only that for most of our journey we hadn't the opportunity."

"So, it wasn't a matter of ascetic discipline," Veit said, smiling over his cup.

"No, not at all! Though I suppose it was penance enough. But I must say," Lorenz continued, feeling wistful, "it was good to pass through lands so like home. And this Heidelberg is a most lovely city."

"You think so?" Veit said, setting down his cup. "I think so, too! I prefer it far to Nürnberg, though its *fine families* are not much better."

"So you still rail against the iniquities of Nürnberg?" Lorenz let out a slight laugh.

"Indeed, I do!" Veit said, pouring another cup of wine. "And why wouldn't I? I have studied at the university here; I am

(I hope) wiser than I was before—so I would feel the disgust all the more keenly. And I have traveled—"

"You have?"

"Yes—my father has insisted on it. 'It is the only way to make you a right-good merchant,' he said to me, in that dour way of his." (Veit imitated his father's stolid monotone.) "He allowed me to stay three full years at the university—some of the best years of my life, I must say—until I became *baccalaureus. Ach!* Those were splendid years! I tell you, I would be most happy, living a scholar's life; the reading, lectures, debates—I loved it all! I fairly begged my father to let me go on, but he said, such was not the path a merchant should tread."

"But you are still here?"

"Not *still here*," Veit replied with sly grin. "Here again. I'll tell you how I managed it."

Veit had been eating with an obvious relish, but now he set his fork and knife down and leaned back into his chair.

"As soon as I earned my degree, my father sent me to our mines in the Tirol, where I spent six dreary months. My brother, Hermann, takes an interest in such dank matters as mining, but not I. For one thing, miners are a most boorish lot—I swear I had not one interesting conversation the entire time I was there! Still, I applied myself to learning all I needed to master the lore of delving and knocking ore from rocks; for, I knew that if I did not, my father would send me back and keep me there until I did. At the end of the six months, he brought me back to Nürnberg, where he kept me by his side for another year. Then, he sent me to Italy. . . ."

"To Italy?"

"Yes. As I am sure you know, Nürnberg merchants do a good deal of business with Florence, Milan, Genoa, and Rome. I was sent to each of those cities to become acquainted with the merchant houses with which our family deals. But, I confess,

Lorenz"—and Veit leaned forward, lowering his voice as if he were about to communicate a confidence—"I spent far more time drinking in the beauties of the art of that land than attending to mercantile business. What you told me Ser Portinari used to say about Italy is true—actually, much truer than he said; he was probably going easy on us *tedeschi*. I cannot begin to recount the glories of that favored land! I tell you, if the new basilica over Peter's bones will be anything like the churches I saw, I can well forgive Pope Leo his indulgence . . . "

"But aren't the Italians horribly corrupt?"

"*Ach!*" said Veit, throwing himself back in his chair again, "I cannot begin to recount the corruptions of that land! Especially Rome—a cesspool of lust and luxury it is! The cardinals have their pick of the most beautiful women—and the prettiest boys! Not that the latter were in any way appealing to me—God, no! But Italian women are exquisite, utterly exquisite! If I had not been a married man, I would have indulged. As it was, I was sorely tried."

"Hold, Veit! Hold it there!" Lorenz exclaimed. He wondered if he had missed something. "You were a married man—you have said nothing yet about getting married."

Veit seemed to deflate at these words. He fell silent. An awkward moment interposed, but then he sighed and said, "Yes, Lorenz I was, and am, a married man. Shortly after I returned from the Tirol, I was wed to Greta Waldhummel."

* * *

"It was a most sumptuous wedding—as much as the Nürnberg council would allow people of our status: for, as you may know, our virtuous city takes care against all exorbitant public display." Veit spoke as if he had a bitter taste in his mouth. "Of course, Greta pushed it to the limit—and, a bit beyond, in my opinion. Beautiful women can get away with a good deal, even in strait-laced Nürnberg.

"You should have seen it! We were married in Sankt Sebald's. After the ceremony, we processed through the streets to her father's house. Greta was beaming—she was the center of attention, and she knew it. As we passed, the onlookers broke out in shouts and applause—and well they might: *ut dea, sicut luna in firmamento, corruscavit.*"

Veit paused and sadly shook his head. "And I confess to you, Lorenz, I was much taken by her beauty. I was like a drunken man. Doubtless, I was aided by the copious amounts of wine I imbibed. And, that night, when first I held her shining flesh in my arms, I felt as if I had reached the pinnacle of bliss."

"As is proper," Lorenz interposed, in priestly fashion. "It is right for a man to joy in his wife." (But as he said it, he found himself thinking, "she, too, must have been at the wedding—with *her* husband.")

Veit reddened. He ran his fingers through his hair. "Yes, and I did joy in her—for about a month. I thought myself the most fortunate of men—I even began to think well of my lot and all Nürnberg. For nearly a month . . ."

Lorenz looked hard on his friend. "But it did not last?"

"No, it didn't last. I wish it had, for now I despise myself—I utterly despise myself! I rejoiced in her body for nearly a month, but then I began to feel the lack of something I couldn't put my finger on. And her character, which had receded into the background of my mind, began to reemerge—her vanity, stupidity, and sheer wantonness. It was not that she was unfaithful to me," Veit quickly added; "no, she appeared utterly devoted. No, it was the fact that she couldn't help being flirtatious, in that entirely insincere way that vapid women have. She *has* to be the object of all desire and envy. I began to think that her marriage to a Scheuerl served the latter, at least as far as other women are concerned. After a half year of marriage, I found I could not stand to be in her presence—even though

I could continue to enjoy her body, wretched me! But I was trapped—I felt trapped!

"You can then understand how eagerly I took up my father's plan to send me to Italy. Of course, she wanted to go with me—but I told her, 'You are with child. You cannot make so long a journey.' The look of disappointment on her face filled me with remorse—for a moment. I nearly resolved to ask my father to put off the journey for a time; but that passed. I needed to get away from her before I came utterly to hate her! Thus, I spent the next year and a half, wandering Italy. When I returned, I found she had given birth. To a son. She had him christened Friedrich, after my father."

* * *

"As I have told you, Italy was a revelation to me. I found there more than beauty and sordid corruption. I discovered a way that I could indulge my desire for study while assuring my father that I was not neglecting our family's business interests—or my wife, for that matter."

Lorenz felt a pang of sorrow for his friend. To be yoked to a woman so inferior in mind and heart—to have to endure her silly prattle: a man of Veit's character, he knew, could scarce endure it, no matter how beautiful the woman was. The expression on his face must have betrayed something of his thoughts, for Veit stopped short. Reddening, he interjected:

"*Ach*, Lorenz!" he said. "You cannot hide what you think of me." Lorenz tried to speak, but Veit waved him to silence: "You despise me—please, do not try to deny it. You despise me for being a bad husband and father. I cannot blame you—for I despise myself . . .

"But though I despise myself, I cannot regret what I have done. In Florence, I met a prominent member of one of the great merchant families there—Girolamo Donati by name. I suppose you haven't heard of him, but he and his family are well known by Nürnbergers, and respected. This Girolamo, I found, is a scholar and something of a poet—we became great friends, though he is several years my senior. When I told him that I wanted to return to the university, he offered to pen a letter to my father in support of my plea. He said he would tell my father that among the *best* merchant families in Italy, a cultivated mind and palate were now deemed as important as solid business sense; and that since I, in his judgment, was blessed with *extraordinary* gifts of mind and heart—I admit he laid it on a little thick, here—he would *recommend* that my father allow me some time longer at the university. And, dear Lorenz, the letter did the trick! My father was so impressed that *Girolamo Donati* would take my part in this, that he allowed me to return to Heidelberg. It is now nearly two years since I've been back."

As he told his story, Veit had grown elated; but drawing to a close, he seemed to deflate. He shook his head sadly. "But, alas!" he sighed. "My time at Heidelberg has now truly come to an end. My father bids me return to Nürnberg. I shall leave here in only a few days."

* * *

But Veit in short order recovered himself. Filling his and Lorenz's glasses with wine, he lifted his own and took the merest sip. He then looked full on Lorenz. "And now," he said, "you must tell me about yourself."

Lorenz was uneasy. He smiled. "There is not much to say," he said. "The life of a monk is, well, retired and uneventful."

"Uneventful?" Veit chuckled. "Yes, probably for most monks. But, it appears, you have been at the center of some rather eventful events. Your Luther, I need not tell you, has become the talk of Germany—and, as I hear, of Rome as well."

Lorenz shook his head and laughed. "But Frater Laurentius has not," he said. "I am but an insignificant *magister* of the rather small and humble Wittenberg University. Scarcely anyone knows my name."

Veit took another sip of his wine and then placed the glass on the table. "Indeed," he said. "And if you do not wish to speak of yourself—a trait very becoming to a monk, I should say—perhaps you will tell me of this Frater Martin of yours."

"That I will, gladly. But I really do not know where to begin. You know, I'm sure, the events that have transpired—"

"Indeed, I do—but I want to know something of the man. Tell me about Luther!"

Lorenz paused and took some wine to lubricate his thoughts. At length he said, "I scarcely know where to begin. It is rather like asking a man to describe his father—for he has been like a father to me. His words have been a balm to my wounded heart, though I daresay I do not yet live by all his counsels. It is like this—no, I will not attempt to describe what he has been to me. I will tell you what he has been to our order.

"I think I can describe him in no other way than to repeat what so many of my confreres have said about him—he is another Sankt Paul. His zeal, his love of Scripture, his very demeanor serve as an inspiration and a goad to us. He has opened the Scriptures to us—it is almost as if we had never understood them before! And it is not only I who say this; even our oldest and most learned confreres say the same. We feel as if, until he broke the bread of Scripture for us, that we had never before tasted the Gospel. He has cleared away the centuries of dross that have obscured the sacred pages—we hear, it seems for the first time, the words of Our Lord, of his apostles, of Paul himself. And now Frater Martin's clarion voice is awakening the Church and stirring the longing of our German people for a true reform, a return to purity and genuine Christian piety."

Veit did not immediately respond. He seemed to be mulling over all that his friend had told him. When at last he spoke, it was with unwonted gravity. "I hear your words," he said. "They echo what so many others have said about Luther. Some of the most learned men in Nürnberg — Pirkheimer, for instance, and my cousin, Christoph Scheurl — say the same about him. But frankly, Lorenz, your words trouble me. I am no theologian, but I wonder how one man can be right and everyone else wrong. The Dominicans speak of him as if he were a heretic — "

"The Dominicans," Lorenz said, with an inflection of disdain; "but they are the worst logic choppers and obstructionists! Look what they've done with Reuchlin. It is intolerable!"

"Is it? I daresay, you have the Nürnberg humanists with you on this; and, I admit, they are learned men — far more learned than I. But the Dominicans, too, are learned men — and I am not so sure they aren't right about Reuchlin . . . "

Veit's words stung Lorenz. "Oh, come now!" he said. "How can you defend them — their filthy libels against so great a scholar are intolerable! And what of the faked miracle in Bern?"

"A most reprehensible affair," Veit replied. "I do not defend it. And those who perpetrated it have been punished. But you cannot condemn all of them for the crimes of a few. And as for filthy libels — well, what of the *Epistulae Obscurorum Virorum?* Reuchlin's defenders have given as well as they have gotten."

Lorenz had to admit the justice of what Veit said; he himself despised the "Obscure Men." And Reuchlin had been as crude as his opponents. It was all the normal way of dispute, of course, but Lorenz didn't like it. "You are certainly right about the *Epistulae,*" he said. "But I don't see how you can countenance the treatment of Reuchlin."

"I do not countenance it, not at all," Veit replied. "I merely point out that fault is not all on one side."

"Perhaps not," Lorenz shrugged, "but in the case of Frater Martin, it is otherwise. If the Dominicans think him a heretic, then they do not understand him!"

Veit smiled. "Well, I will not deny it—for, indeed, I know nothing about the matter," he said. "I will attend the disputation—maybe that will clarify matters for me . . ."

"I think you should."

" . . . And, I may have more opportunity afterwards." Veit smiled as one does who is about to convey pleasant news. "There is some talk of inviting your Frater Martin to come to Nürnberg on his return journey—we'll even provide him a coach, for his comfort. And for yours; for, no doubt, you would accompany him."

Lorenz felt his heart contract. To Nürnberg? No, it couldn't be . . .

Veit's brows knit. He looked intently on his friend. "Lorenz," he said, "whatever is wrong? You blanch . . ."

Lorenz did not answer immediately. He glanced across the room—what should he say? He had intended to avoid saying anything about *her*—and Veit had not brought the subject up. But could he avoid it now? He could lie, say he felt a sudden distemper—but, no, Veit would detect the subterfuge. And, indeed, he wanted to know about *her*, what had happened to her, even if it tore open old wounds that had never really healed. No, he would not lie.

"Pray," he said, "if you have any say in the matter, do not invite him to Nürnberg, for I must accompany him."

Veit did not reply, but Lorenz could see that he understood. Lorenz took courage from it.

"For you see," he said hesitantly, "if I should enter the city . . . the shame, for I might..." He could say no more.

But Veit, in scarce a whisper, as if he were afraid another would hear, finished the sentence for him—"you might meet Beatrice?"

"Yes," Lorenz replied, and then added (irrelevantly, he thought), "and Herr Auer."

Veit did not speak for some moments. He glanced up at the ceiling, and then across the room, at the hearth, as if seeking resolution therein. Then, after what seemed an unbearably long time, he looked full on Lorenz, and striking his fist lightly on the table, broke the silence:

"You need have no fear, my dearest friend." Veit spoke with a warmth devoid of his wonted banter. "You needn't fear. Herr Auer, alas, is dead. And Beatrice —"

"Yes?"

"Beatrice you will not find in Nürnberg."

* * *

Noises from the city, meaningless and vague, came from without the leaded windows; light, flowing through the diamonds of glass, fell on his hands, staining them green and red. The fire crackled in the hearth, while a fly drozed wearily over the remnants of the food set on plates before then. "Beatrice you will not find in Nürnberg." Herr Auer, dead. And Beatrice —

"Veit, whatever do you mean?" Lorenz said at last.

"I mean, simply"—Veit spoke slowly, deliberately—"that she no longer abides in the city. You needn't fear meeting her if you come there."

Lorenz pondered the words. He shot a questioning look at Veit.

Veit avoided it. When at last he spoke, it was with the same deliberation.

"I did not know—indeed, very few knew—of Herr Auer's ailment. He kept it a secret from all but his physician. Even now, I do not know what it was. He might have lived longer, had not—but, *ach!* I speculate. I know nothing . . . "

The two friends shared an awkward silence for some moments. All was quiet, save for the faint sounds of the city from outside the windows. Lorenz's eye caught sight of a spider crawling up the wall.

Veit continued.

"As I was at the time in Nürnberg, I at last gave her your last letter—it was the only time I did so directly, for I dared not trust it to Greta. I knew, of course, what it said, and I was very bad at dissembling, for she asked me what was wrong. I laughed it off, and she pretended to accept my explanation. But I could see I did not convince her. . . .

"I did not convince her—but, perhaps, my manner prepared her. I do not know.

"A week passed; then, another few days. I did not see her or hear anything about her. Even Greta was in the dark. I returned to Heidelberg, troubled but hopeful that all would come off for the best.

"But then I received a letter from Greta. My dear betrothed related that Joachim Mager had visited *Auerhaus*; that he had asked Beatrice for her hand, but that she had refused him. According to Greta at least, Herr Auer was livid with anger. She said he had even struck Beatrice, which I hardly believe. But I suppose his mood was none too convivial when he heard her reasons . . . ."

Lorenz hesitated, then asked—"which were?"

Veit looked him full in the eye. "Fear not, my friend," he said, "I am assured she said nothing of you. She dissembled. She said, she could not marry—She could not marry, for she had made a vow."

Veit's tone carried the smallest hint of rebuke. Lorenz felt a sinking inside. She had made a vow . . .

"What was a pious man like Herr Auer to say to that? He could forbid her, but at the peril of his own salvation. In the end, he acquiesced. He sought to place her with the Poor Clares—Mother Caritas Pirkheimer's bevy of ascetical, well-bred ladies. But she would not stay in the city. At last, Herr Auer agreed to allow her to join the Augustinian hermitesses at Pillenreuth—well within Nürnberg's jurisdiction, but outside the city. There she has been for nigh on five years. I have learned nothing of her since."

"And Herr Auer?"

"Not four months passed before his sickness took him."

Lorenz knew not what to say to this news. He understood. She had loved him. She had remained true to him—for he knew it was not for any vow she made to God that she entered the cloister. She would not break the vow she had made to him, before God. He could not think of Beatrice living so austere a life. She was not made for it; but she cast aside her station, her proclivities, and a good marriage—

He glanced up. He had felt Veit's eyes on him. Veit was studying him.

"Does my news displease you? Or are you happy that she chose the way—the way you have chosen?"

Lorenz shook his head. "I do not know," he said. "I do not know. I feel neither joy nor sorrow at the news."

He did not lie—not quite. He felt no joy or sorrow. He felt dismay.

This was just another fruit, was it not, of his betrayal?

CHAPTER 4

"**D**EAREST BEATRICE—YOU WILL NEVER read these words. But I write to you, for to you alone have I ever been able to bare my soul. You would think me foolish, no doubt, if you knew of it, or you would scorn me, as would be your right. I suppose this letter is like the song I wrote, the song in which I thought I had veiled my love for you. Then you discovered the hidden meaning of the words you heard. Now you shall not have the chance even to read the words I pen."

I met Veit in Heidelberg. He told me all—about your father's death and about you. Dearest one, this was not what I had wanted when I wrote to you, releasing you . . .

I do not know if you have found peace—I pray you have. For many years I have sought peace, but it eluded me. I now write to you what I have never revealed in words to anyone else—not to my superiors, not to the father of my soul, not even to the man who, until very late, I thought my dearest friend. I scarce admitted it to myself, though it sat upon my shoulders like a jeering ape. I now lay it out in black ink: I set out on the way of truth under the veil of a lie—the lie I told to you and the truth I dared not reveal even before the altar of my God. For which, in my conception to new life, I deemed myself stillborn.

But this was not my greatest sin. A far blacker iniquity clung to me, though I for so long did not see it.

I thought I might scrub away the tar of my sin by applying myself to assiduous spiritual labor. I would be a monk. I would live the holy rule of our Father Augustin to the very letter. And I would go beyond the letter, and punish myself in fasting and prayer and spiritual labors. Surely, these would cover my iniquity. Surely these would win me peace! But in them I found no peace, only greater torment. God was far from me, lowering over me, scowling in judgment.

I thought I knew why I found no peace — because I made no confession of my sin. This, I thought, was the source of my distress. Indeed, as long as I would not confess, all my fasting, penances, vigils, and almsgiving were a mockery. By refusing to follow this one command, this one law — to repent and do penance — I was guilty of the entire law. For long I would not admit this. I thought to pile work on work, penance on penance, as if by doing so I could cover that one small sin in a heap of holiness. But in all my labors I found only the one thing from which I fled. I found despair.

And then came the journey to Heidelberg.

You cannot know how happy I was to leave Wittenberg, to journey, though laboriously by foot, through the hills and valleys of Franken, to breathe its air, to drink its waters once again! And then to behold, for the first time, that beauteous maiden, fair Heidelberg, nestled in her bower of wooded hills! I felt as I did when I first saw Nürnberg. I had escaped the boors of Saxony, if only for a time. Immersed in a great event, I could distract myself — as I had so often done before — from despair. It was muted. I made the acquaintance of cultivated men and some of the greatest men in our order; and, to my embarrassment, but also my joy, I saw Veit again. My dear friend, Veit.

But it was by Veit's words that the terrors of hell could break through the thin shell I had formed about myself and immerse me once again in fear and despair.

I knew he studiously avoided mentioning you, as I did. Of course, seeing him, stirred up thoughts of you, but I strove to force them down. But it was all in vain. He told me at last of you and of your father — and thus of the suffering that I brought upon you both.

That night on my bed, I was wracked with fear and terror — would I last until morning? Would I not, that night, be plunged into hell? I cried out to God, but I was certain he would not hear me. I cried out to him, but I knew I could not do the one thing that (I thought) was needful. And even if I did that, did not the tale of my sins weigh in the balance against me? I could never atone. I was among those whom God hated...

He lay down the pen. On the wall, above the scriptorium, it hung, arms outstretched, hands and feet transfixed in the agony of love. It was love that was expressed, he now knew, not judgment — but a love that bestows on the beloved the agonies of hell. "The cross, the cross alone — that is the Christian faith!" "Give me thy righteousness, and take thou my sin." He repeated the words to himself. And then said them again, and over again.

Once more he took up his pen.

I do not understand what then happened. I awoke the next morning, without fear, but not consoled. It was not the old numbness but a grim resolution to push on to the end. I was certain, then, that I could do nothing — my works were naught but dirty rags, useless, destined for the furnace. I said my Mass and betook myself to the disputation.

The words were not new — I had heard them many times before; but it was as if I was hearing them for the first time, or for the first time their meaning penetrated into me. It was not Frater Martin who defended his theses, but a brother from Wittenberg. But the words were Martin's: "Though man's works always appear good, they nevertheless are naught but mortal sins." "The works of the righteous are mortal sins." The sense of these words, which I now understood, shook me to the core. Here I was, dreading damnation for my sins, when even the righteous need fear condemnation—and that for their good works! And, what's more, no matter what I did, or the righteous man does, we are bound to sin. And if we strive against sin, seeking to do what is pleasing to God, we sin doubly. Again, the terror billowed up from within me—what then, I cried in my darkness, has God created us for despair? Hell yawned beneath my feet; there was no firm foothold.

But then I heard the words—

It is certain that a man must utterly despair of himself before he can receive the grace of Christ.

He is not righteous who does much, but he who, without works, believes much in Christ.

If I had not been in the press of men, I would have thrown myself to the earth right then. But in the silence of my heart, where none could hear me save he alone, I cried out—"Give me thy righteousness, and take thou my sin." And all that before had been darkness and despair became light, hope, and indescribable joy.

Why do I write these things to you, O Beatrice? It is not to tell you that I am free from remorse for all that I have done to you. Though Christ has taken my sin and clothed me in his righteousness, sin remains sin; his grace does not change betrayal to fidelity; and I betrayed you. Moreover, I lied before my superiors and before God. But these, though horrible in themselves, were not my greatest sin—the motive for which I sinned. I sinned that I might do righteously. I sinned in the hope that I might please God by my works. But even had I never sinned, if I had done righteously, I had sinned. So steeped in sin are we, so sold to the devil, that we cannot help but sin, whether we do well or ill. Only faith in Christ can make us whole.

And, this is the most painful truth of all — if I had not betrayed you, if I had been faithful to you, I had sinned; for fidelity in man, and any virtue of his, is but a cloak for the self-glorification that seeks its own way rather than the way of God. Man is naught but sin.

Would that you could read the words I write! I would fill you with my new-found hope — that the Holy Spirit is at last, after these many centuries, being so poured out again on the earth that no corner will remain dry from his inundation. Still, that you could read these words — or, better yet, that I could speak to you face to face! But that may not be — not yet. Yet, we cannot cross to one another. The water that separates is deep.

* * *

He lay down his pen. Taking the candle that fed the little orb of light that encompassed him, he rose from his chair and moved across the room to his bed. Blowing out the candle, he lay down. In only a few hours he would rise again, for Matins.

He felt tired, but he could not sleep. He stared up into the darkness. Why had he written the letter? Was it fitting that he do so — he, a priest? Should not he rather suppress his love for her? Oh, yes, he loved her! The years in the cloister could not obliterate that love, though he had sought to deny it, tried earnestly to smother it. And, now several weeks after he had returned to Wittenberg, he no longer sought to do so. Why need he?

The sense of his love grew even as the old malaise had begun to draw round him again. The euphoria of liberation that he had felt at Heidelberg had gradually given way to that old sense of emptiness, though no longer punctuated by recurring, piercing goads of terror. He half longed to feel again those terrors. Would they not be better than this peace — this charnel peace?

Chapter 4

Did he write the letter, thinking that by recalling memory he could conjure up faded joy again?

He had felt that joy the days following the disputation. Indeed, he was not the only one. All his brethren jubilated in what they called the "unveiling of the Gospel." Even that Friar Preacher from Köln, that Martin Butzer fellow, had gloried in the "new age" that he said he now knew had dawned with Luther. A Dominican! And as their carriage jolted out of Heidelberg, Frater Martin himself commented on how "jocund our Frater Laurentius has become." Indeed, he little cared then if their journey would take them to Nürnberg. He knew it would not; that had already been decided. They would, instead, return to Wittenberg by way of Erfurt.

Erfurt! The scene of his greatest struggles, and his betrayal. Despite his joy, his heart had recoiled at the thought of stopping there. His countenance must have betrayed his feeling when he first learned the itinerary; for Frater Martin paused a long moment after telling it, seeming to study him. Then, he said: "fear not, brother. Have faith in Christ!"

But Erfurt meant not only revisiting his shame; it meant seeing Sebastian again. It had been two years since he and his friend had met; but they had kept up a correspondence. With each letter, Lorenz could sense Sebastian's growing unease over his ideas. And in the last letter, Sebastian had all but called Frater Martin a heretic. What would Sebastian say about the gospel Lorenz had discovered in Heidelberg? He could not avoid speaking of it to him. He could hide nothing from Sebastian.

* * *

He had expected rebuke or censure—or, at the very least, a vigorous assault. Instead, Sebastian listened to him with what seemed a detached silence—his hands folded on his lap, his eyes averted, fixed, it seemed, on the ground before him. Except for a few queries for clarification, Sebastian said nothing to interrupt Lorenz's steady exposition of what he called the "theology of the cross." When Lorenz had finished, Sebastian sat in silence for several moments. Then, glancing up at Lorenz, he smiled (the merest flicker) before his face softened into an expression of sadness.

"You call this doctrine *light*—and I know what dark paths you have trodden, my friend. From the day we entered the monastery, I could feel your distress—though its cause I could not discern, nor can I now. I have, though, sought always to accompany you by prayer and, betimes, by exhortation. I have not sought to pry into your mind and heart, nor will I do so now. I see a change has come over you, an appearance of joy and peace . . ."

"But you do not think it true joy, true peace?"

Sebastian hesitated but then said, "no."

Lorenz sought to steel himself.

"But, I assure you, the joy is real, and so is the peace." He did not look directly at Sebastian.

"I will not argue the point with you." Sebastian's tone was gentle.

Lorenz dared not look at Sebastian.

"But you doubt they are real."

"Yes, I do."

"Why?"

They sat in the cloister garden. The sky above was a radiant blue. Clouds moved slowly across the azure expanse. A spring chill pervaded the air. Sebastian drew one hand from his lap and extended it to a blue flower of flax. He pinched the stem between his thumb and forefinger, then drew them up to the base of the flower.

"Peace," he said, his voice scarce more than a murmur, "peace is reconciliation. It is union."

Sebastian still held the flax flower. "He will not pluck it,"

Lorenz thought. And he did not. He let go the stem, and placed his hand with the other again in his lap.

"What you have described to me is not union. It is a separation. Man, separated as if by a measureless gulf from God. You say, Christ gives justice to the sinner. You say, Christ takes on man's sin, but is not made sinful thereby. But neither is man made just—truly just; he is not redeemed. You see, if I take fire to my breast, I am made warm. I become fire. But you would have it that Our Lord takes us to his breast, but we are not transformed thereby. Man remains in himself as corrupt as before. Can this mean anything else but that he remains as separated as before?"

"But this shows God's power—and his measureless love! He loves sinners!" For the first time Lorenz darted his eyes into Sebastian's. He felt he had scored a point against him.

Sebastian, however, did not waver. "Is it power," he replied, "that cannot effect what it purposes? And is it love that does not surrender itself to the beloved?

"My dearest friend, whom I love more than even myself, hear me! You are seeking peace, but you have not yet found the way to peace!"

*　*　*

He awoke to the gentle knock and the voice—*Benedictus Deus!*

> *Et nunc et in aeternum. Amen*

He rose, lit a candle, poured water into a basin, and laved his face. He turned, opened the door of his cell, and joined the brothers, moving in a slow procession to the chapel.

> *Domine, labia mea aperies . . .*
> *Et os meum annuntiabit laudem tuam . . .*
> *Jubilemus Deo, Salutari nostro . . .*
> *Venite, exultemus Domino, iubilemus*
> *Deo salutari nostro . . .*

He joined in chanting the psalm, but his mind strayed through the chapel doors and into the early morning cold. It crossed the leagues of plain, hill, farmland, and water lying between him and Erfurt. In his mind's eye, he stood outside the walls of Erfurt, but he could not yet enter its gates. The hour was too early. Instead, he gazed up into the heavens, still bright with stars. Sebastian, too, was singing Matins. But, even if the gates opened, and he could enter the city, would he join him there?

> Consors paterni luminis,
> Lux ipse lucis, et dies,
> Noctem canendo rumpimus:
> Assiste postulantibus.

No. He could not take that path again. He had found the light he sought ...

> Aufer tenebras mentium ...

He had found joy, and he could find it again ...

> Fuga catervas daemonum ...

He looked up at the heavens, bright ...

> Expelle somnolentiam
> Ne ...

... bright with stars ...

> ... pigritantes obruat.

But did they betoken hope?
Or were they stern sentinels, guarding the heaven of his desire from the night?

THE
BONFIRE

CHAPTER 1

"THE WHOLE FEEL OF AUGSBURG WAS one of foreboding—and his precipitous flight thence would indicate that at least he felt threatened, despite the safe conduct . . ."

. . . The departure of Staupitz and Link from the city (after they had, as I heard, urged him to submit to the cardinal) may have unsettled him. I know nothing more, since I was not his confidant.

You write that Frater Martin treated the document as a fraud. I can tell you, that he has since changed his mind. For my part, friend Veit, I am uncertain. Though I would put nothing past the curia or even His Holiness, I cannot think the cardinal a party to treachery. Granted, I saw very little of him; but what little I saw seemed to confirm his reputation not only for learning but for mercy as well.

But I rush ahead of the account you wished me to tell of what happened in Augsburg. I fear I will disappoint you—for I played only a very small part in the proceedings. But what little I know, I shall relate to you.

As you well know, I did not accompany Frater Martin to Augsburg. Indeed, I would have stayed in Wittenberg had not Frater Johann Lang invited me to accompany him when he passed through on his journey from Erfurt. When we arrived in Augsburg, Frater Martin was already established there, in the Carmelite

111

convent. He had not yet met with the cardinal, for he had been advised to await a guarantee of safe conduct. I can tell you that, whatever the Diet's feelings towards him, and the Kaiser's, Augsburg stood with him—and not only the common folk, but the chief burghers as well. The Elector Friedrich, too, lent him two of his trusted counselors. I doubt anyone would have attempted anything against him then.

What was Frater Martin's demeanor? Was he afraid? Was he resolute . . .

*   *   *

What had been Martin's demeanor?

When Lorenz and Frater Johann arrived in Augsburg, they applied immediately to the Carmelite convent. The prior, Johann Frosch, greeted them with pleasure. "Two more of Frater Martin's brothers come to stand with him against the world!" he exclaimed. "How good God is." Frosch sent a brother to announce their arrival, while he himself led them to the refectory and placed good bread and wine before them. "We shall have cells prepared for you. In the meanwhile, rest from your long journey," he said.

It seemed only a matter of minutes before they were led in to see Luther. He was in a room with vaulted ceilings, books lining the walls, seated at a scriptorium. It seemed he had just laid down his pen and was talking to a man standing near, whom Lorenz did not recognize. Lorenz was surprised to see Staupitz—had he made the long journey from Innsbruck just to be with Martin? When Martin and Staupitz noticed the newcomers, they rose. The unknown man, dressed in rich attire, turned and sized them up indifferently. Lorenz approached Staupitz first and then turned to Martin, who embraced him and then Lang.

"*Fratres*—what brings you to Augsburg?" Martin's eyes were moist. He seemed agitated, even elated. But there was something antic in his demeanor, something unsettled.

"Have you come to see Daniel cast to the lions?"

Lorenz glanced over at Lang. Tears stood in his eyes.

"No, *frater*," Lang said. "We have come to join Daniel in the lions' den."

Martin nodded his head and slapped Lang on the shoulder. Then he let out a small laugh. "There is only one lion, my friend," he said. "And you need not fear him—he has a very particular palate."

He then turned, and Lorenz caught his eye. He thought he read resolution—and fear—there. "It is good, very good, for you to come," he said.

"But let me introduce you to a friend"—and Martin held out his hand to the stranger. "This is Herr Johann Auer, a lawyer of Augsburg and a councilor. He has been aiding me with his sage advice."

Auer bowed. "I do not know," he said, "if my counsel is of any weight. Of greater import is the fact that many here in Augsburg will do anything in their power to help Frater Martin. Indeed, I think the entire city stands with him."

Lorenz recalled that at these words, Martin's eyes softened. He seemed, again, to be reckoning within. He slowly nodded.

"God comforts us in them," he said. "They are my Timothy, Luke, and Epaphroditus." He then let out a nervous laugh—"and, perhaps, they shall deliver me from the lion's maw, or the cardinal's pyre.

"But if not, so be it!"

Then more softly, as if to himself—"but what a scandal shall I be to my poor parents."

How different was Martin's manner the day he received one of the cardinal's lackeys, an Italian by the name of Serralonga. Serralonga was refined; he was glib and loquacious. Lorenz watched the man's hands—they gestured with eloquence as he spoke. They were soft, white, with long, tapered fingers.

Yet, Lorenz thought, those hands could deftly throttle a man, if commanded to.

"As I advised you before—do not think you can sport with the cardinal. He will not run the ring with you." The man's tone was seeming friendly but admonitory. "There is only one word the cardinal wants to hear—"

"I know that word," Martin interjected. "And I will gladly say it, if His Eminence but show me my error."

"Oh, he can show you your error—but he has not come to banter words with you." Serralonga languidly waved one hand. "You must know that the diet, the emperor, the princes—no one will stand with you against the cardinal."

"They will not stand with me, but one will," Martin rejoined. His eyes were resolute. They burned with a steady fire.

"Who will stand with you?" Serralonga chuckled softly. "Saxony? Surely, you do not think he will take up arms on your account?"

"I neither think it nor wish it."

Serralonga waved his arms in an expansive gesture. He moved his head from side to side. "You do not seek the Elector's protection? But without it, where will you be?"

Martin spoke softly, but his tone was taut. "Under the heavens," he said.

* * *

. . . I will let you judge by the events. After I arrived in Augsburg, I learned that Frater Martin, by the advice of counselors, had applied for a safe conduct to the cardinal. This arrived on a Monday. The next day would be the hearing. That evening, Martin called me to his cell; he requested that I accompany him, if I wished. I confess, though I felt the honor, I was fearful. But I noted the spirit that animated him, and it encouraged me. I said I would join him. Yet, I wondered—how could he be so cheerful? For he was, Veit, most cheerful! I couldn't bear not asking him—was he not afraid? He said, "the flesh fears, brother. But I am assured of this—the affair belongs to Christ. If he upholds the cause, it is upheld. If not, then I can do nothing for him, and he must bear the shame."

The next morning, together with Link, Frater Johann Frosch, and two Carmelite brothers, we went to see the cardinal. We were a glum group—all except Martin. He went forth like a warrior to battle. Noting our silence as we left the convent, he turned to us and said, "the will of the Lord be done, brothers. Remember, I pray—even here, in this city, in the midst of enemies, Jesus Christ reigns."

To be in the presence of a cardinal, a prince of the Church, awed me. Of course, I knew Cajetan's reputation as a most learned prelate; and, Frater Martin had assured me, he did not share in the corruptions of the papal court. But these were not foremost in my mind as we entered the chamber; that he wielded the power of Pope Leo, was. He sat behind a small table, dressed in scarlet robes. Behind him, on a peg, hung his red, wide-brimmed cardinal's hat. The cardinal's expression was grave, but he rose when Martin prostrated himself before him, and approaching him, gently raised him to his feet. The cardinal then resumed his seat.

I must say in all justice that Cajetan's manner was kindly, even fatherly. It was immediately clear, however, that he would brook no debate. He demanded that Martin recant his heresies, that he promise not to promote them in the future, and that he should do nothing further to harm the Church. Martin, still with that spirit that animated him when we departed the convent, asked that his errors be specified. Cajetan replied that the theses denied that the Church possesses a treasury of merits won by Christ. When Martin asked where the Church had delivered such a doctrine, the cardinal leafed through a book that lay before him on the table and read a passage from Clement VI that he thought supported his contention. The learned Cajetan, I think, was taken aback by Martin's rejoinder—for he declared that the text, called *Unigenitus,* opposed the clear teaching of Scripture. The cardinal flared at him and demanded a recantation. Martin said he could not recant, not until he was shown how what the pope taught was not contrary to Scripture and the Fathers. It was clear that Cajetan would not, or could not, present such proofs, and he grew the more angry. But Martin stood his ground. And there the interview ended, for that day.

I did not attend the second interview, the following day. Frater Martin had with him, instead, two imperial councilors, as well as Staupitz. I learned afterward that Martin protested that he was not conscious of having said anything against Scripture, the Fathers, the popes, or right reason; and, he offered to submit himself to the judgment of the universities, including Paris. Cajetan, however, would have nothing of it. He had come, he said, merely to induce Martin's recantation. But, in the end, he allowed Martin to submit a written declaration of his position. Again, in regards to the cardinal, I think his desire was sincere—he wanted to get Martin to recant and not merely to be rid of a troublesome monk. Even after the second interview, Martin himself, though he wavered, still confided in Cajetan's honesty and justice.

I was again at Martin's side the next day in the cardinal's chamber. The document he presented to Cajetan was prodigiously long. Essentially, as regards *Unigenitus,* Martin's document said what he boldly declared to the cardinal—"I am not so temerarious that, on account of a single papal decretal, itself ambiguous and obscure, to deny the clear testimonies of Scripture." Such a reply could not, as you must imagine, pacify the cardinal. Casting aside any fatherly pretense, he railed at Martin, urging him to recant. Martin himself could not pierce through the cardinal's din, but at last he did get his attention by shouting (yes, shouting! What else was he to do?) that he would recant if *Unigenitus* called Christ's merits the treasure of the Church. Cajetan, doubtless thinking he had Martin at bay, found the place in the text that he thought supported his claim The cardinal's air of triumph was vexing, my dear Veit—but it was all made up for by his discomfiture; for Martin showed Cajetan—the great scholar, Cajetan—how the text in no way supported his claim. With argument exhausted, the cardinal fell back on peremptory command: "Go and do not come back to me until you are willing to recant!" he snarled.

* * *

No, this was not exactly how it happened; but it wouldn't do to tell Veit everything. "After all," Lorenz reflected, "I captured the essence of the interview."

One could not, doubtless, expect Martin not to feel some confusion in the presence of such as Cajetan.

Still, Martin had dissembled. He must have dissembled, for he knew the text from *Unigenitus* well. He had discussed it with Lorenz and had dismissed it as opposed to Scripture. And when Cajetan quoted the text to him, Martin's reply was, to Lorenz's mind, evasive. The rejoinder was even impertinent.

"Oh, yes! But that text says something quite different. You said Christ's merits *are* a treasure; *this* says Christ *acquired* a treasure. *Are* and *acquire* do not mean the same thing. What, do you think we Germans are so ignorant as to know no grammar?"

Yes, the cardinal had properly interpreted the text, and Martin was trying to maneuver himself out of a tight spot. That much seemed clear to Lorenz. True, Cajetan would not do what Martin asked—prove him wrong from the Scriptures and the Fathers; but Martin did say he would recant if the text said what Cajetan claimed. And then, that request to provide a written statement the next day—Martin was wriggling, that he might not be pinned down.

But, really, given the outcome of a direct challenge, could anyone blame him?

And what of Staupitz? Veit had written that the word in Nürnberg was that Staupitz had abandoned Martin. What could he say to that? After all, he himself knew little of what had transpired, except that Staupitz had released Martin from his vows. What that signified, he could not say. Martin himself seemed uncertain of what it meant—whether, by it, Staupitz was casting him from the order or was acting in his behalf.

The next day, Staupitz departed from Augsburg.

Was it not, then, abandonment?

* * *

As to your question concerning our beloved father, Staupitz, I do not claim to be privy to any peculiar confidence, but I doubt that what he did—release Frater Martin from his vows—represented any abandonment or betrayal. It would be best to disabuse anyone of so gross a charge against the Reverend Father, as he has always regarded Frater Martin with the most tender paternal affection.

I can tell you little more of what transpired—for there is really not much to tell. Frater Martin, as we have said, fled Augsburg secretly, but a full two days afterwards he appealed to the "pope badly informed to the pope better informed." With Martin departed, I saw no point in my remaining in Augsburg. With a brother Augustinian, I made my way—by a more direct route than Martin's—back to Wittenberg.

CHAPTER 2

THEY WERE LIKE AN ARMY ARRAYED FOR battle. Some 200 students, brandishing pikes and halberds, strode lustily through the suburbs of Leipzig, toward the great east gate of the city. They were singing (what songs, he could not remember) as they marched in the winding procession, following the two carriages.

It was a warm day and clear, the Feast of the Nativity of Johann Baptist. Lorenz marked the day and wondered what it betokened. The Baptist had come to bear witness to the Christ—and was that not the very thing that all these men and those riding in the carriage had come to do? And what would be the upshot of it all?

Lorenz turned his head (as he had many times that day) to observe the cavalcade behind him. The weapons, borne aloft, rose and fell with the cadence of the men's marching. Their blades flashed in the sun. He could feel the battle lust quicken in his own heart. As he turned back, he caught Johann Lang's eye—it, too, flashed, and Lang smiled.

He, Lang, with the old Wittenberg theologue, Nikolaus Amsdorf, and a few other professors walked just behind the carriage that carried Frater Martin and, with him, his now seemingly ever-present companion, Philipp Melanchthon. The foremost carriage was laden with Karlstadt—by proclamation the champion of this martial display, but not its hero, at least as far as the singing students were concerned.

As the carriages crossed the moat and passed through the gate, they came alongside the university church. It was then Lorenz heard the loud crack and crunch, as of the snapping of an enormous beam. Startled, his eyes darted to see Karlstadt's carriage wobble and career like a drunken man. A rear wheel rolled off to the left, the carriage pitched sinister, and Karlstadt, thrown from his seat, landed on his rear in the mud. Just behind him, students erupted in laughter. Martin's carriage did not stop, but continued on, taking first place in the procession. Two Wittenberg professors pulled Karlstadt from the mire.

Only later did Lorenz learn the name of the church that witnessed Karlstadt's fall. The *Paulinerkirche*.

* * *

... Actually, Frater Martin had met Eck in Augsburg October last and made arrangements for the disputation then and there. Of course, then it was Andreas Bodenstein—whom everyone calls Karlstadt—who was to contend with Eck; Martin was to have no part in it. Certainly, that was not how it turned out, as you well know. Nor do I think that it was ever in Eck's mind to debate Karlstadt alone, without Martin. His printed attacks on Martin were, I think, goads to prod him into the lists. Whether they had that intent or not, that was finally their effect.

Veit, you have likely not heard of the meetings that Martin had with Carl von Miltitz, of the papal court, throughout the autumn and into the winter of this year. But in case you have, I wanted to dispel any intimation that Martin had acted unbecomingly. Miltitz, as you probably know, came to Germany with the golden rose to woo Elector Friedrich for the pope. Miltitz met with Martin in Altenburg and got him to agree to remain silent and even to publish a tract defending the pope's authority. Well, that was in January. In February, Eck directly challenged Martin to debate (by publishing 13 theses, seemingly against Karlstadt, but really against Martin), and Martin (seemingly in violation of his promise to Miltitz) accepted the challenge by publishing counter theses. As I said, it may appear that Martin broke his promise to Miltitz, but it was not so. Martin promised silence only if his opponents observed silence.

I will get to the disputation itself and address what you heard about what Martin said concerning the pope and councils; but, before I do so, I will give you some account, as you requested, of Melanchthon. "What part has he been playing in Luther's drama?" you ask. Well, an important and, from my point of view, a rather unexpected one. Martin has not known Philipp Schwartzerdt long; not even a year—he arrived in Wittenberg only August last. (By the way, I call him Schwartzerdt, not Melanchthon, because I despise this habit among the humanists of adorning themselves with Greeky or Latiny forms of their names. What? Do they despise Germany so much that they cannot call themselves by their fathers' names? Of late, I have come to prefer my mother's tongue even to Latin—which is why I write to you in German. Away with foolish pretension!)

Schwartzerdt is the prodigy men say he is—I myself have been studying Greek under him, as well as Hebrew, though he is less proficient in the latter tongue. Martin, too, has been his student—though I think Schwartzerdt more beholden to Martin than Martin to him. He has become as devoted to Martin's teachings as I and so many in Wittenberg (and, indeed, Germany) are. But Martin's fast friendship with him is less easily understood. No blood and tears have marked Schwartzerdt's embrace of the Gospel. Indeed, one suspects that his interest is almost purely intellectual; he parses Scripture as if it were Homer. He plays with it. Please understand, I don't mean to disparage him—he is indeed a great scholar, at least in the grammatical and literary arts. His theological penetration, however, is imitative—not that his brilliance does not shine here, as well; but it is a mere glimmer on the waters. It does not seek their depths. One wonders if his self-regard (with which he is replete) does not move him more than the cross. Martin, and others, have, on the contrary, passed through death and hell.

Some of us have wondered at Martin's fast friendship with Schwartzerdt—his junior by some 14 years. (I was amused to learn that he is younger than me by some four years.) Now, I do not claim that age matters—not at all. *Let none despise you for your youth.* Young men may have old hearts, and ancients the minds of children. It is not the disparity between Martin's age and Schwartzerdt's that leaves several of us scratching our heads; it is the latter's school-boy prodigy manner of approaching the mysteries. He has felt no awe. He has known no struggle.

But enough of your "Melanchthon"! You say that folks in Nürnberg "talk of nothing but Luther and Leipzig"—and you ask me about what happened, for I was there ...

* * *

"*Magister!*"

Lorenz turned to see Heinrich Wässerig, running and dodging through the crowd. He was still grasping a pike. When Wässerig caught him, "*Magister,*" he panted, "where will you sup?"

Lorenz said he had not considered it.

"Then, I pray," said Wässerig, "sup with me. I shall pay."

Lorenz laughed. "Then, I cannot refuse," he said.

In short order, he found himself amidst a throng of students, garrulous with laughter. Their spirit was infectious—their battle lust was up; he felt it. Their Achilles was about to contend with the pope's Hektor, and who could doubt the result? He was not surprised that none of them even so much as mentioned Karlstadt. It was all of Luther they spoke.

The tavern they entered was dark and smelt of pork, onions, and stale beer. Some of the denizens—all locals, Lorenz thought—looked at them askance. One grizzled old man slammed down his tankard as they entered, stood, and walked out, shaking his head. Lorenz sat down on a bench before a long table. Wässerig sat across from him.

"They hate us, you know," Wässerig said, his head nodding in the direction of a table over against a far wall. "Leipzig is with Eck."

"I am not surprised. Their university is a very old school, and ours they deem an upstart—and not a little, shall we say, *heretical*. Not only that, but..."

"But that is not all," Wässerig interrupted. "Duke Heinrich opposes us..."

"That does not surprise me either..."

"...And the bishop of Merseburg has declared excommunicate all who participate in the disputation!"

"Again, I am not surprised."

"Then, does anything surprise you?

Lorenz smiled. "Probably not. I am an old campaigner."

A waiter in a greasy apron brought them a platter of bread, one of meat, and a pitcher of beer with mugs. Wässerig poured for himself and Lorenz and then took a long draw. When he set down the mug, he laughed.

"There is someone else who isn't happy with how things are turning out..."

"Pope Leo? Cardinal Cajetan?"

"Doubtless they—but I don't mean them," Wässerig chuckled. "No, our very own Karlstadt! Being pitched into a mud hole and wallowing just like a pig, was a great blow to him. He was none too happy to hear students snort and grunt at him. Matthias Kahl himself declared aloud that that fall betokened defeat at the hands of Eck—and I think Karlstadt overheard him."

"It must have been bitter for Karlstadt, to hear that from his most devoted follower. But," Lorenz continued, "I understand Karlstadt came out of the ordeal dirty but unscathed. That, too, could be an omen."

"Perhaps," Wässerig laughed. "But of what, I cannot say."

Wässerig continued the bantering, and other students joined in. Lorenz ate and drank and withdrew into his own mind. He looked about the tavern, studying the occupants. Besides the Wittenbergers, there were laborers in patched and dirty clothes, as well as students from the university. A confusion of voices — singing, laughing, arguing — blended in cacophony. One figure, however, sitting alone at a small table against the far wall, under a dim lantern, drank in silence. He was dressed as a scholar and wore a slouch hat. He was red-bearded and stocky, but not fat. The man drew Lorenz's interest, though he could not say why. He seemed utterly oblivious to everything around him. It was not until he drained his tankard, that he at last looked about the room. He seemed indifferent to, and disdainful of, it all.

Then Lorenz's eyes and his met. And the man smiled.

* * *

. . . Antichrist.

In you, alone, Veit, do I confide. Breathe not a word of this to anyone. If you consider well what he has written, I think you will understand the context. Of late, too, he has seemed agitated — and this is not to be wondered at. At times he gives us the confidence that no more is at stake than the correction of a few wayward abuses. At other times, his words fill us with horror and dread.

But, yes, he has used *Antichrist* when speaking of the pope — though he has qualified it somewhat. "If the pope is not Antichrist," he said to several of us one day, "then he is surely Antichrist's apostle." I have been at a loss to understand just what he means by such language—does he mean Leo? Or does he mean the office? Though couched in more moderate language, his Thesis XIII troubled even Karlstadt—you say you have read it, so you know of what I speak. Even before the debate with Eck, as late as June he published a further explication of the thesis, giving several reasons for why one should yield to the pope, but denying that the office is of divine origin. But then he went further, declaring that if the pope's primacy should injure the Church, it should be abolished, since what is of purely human right must give way to the Church, not battle against her. So, you see, I was somewhat prepared for what came down at Leipzig, but not fully enough. No, not anywhere near enough.

I shall pass over the debate between Eck and Karlstadt, which began some three days after we had arrived in Leipzig. I shall only say this—though possessed of pure doctrine, Karlstadt proved no match for Eck—a tall, stout, booming man, and, like Karlstadt, possessing the manners of a butcher but (unlike Karlstadt) the debating skills of a sapper. Though I hate to admit it, Eck sliced and diced Karlstadt and left him bleeding on the floor of the debating hall. I suspect Eck could make any case seem plausible, whether he believed it himself or not. His tactic is to deluge his opponent in a sea of facts; the man can quote, verbatim and at length, Scripture, the Fathers, decrees of councils, decretals. Poor Karlstadt had to rely on written notes and books from which he wished to glean quotations. *Ach!* But to no avail. Eck convinced the judges to ban the use of notes and books. Karlstadt, left to his own memory, was no match for the clever (but, I think, unscrupulous) Eck.

It was not until a week following Karlstadt's entrance into the lists that Martin himself joined battle with Eck . . .

* * *

" . . . So, at first, at least, we were all somewhat wonder-struck. Unlike us others, you had your path laid out before you. You could travel it with comparative ease. A wealthy patron, the praise of the masters, the admiration of your peers—why, if you had wanted it (and I thoroughly understand why you didn't), you could have ingratiated yourself with that wispy-pated pagan . . ." He paused, smiled, and then added, "you know who I mean."

"Yes. Mutianus."

"Exactly! *Ach,* Lorenz! Imagine—you could have made the monthly pilgrimage to the Divine Konrad. He would have feasted you with viands, while you regaled him with Latin doggerel. And then there were other delights . . ."

Lorenz took a sip from his glass. It was Rhenish, a very good wine.

"Do you like it? It has become one of my favorites. You wonder, perhaps, how I can afford it? Of that by and by.

"But yours is the really interesting tale. I fear you will find mine neither interesting nor commendable. But back to what I was saying—our friends were surprised, and not a little distressed, by your casting it all away. They could not understand it at all. But that was only because they didn't know you like I do."

Lorenz felt the eyes studying, searching, probing him. He steeled himself. He would reveal nothing.

"Yes, they do not know you like I do," he purred. "Despite the side paths and byways you occasionally have taken, I knew you were meant for a monk. I knew it from the first moment we met. God! I tried to steer you from it, but it was all beyond me. I couldn't contend."

Lorenz thought to steer the conversation from himself. Though he dreaded the result, he said, "And you, Peter—you seem to have done well for yourself."

Peter glanced complacently at his right hand; it wore a ring, set with a large opal. "Yes, quite well," he said. "As you will remember, I was one of the poorer scholars at Erfurt—living in a hovel, getting my food and drink any which way. It was not the existence I savored. Not long after you entered the monastery, I resolved that I would change my condition. And I did."

Peter leaned back in his chair. "You may remember that I taught music to support myself. Well, one day I was able to land a lucrative little position. A widow, well past her prime, but living on a little fortune left her by her late husband—he was some sort of merchant—conceived a desire to perfect her skills at the lute. Well, she employed me. I would visit her house once a week, endure her tedious conversation and hideous lute playing—but, then, she paid well. It was after maybe a month of this that I began to notice how she eyed me, and I bethought myself—maybe I could play her, too. After all, though quite some years older than I, she wasn't an entirely disgusting morsel. I could endure her, as long as it was remunerative. Well, I won't trouble you with details unbefitting a man of the cloth. I will only say, that my fingers played her most skillfully.

"And it has proven remunerative. Most remunerative."

* * *

. . . For four days, Martin debated Eck on the primacy of the pope. He said nothing different than in his explication of Thesis XIII—that the pope holds his office, not by divine right, but by the custom of the Church. He argued from ancient documents, from the Council of Nicaea. Eck had his own authorities. I know not what effect the arguments had on those listening, but I suspect that no one's mind was changed by the evidence, from either side. Duke Georg, I heard, had, before the debate said, "what does it matter where the pope gets his authority from? He's still the pope"—a position quite agreeable with Martin's own,

though the duke is no supporter of the Wittenbergers. I suspect this is because—in part, at least—our
university rivals Leipzig's.

In the end, Eck did what I think despicable.
Instead of adhering to evidence and argument, he
smeared Martin with the opprobrious epithet, "Bohemian." With arrogant smugness (and the manners
of a butcher), Eck said, "I see that you follow the
condemned and pestiferous errors of Wycliffe—he
who said, *It is not necessary for salvation to believe that
the Roman Church is above all others.* And you espouse
the pestilent errors of Hus, who said Peter was never
the head of the Church." I could see this stung Martin, who abhors heresy and schism. He bellowed over
the hall that he was in no way a Bohemian, that he
condemned their schism—and that even if Hus had
been right, he should never have separated himself
from the Church.

But then, following the midday meal, Martin stood
up to say that he had spent his time that afternoon in
the university library, reading the acts of the Council of
Constanz—and what did he discover? That many of
Hus' teachings condemned by the council "are plainly
Christian and evangelical!" Moreover, he said that we
are forbidden by divine law to believe anything that
cannot be established from Scripture—even if the
pope or a council says otherwise. When Eck pressed
him on this, Martin cast aside all caution. In German,
not Latin (so that, he said, he could be understood by
everyone), he declared that councils have contradicted
each other, that any Christian, armed with Scripture,
is of equal authority to a council. Eck, at least, pretended he was scandalized by this confession. Looking about the room as if to say, "do our ears really
hear aright?" he said that Martin had proven himself
infected with the "Bohemian virus." Then, turning to
Martin, he said, with the venom of disdain, "if you
say a council legitimately called can err or has erred,
be to me then a gentile and a publican!"

* * *

"So, Peter, why have you come to Leipzig?"

Peter cocked his head. "To witness the drama of Germany's rebirth," he said.

"Her rebirth?"

Peter laughed. "*Ach,* Lorenz!" he said. "You can still undress my irony. Consecration has not dulled your brains."

Peter smiled and took a drink. He shook his head slowly. "No, you are right," he said. "Not her rebirth. Her dissolution."

"You think then that Luther is dragging Germany into chaos?"

"Chaos? Yes, that is the better term. *Chaos.*" Peter paused, as if he were rolling the word over his tongue, like fine wine. Then he looked Lorenz full in the eyes. "Of course, you don't see it. You're a devotee. You think all these fiery words over indulgences, the treasury of merit, the pope's authority, are really what they appear to be—expressions of a struggle for the purity of Holy Mother Church." Peter snorted and shook his head. "No doubt your Luther thinks the same—do not get me wrong, I think him in earnest. But neither he nor you, nor even that wonder boy, Melanchthon, see things for what they are."

"And what is that, Peter?"

Peter emptied his glass, and poured himself another. "Human events are never what they seem to be, my dear *frater,*" he continued. "Seeking to compass their own ends, men fulfill others. They may think they are acting after their own desires, but they are not. Underlying them—moving the actors and even molding their intentions—there is a Will. Oh, I don't say it is a will like a man's, or even like God's, if you hold to the supposition. No, it is merely a directive principle that determines all men do and think. Its intentions cannot be known, for they are unfathomable. But to those who observe—just sit and observe—its direction can be surmised."

Lorenz forced a laugh. "*Ach*, Peter!" he said. "I have never heard you speak so. You have grown mystical. But, then, I don't think you believe any of this."

Peter shot Lorenz an arch look. "No, perhaps I don't," he smiled. "Perhaps I don't. But what I do believe, you pious soul, is that your Luther may think he is leading the charge for Church reform, but all he is doing is drawing to himself all the forces that for well over a century have threatened to plunge Germany into—your word for it—*chaos*. Up until now, by themselves, all they could do is shake things up a little—but in Luther they have found the center about which they can coalesce and unite their several powers. He is the fulcrum."

Lorenz and Peter's eyes were locked. *What arrogance!* Lorenz thought. *What pretense!*

Peter turned his eyes away. He took another drink from his glass. "Of course, you do not believe me," he said. "But you must admit, at least, that I am more in the current of things than you. Our old friend, Mutianus . . . "

"Yes?"

Peter again took a drink from his cup. He savored the silence.

"He has become quite enamored of your Luther. He calls him—what is it, now?—Oh, yes! *Hercules novus, Hercules Germanicus.* And do you know—perhaps you do not? That Luther has written to him! And in high praise of his paunch-bellied, diminutive self, at least according to Mutianus. *A man most learned, of most discerning culture*—this is what Mutianus himself quoted to me. Of course, perhaps it is not Luther, but the young Melanchthon . . . "

Peter paused, and observed Lorenz under his eyelids.

" . . . but even the great Sun God himself, 'Eobanus Hessus'—you know, that adolescent imitator of Virgilius; *he* has written a *Manual of a Christian Soldier*—when before he cared for no other Christ than Apollo and no godly mother but Venus. Oh, now he is a most devout Christian and on fire for 'reform'! And he is not alone—all the poets have cast aside their Catullus and Hesiod; all are agog over Sacred Scripture. Crotus Rubianus now blathers about nothing but the *Gladius Scripturarum Sacrarum*. Even our old friend, Holzhaupt—though hardly numbered among the luminaries—applies himself to the study of Greek, in order to read the Apostle Paul, and, between whores, talks of finding a rabbi to teach him Hebrew. They tell me the learned merchants of Nürnberg vent of nothing but Luther, when they are not flinging gross and scatalogical epithets at the pope."

Peter sipped from his glass. Lorenz was silent.

"And have you not wondered that the Elector Friedrich—that most pious huckster of relics and indulgences—has made himself your Luther's protector? Luther stands to ruin a most lucrative trade for the old prince; but yet, he shelters him from the wrath of Rome. Have you not wondered why? And, I understand, the elector is not alone among the princes...

"Now allow me, my dear *frater*, to play the prophet. Others will soon unfurl Luther's banner in their war against Church and state. Knights, Franz von Sickingen—you have doubtless heard of his depredations in the vicinity of Worms? How he scythes down the cornfields, sets fire to orchards, lops off hands, severs maidenheads, imprisons priests and monks. He shows tender piety in the crosses he scores with dagger point on his victims' foreheads. He will soon discover his sympathy with Luther's *Evangelium*, if he has not already...

"And let us not forget the peasants, or the Hussites—the Taborites of Bohemia. What has Luther asserted that *they* would object to? Oh, doubtless, you will tell me that Luther is no Hussite—so, you will say..."

"He is no Hussite!" Lorenz could scarcely utter the words. He felt he had no command over his voice. He paused, swallowed,

and then, forcing himself to look Peter in the eye, said, "and
how could Luther embrace the cause of both the princes and
of the peasants?"

"It may seem unlikely," Peter said with a smile. "And he
won't. But Fate, my dear Lorenz does not wait upon Luther.
Luther waits upon Fate."

* * *

. . .Veit, it pains me to hear that you have heard
the tale of Duke Georg's fool. It was a shameful
affair—and, I sorrow to write of it—for both Martin and Eck; but more, I think for Eck. It was widely
regarded as by far the most entertaining passage of
the entire tournament. I could not regard it so.

But lest you have heard false rumor of the affair,
I will briefly describe to you what occurred. Duke
Georg attended the disputations in the company of
his court fool—a diminutive, deformed man, clad in
motley and spangles. He had one eyeless socket. One
day, Luther and Eck took to debating whether this
fool should be allowed to marry; I do not know who
started the dispute. The object of their controversy
sat at the duke's feet, fixing first Martin then Eck in
the gaze of his one good eye. Martin, at least, argued
that the fool should be allowed to marry—though it
was done in such bitter jest that, I doubt not, the fool
was moved to anger, despite the seeming advocacy for
his part. But whatever ill will he felt for Martin was
eclipsed by his palpable hate for Eck. For the learned
Ingolstadt butcher hacked and cleaved at the poor
deformed man—arguing that, to compass marriage
for him, they would have to use direst threats to bring
a woman to altar, thus rendering the marriage null
and void. This was the mildest of Eck's "arguments"; I
will not repeat here what else he said. But, from then
on, how the fool's one good eye glared at him! Day
after day, as Eck entered the hall, the fool beamed
hate through that eye—until one day, Eck, stooping,

thrusting out one shoulder, and squinting one eye, stumped around the hall in mockery of the man. At sight of these japes, the fool's face grew red, and he vomited forth a string of the vilest curses at Eck. The hall erupted in laughter—even Martin and the timid Schwartzerdt did not hold back...

*   *   *

Lorenz laid down his pen.

Even as he wrote, then some weeks after the fool's tirade, the vivid memory of it still filled him with disgust and, what was more inexplicable to him, dread. Just the night before, after he had read Veit's letter, he had again dreamed of it. The fool, twisted in body, one gleaming eye, expressionless like a beast's, standing against his torturers, spewing filthy curses, while the world laughed and mocked. And the more they derided him, the filthier he eructated, until all the hall stank with the reek of the decay of his tortured soul.

CHAPTER 3

DARE THE DEVIL PROPHESY TRUTH? Weeks had passed, then months. Months, then weeks. Leipzig had warned of storm; but it had not struck. Not yet. But the clouds were gathering. Chance drops fell from the sky; in the distance one could hear the rumble of thunder. But as of yet, no storm or torrent of rain threatening to purge the earth with flood. God's bow still hung in the heavens.

Lorenz watched events unfold with foreboding and loathing—Peter Schwach's cocksure smile haunted his contemplation. Could the Devil speak truth? Could Peter, by some necromancy, discern the inner essence of affairs, or, as with some perverse loadstone, resolve gold into rust? On the borders of the West, Franz von Sickingen was baying at Köln—he would tear and rend the city, leave it a bleeding corpse. He would thus avenge Reuchlin. The Dominicans—the "dogs of the Lord," terrified by the wolf's howls—tucked their tails between their legs and scurried away. The mighty Hoogstraten, once prior and inquisitor, was cast down. His blood stained the dust.

"Serves him right!" Thus spoke Lorenz's partisan mind; but his heart was troubled.

And Melanchthon—the scholar who had seemed to care for nothing but his books, the "wonder boy," now snuggled in Frater Martin's bosom, the baby theologian—he was in correspondence with Hutten! Hutten, the iconoclast poet who had pissed on religion while suckling the teat of the Archbishop of Mainz! Hutten, who had suddenly discovered a devotion to the "Gospel"! To the inner circle of the Wittenberg Evangelicals (to whom Lorenz still belonged), Melanchthon conveyed the secrets of these missives. Hutten and Sickingen had a plan. They would appeal to Ferdinand, younger brother to Kaiser Karl (still in Spain), himself not yet 20 years of age; they would urge them, together, with Hutten, Sickingen, and, yes, the Evangelicals, to throw off the pope's tyranny, reestablish German glory, and purify German religion.

Melanchthon spoke neither ill or well of such plans. He merely conveyed them, "to us," the Wittenberg inner circle. The Evangelicals.

* * *

Frater Jürgen smiled self-deprecatingly. "I am but a simple man," he said. "I cannot judge." But the smile passed from his countenance, like sunlight obscured by a sudden onset of clouds.

"I have always trusted Frater Martin—but now . . . "

Lorenz had noticed of late signs of worry and distress in Jürgen; of course he could guess the cause. Distress was palpable in nearly every brother. Nor was it confined to the cloister. The common folk, too, squirmed with dis-ease, though they could scarcely understand the cause. Frater Martin Luther, they knew, was somehow at the center of it; but they could hardly understand what threatened.

Jürgen fingered his scapular. "All my life, you know—the Church, it has seemed like a snug hearth room; outside, nothing but snow, ice, and freezing wind. Even as a child, I wanted to enter the monastery—I loved it that much, you know. Oh, I knew I would never make a priest—my leg, you know; but that was of no account with me! If I could only find refuge in the cloister, I would be happy."

"*Ach,* Jürgen! Nothing has changed. You remain in the cloister; and Mother Church is our mother still. You are not cast off!"

"No, I am not cast off." Jürgen sadly shook his head. "But now everything seems different. I hear distressing news, you know—of what happened in Leipzig. That Frater Martin is now called heretic . . . ."

"Pay it no heed, *frater!* It is but the Dominicans barking at his heels. Neither the bishop nor Rome has condemned Martin." Lorenz spoke with a confidence he did not feel.

Jürgen looked up at Lorenz with the trust of the simple man. "But is it not heresy to say a council can err?"

Lorenz was not sure how to parry the question. He feinted. "It is a difficult question, not susceptible of a simple answer."

Jürgen shook his head again and sighed. "But Martin," he said, "is not as he was. I have always looked to him as a father; and betimes he is as he was, you know—his words full of consolation, gentle, confident in God. You know, it has not escaped me that Martin has undergone mighty struggles. I have not felt such terrors as he; indeed, I am not worthy of such. But to struggle with God that way—and to be so longsuffering with many petty annoyances, including me—I thought him under a special anointing. But now, more often, his peace is gone. His language, his temper . . . "

Jürgen said no more. It was clear he did not want to continue. Lorenz pitied him. He wanted to assuage the fears of this the kindest of brothers. "Jürgen," he said, "I understand your distress. But you must understand—Frater Martin has struggled with God and, like the Patriarch Jakob, has prevailed. And God, as a blessing, has revealed to him what he has withheld from many others for so many years—the essential Gospel. And now Satan and the World are assailing him, for there is nothing they hate more than the Gospel. So, if Martin, amid all his struggles, should walk halt of one leg, we should not be surprised. For God has touched him."

Jürgen glanced up at Lorenz, and both men held each other's eyes for some moments. Then, Jürgen looked away. Lorenz could see he had not convinced him.

* * *

But of what did he need to convince him? Was he himself convinced?

To deny the authority of councils—was that not heresy? To set Scripture against the Church—was that not the very essence of the teachings of Wycliffe and Hus? And what were the fruits of it all? "The drama of Germany's rebirth." Lorenz whispered Peter's words and smiled to himself.

He had just learned that, in October, Martin had received letters from the Hussites in Prague. They called him "Saxony's Hus." Had not Martin at Leipzig called some of Hus' teachings—teachings condemned at Constanz—"most Christian and evangelical"? And, yet, he denied he was a Hussite. "For now," thought Lorenz. Who could say what the next days, weeks, and months would bring? "Neither he nor you, nor even that wonder boy Melanchthon see things for what they are." Again, he found himself repeating Peter's words.

Melanchthon, the boy Schwartzerdt—how he had ingratiated himself with Martin! He had only recently, in September, become a bachelor of theology, and already Martin was often holed up with "that little Greek," as he called Schwartzerdt, discussing theology. He had heard that Martin had said he would abandon his own opinions if they conflicted with Schwartzerdt's. Was it Schwartzerdt who was stoking the flames of Martin's growing radicalism?

For Martin's speech was growing increasingly violent. Oh, yes, at times he could still be the gentle father and confessor, as Jürgen had said; but he was more often agitated with barely controlled rage at the "blasphemies of the Antichrist," the name he now almost always called the pope. And he was predicting that the new age of the Gospel would be inaugurated with fire and sword. And was not Martin at the center of it all? "He is the fulcrum"—again Peter whispered in his mind.

Could the Devil indeed speak truth?

* * *

"So, is it true, Philipp? Sickingen has offered aid to Martin?"

Melanchthon's lips turned in that smile that so emphasized his weak chin. His blue eyes looked towards Lorenz, but not at him. He cleared his throat nervously.

"Yes, it is t-true," he said. "Though I may not give you the source of the intelligence."

Lorenz found the man tiresome. Too much fame, too young, he thought.

"Oh, come now, Philipp!" he said. "You needn't play the conspirator. I can well guess who conveyed Sickingen's message to Martin. It was Hutten . . ."

Melanchthon laughed that nervous laugh of his. "I will not deny what you have surm-m-mised," he stammered. "Nor will I affirm it . . . " he added coyly.

Lorenz felt annoyed. "As you will. But to what end, Philipp? To what end?" He feared he sounded petulant. "Martin has the protection of the Elector—what need has he of a *Raubknecht*?"

Melanchthon licked his lips. His smile disappeared. "I think calling Sickingen a r-robber knight is, perhaps, unfitting; maybe, even, calumnious," he said. "Sickingen has shown himself a f-friend of the Gospel."

"So says Hutten." Lorenz enjoyed the effect of this retort. Melanchthon scowled. "I doubt, though, that the peasants his men have tortured and the peasant women they have violated would deem him so very evangelical. They would likely think the name *Raubknechten* fit the bill more nearly."

"*Frater*," Melanchthon's tone was acid. "I, too, do not approve of such deeds—if the reports of them be true. Sickingen has many enemies who would gladly blacken his name. But we cannot simply dismiss his aid, even if they be true."

"Cannot dismiss his aid?" Lorenz was dismayed. "Shall we make common cause with the Devil?"

"No, not with the D-devil, *Frater*." Melanchthon's spite was rising, Lorenz thought. "But, recall your Scripture. God uses even evil men for his purposes. The prophet Eliseus was told to anoint Jehu. God called Nabuchad-d-danoser his servant . . . "

So, now the *baccalaureus theologiae* was teaching him Scripture! He caught Melanchthon's blue eyes glinting at him, as if to gauge the effect of his words. Lorenz strove to remain composed.

"I doubt not that God may do as he lists. But if he uses evil means, may we? And, I ask again, why need we? The Elector has stood firm with Martin."

"But he may not st-tand firm forever." Melanchthon closed the book that lay before him on the table—the Greek Gospel of John. "Sickingen has offered aid, if there is need."

Lorenz rapped his knuckles on the table. "But don't you see," he said, "that he and Hutten are merely using Martin, and the Gospel, for their own ends? When did Hutten ever care about religion before? Oh, I know he has become so very biblical in his utterances of late and has been railing against Rome with the best of them—but it is all a sham! A pagan he was, and a pagan he remains. The Gospel is naught but a cloak for his dissipation."

Melanchthon was now thoroughly miffed. His hand that lay on the Gospel book trembled, though his tone remained measured. "I pray that you remember, *Frater*, what Martin has said to us on occasion—to all of us. Antichrist's kingdom will not be overthrown save b-by great upheavals and t-turmoil and strife. It must be so. It has ever been so. I need not answer for

Hutten—he will, as he must, s-serve the Almighty's behests. We do not choose the instruments of his wrath; we must merely obey with fear and trembling."

Yes, these were Martin's words; Lorenz had heard them more than "on occasion." And they never failed to fill with him fear, foreboding—and, yes, loathing.

*　*　*

"I can tell you—Martin is terrified of his own shadow! He expects that it will rise up and smite him if he is not vigilant!"

It was one of the first warm days of spring. Lorenz, passing from the parish church, lingered in the marketplace. The late morning sun was a pleasure after the interior of the church, still chilly with the cold of night.

There Karlstadt had accosted him.

He was in a hurry, he had said, and couldn't stop to speak. But stop he did—as Lorenz figured he would.

"His mind is fixed on nothing else—and, indeed, who can blame him?" Karlstadt blustered loudly, waving his fat hands about energetically. "There is probably no other man whom the pope would rather destroy—I needn't tell you that! And, *Frater*" (here Karlstadt lowered his voice), "Martin has learned that they will try to poison him . . . "

Karlstadt's news was not news to Lorenz; but he did not know the source of the intelligence. No, he knew of Martin's fear of poisoning—for just the other day, Martin, very agitated, had said that he had learned that his enemies would send to him a physician, who by magic could make himself invisible. But Martin had been reticent to reveal where he had learned this tale.

But Lorenz could guess who it was. To be certain, he interrupted Karlstadt—"How has Martin learned of the poisoning?"

Karlstadt blinked and gave Lorenz a inquiring look. "Why, don't you know?" he said. "I thought all your circle knew. I wonder... but, no! It can't hurt to tell. Melanchthon knows, as does Amsdorf, I think. It is Ulrich Hutten ... "

Of course! It had to be Hutten. And Melanchthon himself was in on the deal. Doubtless, the two of them were trying to beat Martin into a froth of fear, to get him to accept Sickingen's protection.

"*Ach!* Yes. Hutten, I hear, has written to Martin," Karlstadt continued. "Martin himself told me that Hutten has sent him urgent warnings—mostly, I think, by Melanchthon. 'He is most afraid for me,' Martin told me.

"I don't know what you think, *Frater,* but I think Martin should follow Crotus' advice—write to Hutten!" Karlstadt shook his head sadly. "Indeed, he should, for I fear Rome is about to act—they will excommunicate Martin—and then where will he be? Will our lord, the Elector, dare to defy the pope and the curia? I fear he won't. But Sickingen will. The pope and all his thunderings hold no terror for Sickingen."

* * *

... in Rome all have become fools and idiots, maniacs, sticks, stones, fiends of hell, and the devil himself! I despise the threats of Rome, and I will not be reconciled to it, not for all eternity! I will, unless fire not be to hand, burn to ash all the popish crew. To the winds I cast that humility and submission by which I have suffered the enemies of the Gospel to be magnified.

Such were the words, dearest Else, of the man into whose hands I have entrusted my salvation. He spoke them to us in a fever of passion and, dare I say, hate? I do not record the worst of them. (But why do I not? In writing to you, I write but to myself. Do I fear to repeat them, even to myself?) I wondered—do I alone find them horrible? And should I find them so? Yet, it is not just the expressions of loathing for the pope, for whom I still feel something of reverence—though I should cast that off, as Martin has; for is not the pope the Gospel's enemy? That Gospel that I have received, and which has set me free? I wonder what you would tell me, dearest Else, if you could read this—

So, yes, I confess, it is my lingering sense of reverence for what I should despise that confounds me; but not wholly. If he had, as he always seemed to, founded his confidence in God—which, I think, he certainly has; but, that day, he said nothing of God. He spoke of Sickingen; he spoke of Franz von Schaumberg, who has promised to stir up the Frankish nobles on his behalf. He has, he said, been in correspondence with Sickingen—both Schaumberg and Sickingen have guaranteed protection. "And now I have no fears," he said. "And I shall bring out a book that attacks His Holiness mercilessly, as if he were the Antichrist."

It has all come to pass—the Hussites, the violent Taborites, have taken up Martin's cause, as he has taken up theirs. That blaspheming pagan, Hutten, now spouts Scripture. Schwartzerdt, with the cruel relish of an impudent school boy, tempts Martin on with Hutten's mission to the Archduke Friedrich—maybe the Kaiser himself will be won to the evangelical cause! And now, Sickingen—who in the name of German freedom has tortured and murdered German peasants and raped German maidens, offers, along with the equally bloody Schaumberg, his lance to the cause of "religion."

And Martin's book will be out soon. I have not yet read it. I fear to read it . . .

CHAPTER 4

AND IF I SUCCEED, I SHALL FOR THE *time being become a court jester. And if I fail, I still have one advantage—no one need buy me a cap or put scissors to my head. It is a question of who will put the bells on whom . . .*

So he wrote in the letter to Nikolaus Amsdorf, prefacing the book that "attacks His Holiness mercilessly." It came out, that book, on the eve of the Baptist's nativity, like some forerunner of a terror foretold. The book, an address to the young Kaiser Karl and the nobility of Germany, was everything Martin had promised it would be, and more. It was a fierce attack on "Antichrist," and a call to revolution.

Of course, nothing it said was as horrible or violent as what he had written in that reply to Prierias, just two months before. That was a lashing out of sheer rage, an assault thirsting for blood. "The emperor, kings, and princes, girt about with force and arms, should attack these pests of the world . . . if we strike thieves with the gallows, robbers with the sword, heretics with the fire, why do we not much more attack in arms these Masters of Perdition, these Cardinals, these Popes, and all this sink of the Roman Sodom which has without end corrupted the Church of God, and wash our hands in their blood?"

Wash our hands in their blood! Were these the words of the man who, not even yet a year ago, had in Augsburg cast a resolute gaze on the pyre? Oh, yes, Lorenz had seen fear in his eyes then, but also resignation and stern determination. A lamb he was, meek for the slaughter. But now he was a lion, a-thirst for blood, roaring in vengeance . . .

Or was he, rather, as he said he was, a jester, spewing venom on his tormenters?

* * *

Frater Laurentius,

It has now been some two years since last we spoke. When we parted in Erfurt, it seemed to me that the friendship we had forged in our student days, whose fellowship had grown the more sweet and had deepened and matured in the monastery, when we discoursed on the things of God—that friendship was at an end. I blame you not for this; I fear that my words, uttered (or so I thought) in sincerity of heart, were too sharp and presumptuous. It is so very hard to stand judge over oneself! In the end, God alone shall be the judge whether one has done well or ill. But whether I have done well or ill, I think not my words alone were the cause of our estrangement, which, I now perceive, was long in the making. Not my words, or yours, but the very fact that we have chosen to follow different paths, has sundered us.

I will not flatter you, friend whom I still love from my heart. Even before our last meeting in Erfurt, I thought you were walking astray. From the very first, when I heard Frater Martinus' doctrine, I doubted its soundness. And the more I learned of it, the deeper my doubts grew. When you expounded his "theology of the cross" to me in Erfurt, I felt myself justified in casting a stern disapprobation on it. But, even then, I was willing to alter my judgment. After all, I have held your opinion in the highest esteem; and our superiors—even Staupitz himself—has countenanced Luther. I have never felt entirely certain in my own judgment.

I now have cast aside my uncertainty. Reports of Leipzig, Frater Martinus' disavowal of all obedience to and credit in, not only His Holiness, the pope, but even councils, solidified my judgment of him. It was, however, his address to the German nobility that sealed my mind. It is not only his disavowal of the divine authority of the Church, his denial of the holy priesthood, his subjection of the spiritual power to the temporal, his insinuations, appealing to the basest of passions in the princes, that have confirmed my doubts in Frater Martinus' doctrines—though these, alone, suffice to appall an orthodox judgment. Not these alone, but the very spirit that seems to infuse his utterances; the bile, the contempt, the violence of them, lead me to conclude that it is not the Spirit of God who speaks in him, but the spirit of the Father of Lies, the lord of this world, the City of Man.

It is not with pleasure I write these words. I would rather they remained unsaid. Yet I cannot believe that you yourself have not seen and felt as have I. I confess that I felt something of the beauty in Frater Martinus' theology of the cross—and, given what I know of your own spiritual struggles, I understand why you were drawn to it. Now, however, you must see—you must!—that it is not God who speaks in him. Can a man cast aside Christ's Body, the Church, and cling to her head? *Ach!* I know full well the evils of our age that beset the Church in her head and members—that I do, you more than anyone else know! But one cannot reform the Church and destroy her at once.

It is thus I write to you, one last time, to beg you to sever yourself from this new spirit. It is the spirit of rebellion, of the one who proclaimed, *non serviam.* I will not engage you in disputation; for if, even now, you cannot view matters in the full light of day, no argument, however erudite, however sound, will convince you. I have learned that Frater Martinus will soon publish another, even more virulent attack on the Church; and I doubt not you know it, too, and may even now know its content. I beg you, in the name of Christ and our Holy Father, Augustinus, to cast it aside, to return to the teaching of the apostles. Therein, alone, you will find rest for your troubled soul. Therein, alone, you will find peace.

It is likely, my brother, that we shall not see one another again. Members of our holy order, at least in Germany, have so embraced the new teaching that I can no longer remain within it. With the greatest sorrow I write this, for I have loved our Holy Father's eremites. But I have received leave from our prior in Erfurt, Johann Lang, and our superiors, to depart. I shall begin my journey tomorrow to Köln, where I shall be received into the order of the Preachers of St. Dominic. There I hope to end my days, serving Our Lord in whatever way he sees fit to use me. I bid you, thus, farewell, but in the hope that you shall find your way out of the fellowship of those who would not only rend, tear, and destroy our Holy Mother the Church, but lay waste to her beloved flock in our homeland, Germany.

Your Brother in Religion
and in Heart's Affection,

Sebastian

* * *

In sultry August came the rumors of it. Condemned. The pope had at long last condemned Martin. The bull of excommunication had been promulgated in Rome. It had been printed. It had been notarized. It had been sealed. It would soon arrive in Germany.

In early September, Staupitz and Link arrived in Wittenberg. They had come, Lorenz learned, by application of Miltitz, to persuade Martin to write a conciliatory letter to the pope, to tell His Holiness that he had never thought to attack him personally. "I can write nothing more easily or more truly," Martin said.

It was not long before Staupitz took leave of Wittenberg. Lorenz did not witness his parting with Martin; but, afterwards, Martin was pensive and sad.

In late September, news reached Wittenberg that the bull had, with the bishop's approbation, been published at Meissen. Its bearer into Germany was Johannes Eck. Eck would carry the bull into Saxony.

Soon, the Bishop of Merseburg too published the bull; and the Bishop of Brandenburg followed his episcopal brothers. All that remained was the delivery of the bull to Wittenberg.

But Eck's reception at Leipzig, it was said, was none too friendly. Duke Georg was friendly enough, though even he would not accept the bull as genuine. It was the students who worked misery on poor Eck, forcing him to take cover in the Dominican convent. Eck at last fled like a whipped dog from the city.

The news of Eck's discomfiture at Leipzig seemed to embolden Martin—or drive him mad. Lorenz could not be certain whether it was courage or a gambler's despair that made Martin wager all he had—for what was that pamphlet, that *Babylonian Captivity,* but the final defiance, the flinging away of all caution, the committing of all one's forces in one last desperate offensive? The very audacity of it—one man setting himself against, not just the pope, not just this council or that, but the entire tradition of the Church? This pamphlet, this "prelude" as Martin called it—what was it a prelude to? What did it portend? Civil strife in Germany and schism in the Church? "To begin with, I must deny that there are seven sacraments and for the present maintain that there are but three: baptism, penance, and the bread." What did he mean by "for the present"? What else would this monk seek to overturn?

No, the doctrines were not entirely new to Lorenz. But to see them laid out together in print—to read the audacious claim that, until Luther had rediscovered it, the Gospel had been all but lost—that Rome, the pope himself, whom all thought the pillar and foundation of Catholic truth, was nothing but the envious Antichrist cavorting in the temple of God, proclaiming himself to be God—it was as if the foundation had been pulled away and the temple was collapsing to ruin. *Quomodo sola sedet civitas?* And where would Lorenz flee to escape destruction?

He in dread awaited the bull of excommunication. But he had not to wait long. Only five days after Martin published his pamphlet, the bull arrived in Wittenberg.

CHAPTER 5

"NO, VEIT, MY FRIEND—I CANNOT describe what that moment meant to us, to me. But there is no turning back. Nor did it end there. The students would not see the fire die. Singing the *Te Deum*, they stoked it throughout the day."

Later in the day, when I left the convent, the fire was still burning. In the streets I came across student masquers, decked out in the vilest costumes, driving about in a cart. The cart was full of books—fuel for the fire that still burned before the Elster Gate. I shuddered at the destruction, but I did comprehend the spirit. The strained rope had been severed, by one glittering stroke. All uncertainty was at an end. It really was no surprise. I suppose the horror I felt before, in the weeks and days ere the bull reached Wittenberg, was a foreboding of what he would do. No one could suspect that he would recant—except, perhaps, for Miltitz. He was almost girlishly hopeful. It was all a matter of time; and, I have come to conclude, of the most careful staging on Martin's part. He would perform the decisive deed, but only at the right moment.

What that deed would be, I did not at first know. But then came the rumor that his books had been burned at Löwen and Köln. "I wait now only for Leipzig," he said. But Leipzig did not burn, and he did not wait...

* * *

149

How strange that they should sing the *Te Deum*.

The day was cold. Bitter cold.

Melanchthon had sent out the notice. Melanchthon. Who else, but Melanchthon?

" . . . pious and studious youths . . . outside the Elster Gate . . . the spectacle, pious and religious . . . "

And Martin: " . . . perhaps now Antichrist shall be revealed . . . "

When he came, his eyes were drawn immediately to the bonfire, set just outside the gate, near the *Spital*.

To his left the leper's hospital lay hard by. A wisp of smoke wafted straight into the air, from the place where they burned the lepers' clothes. There was no wind or breeze.

To his right, Frater Jürgen stood but a few feet away, separated from the crowd of students and friars, doctors of the university and masters. He stared at the pyre, unmoving.

Memory tore at his brain.

Turn your eyes to the brazen serpent, Christ crucified. Turn your eyes to him, believe with all your heart that he is our righteousness and our life . . .

But that is the nature of love, my son.

Dear brother, do you yet not understand?

Some survive. Most die of it.

No, Father. I shall die.

You'll push him where he has no intention of going . . .

Herzlieb, ich hab vernommen . . . Wenn willst du wiederkommen . . .

Beatrice, you will not find . . .

. . . our righteousness and our life . . .

Martin stood by the bonfire. The flames were roaring, vaunting against the heavens. Book after book was being cast into the fire. Great, leather-bound tomes, feeding the angry flames.

The flowers wither. The beauty fades into ashes.

Martin's voice rose above the clamor of the fire. He held something aloft. Lorenz could not see clearly what it was. But he knew what it was. It was the bull.

Martin's voice bellowed, like the voice of many waters:

Quia tu conturbasti Sanctum Domini, ideoque te conturbet ignis aeternus!

And he cast the parchment into the fire. Flames licked its sides. They blackened, as if sickened by the plague. The paper curled in on itself, withered, and was gone.

* * *

The friars, doctors, and magisters followed Martin, back through the Elster Gate. Students cavorted about the bonfire. "Feed the fire! Feed the fire! Don't let it burn down!"

Te Deum laudamus...

Lorenz glanced to his right. Jürgen still stood there, unmoving, staring into the fire.

Lorenz turned to the bonfire and the rioting students. He looked again at Jürgen, then back, over his right shoulder. The last of the magisters was passing through the gate.

He hesitated, undecided.

Then, he turned and followed Martin. Back into the city.

PILLENREUTH

CHAPTER 1

BEFORE HIM SHE STOOD, BEAUTIFUL IN the dawn of a cool autumn day—Nürnberg, queen of cities. How long had it been since he had first beheld the wonder of her? Thirteen years? Fourteen? Then, he was a child, awed by the gigantesque glory of her. Now, he was a man, not so taken by her greatness as blandished by her beauty.

Then, he had approached the city from the west, riding over a rough road, in a rich man's carriage. Today, he returned to her, from the east, a poor man, on foot. All the long leagues between Wittenberg and her, on foot. His childhood he had long left behind.

He had arrived at a little village yesterday, at sunset. He had supped and slept in a grimy inn—and contended most of the night in a battle with bed bugs. He had awoken long before dawn and set out in the dark, so eager had he been to see her again. When the sun was just peeking over the horizon, casting his long shadow before him, he halted. The red gleam of morning inflamed the spires of the churches, though it brought as yet no warmth to his cold flesh. He shivered. He rubbed his eyes and drew his hand over his face. His beard was damp with dew.

He was standing before the *Laufer Thor*—the same gate through which he had passed when, so many years before, he had departed Nürnberg. The gate was open now it was light;

but he hesitated. There she lay, across the moat; the colors of Nürnberg waving from the pinnacle of the keep; the gun embrasures in the high walls, but no flash of metal barrels to warn off assailants. Instead, articles of clothing, set to dry in the warmth of morning, hung from the gunnery holes. Nothing to tell him to turn back, to dare not the passage of the water. All was welcome in the dawn of the new day.

But yet, he hesitated. He had come with peace to Nürnberg—to bring her the peace he had himself found. He had been called here to be a messenger of that peace. Yet, he hesitated. Should he brave the passage of the water? If he turned back, all would be as it had been, now, for so long. But if he crossed over, would not everything change?

But if he did not cross, would everything really be as it had been?

And was he not expected?

He moved to cross himself, but then he remembered. His hand fell, as if lifeless, to his side.

He fell in with a crowd of farmers bringing their wares to market in the city. The gate before them burgeoned; the keep expanded in girth, and grew, like a tree, reaching for the sky. He glanced down over the side of the bridge—mist curled up from the water. The guard at the gate questioned each of them and then motioned them to pass. To him: "Whence come you?"

"From Wittenberg."

"Pass!"

He was under the great archway; then, through it. He had passed the city walls. Where now would he go? It was still early—he would not go to the house; not yet. It was still early. They might still be at home.

The *Laufer Gasse* led him directly into those parts of the city where the wealthy dwelt. Nothing had changed since his last visit. The dwelling of the Tuchers reared on his right. He could feel the power of its owners radiate from its walls. Beyond it, humbler dwellings, yet substantial and lofty, flanked the street to north and south. Already, a goodly number of people, most on foot but some in carriages and on horseback, were filling the streets. Most were going in the same direction—toward the *Egidian Platz*. He could espy the spires of Sankt Aegidius rising above the red roofs of the houses.

The street now bent like a dog's rear leg and then forked. He followed the right-hand way. Soon, the houses on either side opened up, and he passed into the wide plaza. The chancel of Sankt Aegidius lay directly before him; the cloister of the Benedictines just to the south of the church. He directed his steps along the way that skirted the northern wall of the church and then turned down the broad way that passed by the great western doors. He stopped and raised his eyes to the two spires, then down to the bronze doors. They were open; people were passing in. Memory flooded his mind. Would he enter? No. Not yet.

He continued into the *Neumarkt*. Farmers and tradesmen were setting out their wares for market day. He glanced about him—hadn't there been a tavern hard by? Yes, there it was! He had entered the city, fasting; he would get some bread and beer. And then, maybe, he would proceed to the house.

But he did not want to arrive too soon.

* * *

He called for bread and beer and cheese. The room, low-roofed and dark, was full with tradesmen, workmen, and some farmers. He looked for a place to sit—he could find only one space, at the end of a long table, farthest from the hearth. He longed for the warmth of the fire, but he saw he had no choice.

The men he sat with smelled of leather, horses, and sweat. It was early, so they mostly ate in silence. They were tired, as was he.

He ate and drank slowly. He was too sleepy for thought, so he contented himself with observation. The tavern was larger than he remembered. Crudely-wrought paintings adorned the walls, depicting rural and city scenes. A few were drawn from the Bible. His eyes flitted from picture to picture. One depicted Adam and Eve — she holding an apple before her husband's wondering eyes. Then, Abraham, knife in hand, poised to kill, but arrested by an angel. He could not figure out the subject of the next picture, to the right of Abraham — a woman, naked, kneeling before a man, as if in supplication. What did it depict? He puzzled over it.

"Can't figure that one out, can ye?"

Jogged from his thoughts, he turned to see, on the opposite side of the table, a large, thick-set man — grizzled beard, hair hanging in curls from his cap to his shoulders. The man was a farmer, come, doubtless, into the city for market day.

The man nodded. "'Tis not many that get the picture the first time," he said. "'Tisn't the sort of thing folks would mostly want to make pictures of, is it? Ye wouldn't expect it now, would ye?"

He did not answer. He knew he wouldn't need to. The man would keep on talking.

"Can ye guess? No? I'm not surprised! Nobody I know of, but one feller, ever did — but I thought ye would know."

The man's garrulousness and red cheeks, like two pomegranates, amused him. He found himself asking, "why would you think I would know?"

The farmer slapped his hand on the table and chuckled. "Why, 'tis your dress," he said "Ye ain't no farmer nor tradesman; that's clear! Why, I'd say ye was a scholar — and not from your clothes only, but from your eyes." The farmer turned to the man next to him — a short, bald and clean-shaven fellow in shirt sleeves and a leathern apron — and slapped him on the shoulder with the back of his hand. "Ain't he got scholar's eyes?" The short man only laughed, shook his head, and took a draught from his mug.

"Why, I'd say ye got scholar's eyes," the farmer persisted. "Ain't I right? You're a scholar!"

He could not help but smile. "Yes, I am a scholar," he said.

"Ye see?" the farmer said, and again slapped his neighbor's shoulder. Then he said, "but, ye be a scholar, and ye can't tell me what that picture's about?"

"I am afraid I cannot."

The farmer laughed. "Well, I couldn't tell neither, the first time I saw it," he chuckled. "And it ain't all that good of a picture, neither. But once ye know it, it all makes sense. It's called the 'Rape of Thamar'—ye know, from the Bible."

He looked again at the picture; now he could see it: Ammon in bed, holding Thamar by her arm; she begging to be spared. It was badly wrought, except for the expression on the man's face. He was resolute. He would not spare her.

"*Ja,* many a feller I've asked, and none's been able to tell me what it's about." The farmer wagged his shaggy head. "But ye being a scholar—but, yet again, ye'd prob'ly know more of them Greek stories than Bible ones, being, as ye are, a scholar and all."

"Oh, I don't know," he replied. He felt his lips smile. "I know scholars, from where I've come, who could tell you that story, not just in Bible Latin, but Hebrew!" He paused. Folding his hands on the table, he looked intently into the farmer's eyes. "And maybe," he said, "I myself am one of those scholars!"

The farmer whistled. "Say," he said, "ye don't mean to say ye can read Hebrew? I've heard of such as ye, and they ain't Jews, neither!" The farmer pondered, then shook his head. "Ye can really read Hebrew?" he asked.

He took a sip of his beer. "Yes, I can, though not as well as some, I confess. Many scholars at my university have taken to learning Hebrew."

The farmer's eyes widened. He wiped his mouth with the back of his hand. But then he shot him a sly look. "And where be ye from, master?" he said. "Where be your university?"

"I think you know," he said. Then, leaning forward, he said in a hushed tone, as if communicating a confidence. "Wittenberg."

The farmer whistled. "*Ach!* I thought so," he said. "Then ye're Evangelical?"

"I don't know what to say," Lorenz replied. And then, conspiratorially, "Am I among friends?"

The farmer looked at him blankly; then began to laugh—so loud that he startled some of his neighbors. "*Ach!*" he exclaimed. "Are ye in good company, here? Don't ye know that not just this tavern but all Nürnberg stands with Luther? Of course, there's some as don't," he added, as if in an afterthought.

"Well, if there's some as don't," Lorenz said, still in confidential tones, "then I'm not sure I want to open my mind. Let it suffice to say that I believe the Gospel."

The farmer gave him a knowing look, and winked. "I understand ye. Ye needn't fear to have old Stephan as your gossip—by God, no! He stands firm on the Holy Evangel, and he don't care who hears him say it! And Luther—God bless him! He has freed us from those ravenous shaven-pated bastards who were eating up all our substance! Yes, God bless him!"

Lorenz looked into the farmer's eyes. It seemed he wanted to say more, but was hesitant. "Would you say that Luther has freed you only from priest craft?" he said, again in a confidential tone. "You know, Christian freedom—some have drawn other conclusions."

The farmer's eyes betrayed understanding. He nodded his head knowingly. "That they have," he said. "But like ye, I won't open my mind."

"But you believe the Gospel?"

"*Ja*," said the farmer, and he slapped his hand on the table.

* * *

It was bright morning when he left the tavern; but it was still early. He would not go to the house. Not yet.

He left Sankt Aegidius behind and followed the way toward the spires of Sankt Sebald's. Wasn't the rector there Andreas Osiander? No, he thought, Osiander was at Sankt Lorenz's. He would soon have to make his acquaintance. It would be Wenzel Link to whom he must first report—Link, who, with Staupitz, had abandoned Luther to Cajetan at Augsburg. Link was at the Augustinian cloister—where, he had heard, the brothers were thoroughly given over to Luther's doctrine. He wondered if they knew what Link had done at Augsburg? But that was now so many years ago. And Martin had forgotten it.

The Augustinian cloister was but a couple of streets over from Sankt Sebald's.

But he would not go there. Not yet. Instead, with a large concourse of people, he followed a street south from the church, toward the *Marktplatz*. As he entered the plaza, he saw it was already set out with booths and stalls; the farmers and merchants were doing brisk business, even this early in the morning. But he did not come to haggle with shopkeepers; he came to gaze, once again, after so many years, on the beautiful fountain.

His heart warmed as he looked on it once again. He recalled the first day he had seen it—a cold winter's day, in Veit's company. He was just a boy then, in awe of everything he saw in Nürnberg. He felt no such awe now; he had grown used to splendor. But the *Schöner Brunnen*—that still had the power to move him. He smiled as he recalled Ser Portinari's scorn. "The work of Goths."

"No, my dear friend," he whispered to himself. "Not gothic—*bellissima* is the word you want."

He turned from the fountain and followed the street that passed behind the *Rathaus* and would lead him back towards the *Neumarkt*. Again he came before the great doors of Sankt Aegidius, and again he hesitated. Should he enter? Memory seemed to beckon him in, but he shook it off. The day would bring enough of memory.

He passed the church by. He turned down one street and up another. He was again among grand houses, some with lawns and gardens. He needed no one to tell him where he was to go; he had walked it so very often he could do it now with his eyes closed. Memory, sweet, though shot through with pangs of sadness and regret—he was not sure he should go on, but he longed to. Despite the fear of the pain of reopened wounds, he longed to visit once again the place where he had been happy.

At last, the lane led him from the street, away from the press of pedestrians, into what seemed a tree-shaded garden. He remembered how, as a boy first entering this lane, he thought he had passed into *Faerie*, so beautiful was the house that then met his gaze—and now, once again, drew his eyes to itself. Now, he felt no hesitation; he would not delay with another "not yet." No matter what sorrow or pain would meet him there, he had to pass through its doors, into its halls; to feel himself, again, embowered by its walls.

He knocked on the great oaken doors. A small window in the right-hand door opened, and a face peered out inquiringly.

"God's blessing!" he said nervously. "I hope I am not too early. I am Lorenz List—Magister Lorenz List."

"Ah, yes," said a voice from within. "The master said to expect you. One moment, please." The small window closed. From within came the sound of the drawing of a bolt.

And, after so many years, he passed again through the doors of *Auerhaus*.

CHAPTER 2

"**T**HE MASTER, I REGRET TO TELL YOU, has had to attend a meeting of the council."

The servant was dignified but cordial; Lorenz instinctively liked him. "He said to inform you that he would return after midday. The Lady"—and here a barely perceptible smile brightened the servant's face—"is indisposed.

"I was bidden, however, to show you your room. If you will follow me, Herr Magister . . . "

Lorenz followed the servant up the steps, then down a hallway until they came to a door. The servant opened it, and Lorenz felt himself looking, as if through an enchanted portal, into his childhood.

It was his old room! Opposite him, across the room, were the casement windows, opening on the garden; before the windows, the oaken table where he used to study and debate with Ser Portinari. To his right, the hearth with the carven mantle blazed with fire. "The master, expecting you today, ordered that a fire be kept burning at all hours," the servant said.

"The master bade me say that you should feel free of the house. Too, might I bring you food and drink?"

Lorenz said no; he had breakfasted. The servant then bowed and went out, carefully closing the door behind him.

He dropped his pack on the floor and looked about him. Had he really returned? Or was this some dream? To his right, against the wall, stood the same small table with the same porcelain bowl and pitcher. Placing his cap on the bed, immediately to the right of the table, he took the pitcher and tipped its contents into the bowl. He laved his face and then, reaching for the towel, dried it. He glanced over his right shoulder, toward the window.

Though hesitant, he approached the casement. He stopped only to run his finger over the wood grain of the oaken table. Through the distortion of the leaded glass he saw the riot of green, red, orange, yellow, and blue that was the garden. With hesitant hand he took hold of the latch, turned it, and pushed the window open.

The air that touched his face was chill, after the warmth of the room. The smell of autumn that came through the open window stirred the sap of his memory. He recalled another autumn, now so long ago, when a young boy and a maid stood by the pond, hand in hand, and beheld a vision in the waters — until it was shattered by the plop of a small frog. He remembered how they had laughed. Nor could the chill of fall dispel the recollection of a warm summer's evening and the phantom of a girl in the moonlight, weeping on the stone bench at water's edge.

He latched the window shut and turned to survey the room. Nothing, nothing had changed! But he had. He was now a man in the place where he had dreamed as a boy. He stepped toward the hearth and ran his hand along the intricately carved mantle. He turned, and strode across the room and lay down on the bed. He had been up since early morning, after a sleepless night. He was tired. For a few minutes he stared up at the ceiling, thinking. Then, his eyes closed.

* * *

He awoke, startled. He sat bolt upright and stared about him with confusion. Then, he remembered where he was. He laughed softly. "It was only a dream," he said.

He wondered how long he had slept. Rising, he walked over to the washing bowl and laved his face. Drying his face, he glanced again at the window. He hesitated, but then turned toward the door. Opening it, he walked out into the hall.

Today he took the steps slowly; but he recalled a day in spring when, a young man, he had taken the stairs more swiftly. His destination, today, was the same as it had been then. The family hall.

Then, the doors to the hall had stood ajar. Today, they were shut. He took hold the door handle and hesitated. Then he turned it and slowly opened the door.

He did not immediately enter. From the doorway he could survey the entire room. Against the far wall the hearth glowed red with a lively fire. He saw that some changes had been made to the room—chiefly furniture that had not been there before. But, on the whole, it was as he remembered it. He took a few steps into the room. To his right, the picture of the absurd old man still hung, but below it was no chair but a wood chest. Just above the chest but below the portrait hung a small painting. He approached closer to see it. It depicted a golden-haired woman, naked. With one hand she pulled at her hair; in the other, she held a dagger, pointed to her breast. He needed no one to tell him her story—it was a popular subject for paintings. "It is Lucretia," he thought.

He turned away from the picture and walked over to the hearth. New fuel had been laid upon red coals. He had just avoided meeting the servant. He watched the flames licking the wood. Absurdly, he wondered how long it would take before they would bite and the faggots sizzle into flame. He turned his back to the hearth and surveyed the room from his new vantage point. There was the place—just to his left—where once a youth had sat, mandore in hand, and confessed his heart in song—just opposite to the pictures of the old man and, now, Lucretia.

However, he had come to see none of this. What had he come to see? Slowly he surveyed the room, his head pivoting from left to right. Then his heart leaped. He had found what he knew he had all along sought. Her. There *she* stood—yes, *she*, arrayed in the beauty that he so fondly remembered. He moved slowly toward her, as in a dream.

The hair was a dark chestnut, pouring down over her shoulders, stray locks like wanton tendrils over her breasts. Her face was fair, but her eyes dark, like her hair; her lips slightly parted.

> *She is my mother.*
> *You never knew her.*
> *No.*

The words and the tone were as vivid as on the day they were spoken. But today the words were not spoken but echoed from the distant past. Then she had spoken of her mother; now he beheld, not the mother but the daughter's image in the mother. This woman was not the girl he remembered—she was older, more mature, but, for all that, all the more beautiful. "So must she be now," he thought, "despite all."

Through a doorway just to the left of the picture he passed into a small room, where doors opened out onto the garden. Autumn was not yet at the full. The gravel path was strewn with a few leaves of red, yellow, and brown, from the trees embowering him overhead. Yet, green grass still grew along the borders of the path, and late flowers were blooming. The lilacs still held their leaves, but they were turning a reddish, dusky brown.

He sat down on the stone bench by pond's edge. Thinking back over the years, he wondered how often *she* had sat in this very place. In good weather, he knew, she had read his letters here—for she had so written. She had come to this place, for here, she had said, she felt closer to him than anywhere else.

Doubtless, it was here she had fled, too, in the days of her trouble—to be near him from her so far sundered.

But what did he seek in the garden? He smiled to himself. He knew—the sweet melancholy of a bitter loss. He had thought to rekindle the vivid flame of his longing and feel again the sadness of an irrevocable estrangement. From the day he had left Wittenberg, he had anticipated this moment; but now that it was come, he found to his disappointment that he felt cold inside. With his fingertips, he gently touched the place where she had sat, next to him, on the day they had confessed their love. But he could scratch no spark from that flint. His heart was unkindled. He rose and followed the shortest path to the garden doors. Into the little side room, through the family room, and into the outer hall he went. But when he had only begun to climb the stairway, he heard a voice calling—

"Lorenz!"

He turned to see, coming down the hallway from the direction of the library, his host.

He said, with more spirit than he felt, "Veit! At last! How good it is to see you!"

*   *   *

"Lorenz, by God! I have found you. My servant, Clemens, told me you had gone to your room, but I didn't find you there. I was just in the family hall, but not seeing you there, went into the library . . ."

They clasped hands. Veit, he could tell, was happy to see him, though his manner seemed a mite constrained.

"Well, then, you just missed me," he replied. "I was in the family hall but then went into the garden . . ."

"*Ach!* I should have known you would go there," Veit said. "You were always fond of it."

The two fell silent. Veit's eyes surveyed him; there was unease in his eyes.

"By God, it is good to see you again," Veit said, a little awkwardly. "But, alas! I have only a short time I can spend with you before I return to the *Rathaus*. I came home to see if you had arrived and to get my mid-morning meal. I trust you too are hungry?"

"It is only mid-morning?" Lorenz said. "I had dozed off in my room and was sure I had slept longer than that!"

Veit laughed. "*Ach*, Lorenz! In this, at least, you have not changed. Didn't you see the clock in the family room — it is quite large, how could you have missed it?"

Lorenz joined in Veit's mirth. He shrugged his shoulders.

"Mind in the clouds, as usual! But, come! Meet me in the dining room in ten minutes. I have had food and drink set out for us."

* * *

" . . . No, my wife will not be joining us. She rarely leaves her room so early. You will see her this evening."

As he spoke, Veit was cutting a sausage. He spoke even as he forked a piece into his mouth.

"You see, Greta enjoys the evening and the night; morning is her time for sleep. I, on the other hand, prefer to sleep in the night and waken in the morning. Of course, my duties as adviser to the council demand it."

"I would have thought you would be sitting on the council by now," Lorenz said with a small laugh.

"No, that task falls to my elder brother, Hermann — who is, I assure you, a most grave councilor." Veit pulled a long face. "You see, he is my father's heir; I am but a younger son. But none of this bothers me in the least. Hermann, you see, oversees the family business, in which I play a much smaller part. This leaves me free to use my university-acquired knowledge of law rather than worry over bills of lading, ledger books, and other such tedium. And my father is content, for he had begun to despair over my business sense. Being a lawyer-adviser to the council is honorable; and since I am rather good at it, I bring prestige to the family. That pleases my father. Moreover, I can live here and not in my father's dreary house. And that pleases me, too."

Lorenz, who was drinking, put down his cup. "Yes, I was going to ask you about that," he said. "How did you come to live at *Auerhaus*? When you wrote me the directions to your dwelling, I was frankly surprised."

Veit lay down his fork with a thud on the table. "*Ach*, Lorenz!" he said. "I should have told you long ago; you, if anyone, really deserved to know. But our conversation when we met in Heidelberg—what is it, now, some six years ago? God! It doesn't seem that long—well, it just didn't turn in that direction, and our letters afterwards were on such different subjects that I just didn't get around to it."

"Yes, and we haven't corresponded now for some years," Lorenz added. "But do not let it concern you, Veit. I would probably not have mentioned it, either, if I were in your place. But, though I wondered at the news at first, I have thought since that it all makes sense. The house would naturally have gone to the Waldhummels upon Herr Auer's death, and it's natural that they would have handed it over to their only daughter and her husband."

"Handed it over? No, not quite," Veit said. "Not as of yet, at any rate. Herr Waldhummel was willing, but my wife's mother has—well, she has other designs. And, if the truth be told, Greta is not fond of the place. But I like it here—and I cannot countenance the thought of a stranger living here, and it cannot stand empty."

Talking of the house, Lorenz could see, made Veit again uneasy. Indeed, waves of unease had passed over his friend throughout their conversation, though Lorenz could see he did his best to conceal it. Veit had been content to let Lorenz ask the questions throughout the meal, but he was, Lorenz could see, eager to ask some questions of his own. Eager, but hesitant. Lorenz surmised the cause.

At last Lorenz thought he would push his friend to unburden himself. "Veit, my friend," he said, "come now, out with it!"

Veit, who had been chewing a rather large hunk of sausage, swallowed hard. "Out with what?" he asked, nervously.

Lorenz felt the master of the situation. "I know curiosity is killing you, but you fear to offend me. But I shall lay bare your trouble."

Veit said nothing. Instead he took a bite of bread.

Lorenz continued: "When we met in the hallway, I could detect your confusion. You had expected to see an Augustinian eremite but instead you were greeted by a man in layman's dress. I can well understand, for in my letter I told you I was coming to Nürnberg on business having to do with the order. It was natural that you would think I was still a member of it. But, instead of a monk, you found a lay scholar."

Veit took a drink of wine and then wiped his mouth with his napkin. He nodded his head. "Yes, my friend; I confess, I was taken aback, though perhaps I shouldn't have been. I know something of what has been happening in Wittenberg—and what is happening here. I cannot say I fully understand it all, though I am willing to learn."

"And you shall!" Lorenz said emphatically. "I don't feel that I have to hide anything. Ask me what you will; I will tell you all."

Veit pressed his lips together and nodded. "Thank you for your forthrightness, Lorenz," he said. "You can read me well; I have never been good at concealment. And, since I have your kind permission, I shall ask about what has been happening in Wittenberg—and, if you are willing, about what has been happening with you."

"As I have said, I am willing. Ask away!"

Veit placed his napkin on the table and pushed back his chair. "I shall," he said. "But not now—I must return to the council. Perhaps we can speak tonight, or tomorrow?"

"I am at your disposal," Lorenz said. "I have much to tell, much of good."

CHAPTER 3

VEIT WANTED TO UNDERSTAND WHAT had happened in Wittenberg, but Lorenz felt he scarcely understood it himself. For was it not far larger than Wittenberg? The question was, what had happened in Germany? Wittenberg was but one piece of flotsam, one remnant of a wreckage carried with a myriad of others on the currents of a vast river, whither no one knew.

And Nürnberg, too, had become unmoored.

It had all begun like a storm in spring. The waiting stillness in the air, the smell of rain; then, a distant rumble of thunder. News had come from Worms — Luther had come under the empire's ban. On his return to Wittenberg, he had been waylaid and spirited away; whither, no one knew. But he was safe, in the keeping of friends.

Throughout the summer, Wittenberg had been quiet. The rumbling sounded from Erfurt. Rumors and then certain reports — stirred by the preaching of Johann Lang, mobs were attacking priests, burning their parsonages. Students, artisans, peasants, all armed, pillaged libraries. Murders in the streets and in homes of the "enemies of the Gospel"; Maternus Pictoris, lying dead in his blood. But in Wittenberg, all was quiet, awaiting the storm.

All went on as before in the life of the monastery — the chanting of the hours, Mass, readings in the refectory, confession of sins. All was as it had been all the years he had lived in the cloister. Daily he rose, prayed, said his Mass, taught in the university, studied. But, despite the appearances and the regularity, the old life had flown from the monastery, and into its empty shell a new spirit had entered. The rabid Gabriel Zwilling rose up among the brethren. Adoring the Eucharist is idolatry! he cried. The Mass is blasphemy—it must be abolished!

Then the storm struck Wittenberg.

First a few, then an increasing number of the Augustinians, then nearly the entire monastery abandoned the discipline of the rule. Zwilling's violence, like a rising wind, was magnified a hundredfold. Like a tottering structure, eaten by termites, the monastery's life collapsed in the bitter gale. Only eight days before the anniversary of Luther's first great defiance, Mass ceased in the Augustinian church. The life Lorenz had known now for eight years was entirely swept away.

The Gospel! The Gospel! Always, the Gospel was the sanction for the destruction. Monks cast off their habits. They wandered the streets declaring God's wrath against the Abomination, as they called it. The prior and the few monks remaining took refuge within the all-but-abandoned walls of the cloister; but even there they were not safe. The prior's former subjects, the renegade monks, incited the dregs of the streets against him. Those wearing the black habit lived in jeopardy of life and limb.

And, despite his doubts, Lorenz remained among his brethren—many of whom, like him, had long since ceased to believe.

* * *

New-fallen snow lay on the streets in the early hours when Lorenz, with Frater Jürgen, had crossed from the convent, toward the parish church. As he set up for Mass at a side altar, Lorenz could hear the tinkling of bells at other altars. He wondered that he, and they, still dared to go through with the ritual.

Jürgen, he knew, still devoutly believed; and it was for such as that lay brother that he kept up the form of the old life. Over the past several months, the distress of this brother, so dear to Lorenz, had been palpable. The ban laid on Frater Martin, whom Jürgen had held in the highest regard; his sudden disappearance; the defections from the monastery—these had shaken the gentle brother to the core. He said nothing; he asked for nothing; but Jürgen's whole demeanor pleaded. Lorenz himself had remained silent about his own thoughts and inner struggles. No man knew his counsels, save for a few. He had not been prominent among the innovators—not for several months. And he had remained in the monastery, following the daily rounds of prayer, teaching in the university, and immersed in study. He wondered if Jürgen at all doubted his devotion to the old faith. If he did, he said nothing.

As ever, he vested, saying the required prayers as he donned alb, amice, stole, and chasuble. Standing before the altar, he hesitated as he contemplated the small statue of the Virgin, holding the Christ Child. It was a tender, playful figure, he thought; Mary held the Child on her right arm; she grasped what looked like a pear in her left hand. Her demeanor was tender as she gazed on him, who, with his right hand, reached to touch her cheek.

Jürgen, he knew, loved this figurine—and it was for this reason that, when he could, Lorenz reserved this altar for his Mass. He wondered if he should so encourage such devotion in the simple brother. Some of the Evangelicals would call it idolatry—though he knew it was not so for Jürgen. The brother's love for Christ and his Mother was simple, but it was pure of material dross—or so Lorenz had thought. But what if it were not so? Was he betraying the Gospel by encouraging such weakness in the monk?

Confitemini Domino quoniam bonus.
Quoniam in aeternum misericordia eius.
Confiteor Deo . . .

Verse and response. Verse and response. As he had said it,
now, for so many years. It was all so perfunctory, without spirit
and without life. But he watched Jürgen out of the corner of
his eye; he knew it was not so for him. But whereas, before,
Jürgen's eyes had longed, now they besought. They bespoke
an inner anguish.

Kyrie eleison.
Kyrie eleison.
Kyrie eleison.
Christe eleison.
Christe . . .

He wondered—why couldn't Jürgen see? Why couldn't he
understand? A storm had struck Wittenberg, but amid its
lowering it flashed with a blinding brilliance—

Oremus.
Excita quaesumus Domine potentiam tuam, et veni: ut
ab imminentibus peccatorum nostrorum periculis . . .

Of course, why, when he himself could see, did he not follow the example of his brothers who had cast off the cowl
and abandoned all to follow Christ? What held him back? No
one said the Mass in the cloister now—but he still said it in
the parish church. Was it just for Jürgen—the brother whom,
brother-like, he should be guiding to truth?

Sequentia Sancti Evangelii secundum Lucam.
Gloria tibi, Domine.

In illo tempore: Dixit Iesus discipulis suis: Erunt signa in
sole et luna et stellis, et in terris pressura gentium prae con-
fusione sonitum maris, et fluctuum; arescentibus hominibus
prae timore, et expectatione, quae supervenient universo

orbi. Nam virtutes caelorum movebunur. Et tunc videbunt
Filium hominis...

He stopped mid-sentence. What was that noise? It came
from without the church. It was like a feral roar, rising in
intensity and volume—but then it as swiftly died away.

> *...venientem in nube cum potestate magna et maiestate.*
> *His autem fieri incipientibus, respicite et levate capita*
> *vestra...*

Again, the noise. It was growing louder. It was drawing nigh
the church. The striking of feet on the stone floor—someone
had run to the church doors, closed for the cold, and opened
one slightly to look out. Almost as soon as he had done so,
he shut it. He shouted, fear in his voice:

"We must bar the door! Someone help me bar—"

But he could not finish. The doors flew open, and outside
what appeared to be a great crowd blocked the sunlight. They
seemed to hesitate, as if afraid to enter; but then, at a shout
they as one body pressed into the church. As they rushed
up the nave, Lorenz could see some held stones; others were
wielding knives. Many were his own students.

Jürgen was now at his side. "What is it, *Bruder*?" he said.
"What do they want?"

"Blood. I fear, blood," Lorenz heard himself say.

The mob, now having moved into the middle of the nave,
halted. One of their number motioned them to silence. Raising his knife and brandishing it, he began to speak. It was
Matthias Kahl.

"Idolaters! So-called priests, I give you fair warning!" he
cried. "Leave this place—or remain, in peril of your life! The
Lord of Sabaoth will no longer abide your blasphemies. We are
his minsters—the wrath of the Almighty! We will tear down
your altars and on the rubble of them raise gallows from which

to hang your stinking carcasses! The crows will peck out your eyes, while your souls roast in Hell!"

"At 'em!"

With a roar, the mob rushed toward the high altar and dispersed throughout the church. Lorenz could see some of the priests were fleeing from the side altars. Students were lobbing stones at them. Brandished knives flashed in the light streaming through stained glass. He turned to see Jürgen lunge toward the altar. The small brother was gathering the statue of the Mother and Child in his arms. Two students tore at his cowl. He fell, the statue under him. He was shielding it with his body.

White anger. Seizing the altar missal — a large book with a cover of wrought metal — Lorenz struck one of the students in the head and sent him sprawling. "Leave him alone! He is an innocent!" he heard himself cry. He turned to strike another of the rioters, but he felt the book torn from his grasp. Something hit him from behind. He lost his balance and fell against the altar. A sharp pain shot through his back and made him gasp; but he managed to crawl toward the little friar; he hesitated and then covered him with his body. He expected at any moment to feel a knife thrust into his back. He tensed himself for the blow. Then all went black.

*   *   *

When he awoke, he was lying on his back, before the altar. He lay there a few moments, gazing up at the fluted ceiling. All was now quiet. "They have gone," he thought to himself. He turned onto his side and then lifted himself up on his right arm. Again, the sharp pain — it came from between his shoulder blades. Wincing, he pushed himself up into a sitting position and breathed — but not too deeply. His head swam. He felt nauseous.

The church was a shambles. Statues thrown down and broken. Altar cloths torn and trampled on the stone floor. Pages of torn missals strewn about. Broken glass.

All was silent — except for the sobs. He wondered where they came from; but then he remembered. Beside him, on his left, Jürgen still lay. His knees pulled up against his chest. A nasty contusion on the side of his face. The small brother was sobbing quietly like a child — and still holding close to his breast the figure of a Mother and Child. From what Lorenz could see, it had suffered little damage. The mother's face still smiled on the child, who rested on her right arm. The hand that had held the fruit was hidden by the friar's robe.

But the little hand that had reached out to touch the Mother's face was gone, broken off at the wrist.

* * *

"Lorenz! Wait, I p-pray, a moment!"

Lorenz turned to see Melanchthon. The small man came hastening toward him.

"Philipp," Lorenz said, "what news?"

"It was I who wanted to ask you," Melanchthon replied. "How are you? When you did not turn up for your Greek lesson, I wondered. But then I heard of that unfortunate event in the p-parish church, and that you were laid up."

Melanchthon's ferret-like face with its supercilious cast normally vexed Lorenz; but today Lorenz thought he detected warmth, friendliness, and sincere concern in the man's eyes. Could it be that Philipp was genuinely distressed on account of a friend's health?

"Yes," Lorenz said. "This is my first day out of bed. I was struck between the shoulder blades by a very large rock cast by a rather angry zealot of a student. It was bad enough that I lay abed three days. But I am better, now, though not free of pain."

"Well, I am glad to hear you are recovering," Melanchthon said. "I was dismayed when I heard what happened; but learning that you were caught up in it only heightened m-my alarm and consternation."

Chapter 3

"You need have no concern for my health, I think," Lorenz rejoined. "Indeed, I am not worried at all about myself, now. I am distressed for Jürgen. He was beaten rather savagely, and he has never been of robust health. He is not recovering as he should."

Melanchthon's face took on a puzzled look. He slowly shook his head. "Jürgen?" he said. "I don't think I know him."

"No, you wouldn't," Lorenz said, trying to stifle his annoyance. "He is not a student, not a scholar. He is a lay brother. He frequently accompanied me to the parish church, where, of late, I have read the Mass. He was with me the other day and was struck down. You would not, I am sure, want to hear the details . . ."

"No, I p-pray you, do not indulge me," Melanchthon replied. "But I shall pray for him — p-poor fellow."

"Yes," Lorenz parried, "poor fellow, indeed." His own wound, and his fear for Jürgen, had been working on him during the days of their convalescence. They pricked him, gave him no rest. And then to have Melanchthon, whom he deemed responsible for much of the unrest, bob his head about that way in apparent sympathy, lanced the sore of his vexation.

"By God, Philipp!" he exclaimed. "He needs more than your prayers! He and those like him, need your sympathy!" He paused, hesitating like a man debating a plunge into cold water. Melanchthon cocked his head and looked with incomprehension on Lorenz. The expression vexed Lorenz the more.

"Must we move so fast?" he said, the more vehemently. "You and I, Karlstadt, perhaps, and others understand what must be done — but the simple ones, what of them? They have not searched the Scriptures like we have; their minds are locked in the traditions of their, and our, fathers. Their stomachs cannot stand meat, they must have milk!"

Melanchthon's ferret eyes darted at Lorenz and then turned away. "But what some of us give them for their milk is really poison," Melanchthon replied. "Your Jürgens believe the Mass will win them salvation—a mere work of men! I do not blame them, for they are simple; but those of us who understand—is it not our duty to tear the poison from their hands before they lift it to their lips?"

"You can tear poison from the hands, but not belief from the mind nor conviction from the heart, Philipp!" Lorenz almost said, *what do you know, callow scholar, of men's hearts, their struggles, their wrestling with God?* Instead, he asserted, "I doubt Frater Martin would approve of such violence!"

"Indeed, he would not approve of violence," Melanchthon replied smugly. "But, as for what's been going on in Wittenberg, Luther *has* seen it, and he approves it."

Melanchthon's words were like a cold drenching to Lorenz. "He has seen it? What do you mean, Philipp?"

"Only that Luther has been in the city, and is generally pleased at what he has seen and heard."

"He is pleased with riot? And what do you mean that he has been in the city?"

"Simply that," Melanchthon sighed. "The day after the riot, Luther entered Wittenberg. No, no one noticed him—he was wearing a great, black beard and was clad like a knight." Melanchthon smiled to himself. "Of course, he was grieved to hear of what happened in the parish church—though I must say"—and here Melanchthon laughed nervously—"he was more vexed that Spalatin had not published certain tracts that he had sent him. But he disapproves of violence; yet, he p-praised the progress the Gospel has made.

"Of course," Philipp continued, "he was saddened by the news of what had befallen you. He would have visited you in the convent, but he dared not go there, for fear of b-being recognized."

Lorenz did not know what to say to this. He was befuddled. Luther in the city! Praise for the "Gospel's progress"! His sadness at the news of it . . . and the *but* that was not spoken, only implied . . .

Melanchthon's eyes met his briefly, but turned away. "Friend," he said, like one who is about to break unfortunate news — "Friend, Luther's gaze sees more deeply than ours does. The Holy Spirit is moving among us in a way he has not done for a thousand years. What is old and error-ridden will soon pass away — it must p-pass away. The Mass will be purged ere long. We must learn to worship God anew, in spirit and in truth. The student mobs sense this — and p-perhaps they are moved by the Spirit; can we know which way he blows? The cold wind is sharp — it goads us to seek shelter. Some of us will gather under the shelter of his wings, but those who refuse . . ."

Those who refuse — as he walked with brisk step toward the convent, he turned these words over in his mind. Did Jürgen refuse? Were the peasants in the countryside refusing? How could they refuse what they did not understand? He himself, Melanchthon, even Martin, had once not understood; but God had drawn them, perhaps not gently, but little by little, to the knowledge of truth. "Why cannot we be like God? Why must we force all this on the simple, whom we ourselves taught to believe the doctrines we now repudiate?"

But, of course — was not Melanchthon right? What can we know of God and his ways? Man's justice is not God's justice; like his mercy, it so far transcends our human categories that we cannot begin to fathom it. The Gospel itself — the glad tidings of God's arcane mercy — had facets and subtleties that he had not apprehended when first he had joyously embraced it in Heidelberg. Its promise of joy, he had found, only yawned on a horror that defied all facile attempts at reconciliation.

* * *

For months now he had wrestled with the horror.

"You say our will is not free, that each of us stands . . ."

"Yes, like a bondsman or slave to God—to God or Satan."

It had been shortly before his departure for Worms that Martin had spoken these words.

"Yet, a slave can will to obey his master or not. But this is not what you mean?"

"No, it is not what I mean." He remembered how Martin's deep-set eyes burned with conviction. Did not his own words terrify him?

"A human master," Martin continued, "can command only the body; God is lord of the soul. A human master can compel only the body, but God compels the will. Indeed, our will would be entirely inert and lifeless were it not moved by God."

"So, when we sin, it is God who compels us to sin?"

"Yes and no. Think of this analogy. Our will is like a saw that cuts only when the craftsman takes it in hand and moves it. If the saw is good, it will make a clean cut. If it is bad, it will cut raggedly. The bad cut is made by a bad saw; a good cut by a good saw. But no cut would be made without the hand of the carpenter."

"But is there not a difference, here, between the carpenter and God?"

"Of course, an infinite difference."

"No, what I mean is, a carpenter uses a saw he did not make. If he cuts with a bad saw, it is because either the saw's maker has failed in his art or because the carpenter has failed in his—by misusing his instrument. But God is the creator of a man's will. If that is perverse, what is the cause?"

"Adam's sin, brother—you must know that!"

"Yes, I know that—but is not what is true of my will true of Adam's too? Did it not stand lifeless and inert in the hand of God?"

"Adam's will was created good and upright ...."

"But he sinned."

"Yes." He recalled how Martin had hesitated, like a man walking near a precipice in a fog. Lorenz himself had feared to take the next step; but the turmoil in his own soul compelled him.

His words were hesitant, reluctant steps.

"But if he sinned, his will—must we not conclude that his will was bad? And if it was bad, who made it so?"

Martin had seemed to steel himself to resolution. "No, his will was good," he said. "But the Spirit did not add to it that it might obey."

It was as he had feared, or near to what he had feared. God did not make Adam's will evil, but then . . .

"Then, mustn't we conclude that Adam could do nothing but disobey?"

"Yes. He must disobey."

"And be damned?"

"And be damned."

Lorenz paused to turn the words over in his mind. But then a thought leaped to life in his mind . . .

"Does not this doctrine fly in the face of Scripture? I see how you might draw it from Paul; still Paul must be weighed against other passages. What of Ezekiel? *I will not the death of a sinner?*"

Martin did not immediately answer; it was as if he were uncertain. He looked intensely into Lorenz's eyes. Then he nodded.

"Brother," he said, "you must know that here Ezekiel speaks of God's manifest will—the will he reveals to us. He speaks not of God's hidden will, terrible to us, but still to be adored in silent awe—for who can fathom it? Why do some embrace God's promise, while others spurn it? Is it not because God, by arcane counsel, ordains that some will believe, even so that they can do naught else? Some he moves to believe, others he moves to sin—though the sin is not in God but in them."

"But if God is so very other, how can we cling to his promises?" (He tried to suppress his anxiety.) "Christ said, *he who believes and is baptized, shall be saved*; but do those words reveal his manifest or hidden will?"

Martin shook his head. "Brother," he said, "God's will is unfathomable. Look rather to the cross—what does the cross tell you?"

Lorenz lowered his eyes. "The cross speaks of hope and mercy," he said. "But your words speak of something very different."

Martin's intense gaze softened; fellow feeling shone in his eyes. "But that *is* the cross, the ever-present fear of God's terrible will," he said. "From it faith is born. We must cling to Christ's promise, even if all reason screams out in protest—as it does, dear brother, as it does. We can do nothing but believe the promise, that Christ will fulfill his promise. That is our only hope."

But if that is hope, Lorenz thought, it is not far from despair.

* * *

The figure of the woman and child stood on the small table beside the bed. She still held the pear fruit in her left hand. The boy child, resting in the bend of her right arm, still strove to touch her face. But the child's hand was broken off at the wrist.

Two men, passersby he had haled, had carried Jürgen from the parish church to the convent. Lorenz himself had carried the statue. (He had searched, but had been unable to find the boy-child's hand.) He recalled the smile on Jürgen's face when he saw the statue on the small table beside the bed. Even now, as they were conversing, Jürgen's eyes strayed betimes to the figurine.

"Yes, I am in pain; but I am content." He paused, then said, "I have not long, you know."

Lorenz shook his head. "*Frater*," he said, "your injuries are not serious. They cannot be life-threatening. You will recover."

But even as he said this, he thought how Jürgen had waxed the more pale over the past few days. How weak he now seemed.

The small brother smiled feebly. "You speak," he said, "like someone who says, 'do not worry! All will be well!' But, *Frater*, I am not worried. I hope soon all *will* be well."

Lorenz did not know what to say to this. He merely nodded his head.

Jürgen continued. "I fear, however, that I have not yet thanked you for bringing Our Lady to me." He glanced toward the statue. "She comforts me. It is sad that Jesus has lost his hand—but you know, I can imagine it there."

Again, Lorenz did not know what to say. He did not want to encourage "idolatry," but then again, he wasn't at all certain that it was idolatry with Jürgen.

" . . . And, I have not thanked you for another thing; how you tried to save me from those ruffians. You were a true father to me. I can never repay you, except to ask Our Lady and Jesus to bless you."

"That would be repayment enough, *Frater*," Lorenz said.

Lorenz looked down at his own hands, clasped on his knees. Was he doing right by encouraging the very attitudes he had himself come to see as false? Shouldn't he be speaking of faith to him, telling him of the Gospel? He had started to, betimes, in the past, but a caution had silenced the words before they passed his lips. Perhaps he should just force himself; it were an injustice to deprive any man of truth. But when he lifted his eyes, he saw that Jürgen was looking steadily at him. He knew he could not carry it through. Instead, Lorenz smiled at him and began to rise, "I fear I must leave you," he began to say . . .

"But *Frater*, one more thing," Jürgen interposed. "Think me not too bold, after all you have done for me, to make one more request. I would ask someone else, but I know they would not do it for me. Even if they did, they would just pretend. I . . . I know that you also do not believe in it anymore, but I know that you would not pretend."

Lorenz knew what Jürgen was asking. He could, he knew, try to convince his small brother that it was all unnecessary; but he thought that pleas of that sort would be lost on Jürgen. So, he nodded and said, "Yes, *Frater*, I will hear your confession."

A broad smile brightened Jürgen's face. "Thank you, thank you, my father!" he said.

Lorenz too smiled. He felt unaccountably happy. He would do for Jürgen what he requested. And despite his own opinions and doubts, he would not "pretend."

CHAPTER 4

AGE HAD NOT DIMMED HER BEAUTY. Yes, she was no longer the lithe girl whose loveliness had once ensnared his boyish heart. Less nymph-like she seemed and more buxom; but her modest Nürnberg gown scarcely concealed her shapely, well-proportioned figure. A wisp of her hair, harvest hue, having escaped from her matronly wimple, dangled wantonly over her cheek. Her skin was like freshly churned butter and flawless. As she offered an exquisite hand to him (long, tapered fingers, bright with rings), her blue eyes' glance was bold.

"Lorenz—or should I say, Herr Magister List? I am most glad to see you again!" Her tone was languid, like a sultry day in summer.

"Frau Scheuerlin," he said, bowing slightly.

"O, please!" she said with a laugh and a waive of her hand. "I don't know how I should address you; but do you call me Greta, as of old. Are we not like cousins?"

He shrugged his shoulders. "I suppose we are," he said. "Then please call me, too, by my Christian name."

"Yes, I shall call you Lorenz."

At the evening meal, Veit said little; the woman he addressed as "wife" carried the conversation forward. Lorenz's first impressions of her had been favorable. The years had mellowed her, it seemed; the flightiness of youth was gone, and in its place reigned grace and poise. Consciousness of her great beauty, perhaps, had made her self-regarding. Indeed, after a while, her demeanor seemed somewhat too studied. It seemed to Lorenz almost that she was playing a part.

To Lorenz's wonder, her conversation turned not on airy nothings but on theology. She was, she assured him, decidedly Evangelical. "As you probably know," she said, "my husband is not; but I am, as are my father and mother." She seemed intensely interested in whatever he could tell her about Luther and that "brilliant young man," Melanchthon. "I had not known that you have been so intimate with both," she said, prettily arching her eyebrows. She said she wanted to know *everything* about what had happened in Wittenberg. She had heard of all the upheavals in the town—but, of course, such is to be expected (she said piously), for the Devil will ever seek to deceive men and twist what is good to his will. Still, she did not think the like would happen in Nürnberg, for the counselors were wise men and would direct everything with due care. They would never allow *fanatics* to sully the Pure Word. No, Nürnberg was a *very* different place . . .

"Still," she said, "there is a good deal of unrest amongst the peasants outside. We do not know where *that* will end!"

Despite himself, Lorenz found her intoxicating. She had cultivated a grace that yet could yield here and there to a girl-ish charm. Her eyes were bold, but in their boldness, inviting. He thought he should not look long on them, but he found himself drawn to them. Her gestures and mannerisms, too, he found utterly amiable. The wisp of hair, dangling from her wimple and lightly brushing her cheek, was the final flourish that completed the vision of delight.

When at last Veit's voice intruded on hers, the sound was jarring: "Wife, I pray, have mercy on Lorenz. You press him so with questions that he can hardly eat. Have done!"

Veit's intervention vexed Lorenz; but it seemed not to trouble Greta at all. She put on a little pout and, holding out her hands in a pleading gesture, begged his pardon. "My husband," she said, "is always so quiet at meals — and he rarely takes me from the house! Perhaps I am an idle gossiper, but I do enjoy a good conversation. You would not expect it, Lorenz, but Veit has grown so very grave; he's always thinking on deep matters, no doubt! Why, I didn't know until a fortnight back, when he told me that you would be coming to our house, that you had been in correspondence! And as for the reason for your visit, he told me nothing."

"Well, that may be because he himself does not know," Lorenz replied. "You see, I myself have been somewhat secretive on that score."

Greta put on a coy smile. "Well, then, I will not trouble you with questions," she said. "But you must know how tantalizing a secret can be!"

Lorenz laughed. "There is no secret," he said. "I have come to confer with Wenzel Linck, Osiander, and some others. The Marshal of Weissenbrücke has requested an Evangelical preacher from Luther, and Luther chose me."

"Weissenbrücke," Veit said. "That's where you went to school . . . "

"I did — that is the reason, no doubt, that Luther chose me, though he said nothing of the sort."

"And you could not resist the call of your old home?" Greta said.

"No, not of my old home. I could not resist the call of Nürnberg — and my friends," Lorenz replied. "Before I depart, Linck would like me to preach to the Augustinians for a time. I suspect I shall be here at least a month. And I am certain I will not remain for good in Weissenbrücke."

Greta smiled. "Then you will return to Nürnberg?"

"I don't know, but that is what I hope."

Lorenz felt a pleasant refreshment; he had expected to find Greta as he had remembered her—vain, frivolous, and pettily cruel. But instead, he found a woman, a wife and mother, whose cultivation and poise complemented her great beauty. He wondered how Veit could find her so distasteful, as he clearly did. She seemed a mate on whose account any man would deem himself most fortunate. Indeed, Lorenz was enjoying her company more than he was gloomy Veit's. Moreover, he found that her loveliness kept drawing his eyes like a lodestone.

She had finished the last of her wine and had set down her glass. "Lorenz," she said, with a shy smile. "I hope you will not think me nosy; but, when you said you would be preaching to the Augustinians, I could not help wondering if you might do the same for their hermitesses at Pillenreuth?"

Veit, who had lifted his glass, set it down rather hard on the table. "Wife," he said irritably, "do not tread there!"

"Husband," she replied, with a sinuous pout in her tone, "I see no harm in it! Mother and Father are very troubled, and so am I. I thought that, if Lorenz was going there, he could help..."

"Help?" Veit's tone was sharp. "I don't think it is just *help* you are seeking!"

"But I am," she replied, a gentle complaint in her voice, as if she were pleading against an unjust accuser. "You cannot understand, for you do not yet accept our views. But you should at least be fair to us..."

"Veit," Lorenz interposed. "Feel no vexation on my part. I do not object to Greta's question."

Indeed, he did not. Rather, the mention of Pillenreuth thrilled him. He had longed to ask Veit, but embarrassment and shame had held him back. He had had no intention of broaching the subject with Greta—but now that she brought it up, he saw he might learn what he wished to know without exposing himself too much.

"Thank you, Lorenz," she said. "I asked whether you might preach at Pillenreuth because, well, you know, Mother and Father are very Evangelical, and our Schwester Agnes . . . "

She paused. Her eyes had been cast demurely down, but now she flashed a quick glance at him.

" . . . our Schwester Agnes," she resumed, "is there."

He hardly dared ask, for he had guessed; but he forced his lips to form the question, "Schwester Agnes?"

"Yes, that's the name she took," Greta replied. "But you must know of whom I speak! It is our very own cousin and friend, Beatrice . . . "

("No, not Beatrice; but Else. *Else mein.*" He did not speak the words, but they resonated in his mind.)

" . . . so many in Nürnberg who have embraced the Pure Word are most troubled in conscience that they dedicated their daughters to the monasteries. They are demanding that the council allow them to pull their daughters out. Though Father and Mother themselves did not dedicate Beatrice, they feel responsible for her, now that her father is gone . . . "

(*They* responsible? No, he alone was responsible—and didn't this fact alone require that he do something?)

" . . . Father has been one of the chief ones to demand that the council give the permission. Indeed, he has been talking with your own Wenzel Linck about what to do. One of the chief problems is the prioress . . . "

(He could scarcely believe that the opportunity had presented itself so soon. He had not thought that it would present itself at all...)

" . . . she is a real horror! Like that Caritas Pirkheimer, whose monastery Uncle had wanted Beatrice to join. It would not have made any difference, spiritually speaking—but at least she would have been in the city. A monastery outside the city is no safe place, given what the peasants are up to."

Lorenz had only been half listening to her; but at the suggestion of danger, he looked up—and caught her eye. All the while she had been scrutinizing him, he saw—though at once she tried to conceal it by glancing away. But in that brief moment in which their eyes met, he detected the glimmer of the old Greta. He smiled to himself—he had almost been taken in again.

"Greta," he said. "I am sad to hear about your parents' distress—but they really cannot be proposing to force anyone from the monastery?"

Greta, whom he suspected knew that she had been discovered, recovered herself adroitly. ("A real artist," he thought.) "But why shouldn't they," she said, defensively. "You yourself know that monasteries are full of idolatry and even vice! It would be for the salvation of her soul!"

"First," he said, "I know no such thing. Secondly, no one can force another's conscience. It would be wrong to do so, even to save a soul. I could have no part in such violence."

She smiled. "No one is asking you to do anything violent, Lorenz," she said. "But what about trying to persuade someone? That wouldn't be violent, would it?"

Lorenz met her smile with his own. "No, persuasion would not be violence," he said.

* * *

"I beg your pardon, Lorenz."

Greta had gone; the men were alone. Veit poured Lorenz some more wine. "Greta is such a cat!"

"Yes, and she played me like a mouse . . ."

"She almost had you in her claws . . . "

"But I escaped."

"No, not quite." Veit took a sip of wine. "You weren't devoured, but you were clawed. *Ach!* I should have warned you that she

192

might bring up Pillenreuth—and Agnes." Veit's voice trailed off on the last word.

"Veit, my friend," Lorenz said. "Do not fear to speak of Beatrice. I am not so fragile that I shall break at the sound of her name."

"Well, I suppose it has been a long time. Greta was trying to sound your heart—she is convinced that you still pine for her cousin. But all wounds heal in time, I suppose."

Lorenz could detect a note of censure in his friend's tone; but he would not try to correct the misconception. Instead, he turned the conversation elsewhere.

"Veit, I can see—and what Greta has said only confirms it—that, well, with you, friendship contends with disapproval of—of what I have done."

Veit averted his eyes. "Disapproval?" he said. "No, I don't think it is disapproval. Incomprehension, perhaps—and not only about what *you* have done. About everything that is happening."

"Then Greta is wrong—you are not utterly opposed to the Evangelicals?"

"No, Greta is right," Veit looked directly at Lorenz. "Or shall I say, at least as far as my perception goes. Thus far I have seen nothing about the Evangelicals that could convince me that they are of God."

Lorenz had no immediate rejoinder to this. He understood.

"Veit," he said, "do not hesitate to explain yourself. You will not offend me."

Veit took another sip of wine and smiled. "You will scarce believe it," he said, "but I was beginning to feel reconciled to Nürnberg, not long after I returned—you know, after our chance meeting in Heidelberg. I could even tolerate Greta; after all, she is beautiful, and she has given me two children. Indeed, it was not long before she was expecting another. I found, too, that Nürnberg had a vibrant intellectual life—something that I of course knew before but had never taken advantage of. I decided I would join the *Sodalitas Staupiziana*—you've doubtless heard of it, a group of our city's intellectual elite inspired by Staupitz. I will not claim I was among the leading lights among them, but I could hold my own. Of course, it was from them I first encountered Luther's teachings—the *Sodalitas* was already becoming a center of Evangelical interest."

"And, what did you think of what you heard?"

"Well, of course, I sympathized with his attacks on the abuses; but that was nothing unique, for others have said the same thing. The teaching on faith at first seemed plausible—but it was when he began to carve away at the sacraments that I began to find grounds for disagreement. Then he began calling the pope *Antichrist*. It was not long before I was certain that I could never be a Lutheran."

As Veit spoke, Lorenz studied him. He felt his friend was not telling him everything. "But it was not mere theology that has inspired your aversion to the Evangelicals," he said.

"No," Veit replied, "it was not only theology. You see, Lorenz, I am finally no theologian or philosopher; I am a lawyer—and what I saw as a lawyer was that Luther was not intent on correcting this abuse here and refining that doctrine there; he would level the Church to its foundations, and with the Church would fall the empire and all peace and security in Germany.

"Moreover, who can read Luther's tracts—which, by the way, are written in plain German, so that any peasant with a few letters can read them; who can read these, I pray, and not see that their effect is to incite the wicked and unstable to all manner of violence? Did they not stir up Sickingen?"

"Well," Lorenz interposed, "Luther has disavowed what Sickingen did . . ."

"*Ach!* One can easily disavow after the fact—after the damage has been done. But who would believe it?" Veit's manner was growing more vehement. "And what of the peasants? In the name of *evangelical liberty* and the *pure Word*, they are raising *Bundschus* all over Germany—some not far from this very city! But that is not the worst of it, not by far! Nürnberg and her sisters—the august imperial cities—have been playing a double game. Our *honorable* members of the council have become so very evangelical. Their *Christian freedom*, as they call it, will turn them a very tidy sum when they can freely dispense of church properties. They want the power to interpret the *pure* Word only that they might pluck the wealth from the *impure* monasteries. And what will they do with all the new wealth? Will they help fund a war against the Turks? No, that they will again refuse, as they did this past year at the diet! Gesturing with one hand, they will bleat about the hardships and injustices they suffer, while the other hand grabs their Judas gold from the king of France!"

Lorenz did not know what to say to all this. Was it not true? Yet, there was more to be said—was there not more to be said? But how to say it?

Veit, who had emptied his wine glass and was staring into it as if he would discover therein the secrets of the lodestone, slowly shook his head. "And then there is my wife," he said. "How easily she cast it all away! Oh, I know—what could I expect of her? But I had only just begun to take pleasure in her again! But"—and here Veit laughed—"I suspect that, if it were not this, it would have been something else. Still, it is all so very confusing, Lorenz. What has befallen us? Can you, with all your Evangelical conviction, answer me that—what has befallen us?"

CHAPTER 5

FRATER JÜRGEN'S *REQUIEM* WAS THE last Mass he had said. He had not known that it would be that day when he doffed the chasuble; but it proved to be so. He remained in his cell in the monastery. He continued to wear the habit as before. He ate in the refectory with what remained of the brethren. But he no longer sang the hours with them; he prayed, alone, in his cell. And he no longer said the Mass.

"Antichrist is to be broken, but not by the hand of man." These were the words Martin sent to Wittenberg not long after his return to—to wherever he was in hiding. Yet Melanchthon had said that Martin had been in the city and had been pleased with what he had seen and heard, though he deplored the violence. But, whence the violence? Words can inspire violence; they can prick, prod the spirit into frenzy. Scourge a hated man with words; flail away at his reputation until it hangs festooned about him in bloody ribbons; render him loathsome, and the mob will tear him to pieces! But it will not be your victim alone who will suffer. It will be the innocent, simple one—he who "refuses"—who will slake the blood lust of vengeance. And none will mourn for him. For is it not the secret counsel of God?

Of course, it had not been Martin who had been stirring the pot in Wittenberg. It had been Zwilling. It had been Karlstadt. They had been brewing the soup while Melanchthon dithered and wrung his hands. It was Karlstadt who defied the Elector's decree; and Zwilling, the day before, the Eve of Christmas, whose preaching stirred the mob to riot in the parish and call down in drunken song the visitation of plague and hellfire on the Castle Church. And Karlstadt's japes the day after, and the day after that, had been by his own counsel. Solely by his own counsel.

Was it on account of these that Jürgen lay cold and rotting in his grave? Was not their clamoring alone merely the echo of words sounded by another? Of the man who, in the vehemence of his zeal, had proclaimed himself the voice of God?

Lorenz had turned his back on all that he once held sacred. But where he would turn now, he could not say.

* * *

In defiance of the Elector—

His command had been clear—no change, only discussion. No change, until all could agree. But Karlstadt would pay no heed.

Did all Wittenberg gather in the parish church that Christmas morning? It seemed so; the church was filled to overflowing. What had they come to see?

Karlstadt, clad only in a plain, black scholar's robe, stood before the altar. He read the Latin prayers. But when he came to the consecration, he laid aside the Latin:

> *Nehmet hin und esset: das ist mein Leib... das neue Testament in mein Blut...*

With dismay, Lorenz heard the sacred words spoken in the common speech! How dared Karlstadt?

And the town council of Wittenberg also dared. Mass, they said, was thenceforth to follow Karlstadt's form.

In defiance of the Elector.

* * *

How old was the girl? She was small, thin, and pale. She seemed lost in the shadow of the substantial Karlstadt. His bovine bulk, Lorenz thought, would crush her.

How old was she?

Karlstadt was not far shy of two-score years; she appeared to have just emerged from childhood. Was she not more than half his age?

She shrank beside that bull of a man; she glanced nervously at the notables gathered around them. Melanchthon was there; so were many of the Wittenberg professors. She was not beautiful, even pretty. Though of noble blood, she was not rich. But Karlstadt relished her.

Karlstadt had said his motive was to rescue poor, miserable priests from the captivity of the devil. (It brought Gottfried to mind — but Gottfried had made no pretense: his was fornication, pure and simple. He broke his vows, but made no bones about it.) "I observe that marriage is allowed to the clergy," so Karlstadt had written the elector. "And I will marry Anna Mochau . . . I pray Your Grace approves . . . "

But he did not await His Grace's approval on Christmas; nor did he now, on Stephen Martyr's day.

Thus were they were made handfast. They would be married within a month — on the feast of St. Sebastian.

* * *

Melanchthon confessed himself "strangely moved" — but that was Philipp, blown about by every new wind. A brilliant fellow, but unstable.

They arrived, those "prophets," on the day after Karlstadt's betrothal. Lorenz did not bother to go hear them, these men from the border lands — from that little barbarous outpost, Zwickau. Their leader was a cloth weaver — Storch by name. He and his two companions drew large crowds wherever they preached. That was to be expected of the common sort . . .

"They have an unction—a p-power, a presence," Melanchthon told him. "I can scarcely say how deeply I am moved by them."

"But come, Philipp," Lorenz said, "test the spirits! You say they do not appeal to Scripture . . ."

"No, they do not—and that troubles me! But you must hear them speak—their words are not their own . . ."

"Yes, but they might be the Devil's."

"And thus," Melanchthon said, "I am deeply troubled—stirred and troubled."

* * *

It was not the prophets that had most deeply troubled Lorenz, nor the iconoclastic fury of Karlstadt and Zwilling, inciting the mob to break images and overturn altars. It was the barrenness of his own heart. Jürgen had been his last tenuous connection with the Old Church. Oh, even before Jürgen's death, he had ceased to believe any of it—the words informing a transubstantiation, absolution of sin; the touch of hands conferring benediction. Yet, for Jürgen he had believed; for the sake of his timid, erring brother, he had believed.

Had it been a sin to confer on him that last, furtive *absolvo te*? Had it been sacrilege to consecrate the bread and wine? Yes, it had been. Yet, it had been for Jürgen that he had performed the pantomime. He had jeopardized his own soul, for Jürgen's sake. And though he should repent of it, he could not. He did not regret it.

He had thought that with Jürgen dead, he could cast it all off—the Mass, confession, monastic discipline, all that jugglery of the Devil. He would be free to follow the Gospel! And, indeed, he no longer said Mass or heard it said; but it was not liberation he felt. It was emptiness.

He could not cast off the habit, as so many of his brothers had. He remained in the monastery, followed the rule as he may, when even those brothers who remained ignored it. Why? None of it could fill the void. He half longed for the ancient terror, the fear of God's storm-lowering countenance. "Faith alone" had comforted him—but was it too much comfort?

* * *

The hot, sweaty bodies were pressing on him from all sides. The brawny farmer, tall, thickset, with a blonde beard covering his chest, was shaking one fist in the air and shouting with garlic-laden breath in Lorenz's face. "Devil's spawn! Antichrist!" It was absurd, he thought, that he should die a martyr for what he no longer believed.

It was the habit; he had come to the preaching in a habit. A foolish thing to do.

He had heard so much about this preacher, Niklaus Storch. He was a tall, thin man, with large hands by which he gestured ponderously slow as he spoke. His beard was a dark brown, almost black, as was that hair that hung straight to his shoulders. He dressed like the weaver he was. His green eyes squinted, as if they were nearsighted. But his voice belied his unprepossessing appearance. Its mellowed tones were many-faceted. Betimes they were placid; but they could swell and rise with the vehemence of a mighty wind that can shake the ancient trees of the primeval forest—or tear them up by the roots.

Despite himself, the preacher's words stirred him to the depths. It was not the words themselves, for Storch's words were not always well chosen nor was he very eloquent. It was not the words, but the conviction that infused the words that moved Lorenz.

Wittenberg, Storch declared, had cast off Antichrist, but not all of his works. Christ's kingdom had not yet been founded there. "Where is Christ's kingdom?" he cried. "Is it in Rome, in Wittenberg, or is it"—he said with a sudden, broad smile—"in Zwickau?" The people laughed. "No, ye're deceived, brethren, if ye think ye can turn over a stone or sweep the threshing floor and there find the Kingdom. It's not hidden under a blanket. It is not under the earth for ye to dig it up. Where is it? Do ye really want to know? Well, I can't tell ye. Ye must find it for yourselves!"

Storch, however, could tell them where the Kingdom of Christ wasn't. It wasn't where one man lords it over another, for every man is equal in the Kingdom. It wasn't where men live by laws, for every man is free in the Kingdom. It wasn't where men worship God with outward forms and in houses of stone, for men live by the spirit in the Kingdom. "And 'tisn't where one man says 'mine' and 'yours,' and another says 'yours' and 'mine.' For all share all things together in the Kingdom!"

The Kingdom was coming, Storch insisted, and the sign was the spirit with which he preached. "If ye will only heed — God speaks to man in his inner heart. Ye hear the word with your ears, but ye must understand it with your spirit. *Ach!* Give heed to his prophet and open your hearts to the spirit's inspirations! Then, and only then, will ye perceive the mystery of the kingdom of God!"

That kingdom was coming. It was upon them. Rulers would be torn down from their thrones. The pope would be toppled into hell, pulling down all his followers with him. "On that day," Storch's voice now rose in a tumult of inspiration, "on that day, God will gather the priests of Babylon and trample them in the wine press of his wrath! It matters not if they have taken wives; for the slaking of the lust of the flesh will not spare them. They will all be slaughtered by the breath of God's mouth, ever' last one of 'em!"

The crowd roared with glee and clapped their hands. This was the sort of talk that pleased Wittenbergers!

It was then the tall farmer caught sight of Lorenz and came at him, shouting, "Antichrist! Devil's spawn!" The man grabbed

Lorenz's cowl and threw him to the ground. Others around Lorenz joined in with the farmer—"kill the dirty priest! Kill him!" "No," others shouted, "take him to the preacher! Let him judge him!" Lorenz felt himself pulled up off the ground and dragged to where he was cast down at Storch's feet. Still the cries rang out, "Kill him! Kill him!"

But Storch's voice rose above the rest, demanding silence. When the clamoring had subsided, he looked down at Lorenz, lying at his feet. "What do ye here, priest?" Storch asked savagely. "Come ye to spy on us—don't lie, dog, for I know ye have! Ye have stirred up the wrath of these good people—but the unction within me forbids what they seek—your death." Storch then addressed the crowd, "For ye must know, it is Christ who shall slay the wicked—we, my brothers, should not stain our hands with blood—not yet! We can only wait and long for the day when Christ shall hurl these shaved-pates into Gehenna! Then we shall laugh and be glad, my brothers! Laugh and be glad!"

"And as for ye," Storch said, addressing Lorenz. "Do not burden our eyes longer with that frippery of the Fiend. Come only when you have cast off the Devil's livery. Begone!"

* * *

"It was not for fear of the mobs that I did it—I assure you, Veit, it was not. Casting off my habit was like flaying off my own skin. I had not realized what a monk I had become."

He knew he did not have Veit's sympathy, though he still had his friendship. Veit, he knew, was trying to suppress his censure.

"Then, why did you do it?" Veit said after a long pause.

"I was in a way forced to it. Our convent disbanded, just ceased to exist. I was a monk without a monastery."

Veit said nothing, but Lorenz could read his thoughts. Veit was transparent.

He forced out a laugh. "*Ach*, Veit! Come now, say what you want to say. You will not offend me."

Veit ran his fingers through his hair (not the first time that night). "What do I want to say?" he said.

Lorenz shook his head. "Simply that I could have left Wittenberg and joined another house of our order. And that is surely true—but, Veit, how can I get you to understand? I did not believe in any of it anymore. Doffing the habit allowed me, at long last, to stop playing the hypocrite."

"But what of Luther?" Veit was agitated. "You said that he donned the habit once he returned to Wittenberg."

That was true—and, then, it had seemed a betrayal. Not only had Martin resumed the habit but he had reinstituted the Latin Mass—"for the sake of the weak," he had said. What he had lauded while in exile he excoriated upon his return. Karlstadt had been cast out; Zwilling, tamed. Of course, the iconoclasm and mob violence had troubled Lorenz—but who had inspired it to begin with?

"Yes, he did, but he did not ask anyone else to do so. And he has, as you know, since abandoned it."

Luther's return to Wittenberg had indeed been brave, Lorenz had to admit to himself. But in compare to the likes of Thomas Münzer, Niklaus Storch, or, even, Karlstadt, Martin had seemed vacillating. But perhaps he did it to still the nerves of that jittering Melanchthon.

Veit rose and walked to the hearth (they were in Lorenz's room). Crouching down, he picked up a faggot and threw it onto the fire. He stood and looked into the fire, his arms folded across his breast. "*Ach*, Lorenz," he said. "I cannot say I understand any of this . . . "

"Nor do you approve . . . "

"No, I don't approve," Veit said with resolution. Then he turned and looked full on Lorenz. "What will you do?" he said.

"You know, Veit," Lorenz said, puzzled by the question. "I shall complete my preaching to the Augustinians here and then, shortly before Christmas, go to Weissenbrücke."

Veit shook his head. "No, that is not what I mean. What will you do about—about my wife's parents' request? I know they have spoken to you."

Veit's laborious circumlocutions whenever he spoke of Greta or the Waldhummels were amusing; but pity for his friend now overcame any humor he might have felt at it. This matter deeply affected Veit.

"Veit," he replied, "if you were me, what would you do? Duty demands that I make the attempt."

Veit shook his head. He turned, crouched before the fire, took another stick, threw it on the hearth, and watched it catch fire. Lorenz knew what Veit would say, but for friendship. It was a question, indeed, that he had been asking himself over and over again. "Is it truly duty that compels you?"

Lorenz did not want to answer that question.

CHAPTER 6

LORENZ HAD SPENT THE LAST FORT-
night in Nürnberg conferring with Wenzel Linck,
once the prior of the Augustinians there but now the
preacher at the Hospital church. He had heard much of Linck
before coming to Nürnberg—indeed, had met the man some six
years before, in Augsburg. Report and their brief acquaintance,
however, had not prepared him for the man. The tedium of him.

Wenzel Linck was loquacious, but with little to say of worth.
His conversation was capacious, but without depth. What he
could touch on in a single harangue (his wonted mode of communication) was encyclopedic, but incoherent. He was utterly
obtuse—he could not divine the mind or heart of an inter-
locutor, even if he allowed him to finish a sentence. Linck's
devotion to Luther was staunch, but bloodless.

At their first meeting, Linck launched into a discourse on the
Scheuerls and Waldhummels, though he scarcely knew them.

"So, you are residing with the Veit Scheuerls? I wonder at
it, indeed I do! Oh, Frau Scheuerlin is a true Christian, but
her husband is one of the worst papists in the city—I am
surprised he would let you pass his door!"

"He is an old friend . . ."

". . . But maybe the Spirit is moving through him at
long last! His cousin, Christoph, is little better, though he
was among us once—inscribed even in the pope's bull of

205

excommunication—though, it is said, by Eck's discretion, not Leo's. But such is the papal tyranny! And Veit Scheuerl was once one of the *Sodalitas,* if you can credit it! His father and brother are Evangelical, though one of the brothers is a monk and, I hear, a rabid papist. The mother is locked in superstition, like the son. *Ach!* 'Tis written, that in the last days some shall depart from the faith, giving heed to seducing spirits and doctrines of devils—we are living in that time, most assuredly! And if it were not enough that we have to deal with Antichrist—we now have to contend with wolves like Karlstadt, Münzer, and Zwingli, distorters of the Word...

"... But Frau Scheuerlin—a most devout woman! And her parents, united in devotion to the Word! Herr Waldhummel has borne witness to the Pure Gospel before the council, urging them in season and out to put away all diffidence; for 'tis not enough, nor pleasing to God, merely to *permit;* they must also *promote* and *mandate!* Blasphemy still echoes in the churches of this city! It is the duty of the magistrates, as true Christians, to restrain the evildoers, prod the indolent, correct the refractory!

"... And Frau Waldhummelin! A veritable lioness for the Lord! How she stirs the gentlewomen in the town against the blasphemy of the convents! *Pull your daughters from out those dens of iniquity!* she urges them! And I probably need not tell you, for you know the family, that Frau Waldhummelin has a niece at Pillenreuth, her husband's sister's daughter and the offspring of the late Urban Auer, once a lawyer of the city and a notable scholar! Alas, that I knew him but little!"

A knock at the door interrupted Linck. "Enter!" he called with a touch of annoyance, and a woman came in carrying a platter with a flask of wine, two cups, a loaf, and a small round of cheese. She was quite some years younger than Linck—and, if Lorenz did not know better, he would have taken her for his daughter. "*Ach!* Magdalena!" he ejaculated. "God's benison on you for this! Set it down on the table here." Then gesturing to Lorenz, he said, "This, my dear, is Herr Magister List, but newly arrived in the city from Wittenberg!" The woman curtsied. "Herr List," Linck continued, "my wife, Magdalena!"

When the woman had departed, Lorenz seized the moment to redirect Linck's loquacity. "Herr Linck," he said, "tell me, I pray, of Weissenbrücke."

"There is not much to tell," Linck replied, his mouth full of bread and cheese. "The Spirit has convicted the heart of the marshal of that fair town and region, Herr Sigismund—he has come to Nürnberg many times to hear the preachers. They have converted him to the Pure Gospel! But his people are still enmeshed in the snares of papistry; and he desires a preacher to come among them, to draw them from darkness into light. Thus, he asked for you."

Linck's last words amazed Lorenz. He wondered if he had heard Linck aright. "He asked for me?" he said. "You mean, of course, that he asked for a preacher and . . . "

"No, what I mean, is," Linck said with a tinge of impatience, like a schoolmaster trying to drive home a lesson into a dull mind, "Herr Sigismund asked *for you*. He said specifically, 'Lorenz List, *magister* at Wittenberg.' I had no doubt about whom he meant. Didn't Martin tell you?"

"No," Lorenz replied. "He said nothing about this to me. Why did the Marshal ask for me?"

Linck took a long draught of wine. "That I cannot tell you," he said. "And I did not inquire. I was content merely to hear that he longed for the sustenance of the Pure Word."

And Linck cut himself another hunk of cheese.

* * *

"She told me of your reluctance—though she used the term, *refusal*. I did not countenance it, of course—the good woman, I said to myself, must be exaggerating! It must be *reluctance* she

meant—for why would anyone *refuse* such a pious request? Nevertheless, even if you did not *refuse*, I do not quite understand
your *reluctance* to accede to so just and evangelical a request."

It was his second meeting with Wenzel Linck. He had come
to discuss the sermons he would preach in the next week to
the Augustinians. But, instead, he found Linck preoccupied
with another matter—and addressing him like a disappointed
father. Lorenz was piqued at Linck's tone—after all, he was
not a child; and though the junior of the man by many years,
he was not his inferior in learning or position. He decided he
would leave Linck to wonder about the cause of his *reluctance*.

When Lorenz offered no clarification, Linck cleared his
throat, shook his head, and continued.

"I am surprised," he said, "very surprised! For I assume
that your silence speaks assent to my surmise. I am puzzled,
too—why didn't you tell me that you had lived in Nürnberg
and been a denizen of *Auerhaus* for some two years? I recall at
our last meeting that we spoke of Auer. Frau Waldhummelin
told me that he had behaved like a father to you and that
you and the young lady in question had been like brother
and sister! You can imagine how foolish I felt to have known
nothing of this history—I believe Frau Waldhummelin herself
wondered that you had told me nothing about it! Of course,
this news only deepens my dismay!"

Lorenz felt little compunction for Linck's dismay. After all,
the affair was really none of his concern. And what an annoyance that Frau Waldhummelin was! She could not prevail with
him, so she appealed his refusal to a higher court! Why could
they not leave him in peace?

" . . . It is our calling to seek out the lost, to pluck souls from
hell! And if our duty is clear as regards all men, is it not all
the clearer as regards kin, or those who are like kin to us? This
woman, the daughter of the man who treated you paternally,

is in jeopardy of losing her soul! She is captive to the Law and subject to its judgments and decrees! And yet you will not lift a finger to free her! Frau Waldhummelin—yea, and her pious daughter, Frau Scheuerlin—ask you merely to speak to her, to help her to open her eyes to the Pure Gospel! They deem that you, more than anyone else, might do what they have been powerless to effect—and yet, you are *reluctant*. I do not understand it . . . "

" . . . Nor will I explain it to you," Lorenz thought to himself. For, how could he tell this pedant what lay behind his *reluctance*? How intensely he longed to do the very thing he had refused to do! To speak with her again! To see her face and hear her voice again! It was the intensity of this longing that repelled him—indeed, it frightened him. How dared he, who had abandoned her, seek her once again? What right had he to disturb her peace? He could, of course, easily assuage such qualms—but he could find nothing to soothe his deeper fear. If he went to her, if he sought her soul, what would be his motive? Would he be working on God's behalf or his own?

CHAPTER 7

THE RED-ROOFED CITY FELL AWAY BEFORE
him. He was peering into the south, beyond Sankt
Sebald's, across the ribbon of the Pegnitz, to the southern walls. His eyes sought to pierce through the mists that hung
over the city—but he knew that, even if he had the gaze of
an eagle and the day were clear, he could not see the village
with its cloister. They were just too far away.

He traced with his finger the horseshoe groove on the edge
of the wall. Eppelein.

That day in late October (it was near All Saints') he had
climbed the slope of the rock of the lordly castle, just as he
had done so many years ago, with Veit, on a far colder day
than this. Then it had been a journey of innocent wonder.
All had then been new—the city with its aspiring steeples,
its massive but elegant towers, pennants streaming aloft, its
cacophony and song. And friendship new found. Like a mystery, Nürnberg had held promise of layer upon layer of new
discovery. He felt he could spend a lifetime exploring her and
never exhaust her marvels—just like a woman.

But today he cared nothing for Nürnberg. He felt he had
come to the bottom of her; there was nothing more to discover.
Of far greater allure was what lay beyond the river, beyond
her walls, over the miles of farm and forest land—the little
village of Pillenreuth and its cloister.

He longed to accede to their importunities—Greta's, the Waldhummels', Link's—for they were merely the articulation of his own desire. But he resisted them, resisted the urgings of his own heart. He did not trust any of it.

Really, though, it was all so easy. So very easy. For why had he been sent to Nürnberg, if not to seek and save what was lost? He had been entrusted with the message; he was its minister. What he himself had been given, was he to gather it in, like a miser, to himself? Dared he hoard it, cover it with a bushel basket, bury it in the earth? Its riches were not his alone—they belonged to peasant, townsman, lord, and emperor. And did they not belong, just as well, to her?

And was his purity of intention important? God uses even wicked instruments to work his will. If he proved to be a vile sinner, was there anything new in the revelation? To withhold the Gospel because of his unworthy heart—if every preacher did so, the Gospel never would be heard!

And when one finally came down to it, was there aught wrong in claiming what was his own? Was she not his wife—for even the papists must say that only death breaks the marriage bond, even for those freed to follow the "higher calling"? And it had been falsehood, lies, that had induced him to free her. And, now that he knew the truth, was not everything different? Indeed, all was different. He, too, had been freed...

The sun overhead had just passed the apogee. Its fires could not burn the mists away, the mists that hung over the city, over his heart. He longed for clarity, to see every distinct line, to caress with his eyes every texture...

How ludicrous. He laughed to himself. "Fool," he thought, "quit pretending!" He knew that it was not the impurity of his intentions, the comprehension of his desire for her masquerading as religious zeal, that had dissuaded him. He had known all along (though he scarce had admitted it to himself) what fueled even his desire to come to Nürnberg. He had not come to preach the "Pure Word"—he had come because, here, *she* was near. But if that were so, why did he now refuse to go to her? He could "deliver" her and make her his own—but yet he would not. Why?

That, too, was perhaps becoming clear to him. Was his refusal to go to her—was it not for the same reason that he had said Mass for Jürgen, administered *viaticum* to him, anointed him? He had then, he felt, played fast and easy with his own convictions. But even though he admitted this, and his conscience had tormented him on account of it, he still thought, even now, that he could have done nothing else. Nor, he thought, could he do anything in regard to her. Though he longed to, how terribly he longed to!

For what could he give her, in exchange for the peace of her cloister? He had himself, even as a monk, never known that peace, though he surmised he knew of some who had. But she, surely she, knew that peace—and could he bring himself even to the attempt to tear her from it? The honeyed words he would be forced to employ would turn to gall on his tongue.

The mist did not obscure Sankt Sebald's—she lay below, down the declivity of the rock, and beyond; her green, copper spires aspiring. Farther away, he could descry Sankt Lorenz's, across the river.

Peace! He had thought he had found peace. "The cross, the cross alone . . . " Yet, he should have known, if he had been listening. There is no peace in a cross. *This is the cross, the anguish of fear that Christ is false. You will not escape this anguish, this terror. . .* He had thought that this anguish of fear was but a temptation to waiver—a chimaera sent by the Fiend, a *scandalum*. But, no—the kindly face, the hand beckoning across the storm-tossed water, the father hastening to embrace the wayward son: these were but masks hiding the true face. The eye-holes were dark.

Once again, he had confronted the unfathomable God, the being whose self-revelation is a concealing. This God called man to a trust without confidence, a faith without assurance—a leap into the dark that could land him on firm ground, or plummet him into an abyss. This was the "Gospel" to which he had committed himself, for which he had once again broken a vow. He could not turn his back on it, nor must he bury it in the earth.

But Jürgen could not have suffered the terror of it. And neither, he thought, could she.

Still, how he longed to go to her! But he dared not.

* * *

When he returned home later that day, Clemens met him with a note. Opening it, he read:

> *Herr Magister,*
> *I called on you this afternoon, but you were not in. I shall call on you tomorrow, about the ninth hour. I have a matter of some importance to discuss with you.*
> *Eberhard Waldhummel*

Lorenz knew what the "matter of importance" was. It had been broached first by Greta. Then her mother had sought to enlist him.

He thought back to that afternoon.

When Frau Waldhummelin strode into the family hall, he noted immediately that the years had not softened her; if anything, her angularity had grown sharper and more decisive. No pleasantries passed between them (it must have been difficult, he thought, for her to deal with someone of his station). She launched immediately into her subject.

It was only her devotion to the Pure Word, she had assured him, that compelled her to call for his intervention in this most "delicate" matter. She could not idly sit by, she told him, while her niece's salvation hung in the balance. She knew (for

"Frau Scheuerlin had told her") that he and her "poor niece" had been "like brother and sister"—a situation, she admitted, that, at the time, she had surmised but did not fully approve, yet which, in hindsight, she averred, had the "marks of Providence" about it. (So Greta had not revealed all—Veit must have threatened her good, he thought.) She herself had gone to Pillenreuth, pleaded with her niece, had been forced, at last, to use "hard words," but all to no avail. Her niece remained "as hardhearted as Beelzebul," locked in pride ("she had been stiffnecked, even as a child"), a slave to works and to her own stubborn, self-will! It was only the "comfort of the Gospel" that she wished to impart—the wondrous mercy of which she herself had partaken. She *hoped* that it was only her niece's pride that resisted, nothing worse—for she had heard of all the corruptions of the monasteries, shocking tales that, as a lady, she would not repeat: he could not drag them from her! But, of course, having been a monk, he knew, he must know... In any case, she was certain that he shared her zeal for the Gospel and for the soul of one who had been, though now many years past, dear to him. Would he not plead with her? She could easily get him in to see her—despite the tiger prioress, a veritable harridan, a real harpy! Her husband, after all, sat on the council; he had authority, he had power...

He fairly enjoyed the look of scorn that passed over her hard features when he refused. She departed from him with utter disdain, shaking her formidable head.

Yes, he knew what the "matter of importance" was. He doubted, however, that Herr Waldhummel would descend on him with claws bared, as his wife had done.

* * *

And he was right.

The next afternoon, when he met him in a small drawing room, Herr Waldhummel seemed to be suffering from indigestion. He was no more willing to be there, it was clear, than Lorenz was to speak with him. The rather tall, square-shouldered man sat on the edge of his chair, his legs spread apart and his large hands grasping his knees, as if he were poised to spring up and flee. His eyes never once fixed on Lorenz but darted about the room. He spoke in that measured monotone a man adopts when he reads figures from a ledger.

Herr Waldhummel assured Lorenz that only the deepest anxiety for his niece compelled him "to come here today." (Lorenz smiled to himself—anxiety for his niece or on account of his wife, what she would do to him?) She was, after all, the daughter of his departed sister—and the very image of her! And Urban Auer had been among the most respected counselors the city had known. Moreover, she had entered the monastery in the most unusual of circumstances—her father had promised her in marriage to one of the foremost younger men of the city, a man of noble parts and not a little learning; a man now highly respected in the city and a most devout adherent of the Pure Word. Why she had done so was out of reckoning! And after her father (with his own and his wife's endorsement) had so satisfactorily closed the deal! Indeed, a Mager was more than she could normally have bargained for in the matter of marriage. But she threw it all away! And what did she make on return? A dreary life in a provincial convent.

It all really made no sense! And now, when she had the Gospel to render the contract null and void, she clings to her poverty! Of course, she is now past 25 years—who would marry her? True, her Waldhummel and Auer inheritance is nothing to sniff at; but there are plenty of wealthy heiresses in the city, younger, and doubtless (now) more lovely to behold—he had not seen her, but Frau Waldhummel had said she has greatly fallen away. Nevertheless, she could find some man who would be happy to take her. And if not, she, at least, would be rich.

Lorenz wondered what this meandering monologue was leading to. Waldhummel clearly thought his niece had made a bad business deal—did he come here merely to express his dismay? If so, Lorenz wished he would have done and leave him in peace. But Herr Waldhummel's harangue merely proved to be an attempt to soften the ground. After a few more minutes of it, he at last launched into his pitch.

"I do not claim," he said, "to be a theologian. Don't misunderstand me—I am, I assure you, Evangelical; but I am a man of affairs. I leave the theology to others. My wife tells me that you have refused her offer—but I do not blame you; you doubtless have your calculations. And to be quite frank with you, I would rather leave her alone; but there are considerations. I am privy to information that, I think, you may not know and which you may want to be apprised of."

Lorenz expected that he would have merely to endure another long assault on his sense of duty, an appeal to friendship or the memory of his patron. But Herr Waldhummel touched on none of this. He spoke in that gray monotone of his, but his words succeeded in chilling Lorenz to the core.

The *Bundschu* had reappeared in the neighborhood of Nürnberg. It was printed in rude pamphlets, scrawled on walls; it had been seen in the city itself. "Here is a sample of what *Armer Kunz* is handing out," he said, as he passed Lorenz a folded piece of paper. Opening it, Lorenz beheld a crude woodcut of a peasant holding a banner displaying a crucifix and a peasant's boot. In the background, a castle engulfed in flames. Below the picture were written the words:

> *Bauern, auf!*
> The Lords have driven you like cattle!
> The priests have sucked you dry!
> Freedom!
> Pillage the Castles!

Drive out the Parsons!
And on the Cloister's Roof
Set the Red Cock!
Bundschu!
Bundschu!
Bundschu!

Such pamphlets were being passed out not only in the Alt-mühl and the March of Weissenbrücke, but in the villages just outside of Nürnberg. "Travelers coming into the city say they can sense a violent anger in the villages. They say it is smoldering but will sooner or later burst into flame, and then we shall have a full-scale rebellion on our hands, much like those in the South. Its effects on trade could be dire. No one, of course, can predict the extent of the rebellion or the magnitude of its destruction; but this much, I think, can be predicted: that the cloisters will not be spared. And a woman's cloister will prove a most tempting target for the peasants."

Herr Waldhummel's words were measured and matter-of-fact; but they struck home. Images of what he had been told about the Hussite rebellions in Bohemia rose in Lorenz's imagination. Burning buildings, desecrated churches, sisters violated and then left for dead among the smoking ruins. That *she* should suffer such—no! Please God, no!

"And even Pillenreuth is in peril?" he managed to say.

"Yes," Herr Waldhummel replied. For the first time he looked straight into Lorenz's eyes. "I think we understand one another," he said.

"How imminent is the threat?"

"It is on our doorstep—hence, in part at least, my wife's sense of urgency."

Lorenz merely nodded.

Herr Waldhummel glanced across the room at the clock; it had just struck the hour. "I have an appointment in another half hour, so I cannot stay longer," he said. "I think, though, I have sufficiently explained matters to you."

Lorenz nodded.

Herr Waldhummel rose. "Then, what answer may I bring to my wife?"

What answer? Lorenz knew there was only one answer. He too rose.

"Tell her," he said, "to arrange a meeting. I will accompany her to Pillenreuth."

CHAPTER 8

I T WAS COLD THAT MORNING; A HEAVY
freeze had descended on the city in the night. As the
carriage drove onto the *Fleisch Brücke,* Lorenz glanced
through the window at the Pegnitz. It was partially frozen.
Across from him sat Frau Waldhummel and a maidservant,
well bundled up in coats and blankets. The lady's face, with
its sharp nose, was colorless. Her eyes were cold.

His blanket he let fall to his lap. He scarcely minded the cold.
The carriage skirted Sankt Lorenz's on their left. It continued
down a broad way until it came to the *Frauen Thor,* through
which it passed from the city into the open country beyond.

Scarcely five miles now lay between him and Pillenreuth.
What lay at journey's end? He felt both expectation and dread.

The memory of his former resolve to leave her in peace
prodded him. It had seemed right, though it flew in the face of
his deepest convictions. Herr Waldhummel's report of peasant
unrest and what it could portend for a cloister of women had
shaken his resolve—indeed, at the time, he thought he had
no other choice than to ally himself with Frau Waldhummel's
plot to lure her from the monastery. Yet, even now, when he
considered what could happen, he felt a deep reluctance.

He wondered—was it really fear for her that now drew him
to Pillenreuth? Had his all too palpable desire not seized on
that fear as a pretext? Perhaps he had been too precipitate;

perhaps he should have let a day or two pass before he decided. Instead, he allowed himself all too easily (it seemed now) to be goaded into a decision he would probably regret. For he would be used in a none-too-subtle game of manipulation—a game he despised yet was willing to play.

Not far outside of Nürnberg, the road passed into a wood. Frozen snow lay in patches among the denuded trees. In the distance he could see a hut standing amid a clearing. Smoke was rising from it. At length, the forest fell away, and the road turned south, skirting an open field to the east. Snow lay in the furrows. Barren. So very barren.

He doubted the spring.

* * *

He stepped down from the carriage; dirty remnants of snow crunched underfoot. A cold mist hung in the air. He pulled the lapels of his coat more firmly under his chin. He followed Frau Waldhummel into the nuns' chapel.

A servant had gone before them to announce the arrival to the prioress. She must have expected their coming, for the servant returned in short order to announce that the prioress awaited Frau Waldhummel at the small grate in the chapel, which communicated with the cloister. "Do not follow me, yet," Frau Waldhummel whispered to Lorenz. "Find a place you can see me clearly, but yet remain hidden. When I want you, I shall gesture."

Lorenz followed a side aisle and found a place behind a pillar where he could see Frau Waldhummel but yet keep himself unseen by anyone through the grate. It was cold in the chapel; he wished he could walk about to warm himself—and to stave off anxiety.

A chair had been brought for her. She sat unmoving for some minutes in front of the grate; but then she nodded her head—the prioress must have come. He saw Frau Waldhummel speak at length, regally gesturing with her right hand. She then stopped and appeared to be listening. She shook her head emphatically. She pointed into the chapel and began to speak; but, it appeared, she was cut off. She then shook her head again and reached into a pocket of her coat and pulled out a folded piece of paper. She unfolded it, held it up to the grate, and then pointed at it with her index finger. She held the paper close to her face and appeared to be reading it aloud. She leaned toward the grate, waving the paper, refolded, in her right hand. She then sat back in her chair, placed the paper again into her coat pocket, and smoothed the skirts of her gown.

Several minutes passed. Lorenz found himself staring at the grate and thinking of what lay beyond. Frau Waldhummel remained sitting, her head bowed, as if she were napping. He then heard the noise of metal grating on metal; slowly, a door to the right of the small grate opened. Frau Waldhummel rose and turned as a dark-robed figure passed into the chapel. It curtsied to the older woman, who merely nodded her head. As the door closed with a clang, Frau Waldhummel gestured to the other to follow her to the opposite side of the chapel, away from the grate and the door. They were now only a few feet from where Lorenz stood.

Frau Waldhummel saw him. With a furtive wave of her hand, she beckoned to him. He stepped out from behind the pillar.

* * *

Frau Waldhummel, who had been speaking with some heat, glanced at Lorenz as he drew near. Her companion turned with a look of exasperation, giving way to frightened surprise. She turned again to Frau Waldhummel. "Why have you brought a man here?" he could hear her say.

He was close enough now to touch her. She turned to face him, but stepped back a little. Her eyes ("they are still beautiful," he thought) spoke fear. She glanced at Frau Waldhummel, and then back at him. Then her lips parted slightly; her look of fear softened to stunned astonishment. She whispered, "It is you."

At long last, after so many years of longing, he could look into her eyes again; he could hear her voice. He felt like one parched with thirst, drinking at last from a cold and limpid spring. He knew he still beheld her across a wide water—but, yet, he beheld her! Even if he could never cross that Lethe, he felt he could be content with the vision of her.

Indeed, he feared to speak; for so a rude a sound as his own voice, he thought, would shatter the vision, like a stone cast at an image in still water. And what might she say to him in reply? Would she welcome him, or spurn him? Would she dance him across the water, or thrust him eternally away? He could detect nothing in her eyes, save anxious wonder.

How long they stood thus, he could not say. They were alone, embowered by the vaulting chapel; he felt, rather than saw, Frau Waldhummel slip away. He knew he must speak, but what would he say? He had practiced what he *would* say, but all memory of it was gone.

* * *

"Yes, it is I," he said at last. "I have come that I might . . ."

But she gestured him to silence. "I pray, say no more! Say nothing more!" She turned away, folding her arms across her breast and bowing her head as if she felt a deep, inner pain.

Pleading had been the timbre of her voice—it was not wrath that spoke, or disgust, or disdain. Pity filled his soul, but so did longing. He knew not whether to be silent or to speak.

They stood thus for what seemed a long spell. When he summoned again the courage to speak, he could only say, "I beg you, hear me!"

He could scarcely hear her reply. "Hear you?" she said. "What have you to say to me, or I to you? Too much separates us. What I was, I am no longer. What you are, I do not know."

Again, silence. The winter silence. If it were spring, one could, perhaps, hear birdsong through the open church doors — or from recesses of the vaults overhead, where birds build their nests in spring. Now, when he spoke, he could see his own breath. All was cold. All was dead.

"I scarce know myself," he said at last. "When I was as you are now, even then I knew not myself. What I am now, God only knows."

Still, she would not look at him. "Then, it is as I fear," she said. "I had thought, when I first saw it was you, that it had not been as I had thought. That you had ... I could have forgiven you that. But this — this is a most cruel divorce."

He understood her — there was a time when the same horror had seized his own heart. And even now betimes between sleeping and waking, he felt it still.

He felt a growing despair and desperation. "Please hear me," he pleaded. "And look at me — turn away from me no more! It is not as you think. Beatrice!"

He reached his hand across the void. He gently touched her shoulder. He could feel her shudder. But then she slowly turned to him. And their eyes met.

He breathed deeply and sighed. Everything that he had planned to say to her was meaningless. It was not to the point. He knew he could not play that game. He must not deceive her again.

"I am not," he said, "as you have thought me; but I am he whom once you knew. No, that is not right — for I have passed through hell. I have felt the terror of wrath; but more than anything else, I have languished in regret — what I did to you. And though I have found release, I feel as yet no peace."

Her eyes (oh, the beauty of them!) — they were so very beautiful in their sorrow and, yes, pity. They were no longer guarded; they spoke nothing of fear. Only sorrow.

"Lorenz"—she said his name so gently—"you have found release, but yet feel no peace? If it is for your regret, be, I pray, at peace. I will not say that I felt no sorrow then—it was most bitter; I cannot hide it from you. But I have accepted it as the will of him who, though he wounds, heals."

She lowered her eyes, but she did not turn away. A flicker of a smile passed over her lips, then was gone. "It is not that I thought so at the time," she said. "And, I confess, at first I bitterly reproached you. But as I thought more on it, reading your last letter over and over again, I felt I could see your heart. It was hopeless, perhaps, our union. You wanted, I saw, to save me from disgrace. I knew how you loved me—how painful it was for you to release me. Only one thing, I fear, I do not even now forgive you for—thinking that I would ever be unfaithful."

Her words stung him. He had doubted her fidelity? He recalled the words of his last letter: "Obey your father, trouble him no more . . . " Yes, yes, of course; it was clear. His urging her to forget him, to marry another, to forswear her vow; the supposition that she would do as he bid—was that not an aspersion? He should have known she never would.

He dared not look at her; he cast his eyes across the chancel of the church, toward the high altar. Would his sins forever sprout, like rank weeds, from his memory?

"Yes," he said, "I thought you unfaithful—or that you would prove so, though I did not think so then. I did not want to burden you more . . . "

But was not even that a lie? It was a vile lie. And what was he urging her to now?

"Lorenz"—her voice, speaking his name, drew his eyes again to her. And again their eyes met.

"Lorenz," she said, and her glance bespoke neither fear nor anger, only pity. "I know and I understand. And I reproach you, when I should reproach myself. Would I have remained faithful?"

"*Ach!* Do not speak so, I was unjust . . . "

"No, pray, hear me," she said with an earnest sorrow in her tone. "You have confessed, now I must. Please, hear me! What I chose—this place, this life—I chose, I fear, not for love of God, but from fear. Yes, I was determined, come what may, to unite myself to none other than you. But I knew my weakness. Could I have lived alone, holding you in my heart, as I had purposed to? Could I have long withstood my father's demands? Could I have lived with no one to love me? I was young and, perhaps, foolish; but, I was young and weak. I feared I would falter in my resolve . . . "

She hesitated, as if calling up resolve. She sighed.

"It was this fear that inspired me to think—and I convinced myself that surely it was from God—it led me to think I could fulfill my vow to you by a lie. I thought that, though the deep water sundered our bodies, in this way our spirits could reach out and touch each other and mingle in a higher union; and in the end, we could consummate in death what had been unfulfilled in life. Thus, I told my father that I could not marry, for I had pledged myself to another. I said it was God, but it was not. It was you."

She paused. She enfolded her scapular in her hands.

"*Ach*, Lorenz! I fear I dissembled; but, at the time, it did not seem so—and now I wonder at it. Yet, it seemed to bear fruit. When I prayed the Office, heard Mass, I felt that we stood side by side, joined forever in the sweetest of marriages. We became as a brother and sister frolicking in the hall of our Father." A smile brightened her face, and then faded. "We were united by a deeper bond than that of the flesh. And over time I felt I needed nothing of the flesh; for bodies but press one on the other, but our souls—yes, I thought our souls had become truly one."

Her words astonished him. Those years of his struggles in the monastery, when he strove to forget her, not to think of her, she had been reaching across the void to him. And what she had thought was union had proved but another deception.

He feared to ask the question, but he knew he must. "And it is otherwise now?"

Her brows knit and her countenance darkened. "Yes," she said. "It is."

He nodded. He understood.

Should he not leave her alone? He had caused her enough sorrow. He thought he should leave her, but he felt he could not. He could not lose her again! And what he had come to do, was it not for her good? Yet what could he say to her that would not seem like cozening? Still, he had to make the attempt. He felt he needed to make the attempt, and not for the Gospel, not for her soul nor the safety of her body, but because he wanted her. Oh, God, how he wanted her! But had he any right to her?

That, however, was a tired question, a relic of the old lie. More real, more immediate, was the desire that, like a welling sorrow, enveloped his heart. He looked into her eyes; he could see uncertainty in them, and fear. He reached out and took her hands in his. She did not resist him, though her hands trembled. He tried to speak, but the words failed in their utterance. Again he tried to speak, and this time the words came.

"Hear me, I beg you!" he said (wildly, he thought). "It is otherwise, it had always been otherwise! We have been deceived, you and I, but we need be so no longer! *Ach,* how I have longed for this day, to see you again, to hold your hands in mine—and you have longed for it too. I hear it in your words, see it in your eyes! We may be again what once we were! Come with me—God does not will our separation. Nor do I or you!"

He could read, for a moment, confusion in her eyes. Uncertainty flickered in their depths, a spark of the old love that could be quickened into flame, if only he could conjure up the right word. But that word did not come. And as he looked into her eyes, he saw the small flame flicker once more, and it was gone. Slowly she withdrew her hands.

"No, I do not wish it," she said at last, in scarce a whisper. "I cannot, I will not be foresworn. Do not ask this of me. I will not, again, betray my first love."

A feeling of desperation seized him. He had to convince her, to find the right words to shatter her resolve. But the words would not come. All he could utter was a plea—but it, too, was an old word, meaningless in the shadows that darkened around them.

"But, you are my Beatrice!" he whispered. "You are Else!"

She stood, unmoving. She still looked on him—and for a moment he could detect a wavering; but it flickered as soon away, and she withdrew into an inner sanctuary, behind a door, bolted and locked. Slowly she shook her head. "No, I am not Beatrice," she said at last, and there was resolution in her tone. "I am no longer Else. I am Agnes, only Agnes."

The door, firmly shut, was bolted and locked, and she was on the other side. There was nothing more to say—nothing more, but a valediction. And he found it strangely easy.

"Then, go in peace," he said, "I will trouble you no more."

And with the dying of his voice, she turned from him and walked toward the small door through which she had entered the chapel. She knocked twice, and it was opened for her. She passed through, never once looking back. And the door closed behind her, with the screech of iron grating on iron.

THE
HOMECOMING

CHAPTER 1

A COVERLET OF NEW-FALLEN SNOW LAY on the streets and blanketed the rooftops. Lorenz pulled his hat more firmly down on his head and adjusted his scarf. It was cold, but not bitterly so; still, the snow kept falling. This was no day to be walking out; it was a day to be sitting by the hearth, sipping mulled ale and reading a book. Still, he was expected. He could not beg off or send his regrets. He was expected.

He stepped off the front-door stoop; his boots sank into the snow. It would be a difficult trudge, and when he reached the end of the town, it would be all uphill. He had greased his boots, but he feared his feet would not be spared a good soaking. With a sigh, he began his journey.

The *Farbestraße* was narrow — as were all the streets of this town; so different from Nürnberg of the wide ways. The houses on either hand reared two or three stories above the street. They glowered over him, many-windowed Arguses, though, today shuttered as if in sleep. They could not see him pass.

He labored along the *Farbestraße*, wondering if it would ever end. It was a far longer way than he remembered. When at last he came to the curiously-arched bridge spanning the river, he paused to rest. He was almost to the *Marktplatz*. It would be the first he had seen of it since his return to Weissenbrücke.

* * *

Then he had entered Weissenbrücke through the southeastern gate; he had followed streets that did not pass through the *Marktplatz*. That was two days ago. Since then, he had been holed up in his Tante Ursula's house, to rest and await the summons. He thought of it, of course, as her house—as he would, even had Onkel Georg still been alive; and though now her son, Adolf, was its nominal lord, and was married, it was clear to whom the house belonged. Tante Ursula remained its tutelary deity.

It was Adolf who greeted him when he arrived; but the son (who resembled his deceased father) did not dally with him in cousinly conversation but directly led him into The Presence. She sat, enthroned, on a well-cushioned chair, before the hearth in the main drawing room. Lorenz at once saw . she was not the woman she had been, at least in appearance; she seemed shrunken, and her skin hung loose on her bones like wet clothes on a line. But when she spoke—which she did as soon as they entered the room—he understood what appearances can belie.

"Who is it, Adolf?" she barked with a growl of command.

"It is Cousin Lorenz, Mama—you know, Onkel Johannes'..."

"*Yes, fool*, I know who Cousin Lorenz is—I am not so old and forgetful as all that. Ask him into the room!"

She fixed her squinted eyes on Lorenz as he came toward her and greeted her—and, "Hmph!" she said, "What brings you to visit your kin? Your father, I hear, hasn't seen you in years. Here, sit down there," she commanded, pointing to a chair just to her left.

"It is very good to see you, Aunt," he said as he sat down.

"It might be good to see you," she replied, "if my eyes worked better." (She snorted a small laugh.) "And don't be telling me how good I look—I know what an old scarecrow I've become. Old folks don't look good, and that's a fact!"

Lorenz did not gainsay her but inquired after her health. "Mostly rotten," she retorted. "I've got the gout and my eyes—well, I've told you about them. No use beating a dead rat! But you, what are you doing here? I figured when you left for Nürnberg all them years ago, you'd not be coming back here."

"I have business in the town," he said.

"Business? What kind of business could you have here?" She leaned closer to him and squinted at him. "Seems you're wearing some pretty nice clothes there—what are you, some kind of lawyer?" She grimaced a kind of smile. She was missing two front teeth.

"No, Aunt, I am not a lawyer, and these are not such nice clothes."

"What are you, then?"

"I am a scholar, a *magister.*"

She snorted—"a scholar, a *magister!* I guess there ain' much money in that!" She cackled and sat back into her chair. "Looking for a living, no doubt," she said.

"No, Aunt," he said. "I've been asked to come to Weissenbrücke, by the Marshal."

Tante Ursula's eyes opened wide. She whistled. She wagged her head. "The Marshal!" she cooed. "Well, I never ..." She adjusted her formidable girth in the chair.

"Of course, you know, your Onkel Georg—the Marshal (not this one, but his father, God rest him)—used to ask for him, too. He used to say, 'why, Georg, you're the best master carpenter for miles around—Nürnberg herself ain' got better!' And your cousin Adolf is nearly as good as his father, and he would be used, too, if *this* Marshal had any sense; but he don't seem to care for such things as master woodworking. I hear he's all in a dither over that Luder fellow who's been causing so much fuss."

Lorenz smiled to himself. "You don't like that Luder, Aunt?"

"God, no!" she sniffed. "I'm with the old Church! *Ach!* It's good enough, ain' it? No use throwing off a good thing, even if it ain' perfect. Why, my gossip Berta Stimmelose, who gets around more than I do—I can't get about much these days for my ailments—Berta tells me what's happening with folks and she says that Luder wants to smash all the statues and turn the churches into stables! *That* won't make much work for a master craftsman used to working for the Church, will it now? The old Church always gave my husband good work—and now there ain' nothing left for his son. Times are hard enough . . . " She pulled a handkerchief from her bodice and lustily blew her nose.

When she had wiped her nose, she squinted at Lorenz and nodded her head. "I suppose you're looking for a place to stay?" she said.

"No, Aunt. I shall stay in an inn until the Marshal calls for me. I only came to call on you . . . "

She interrupted him, "Nonsense! You're kin, and you'll stay with us! What would people say if they heard Ursula List had turned her own nephew away? No, you will stay with us!"

She picked up a bell and rang it decisively. A maidservant entered and was told to prepare a room "for my late husband's brother's son." In the meantime, he could go to the kitchen and get a bite to eat. "Anyway," she said, "I can't talk no more right now, I'm about ready to nod off."

Lorenz rose, thanked his aunt for her kindness, and turned to leave the room. When he had reached the door, she called him to stay.

"Tell me," she said. "You ain' mixed up with any of this Luder business, are you?"

Lorenz paused and smiled. "I am, Aunt," he said.

She grunted and was silent. Lorenz waited to hear her verdict, and he did not have to wait long. She shook her head.

"Well, that ain' so good," she said. "But," she said after another long pause, "it may not be all that bad—it might be useful to have kinfolk in that line, if things change."

"I shall do my best, Aunt."

"No doubt you will," she said, nodding. "You were always a good lad. Now get you gone! Have something to eat! I don't think I can keep these old eyes open another minute."

* * *

Lorenz laughed as he looked at his image in the river. "Well, that ain' so good!" he said to himself. He shook his head and resumed his journey.

After crossing the bridge, the *Farbestraße* veered to the left and then discharged itself into a large square—the *Marktplatz*. Lorenz paused to take in the sight, so familiar from his youth. To his left reared the *Marienkirche*. A little further to the west of the church was the cloister of the canons, where he had attended school. Across the square from the cloister sat the old *Wirtshaus*. In the midst of the plaza, though more to the west and north was the octagonal fountain where first he had heard Bruder Heimrad speak. Bruder Heimrad! Of course, he had not expected to find him in the city, and Tante Ursula had told him that he had died some three years after his own departure for Nürnberg. "And it's just as well," she had said, "for he'd never take to the goings on of these days!"

No, he probably would not.

Lorenz crossed the plaza toward the fountain. Clearing the snow from a portion of the basin's wall, he sat down on it. He tried to remember—could he picture Heimrad here, weaving stories for the peasants and townsmen? And what of the day when the old man spoke of his own inner struggles—and that to a mere stripling of a boy? He closed his eyes—but, yet, he could not picture it at all. Of course, Heimrad never sat here in such weather...

He opened his eyes and looked out across the square, toward the *Marienkirche*. He hesitated, but then rose and crossed the square. He climbed the steps of the church and, pushing the great bronze door, entered, halted just within the threshold. He had seen churches more glorious, but this one still ravished the heart. *Quam dilecta tabernacula tua, Domine virtutum* — the words of the psalm sounded in his imagination. *Quam dilecta,* he repeated to himself, but then paused in thought. He turned and left the church.

It was just as far from the *Marktplatz* to the foot of the *Burg* as it was from Tante Ursula's house to the *Marktplatz* — not really very far, in good weather; but in this snow, it would seem three times the distance. The snow began to fall more heavily. He wished he could turn back — but he was expected. He could give no good excuse . . .

He was breathing heavily, and sweating, by the time he reached the town gate, nigh where the river entered through an arch and portcullis into the town. Passing into the open country beyond, he followed a snow-covered road, but it was not long before he came to a bridge arching the river. The river itself skirted the base of a steep hillside, the *Grauenberg,* upon the summit of which reared the castle. He crossed the bridge and immediately began the ascent of the hill, following a road that, beginning at the south, wound round about the western side of the hill, curving around its northern fell, and entered a gate in the wall facing due east. The grade was none too easy; but the wind had blown much of the snow from the road, and the storm had abated.

When he reached the gate, he pulled a document from inside his coat and offered it to the guard. He was waved in. The way now ran between the first wall on his left and the second wall, above him, to his right. He passed along the southern side of the hill and then turned north, until he came the gate in the second wall, facing due west. The guard there, seeing his paper, told him to proceed to the main house, where he would inquire—not at the main door, but at a postern on the left side of the house.

The main house where the Marshal dwelt with his family, stood on the northernmost side of the hill. It was an ancient pile, rising some four stories, with a steeply pitched roof of red tiles. The postern he sought lay in a small courtyard outlined in part by the house and the chapel, which ran perpendicular to the house. He could just see the peak of the keep, copper-sheathed, rising behind the house. He took the heavy knocker in hand and struck the door plate twice.

The door was opened by a servant, who, upon hearing his name, led him into a small room, upon the far side of which was another door. The servant knocked on the door, opened it just enough to speak with whoever was within, and then gestured for Lorenz to enter.

He passed into a large room. Tapestries depicting the hunt hung from two of its stone walls, but on the right was a large bookcase, weighted with heavy tomes. In the center of the room stood a large, wooden table, with high-backed chairs set across from each other. Other chairs, cushioned, were placed about the room. On the far side of the large table was a wide hearth alive with a brisk, roaring fire. Before the hearth, his back turned to Lorenz, a man stood, warming himself.

The man, wearing a coat lined about the collar with ermine and falling to just below his knees, seemed not to notice Lorenz's presence. He did not turn to greet him but took a fire iron in hand and knelt to stir the coals. Putting the fire iron back in its bracket, the man adjusted his coat, and then at last turned to face Lorenz. He uttered no word of greeting; he merely smiled.

The man's long red hair and thick beard, falling to his chest; his portliness, the heaviness of his bloated face, at first forbade recognition. But Lorenz could not mistake that smile, redolent not of mirth or good pleasure or friendship, but of something more enigmatic. That smile, and that smile alone, jolted Lorenz into recognition. He was much changed from the last time Lorenz had seen him, some seven years before; but his identity was now unmistakable. He was Peter Schwach.

CHAPTER 2

"LORENZ, I PRAY, BE SEATED!"
Peter motioned toward one of the high-backed
chairs placed by the table. Lorenz was glad to rest
after his long walk. Peter sat down across the table from him.

With only a few feet now separating them, Lorenz could
better observe his once friend. The old Peter had possessed
a thin and somewhat starved appearance; this Peter had evidently been eating better meals. His face had grown fleshy;
his blue eyes were watery. Though his hair hung long over his
shoulders, it was receding at the hairline. His pudgy hands
were white and soft; their fingers, bedecked with rings. The
cuffs of his coat were shiny and somewhat worn.

"Well met, Peter," Lorenz said. He paused and then laughed.
"I suppose this solves the mystery," he said.

Peter pursed his lips. "The mystery," he said — "what do
you mean?"

"What Wenzel Linck told me — that I had been asked for
by name in Weissenbrücke. I could not understand how that
could be."

Peter cocked his head and smiled — "Why, because you do
not think your fame has spread to Franken?"

"Even so. My fame, as you call it, was not great, even within
Wittenberg. That it had come to the attention of anyone outside that city, especially in faraway Franken, was hardly to be

suspected. But now that I meet you here . . . "

"You understand how you have been preferred," Peter said. He laughed. "Really, there's nothing underhanded and disreputable in this, my dear Lorenz—after all, friends must help friends in this world. When the Marshal mentioned bringing an Evangelical preacher to Weissenbrücke, my mind immediately lighted on you. I could think of no one better."

Lorenz, too, smiled. "I could think of several better," he said. "Perhaps if you had consulted me . . . "

"If I had consulted you, then I had never brought you here. Your modesty, my dear Lorenz, would have hindered you. Instead of my old friend and fellow Frank, I would have had to bear with some Saxon droner and verse chopper that you would have thought preferable to yourself. I admit my means of getting you here were somewhat backdoor, but they worked, did they not?"

"Indeed, they did," Lorenz said. "But maybe now you could tell me what exactly the Marshal wants the illustrious Lorenz List to do in his glorious city?"

Peter's smile contracted into a frown at the words, *glorious city*. But in a trice, he recovered himself. "All that in good time. But first let us renew old friendship." Peter rose and walked over to a small side table where, from a tall and shapely glass carafe, he poured two glasses of wine. These he brought to the table, handing one to Lorenz. Sipping but a little, Peter sat back in his chair and made as though he were studying his guest. Then, "it's been some six or so years since we met by chance in Leipzig—what have you done since?"

"I haven't done much," Lorenz said warily. "I have merely led a scholar's life."

"Indeed?" And Peter sipped his wine. "But last time we met you were a shaved-pate; now you evidently are not—surely there is a story there."

"There is indeed a story, but not a very interesting one, I'm afraid," Lorenz replied. "It is merely a matter of theology, the sort of thing that . . ."

"That I wouldn't be interested in," Peter interjected. "But, my dear *magister,* that was the old Peter! I am very much changed. I have grown very pious—and am solidly Evangelical." Peter smiled.

Lorenz took a sip from his own glass. (It was a good wine, though not of the finest.) "Really?" he said. He was dubious.

Peter laughed. "*Ach,* Lorenz," he said. "I should know I cannot deceive you! You know your old companion in sin too well. But I must protest that you are not entirely just in your supposition. I am quite sincere in my conversion—for the nonce. My conscience, you see, is captive to that of my master."

"The Marshal?"

"Indeed! After all, what kind of servant would I be if I did not support my lord in matters that touch his interests so deeply? I was employed on the supposition that I was a very devout Evangelical, and so I shall remain—for as long as my master pleases."

Peter took the slightest sip from his glass and set it down. "But you wonder, perhaps, how I came into his service," he said.

Lorenz gave a little nod.

Peter sat forward in his chair. "Well, I am not so self-effacing as you; I shall tell you . . ."

* * *

Peter reclined again in his chair. He rested his folded hands on his stomach. He began, "some years back, I formed a liaison with a certain widow of Erfurt, whom I had been teaching music . . ."

Lorenz did not wish to hear the details of this "liaison." He interposed: "Yes, you told me of her."

Peter, raising his eyebrows (and seeming a tad annoyed at the interruption), said, "I did?"

"When we met in Leipzig."

"*Ach!* Yes, that was shortly after I had, shall we say, initiated her into the deeper mysteries of the musical art."

"I believe that is so."

"Well, then I shall skip some of the details of my story, since you have already heard them," Peter said peevishly. "As I may have told you then, the liaison proved very lucrative for me, *because,* of course she could not marry me. She was, however, quite lavish in her gifts; and she took great pains to introduce me to some of the right people in Erfurt. It was through them I made the acquaintance of Herr Sigismund. You see, he was on his way to Wittenberg to confer with your Melanchthon on pious matters—it was but shortly after Luther had disappeared—and he stopped off in Erfurt on other business. It turned out that he was in need of a *legis peritus* to advise him. My connections in Erfurt thought they would finagle an audience for me with his lordship—they knew that I was from Weissenbrücke and thus thought I would be a shoe-in for the position. Some of my cronies knew, too, that I was growing tired of the widow and they thought I needed a change of scenery." Peter leaned forward and said in a confidential tone, "It was growing quite tedious, Lorenz—she was intensely jealous; I couldn't even look at another woman! And she had a rather toothsome serving girl . . ."

"So, you met with Herr Sigismund and he employed you?"

"Precisely, my dear Lorenz," Peter said, leaning back again into his chair and propping his hands again on his belly. "I was just coming to that. He was quite impressed with my lawyerly credentials and was pleased with my stout Lutheran devotion. Moreover, he understood that I was pliable . . ."

"I'm surprised the widow let you leave Erfurt."

Peter shook his head sadly. "Indeed, she was none too content with the business, I can tell you," he said. "She would,

I'm afraid, have created some difficulties, but fate or the Good Lord intervened. You see, she died rather suddenly." Peter nodded complacently, but then frowned. "Of course," he said, "she left me nothing, for all I had endured with her. But then I had the new position, so all was not lost."

"And now," Lorenz said, "you are counselor to Sigismund, Herr von Weissenbrücke and, I suppose, a man of some importance."

Peter leaned forward in his chair and shuffled some papers. "Yes," he replied, "his lordship reposes the utmost confidence in me. His servants wait upon my command—the women as well as the men. And, may I add, dear friend, that Frankish women are as delectable as ever?"

"Well, Peter," said Lorenz, "it seems you have done well for yourself. It must be gratifying to have a man of the likes of the Marshal of Weissenbrücke as one's patron—and, moreover, to have become a great man in the town where one lived as a boy."

The sudden darkening of Peter's countenance told Lorenz that he had struck the mark.

* * *

"It is very cold today, is it not?" Peter said. He pushed back his chair, rose and stepped to the hearth. As he warmed his hands before the fire, he said "But enough of my story. I now turn to yours.

"Our patron has been most eager to find a learned and *moderate* Evangelical. He has an ill opinion of the distempered preachers he's heard of. He wants the Church in his domains reformed, but he wants someone who can guide the reform without setting everything on its head."

Peter turned and faced Lorenz. "You see, matters are very delicate here in Weissenbrücke," he said, as it were, confidentially. "Ever since the days of our patron's great-grandfather there has been rivalry and tension between the city's council and the marshals. You see, the city's walls used to enclose this castle; but during the great-grandfather's reign, the townsmen revolted and forced the Marshal to build a wall separating the castle from the town—you walked through the gate of that wall today, no doubt. Ever since, the council has been pushing for greater independence from the marshals—no doubt, they are bucking for free city status. It is our job to make sure they do not get it."

"Our job?" Lorenz said, as if he did not understand Peter's meaning.

"Yes, ours—if you decide to remain and serve His Lordship."

"But I do not understand. I am a *magister;* and, I suppose, you would call me a preacher. I have no skill in political matters."

"Oh, please, Lorenz!" Peter said with a frown. "I believe you understand me well enough. But I shall flesh out the business for you, if I must."

Peter stepped back to the table, took a long sip from his wine cup, and set it down. He continued.

"Ever since your Luther began stirring up the hornet's nest, the town council here has been all afire for the 'Pure Word,' as you all call it—indeed, it's all they talk about! Now, mind you, I am not so convinced that they are as intent on laying up the treasure *that perishes not* as they are in scheming to become the thieves that break in and steal—and Herr Sigismund shares my opinion. They have set their eyes on some of the rich religious foundations of the city, including that of our old friends, the *Marienkirche* canons. The *Pure Word* demands that these, including their land holdings outside the city, be *reformed* and brought, of course, into the full possession of the Most Christian Council—and they cite old Luther's own words as their warrant. The council's only intent, *of course,* is to redirect these resources to the purification of the Church—for which there will have to be a purging of the temporalities. The council will find a more evangelical use for the wealth, no doubt. Do we understand each other thus far, Lorenz?"

Lorenz nodded. He understood it fully.

Peter continued. "Our patron has, himself, been waxing more Evangelical over the years — but, please understand, for somewhat different reasons. He understands the tenderness of the councilors' *conscience*, and he sympathizes. But, he, too, has a tender conscience that will not allow him to countenance any diminution of his own religious duty. That was the motive behind his journey to Erfurt and Wittenberg, now some four years since. It was for this, in part, that he brought me to Weissenbrücke."

"And you, no doubt, have proven a most sympathetic councilor, Peter."

Peter smiled. "I have, indeed, friend; as I have told you, I have myself grown quite Evangelical. But, alas! I can only counsel; I cannot effect. The difficulties are indeed great! You see, it is not the council alone that has discovered the new faith, but the guilds and the city rabble; but their taste is decidedly more incendiary than the council's. Preachers, tainted with the doctrines of old Karlstadt and Münzer, have come among them. There have been street riots, priests have been assaulted, and mobs even broke into the Franciscan church, smashing its windows and destroying its statues. His Lordship has been able, thus far, to restore order, but the city is seething. And then there are the peasants . . ."

"Yes, I have heard the rebellion is spreading . . . "

" . . . like a wildfire — though here as of yet, it is merely smoldering," Peter said. "Swabian incendiaries have been infecting our peasants; there is talk among them of abolishing certain feudal rights, which, they say, are but recent impositions . . . "

"As indeed some of them are, Peter. You know that."

Peter again sat down. "Indeed I do," he replied. "But whether they are of ancient right, just or unjust, is not my concern. I serve my master, not abstractions."

Peter paused, sipped his wine, shot a brief, probing glance at Lorenz, and continued.

"It is not only the Swabians that are making trouble. Some of the poor, unbeneficed priests are stirring up the peasants. There is one fellow—one of those ignorant peasant clerics—who serves the *cura* in some village on the Tiefer Bach, some two-score miles from here: he has been preaching what he calls the *pure Gospel* of Christian equality. The *cura* is beyond reproach, 'tis said, though in his younger days he was none too strict with his vows: he kept, they say, a woman and had several children by her. But she is dead, and he is too old for anything save holiness. Moreover, he is too old to keep this priest in line . . ."

As he told his tale, Peter was, as it were, studying the rings on his left hand; but then he shot another glance at Lorenz. Lorenz tried to mask his feelings, but he knew Peter saw right through him. The Tiefer Bach; the village, with the small, onion-domed church hard by that stream, the cemetery with *her* grave. Old Gottfried, too old for aught save holiness . . . and what of the others?

"Our patron," Peter continued, now taking up a document and casually observing it, "has been reticent to move against the priest, fearing what *Armer Kunz* might do. These are very perilous times, and one must move warily. It is this same, shall we call it, *prudence*, that has made him hesitant to deal with the town. Herr Sigismund is beset with peril on all sides." Peter laid down the paper and looked directly at Lorenz. "And this is where you come in."

Lorenz forced a casual laugh. "Where I come in?" he said. "What can a preacher do where princes and sage counselors fail?"

"A fair riposte, my dear Lorenz! You have struck close to the mark," Peter purred, "but not on the money. You see, *sage counselors* advise and plan and, yes, direct; they do not themselves act. And princes, well, they follow our counsel—if they are wise. And my counsel has been to, at long last, reform the Church here—but upon the moderate grounds that would win the council over. Those sage nonentities want nothing to do with radical notions, either of the townsmen or the peasants. They want nothing to do with the old Church, for that would not fill their coffers. I told Herr Sigismund that by proclaiming a reform of the moderate sort he could join forces with the council and draw in the more reasonable members of the guilds—and all of them together could share in the swag."

"You used those words . . ."

"No, not exactly those words, but that was my general drift."

"And that is why I am here—to bring about the reform?"

"Indeed, Lorenz. You always were a sharp one!"

"Yet, my dear Peter, I am no public orator—I haven't the skill to woo crowds with alluring words."

"But you have knowledge and, dare I say, wisdom." Peter appeared to grow serious. "Lorenz, I did not ask you here to be a street preacher—you can get others to do that. I want you to guide events and govern the new Church structure along the lines I have proposed. We are giving you a priceless opportunity to fulfill your calling, to bring the Gospel to the town and county of Weissenbrücke. The care of souls . . ."

Lorenz laughed. "Come, Peter," he said, "since when do you care for the care of souls?"

Peter smiled. "*Ach*, Lorenz!" he said. "Did I not tell you that I have become very Evangelical? But, no—I cannot lie to you. I care nothing for souls; but I do care for the advantage of my patron—which, of course, accrues very much to my own benefit. But really—does my intent matter? Whatever I want, I shall not hinder you in the course you will take."

Lorenz stroked his beard thoughtfully. "*Ach*, Peter!" he said at last, "you know I could not refuse such an offer, not without betraying what you call my *calling*. I can only accept your proposal. Shall I meet with the Marshal?"

Peter slapped the table. "*Ach*, very good, Lorenz!" he said, with a sinuous pleasure in his tone. "Yes, you shall soon meet with him! But before you do—well, I must warn you of one snag in our proceedings."

"And what is that?"

"The Countess, Herr Sigismund's wife," Peter said with a note of repugnance. "She is very devoted to the old Church—and very close to our old preceptors, the *Marienkirche* canons. They have so confirmed her in her superstitions that she is using all her feminine influence to hinder the Marshal from fulfilling his pious intentions. She is very strong willed, and beautiful, to boot. And, alas, she has proven very persuasive."

"But if she has thus far been so persuasive, what of a sudden has set his resolve?"

"Fear of revolt, pure and simple," Peter said—"and the news that *his* lord, Casimir von Brandenburg, is favoring the reform—albeit not openly yet. Still, even though our patron is willing now to move forward, everything has to be done in such wise that it appears the people are being won over by conviction, not coerced—the Countess will not countenance coercion. There must be street preaching—doubtless there are skilled orators among you in Wittenberg; you can bring them here. And there must be disputations. I think you could see to those . . . "

"I could, indeed," Lorenz said, rising. He paused and thought on what had been said. "I think we understand each other, Peter," he said at last. "When shall I meet with Herr Sigismund?"

Peter did not rise. "In a few days — he is currently visiting some of his estates outside the city. So, in the meantime, rest from your journey and reacquaint yourself with the town. You are still with your aunt?"

"I am."

"Well, we shall find you rooms of your own, closer to the *Marktplatz*."

"Thank you. May I go?" Lorenz was eager to be free of Peter

Peter rose, "Yes. I shall summon you when Herr Sigismund wishes an audience."

*   *   *

Lorenz bowed slightly, turned, and walked to the door. But he had scarcely opened it, when he heard Peter call him. "Lorenz, one more word."

"Yes?"

Peter said nothing immediately but fixed his eyes on Lorenz. There was something strange, almost fey, in Peter's expression. "I think you would ask a thing of me," Peter at last said, with a faint smile.

"And what is that, Peter?" Lorenz forced a laugh, though Peter's expression made him uneasy.

"About your old mentor, Heimrad, where you might find him."

Those lips, uttering that name! But the smile had disappeared from Peter's lips. He seemed grave. Lorenz hesitated and then nodded.

"I was told he had been buried," Peter said, "outside the city, in the cemetery of a village church. Right from the start, the foolish peasants called him a saint — which may have been the thing that induced the late marshal, Herr Sigismund's father, to transfer his uncle's remains to the family tomb in the crypt of the *Marienkirche*. A saint in the city could attract pilgrims."

Lorenz nodded. "I thank you, Peter," he said, and turned again to go.

But once more Peter stopped him. "Lorenz," he said. Again, that almost smile was on his lips. "If you will take my counsel, visit him soon. There are not many days left."

For a moment, Lorenz and Peter stood, looking at each other across the room. Then Peter sat down at his desk, took up a document, appearing to study it. Lorenz, turned and walked out of the room, closing the door behind him.

CHAPTER 3

THE CRYPT OF THE *MARIENKIRCHE* WAS dark. But for the tiny flame of the sanctuary lamp and a few flambeaux, the vast room was lost in shadows. The unsteady light of a torch hard by only barely illumined the inscription:

HEINRICH III,
MARKGRAF VON WEISSENBRÜCKE
HEIMRAD
PECCATOR
✠

Lorenz was happy that, though his kin had added the former name and title, they had kept the inscription that Heimrad had doubtless desired: *Heimrad, a Sinner.*

Lorenz knelt and traced the letters of the name with his finger. He then lay the palm of his hand on the stone. He smiled to himself—did he really expect to feel a heartbeat? He stood and contemplated the stone.

Why had he come here, anyway? Heimrad was gone. Had he come here on pilgrimage—like the peasants and poor folk who left the offerings on the tomb, flowers and little trinkets made in the shapes of a leg, an arm, a heart? "So, Heimrad is thought to work miracles," he mused to himself. "Strange. He would not have welcomed such attentions in life."

Why had he come? He was no nearer to him here than in

Wittenberg. He could not hear his voice nor see the shining mirth in his gray-blue eyes. The tongue of the teller of tales was long stilled. The hand that had been so open lay cold in the tomb. No, the rotting effigy lying in the crypt beneath the stone was not Heimrad. He had departed.

No one was there now, save himself—Lorenz List, surrounded by the dead; yet, Lorenz could imagine the poor folk who visited the tomb. They would come, begging from the "holy man" some boon; and if they deemed their prayers answered, they would return with an offering in thanksgiving. In either case, they would kneel and kiss the stone, then cross themselves, and depart. Lorenz half wished he could do as they did, but he dared not. Had he not cast all that away?

Again, he knelt and brushed the inscription with his finger. The stone was cold, so cold. There was no life in it.

*　*　*

Yes, it was the eyes. In the eyes was the resemblance. Yet they were so very different, those eyes.

He had been summoned. This time, a carriage had come to fetch him at his new residence, on the *Marktplatz*. The day was cold, for it was January; but there was little snow on the ground. He thought, that day, he would have preferred to walk.

It was some three weeks since he had first spoken with Peter. He had twice visited him since but had not been summoned before the Marshal. Lorenz began to wonder if Herr Sigismund had not changed his mind and he would be sent away. The prospect did not distress him.

But then, just a few days ago, the summons came. In two days, a carriage would come at sext and take him to the castle. Herr Sigismund would grant him an audience.

Now, he stood before him.

Herr Sigismund was a young man, tall and rather too thin, but handsome, with thick dark hair and the beginnings of a beard. His mien was grave. He betrayed no mirth; he seemed none too pleased with his guest. Yet, though he was not jocund, he was civil. He was sitting upon a rather large chair — something of a small throne — in the castle's audience hall; and when Lorenz entered, Herr Sigismund nodded to him and asked how he had been faring, whether he had been provided with all he needed or desired.

"Yes, I am quite content. You have been most attentive, *mein Herr*," Lorenz replied and bowed.

Lorenz had wondered if he would see any family resemblance to Heimrad in the young man; and at first he saw nothing. But then he noticed the eyes — they were less deep set than Heimrad's had been, but their shape and hue, Lorenz saw, were those of his departed mentor. Yet, he noted, there was this difference. Heimrad's eyes had been expressive of his various moods — sorrow, compassion, but, mostly, a steady joy. But they had never evinced what Lorenz read in Herr Sigismund's eyes — wariness.

"So, I am told that you were closely acquainted with my great uncle — the saint" — Herr Sigismund's lips bent into a small, ironic smile. Lorenz knew who must have informed the Marshal of this — the man who stood beside him.

"Indeed," Lorenz replied, "I was privileged to have known him."

"He was something of a mentor to you, eh?" The Marshal said this with the shadow of a sneer.

"Yes, he was," Lorenz replied. He would have said, *no, more like a father than a mentor*, but the Marshal's demeanor stymied him.

"I wonder what he would think of our proceedings here?" This Herr Sigismund said, as if to himself. Lorenz did not reply.

"I trust, my counselor here" — Herr Sigismund gestured toward Peter, who stood beside Lorenz — "has explained our situation sufficiently." The sudden change from a kind of ironic banter to wistful introspection, ending in that matter-of-fact, business-like tone unsettled Lorenz. How could the man change moods so quickly? He managed to answer, "he has."

The Marshal's manner grew solemn. "I have committed myself to the Gospel; there is no turning back," he said. "Indeed, if I did falter, the people would take it in hand themselves. That must not happen!" Again, Herr Sigismund was speaking as if to himself. Lorenz, however, thought the Marshal's words begged a response.

"I rejoice that God has found in your lordship so zealous an instrument to work his will." (As he spoke these words, Lorenz could not but feel their timbre false. But wasn't the whole proceeding a farce?) "The true Gospel will admit of no excess, such as many sectaries demand. The Master himself, as well as St. Paul, demand obedience to authorities ... "

Herr Sigismund interrupted him. "You say the right words, *Herr Magister*," he said, again with that ironic smile. "*Obedience to authorities* — the phrase rings sweetly in my ear. I suppose I need not tell you that there are those calling themselves *evangelical* who think it no sin to set themselves against us."

"Indeed," Lorenz answered (again in that false tone as he thought it). "But we — Herr Doctor Luther, Philipp Melanchthon, myself — condemn those who would lift the heel against those whom God has anointed to rule. Moreover ... "

"Moreover, what?" Herr Sigismund's temper flared. "Can there be aught besides this? Are not ... " He fell silent; he seemed to be trying to master himself. Then, with a wave of his hand and a gasp, he said, "I pray, continue ... *moreover* ... "

" ... We, we hold that, though we must keep to the sure path of reform, we have to look to the weak and ignorant. We should not quench the smoldering wick ... "

Herr Sigismund laughed. "Not quench the smoldering wick," he said. "That's fine! That's very fine! We must move surely, but steadily. Yes, I think we shall get on well together, my good *magister*!"

As they left their audience with the Marshal, Peter leaned close to Lorenz. "You did well, very well, my dear Lorenz," he said. "You can play the part of a courtier. *Moreover,* I think His Lordship was quite taken with you . . . "

* * *

"What would you think of the 'proceedings here,' Heimrad?" He knelt by the grave. "I have come here to do what, I fear, you would not approve. But what else am I to do? *Alea iacta est.*"

He sat down beside the tomb. He turned his head slightly aside; the torch's flame still burned bright. He looked down at the tomb, just to his right. His shadow fell across the inscription; but one word was still touched by the light. *Peccator.*

"When I was a child," he thought, "I would have been content to be here. This church, this town, seemed utterly glorious. But then I left, by your counsel, Heimrad; I saw Nürnberg and forgot Weissenbrücke. And in Nürnberg I met her from whom I am parted, I now know, forever. But if I had followed your counsel, Heimrad . . . "

He reached out his hand and, with his forefinger lightly touched the inscription, HEIMRAD. He rose, and looking for the last time at the tomb (he was determined never to visit it again), he made his way into the upper church.

The light of the sun, setting behind the rose window at the rear of the nave, cast a colored radiance over the stone floor. Yes, he had seen grander churches since leaving here, but the *Marienkirche* still spoke to his heart. And it was a lovely church, as yet untouched by the stirring tumult in the city. It would be his task, maybe, to preserve it, keep it from harm.

This, at least, would be a motivation; his heart, he knew, was not in the work of "reform." His desire was not to hemmed in *here* by the haunts of his childhood — oh, yes, he understood Peter, despite his bravado. It was painful to return to where one had been nothing and to be nothing again. Sinking, Peter was dragging him down with him.

Still, that was not the whole story. Would he really mind coming back to Weissenbrücke, if it had not been for... He had been at the center of things in Wittenberg—vile, diminutive Wittenberg, a town that, compared to this Weissenbrücke, was misshapen and slovenly; yet, was it not the stirring ground of the revolution that was sweeping through Germany? In Wittenberg, he had been a respected *magister* and a member of the circle surrounding the greatest man of the time. Yet, he had come to feel restless and discontent there. So, when Luther had called him to come *here*, he did not hesitate.

Yet, it was not for Weissenbrücke or for the Gospel—it was not these, he knew, that had struck the spark from the flint. It was the chance to be in Nürnberg again, if only to pass through it, to relive his happiness there, if only in memory; to be near *her*, even if he should never lay eyes on her. And now, since he had seen her, and she had turned from him, closed the door and latched the bolt, he felt no more purpose, no unction. He wanted to be neither here nor anywhere. He felt dead inside.

He turned his back on the high altar and strode from the church. Passing through the great portal, he looked out on the *Marktplatz*. It was late afternoon, and the shopkeepers (it had been market day) were beginning to close up their booths. It was cold, but he stood at the top of the church steps and watched them. That was the life for men, he thought; being a fishmonger or a farmer or a merchant, bringing his wares to market. These men and women would return home, eat their meager meals and then enjoy the sleep of peace. No "high thoughts" to trouble their dreams. No grave responsibilities for which they were unfit, by which they would be judged.

Judged? That was an old, worn-out word, was it not?

No, he thought, it was an apt word for him. So very apt.

* * *

Could it be? Could it really be *him*? What would he be doing here?

He thought it barely possible—but yet, the gate of the man, resolute but without direction, moving from one booth to another, not in a slow, meandering fashion, like one taking the air and glancing over the wares, but in straight laterals from the line of his procession, taking a gander at one booth's offering, shaking his head, and then, striding a little farther, veering off to left or right, eyeing the offerings of another, nodding his head, but without pulling out his purse. And his demeanor, tall but stout, straight-shouldered as if brazen to defy the world, but too cock-strutting—did it not bespeak the man? Indeed, could Germany hold another like?

Lorenz hurried down the church steps and, passing between two booths, followed the man down the makeshift avenue formed by lines of sellers' stands to left and right. Now that he could see the man at closer range, he thought, "It must be he!"

Lorenz had to duck behind a booth; the man had stopped before a fishmonger's and was haggling. If he but turned his head slightly, he would see Lorenz. The haggling was unusually long-winded; the man was determined to get his price, while the fishmonger seemed just as resolute to get his. Lorenz could not see the man's face—he had a fur cap pulled down over his ears and a high collar to his coat. But, as he watched the contest, he smiled to himself. It had to be he!

When the bargaining was at last done, and the man walked away with his fish, he did not stop or even look at other booths around him, but strode resolutely forward. It was not hard for Lorenz to follow him, for few were now walking the streets. His quarry passed down a narrow and winding thoroughfare where stood some craftsmen's shops and dwellings. The man pursued his way some three hundred yards and then turned abruptly down what appeared a small alleyway between two blocks of houses. Lorenz hastened his step, to make sure he did not lose sight of the man. He turned warily into the alley just in time to see the man pass through a side doorway of a tall, three-story house.

What was he to do now? If he turned and returned to his room, he might never find out if his surmise was correct. But if he dared to knock on that door, and his hunch was mistaken—how would he explain himself?

Lorenz chose the bold course; after all, he was almost certain his hunch was correct. He approached the doorway, hesitated, and then knocked.

No answer.

He knocked again, this time harder. Then he heard a voice from inside, "Who is it?"

"A friend."

There was a pause; then he could hear a bolt drawn. The door opened a crack. A moment passed. Slowly the door swung open. He could now clearly see the man's face staring out from the darkness within. The man gaped. Astonishment, it seemed, had struck him dumb. But when he had found his voice—

"Lorenz," he said, "what are you doing here?"

CHAPTER 4

"WHAT, ARE YOU GOING TO KEEP A friend standing outside in the cold, Karlstadt?" Karlstadt—for it was he—eyed him with suspicion. "What do you want, Lorenz?" he said. "How did you know I was here?"

"That is simple," Lorenz replied. "I saw you in the *Marktplatz* and followed you home. Now will you let me in, Karlstadt? It's cold as hell out here."

Karlstadt appeared uncertain and to consider the matter. Then he nodded his head slightly, shrugged his shoulders. "All right, you may come in," he said, opening the door wider. "But for God's sake, don't let everyone know I am here."

The room was small, dark, and rather cold. Only the feeble flame of a tallow candle provided any light. The room was furnished with only a table, a chair, and a bed against the farther wall. Karlstadt sat down upon the bed and motioned Lorenz to take the chair. "It is the best hospitality I can offer you," he said.

The two men sat in an awkward silence for some moments, until at last Karlstadt said, "I heard the Marshal brought an Evangelical preacher here. I did not expect it to be you, Lorenz."

"I can understand your surprise," Lorenz replied. "I have never been much of a preacher. I am not quite sure what I am doing here myself." He did not want to say anything about Peter Schwach. "What brings you here, Karlstadt?"

259

Karlstadt shook his head and vehemently scratched his scalp. "What brought me here? *Who* brought me here?" he said with a growl. "Who else, but that frothing-at-the-mouth cur — the pope of Wittenberg!"

Lorenz feigned astonishment. "Karlstadt," he said, "you don't mean Luther?"

"Who else could I mean?" Karlstadt snapped. "The great pontiff himself, enthroned on his privy, shitting his decrees as if all the world had to lap at his ass! He's torn down one tyranny only to set up another — and to think that I conferred the doctor's cap on his haughty head!"

Lorenz found Karlstadt's ill humor amusing. "But surely you don't mean that Luther sent you to Weissenbrücke?" he said

"No, he didn't send me here — don't mock me, Lorenz! You must have heard how he played the lord bishop against me — saying I couldn't preach or teach without his leave; how he slandered me — claiming I was concocting violent revolution with Münzer. Weren't you with him in Jena?"

"No, I wasn't . . ."

"Well, if you had been, even you, who love him — as, I confess, I once did, as we all did — even you would have smelled the falsehood — the utter lies! And why? Because I claim the right to interpret Scripture, just like he does! But he alone is infallible, it does appear! And then he got the Elector to drive me out of Orlamünde — you didn't know of that?"

Lorenz nodded. "Yes, I knew of it — and, I confess, I was glad of it, Karlstadt. You were tearing down images and forbidding music. And as for polygamy . . ."

"That is because . . ." and here Karlstadt leaned forward, shaking his finger at Lorenz. "You say you follow Scripture, and Scripture alone; but you interpret it according to the traditions of men. Why, Abraham had more than one wife, and have you not . . ."

Lorenz did not want a debate Scripture with Karstadt — "but,

Karlstadt," he interrupted him, "were you not preaching insurrection with Münzer?"

"By God, no! No, by God!" Karlstadt pounded his knee. "The kingdom of God is not built so—that's what I told Münzer! You can't advance God's truth that way. Luther cannot cite one thing I said to defend this calumny!"

"But your donning peasants' clothes, and casting aside your doctorate, taking up farming, living like a peasant. That could seem revolutionary for a man of your station—and isn't Münzer stirring up the peasants?"

Karlstadt barked—"*Ach*, Lorenz! That he is—but I had nothing to do with it! See how Luther has poisoned even my friends with his lies?" Karlstadt threw up his hands, as if in despair.

Lorenz paused, as if he were soberly considering the matter. Then, looking at his friend and nodding, said, "Well, I'll believe you, Karlstadt—I never really could picture you as *Armer Kunz*. But tell me, you left Orlamünde and came here? Why?"

Karlstadt resolutely shook his head. "No, I did not come here—"

"But, Karlstadt, it seems you are here now . . ."

"I did not come here immediately," Karlstadt growled. "I have been here only some three weeks. I didn't intend to come here at all. I went first to Strassburg, and then to Zürich. From Zürich, I came to Rothenberg—but enemies of God on the council in that pestilent town drove me thence. I hope to return soon—God's Spirit works mightily among his folk there. For the meantime, I am here."

Karlstadt didn't say why he came to Weissenbrücke, nor would Lorenz ask him a question he would surely not answer. Lorenz surmised that Karlstadt had an ally in the city—someone for whom the new Lutheran preacher might cause trouble.

And this was, of course, true—as far as Lorenz's new duties went. It was the likes of Karlstadt that the Marshal most desired to be rid of—men who stirred up the common folk against authority. Lorenz could very easily have Karlstadt seized surreptitiously—and he really ought to, of course. Yet, though he had never really liked Karlstadt, he felt an odd affection for the man. Rather like an unpleasant kinsman.

"Karlstadt," he said, after a pause. "I feel I must warn you— you really shouldn't stay in Weissenbrücke . . ."

Karlstadt stiffened. "Lorenz," he said. "Would you drive me hence? Or would you . . ."

"I would," Lorenz interposed, "but the first, not the last. You see, I am now the Marshal's preacher, and I stand with Luther. I shall be frank with you—I find your teachings detestable, damnable! I have come here to bring the true Gospel, not some Hussite doctrine of insurrection. Whether you, with Münzer, propose violence is irrelevant, for your doctrines are incendiary! You are stirring up the common folk against their rulers, who govern by God's decree. You may not stay here—I am giving you warning to leave. If you do not, I shall have to do my duty."

Karlstadt's cheeks, which had at first blanched, now flamed a fiery red. He pounded his fist on his knee. He cried out, "My teachings damnable? Incendiary? *Gott!* What of your Luther's furtive rutting with the Roman whore? *Ach!* He shouts 'antichrist' until he chokes on his own bile, but will he clear the shit from the stables? No! Like Jehu, he keeps Jezebel's idols—and becomes himself another Achab! Oh, he has written of the freedom of the Christian, but he has made himself pope, that is what he has done! His pride rises like the fumes of a dung heap to heaven—and like the Antichrist, he makes war on God's elect! And as for incendiary . . ."

"Karlstadt," Lorenz commanded, "enough!"

But Karlstadt ignored him. "No, you will hear me—you have slandered me, so you shall give heed! Who has been more incendiary than that Wittenberg firebrand? He has incited the common folk against the priests and monks, against the bishops—against the princes themselves! His words have set fire to Germany! He calls me incendiary only because he fears to lose his power—he fears a rival. But it is not Andreas Bodenstein he battles, but the Lord Sabaoth!"

Karlstadt's words stung Lorenz—he had to confess there was much truth in them. But he would make no admission—not to this butcher theologian turned farmer. This dull pate could not get the better of him! "Andreas, be silent!" he shouted, to be heard above Karlstadt's din. "I will not argue with you—you stand condemned in a higher tribunal. I am not holding a disputation with you, nor do I retract anything I have said. I am warning you—leave this city and county! I will not have you stirring up the common folk against God's anointed."

Karlstadt opened his mouth wide and laughed. "*Ach*, Lorenz, you fool!" he exclaimed. "Do you think that it is Andreas Bodenstein you have to fear? The bells on your fool's cap have rung you deaf! Your devilish pride has blinded you! You may shake your bauble scepter at me all you want, you may drive me hence—you may kill me! But in my place will rise thousands more! This backwater is already swarming, not with Karlstadts—you could wish it were, if you knew. *Ach!* Only if you knew! The folk are thirsting for the Gospel, for freedom from that tyranny that is crushing them! And not just this town, but all of Franken is stirring—the *Bundschu* is here, but it is not I who have been scrawling it on walls, carving it in tree bark, or stitching it into banners. The peasants—yes, your own people, Lorenz—you bloody traitor! The peasants are sharpening their scythes and priming their guns. The fields are ripe unto harvest, and when they are scythed down, blood shall flood the land!"

Karlstadt's vehemence shook Lorenz, but he remained self-possessed. "Do you dare," he said sternly, "threaten the Marshal, Karlstadt?"

Again Karlstadt laughed, a humorless laugh: "No, Lorenz! I threaten no one, but the priests and their lord, the Devil. I do not speak of what I would do, but of what will certainly come to pass. Wherever I go, I counsel peace: the triumph of the Gospel, I say, will not be won by bloodshed. But none listen to me; nor will they listen to you, with your watered-down Lutheran milk. The townsmen are stirring, the Frankish peasants will not rest until their grievances are met, or the whole land is laid desolate! It is not Karlstadt that stirs them, but God!"

"And you," Lorenz said, "you would resist the will of God by counseling peace?"

Karlstadt shook his head. "*Ach,* Lorenz," he chuckled, "you would cause me to stumble with your subtleties. Hear me! I give God's manifest will as my counsel. His hidden will—well, it is not my business!"

God's manifest will, his hidden will—what, even Karlstadt? Lorenz fought them, but Karlstadt's words horrified him all the same. God was inciting the peasants, threatening destruction to Franken—but to what end? But that was a foolish question—who could plumb God's counsel? And who could stay or stymie it? Certainly, not Lorenz List.

But, yet—was it not his duty to try to stay even the hand of God? He thought of his home village, of his father; brother, Sebald; his sister, Inge (how much he had thought of her since coming to Weissenbrücke!) What Peter Schwach had said of the peasant priest preaching insurrection—who else but he should stand in the breach between God's inscrutable will and *them*?

But he, Lorenz List—dared he struggle with God? Or was it God himself who was coaxing him to the fight—a wrestling on the field of Phanuel?

Quod nomen est tibi? But even in the depths of his heart, Lorenz heard no answer.

264

CHAPTER 5

KARSTADT DEPARTED WEISSENBRÜCKE within the week; it was only some weeks later that Lorenz learned that he had returned to Rothenberg. "Well, Rothenberg can have him," Lorenz thought to himself on hearing the news.

Yet, Lorenz knew he could be thankful to Karlstadt for this—the tempestuous, vacillating man had instilled him with a purpose. He could not have cared less for the "reform" of Weissenbrücke—just to save the Marshal's hide! Hadn't his father and grandfather before him driven the peasants ("yes, my own folk," Lorenz mused) like swine to the slaughter? Ancestral rights, ancient custom, trampled into the mud the folk tilled to enrich their haughty taskmasters! And these men, using the sacred to shore up their profane despotism! They merited a fall.

Yet, Lorenz knew, even if the peasants triumphed for an hour, they would be crushed within a day. Herr Sigismund might not survive the deluge, but the peasant bark would never come to rest on the mountains of Ararat. Sigismund's feudal lord, the Markgraf von Brandenburg-Kulmbach, Casimir, Lorenz knew, had appointed two preachers to bring the Gospel to his land—and it was this intelligence that had convinced the Marshal to embrace the Lutheran cause, or so Peter had assured Lorenz. Nevertheless, though Casimir might deal gently with the peasants who eschewed radical revolution, there would be no mercy for those who followed the piper.

No, Lorenz admitted to himself, it was not Weissenbrücke's salvation that moved him, but the safety of his family and home. If he could tease his folk into neutrality, he might save them. But the path to his village passed through Weissenbrücke. If he could establish a foundation for the reform here, he would be free to confront the threat to his people.

But if God willed otherwise? It mattered not to Lorenz. For his folk, he would fight even God—like Jakob did at Phanuel.

Quod nomen est tibi?

* * *

It was fortunate that Doctor Paulus was dead. Lorenz knew he could not have withstood him in the disputation. It was certain which side he would have taken.

As it was, the champion for the Old Church was the dyspeptic *magister*, Pater Hilarius. He was a diminutive man, rather round in the midriff, and entirely bald. He was not ill spoken, but he was a thorough scholastic, and rather fond of *very* subtle distinctions. It was for this reason that the party of the Old Church chose him. They thought him a formidable disputant.

Yet Hilarius, though quoting scripture from memory, was pedantic in interpretation. His explanations were like the dry bones of Ezekiel—there was no life in them. Lorenz used this weakness to his advantage. He bedewed his own speech with the water of refreshment—he spoke of the longing of the soul for forgiveness and peace, of the terror of Scripture when it rages against the sinner, but of its consolation when it whispers to the trembling heart, "be still, and know that I am God." Hilarius' interpretations were magisterial, very correct, and (Lorenz had to admit) quite compelling. But they were dead. The spirit that had uttered them had fled.

The disputation was held in the *Marienkirche*, at the Marshal's express command. Indeed, Herr Sigismund himself was present, with the Countess. Lorenz had the lordly couple clearly in view as he spoke, for they sat enthroned before the large concourse of people who had gathered in the church. Herr Sigismund seemed most intent on the discussion, and would smile when Lorenz skewered his opponent with a deft thrust. Yet, Lorenz wondered at the man's eyes; it was as if they were looking inward; and whenever he smiled, Lorenz noted a hint of self-deprecating cynicism in the expression. The Countess did not change her expression from the moment she assumed her seat. She sat, stock still, her eyes cast down, her lips pressed firmly together, like one who had been subjected, against her will, to some great indignity.

* * *

"The Marshal was very much pleased with your performance yesterday, my dear Lorenz." Peter's smile was generous, but his eyes were cold, almost hostile, or so Lorenz thought. "He said to me afterward that you had castrated that pig with consummate dexterity."

"Please relay to His Lordship my humble thanks," Lorenz replied. "I suppose the Countess was not so effusive in her praise . . . "

Peter poured himself a glass of wine. "No, no, my clever theologue. You were eloquent and, shall we say, even seductive—but not such as to warm that cold heart. She is utterly insensible—willful and cross. I don't know what Herr Sigismund sees in her."

"She is quite lovely, as I am sure you have noticed, Peter."

Peter smiled and leaned back in his hair. "Yes, she has a most shapely form, does she not? Her breasts are utterly exquisite and"—Peter paused and cocked his head. "Don't give me that disapproving look, Lorenz. A man may look and imagine, without touching. You needn't fear: I shall not attempt to seduce her." Peter laughed.

("Yes, laugh, Peter," Lorenz thought. "I know, and you know, she utterly despises you.")

But, of course, Lorenz knew she had no great regard for him, either. Indeed, she remained the one great obstacle to his goals. It was as if the Marshal were poised, ready to plunge into the new order of things, but for this one hindrance. This hindrance, Lorenz knew, would not go away, so he had to dilute its influence. Though the Marshal regarded him highly, Lorenz knew his own influence was not enough.

"Has His Lordship given any more thought to my proposal? I trust you have been urging it, Peter; it would be to all our benefit."

Peter took a sip of wine. "It was this I wanted to discuss with you — I did not invite you here just to inflate your head with praise. He has given it much thought, as I have urged it seasonably, and he has agreed. Have you made preparations?"

"Indeed I have," Lorenz said. "I have sent already to Nürnberg and Wittenberg and have secured a *magister* from the latter and two preachers — former Augustinians, like myself — from the former. Both Luther and Wenzel Linck have been most eager to help."

"How soon could they arrive?"

"They will come as soon as we send for them."

"Then send for them!" Peter paused and began writing on a sheet of paper. Without glancing up at Lorenz, he asked, "And have you given any thought to our peasant problem?"

"I have." Lorenz wanted to wait until Peter stopped writing; but when Lorenz hesitated, Peter said (with a wiggle of annoyance in his voice), "Well?"

"We can't do anything until at least the Nürnbergers arrive — it would probably be best to wait until Wohlgemut Kraft comes ... "

"Who is he?"

"The *magister* from Wittenberg."

"Oh."

"I feel it is my duty to oversee and direct them for a time, though I doubt it need be long. Then, I shall probably leave Kraft in charge of things here, and myself go to the Tiefer Bach."

Peter laid down his pen and looked up at Lorenz. "Hmm," he said. "I suppose that makes sense—you know those people better than any of us."

"That is my thought."

"But, take heed, my zealous apostle"—and Peter leaned back into his chair—"I am not sure the Marshal will want to give you up—he is really taken with you, as I have said. He'd sooner send me, I think. You know, of course, the danger . . ."

"I do."

Peter snorted a mirthless laugh. "A regular martyr you are, my dear Lorenz. I can't say it is one of your most endearing traits. Indeed, I cannot understand it at all! But my advice is that you explain your intent to Siggi yourself—he won't warm to it, coming from me."

"I was hoping you would broach the matter . . ."

"No, Lorenz!" Peter's tone was taut; his eyes flashed indignation. "Right now, he doesn't even want to discuss the peasant problem. Just this morning, in counsel, I gently introduced the subject. He flared at me, and abused me before everyone—I came near to resigning. The words he used, the epithets he hurled at me . . ."

"It sounds as if he's frightened."

"*Ach!* He is, Lorenz, he is!" Peter said; and then, as if to himself, "But that doesn't excuse the insult! I may not be his equal in birth, but my learning . . ." Peter paused, as if trying to collect himself. Then he continued: "And the others—how pleased they were, to see me so discomfited! They dared not display it openly—but their lips, twisted in that contemptuous way of theirs . . . Why, if I could . . ."

Peter left the thought unexpressed. Though he could understand why the counselors would despise Peter, Lorenz nevertheless pitied him. He knew what it was to feel such contempt; and to have it coupled with one's own self-contempt is the more bitter.

"Then perhaps I should wait to mention the matter to him," Lorenz said after a short pause.

Peter nodded. "Yes, you should—though I doubt he would abuse *you*." Peter had resumed his smile. "But, yes, I should wait, if I were you."

Peter again took up his pen and began writing. Without looking at Lorenz, he said, "I have some pressing business. I think you had better go."

Lorenz nodded and, without saying another word, rose and left the room.

*   *   *

"So, you'll be leaving Weissenbrücke—for where?

"...Your father's village? I don't see the point in *that!*"

He had come to bid farewell to Tante Ursula. He would be leaving the town in a few days.

"You've got a good thing here—why give it up? Why, I hear the Marshal has taken a real liking to you—just like his father did my husband, your uncle, God rest him. That ain' something to give up!"

"I'm not giving it up, Aunt. I shall be back, no doubt. There is unrest in the countryside—that is why I am going home." He thought how strange it was for him to utter the word, *home*.

Tante Ursula adjusted herself in her chair, took out her handkerchief, and wiped her eyes. "*Ach,* I have heard of what's afoot on the land," she said, with a snort of contempt. "Them peasants can't be content with the gifts God's given them—they have to revolt and make such nonsensical demands! And how the lords have let them tear up and down the country, pulling down castles and monasteries! Well, I figured it was just like them Swabians: pure savages they are, pure savages! But I never figured our own Frankish peasants would start ripping around that way. But then, a peasant is a peasant; you never..."

"But that is why I am going to the countryside, Aunt. The Frankish peasants haven't done anything yet—and it is my task to make sure that they don't."

"Well, I suppose you know them people—your father *is* a peasant, and you was born that way, though you've done better for yourself, like your Onkel Georg did, God rest him! And you've kept them woolly-pates in the city in line with your preaching. They ain' destroyed nothing in the *Marien-kirche* yet—though I wonder if this marshal would do anything about it if they did. He's none too open-handed with the artisans, like his father was, God rest him! Why, the Franciscan church is still a shambles, and nothing, nothing has been done!"

"Herr Sigismund has had many matters to occupy him, Aunt. But I am sure that when everything calms down, he'll turn his attention to such matters as repairing churches..."

"Well, God bless him if he does! Why, his father, and his father before him, was very openhanded with the artisans. Your Onkel Georg was one of his favorites, as my father was before him. But this marshal is different: he's mixed up in all this newfangledness..."

"As am I, Aunt."

"Yes, yes, I know—and I don't think I approve of it all, either! Things was fine the way they were, from where I sit. But I must say" (and here her face wrinkled into a smile) "the way you dressed down that Father Hilarius—I heard all about it from my gossip, Berta Stimmelose—why, it was grand! I never did like him, always so cross and complaining. He was none too friendly to your Onkel Georg, either!"

Lorenz rose. "Well, Aunt," he said, "I fear I must be going. I would like to stay longer, but—well, you know how it is."

"Yes, I do, nephew—no doubt tired of hearing an old woman blather and repeat herself. I know how it is."

"I probably won't be able to visit again before I leave."

"That's alright, that's alright! Go do what you have to do—but hurry back! Don't let them peasant maids turn your head" (and here Tante Ursula winked). "Remember, you belong here, in Weissenbrücke."

EVERY STEP OF EVERY MILE WAS A progress into what-had-been. He was returning into a land that had once been palpable but which, for years now, had shimmered only on the borderlands of dream. And was he himself now any more substantial than a dream?

A boy walked beside him, and he was growing into that boy. Every step of every mile, he sloughed off the layers of years that separated him from that boy. The *schola* at Weissenbrücke had become an expectation of hope and vague fear. Nürnberg was now but a tale of wonder told by beguiling travelers. And Else—she was an image of dream-beauty remembered upon waking only as a trembling of desire.

He was growing from Lorenz List, Wittenberg *magister*, back into Lori, a bumpkin child lisping a rude German and, barely, a bookish Latin. He was no longer the companion of the resplendent Luther, the prophet of a new age, but the smudgy son of Johannes List, the peasant farmer. With every step of every mile, as he grew smaller, the image of his father loomed ever larger. He was, once again, the boy sitting by the hearth, just out of eyeshot, listening to the jawing of the men, hoping his father would not see him.

And he was, once again, Inge's brother. With every step of every mile, the image of dream-beauty was delineating itself into the form of Inge—Inge as once he knew her. Yet the new form was enveloped by a fog that obscured remembrance. She would not be as she once was to him; he could not slough off that one layer of what he would become. Not the sharpest blade could pare off the skin of the youth who had sat by the river, mourning the death of his childhood.

* * *

The road now began its climb up the low ridge. He followed it with slower step—it would not be long now. Every bend and turn brought recollection. Every tree or stone was like a long-sundered acquaintance—he recalled their features, but they knew him not. The forest floor to right and left was bare of undergrowth, but the trees were budding with new life. Patches of old snow clung on in the shadowy places.

The road did not pass over the summit but took an easier grade about its base. But at the bend, where the road turned toward the east and began descending, he could see the valley of the Tiefer Bach below him. The stream was hidden from view, as was most of the village, by the trees; but to his left, east of the village, he could see the church, its blue cupola, cross surmounted.

It was here, at this last turn of the road, that he hesitated. Should he go on? His mind gave a ready answer: "Of course! You bring salvation to your folk." But his heart spoke otherwise. The blue cupola, he felt, forbade his passage—it would lick the sky in wrath if he took another step. And the dead, buried in the mold of the churchyard, would rise in anger against him. And with them would stand his mother.

He shook himself and forced out a laugh—it was naught but the absurd fancies of childhood, or a temptation of the Devil! Still, he hesitated. It was at last only the recollection that he was sent here by the Marshal and that he could not return to Weissenbrücke with the tale that ghost-fear had kept him from his obedience that set his resolve. He stepped forward onto the downward path.

*   *   *

The road crossed the Tiefer Bach by a small bridge, nigh to the church, which stood on a rise, girdled by the stream. On the church's north side, ranks of grave markers pierced the mold, following the hillock's contours, curving round the half cylinder of the apse. He could descry where his mother's tombstone rose; but he would not visit her. Not yet.

He crossed the bridge and stood on the farther bank. He was weary; it had been a long day's walk. Yet, despite his body's exhaustion, his heart leaped within him as he looked down the road, into his natal village.

Nothing, it seemed, had changed, except that a new house now stood at the head of the path, this side of the row of village houses. As he passed down the street, to left and right he saw the old, familiar sights—the carpenter's and blacksmith's shops, some farmers' houses, the tinker's. From doors, a few people eyed him with suspicion; he did not recognize any of them, except one old woman—how age-altered Frau Loesel had become, he thought! At last he came to the inn, *Zum Bachkrebs*, where he hoped to get food and drink and lodge for the night.

*   *   *

The common room was dark, and it was still too early for much custom. The proprietor, Balthas Hecht, greeted him warmly, though he eyed him with a little suspicion. Hecht was much changed from the young man that Lorenz remembered—he had grown stout and bald and, when he spoke, Lorenz could see he was missing some teeth. Hecht's eyes were screwed into a perpetual squint. Lorenz called for bread and cheese and beer.

When the proprietor had brought Lorenz his food, he bustled about the tables, wiping them, arranging the benches, trimming the lamps. As he appeared to be rubbing at a particularly stubborn spot on one of the tables, he observed casually, "We don't get many strangers here—may I ask whence ye come?"

Lorenz swallowed his food, took a sip of beer, and said, "You may. I come immediately from Weissenbrücke, but my home for many years has been Wittenberg,"

Hecht paused in his rubbing, and said with some interest, "Wittenberg, ye say? Wittenberg!" he repeated, more contemplatively. "And what brings ye here?"

"Business."

"Oh, business," Hecht repeated, nodding his head. He paused and added, as if nonchalantly, "Will your business keep ye long here?"

"Perhaps."

Lorenz smiled to himself. "Poor Hecht," he thought. "Curiosity is eating at him. Shall I heighten the mystery?"

He said nothing more as he ate his meal. All the while, Hecht kept up his bustling about, casting ever and anon furtive glances at his customer. When at last Lorenz had finished his food, Hecht hurried over to take his platter. "Can I get ye something more?" he said, wide-eyed.

"No," Lorenz replied (he noted the downcast look in Hecht's eyes). "Well, maybe—yes!" (Hecht's eyes brightened.) "I suppose a publican would know most of the folks hereabout."

Hecht stammered, "Yes, yes, I would. I'll tell ye anything— that is, if I can, ye know, honestly . . ."

"Do you know of a List family in these parts?"

"The Lists?"

"Yes, I was told this was their village."

"It is—yes, it is, though there be only two hereabouts now. That is, there is a daughter, but she's married, ye see . . ."

"Yes, I see." Here Lorenz finished the last of his beer and called for more. ("Oh, bother!" Hecht muttered as he waddled away.) When the innkeeper returned, Lorenz took a long draw from his mug. Only then did he continue.

"You see, I am not interested in the daughter, at least not directly; but in two men—one, named Johannes (the father, I'm told) and his son, called Sebald."

"*Ach!*" exclaimed Hecht (now simply trembling with curiosity) "Johannes List and Sebald! Yes, yes, I can tell ye anything ye want about them. They're good men, they are—though ye don't see much of old Johannes, since he stopped being headman. Keeps to himself, he does—though he still works his place, with his boy. But he keeps to himself. Ye don't see much of him, yes . . . "

Lorenz took another long draw from his cup. "I trust, then, they are both in health?"

"*Ach,* yes!" Hecht chirped. "Very much so! Even old Johannes, though he's getting up there, ye know. Of course, no one sees much of him . . . "

"Well, that's most welcome news," Lorenz added. "For, you see, I need to speak with them, though I would rather speak with the young man first." And here Lorenz lowered his voice, beckoning the publican to come closer. "I've come with a message for them—from Wittenberg."

"From Wittenberg?" Hecht said, beaming wonder.

"From Wittenberg!" Lorenz replied, with decision.

Hecht emitted a little whistle.

"Can you help me?"

Hecht gave a little leap backward. "*Ach,* yes—can I help ye. *Ach,* yes! I can point ye to their farmstead—it's not far, only at the end of the village! But wait!—" as if a thought had suddenly struck him—"You're in luck today—yes! Sebald should be joining the lads after work here—this very evening! Oh, it would be so much more convenient for ye, if he came here, rather than ye going to the *Hof.* Ye must be tired, after your long journey. Ye could rest until this evening . . . "

Lorenz understood Hecht's solicitude for him; having him meet Sebald here would give the village matter to talk about for months to come. And, he thought, it would serve his own purpose, too. He did not want to face his father until he had spoken first to Sebald.

After a short pause, Lorenz nodded. "No, that is a very good idea you have—for I am tired, as you noted, and the message I have will require some explanation. No, your plan is very good—but you are sure he will come here tonight?"

"As sure as I am that my beer is the best for miles around," Hecht said with a genial smile that puckered his fat face.

"Very well," Lorenz said. "It is settled. But I must warn you . . . "

"Yes?"

" . . . That you say nothing to him, or anyone else, about what I have told you. Do you understand?"

"Oh, yes . . . "

Lorenz pointed to a small table in a dark corner of the room. "I shall sit over yonder tonight," he said. "All I ask of you is that you direct him over to me—say only, 'that *gentleman* would like a word with you.' Say nothing more. Do you understand?"

"I do—oh, ye can count on Balthas Hecht!"

"Very well. Do as I ask, just as I ask it, and you will be rewarded." Lorenz pulled out his purse. "Now, please show me a room, so I can rest. Call me, I pray, before you expect his arrival."

"*Ach!* Worry not, good sir—I shall do just as ye ask. Ye can count on Balthas Hecht!" the proprietor said with a smile and a decisive nod of his head.

CHAPTER 7

L ORENZ AT ONCE RECOGNIZED HIS
brother, for his resemblance to their father. He was
tall, broad of shoulder; his face was angular, with
deep-set eyes and dark, prominent eyebrows. Dark hair grew
abundantly over a high forehead, and his beard was thick for
so young a man. Sebald List's manner with his companions was
at once jovial but restrained—like Johannes List's demeanor
must have been in his youth. He seemed the master of the
situation and the leader of the young men. It was obvious
that, though they were familiar with him, they respected him
and sought his approval.

Even Balthas Hecht—Sebald's senior by not a few
years—approached the young man obsequiously. The proprietor spoke, gestured expressively, and then pointed discreetly
toward the far corner where Lorenz sat.

The young man seemed to lose some of his strut as he
approached Lorenz's table. His tone sounded uncertain as he
asked, "you would speak with me, sir?"

"You are Sebald List?"

"Yes."

"The son of Johannes List?"

"Yes."

"Then, please sit down."

Lorenz knew he could not unburden himself in that room;

279

the men kept glancing with furtive eye in their direction. He thus spoke softly.

"I have a message for you, though I cannot deliver it here." He watched to gauge Sebald's reaction. "It is from your brother, Lorenz."

Sebald's eyes widened, though otherwise he kept his composure. "My brother, Lorenz!" he said, in a whisper. "This is the first that . . . " He shook his head. At last, looking directly at Lorenz, he asked, "What is it?"

"As I said," Lorenz replied, "I cannot tell you here. Is there someplace we can speak in private, tomorrow? I would speak with you, first, without your father."

Sebald nodded. "Yes, of course. You had better do that," he said. "I would ask you to our dwelling, but as it stands — you would be sure to meet my father there, and of course the hands . . ."

In the end, Sebald and Lorenz agreed to meet at the ruins of the old castle, on the summit of a hill, just to the west of the village. Few of the village folk ventured there, for it was thought to be haunted. There, they would be alone.

* * *

Standing by the jagged edge of the wall, one could see directly into the heart of the village, below. Lorenz could take in the entirety of his father's farmstead — the outbuildings, the house itself, and the linden tree, leaves infant-green, that grew outside what had been her window.

"It took you all unawares?"

Sebald nodded. "I couldn't hardly believe it when you told me you had a message from Lorenz. That you are Lorenz — I never expected that."

Lorenz had imagined how it would be when he revealed himself to his brother. Of course, Sebald would not remember him — he had been but a small child when Lorenz left the village. But how would he greet his brother? Lorenz had hoped for something more than surprise and wonder.

"I suppose I have come upon you all unawares—I should not have done so," Lorenz said. "I have been remiss in not writing. But my last letter, doubtless, did not please our father." Lorenz paused and looked out over the village. "Has he spoken of it?"

Sebald shook his head. "No, he has not spoken of it to me. In fact, he has not . . ." But Sebald left the sentence unfinished.

Lorenz was not sure he wanted to hear the rest, but he prodded his brother, "Yes? Don't be afraid to speak."

Sebald's eyes were expressive. They bespoke some embarrassment. "I was going to say that he has said very little about you."

Lorenz nodded. Again he looked out over the village. He could guess what his father said of him—when he spoke of him. "And when he did speak of me, what he said was something like, 'that good-for-nothing monk.'"

Sebald nodded. "Yes, something like that," he said.

"And what will he say, do you think, when he discovers I am no longer a monk?"

Sebald shot Lorenz a quizzical look, as if the discrepancy between account and palpable fact had just occurred to him.

"You wonder that I am not dressed like a monk? That I will explain by and by—though with a very little thought you can, I think, guess the riddle. You have probably heard of the like, with others . . ."

Sebald looked steadily at Lorenz. He lowered his eyes and nodded.

"Well, brother," Lorenz said, more to himself than to Sebald, "We will find, perhaps, that the news will please our father the better. You see, I am now something of the great man he wanted me to be. You see, I am a *magister* of Wittenberg, the companion of some of the greatest men our time, and under the employ of the Marshal of Weissenbrücke. I have come here under his warrant. It is not quite what Father wanted, but it is something . . . "

The two men fell silent. For the first time, Lorenz questioned the wisdom of his coming here. It had perhaps been better had someone else taken on the task. He wondered if even his brother would stand with him, or if his father would oppose him—it was likely, for even if Johannes were sympathetic with his cause, resentment from the past might prod him contrary. Could he make headway, when his own father and brother opposed him? He would not test it now.

"And Inge?"

Sebald smiled. "She has spoken of you often—it is from her that I heard most about you."

Lorenz smiled. "She was a dear sister to me . . ."

"To me, too," Sebald nodded. "You see, she took care of me when I was young. Even after she was married, she was good to me. I stayed often with her and Eitel—you know, she married Eitel Moeller?"

Lorenz nodded. His old resentment—why should it bother him now?

Sebald laughed—it was a manly laugh. "She treated me like her oldest boy, scolding me when I did amiss," he said, pulling his own ear and lightly smacking himself on the rump. "She made sure I got some reading and got father to send me to the priest, Gottfried. When I didn't want to study, she told me to be like our brother, Lorenz—'that great scholar,' she used to say. But I was never so good a student. Gottfried himself said I was none so smart as my brother!" Again, Sebald laughed. And then, as if in afterthought: "She was not sad that you became a monk."

Lorenz smiled at his brother. "That subject again?" he said. "You are curious, aren't you, brother? Well, I will assuage your curiosity, by speaking of the matter to our father. He is the first who should know whether the education he obtained for me was ill-used or not. Shall we go to him now?"

Sebald pondered for a moment, then said, "he will be at home now — he is always at home, hardly ever goes out into the village."

"Then let us go to him," Lorenz said. "And then, I wish to see Inge. I have much I need to say to her."

*   *   *

The *Hof* seemed shrunken and mean. Distorted memory had magnified it, plastered over its unevenness, brightened its colors. "Apotheosis of a cow yard," he mused to himself.

His father, too, had shrunk and withered, like a last season's apple kept too long down cellar. He was a vigorous man in his forties when Lorenz had left him; but that was some 20 years ago. The years had not been gentle with Johannes List. He still had vigor — Sebald had said he yet worked a full day, though more slowly than had been his wont. Johannes' hair and beard were full, though now ashen white; he had not grown bent or stoop-shouldered; yet, looking into his father's eyes, Lorenz felt as if he were peering into the windows of a long-abandoned house.

Johannes' manner, however, had not been gentled. "So, you've come back?" he said gruffly, when Lorenz stood before him in the hearth room. "Where's your monk's robes and your beads?"

Lorenz winced; his father still had the skill to find the wound and prick it. "I have abandoned them now these three years," he replied, like a timid son who dared not tell a lie.

"Abandoned them?" Johannes laughed. "I didn't think they let you do that. Shouldn't you be locked up for such doings? 'Twas the way before now. Why, I can remember some whoreson priest run off with a nun from Klosterneubrunn. 'Twas said they were heading for Schweiz, but they got caught. Both were flogged and pilloried. I reckon that if he was a priest like Gottfried, he could've got away with having a woman—wouldn't need to seduce a nun now, would he?"

Johannes eyed his son archly. Lorenz did not respond.

"Was it a woman that got you to doff your cowl and jump into—breeches?"

Lorenz's heart recoiled at the question. It was too close to the mark. But it did not strike it.

"No, father. It was not a woman. I was a cloister brother at Wittenberg and a *magister* in the university. The monastery disbanded and I—well, I saw no more reason to continue a monk's life."

"I daresay you didn't," his father grumbled. "I can't reckon why you did it in the first place—you had a fine situation with that Herr Auer in Nürnberg. You could've made something of yourself, instead of becoming one of those beggar monks! I spent some good money sending you to school, and I thought everything was set. But now I reckon you're just a poor wanderer begging for scraps. If you've come here looking for handouts, you can just . . ."

Lorenz would not let his father finish. "I have not come here looking for scraps, Father, and I'm not a beggar!" The vehemence of Lorenz's reply seemed to check Johannes. He stared at his son as if he had for the first time noticed his presence.

"I'll have you know, father," Lorenz continued with the same fervor, "I have come here under a warrant from Herr Sigismund von Weissenbrücke. I have not come here to beg!"

Johannes grr-umfed. "Some favor," he said acidly, "to be sent by the Marshal to some backwater like this."

Under his father's scorn, Lorenz felt as if he were himself reduced—to a childish diffidence. Sullenly he retorted, "the Marshal did not send me here—I chose to come here. I could have remained in Weissenbrücke or returned to Nürnberg..."

"Then, you should have stayed there or any place else instead of coming here!" Johannes was working himself up to a peevish rant. "I know your kind! Gottfried has told me all about you—your dicks can't poke through your cowls, so you take to wearing breeches with cod pieces, the more easily to do your business. And you come around and stir up the peasant folk to bloody deeds with all sorts of wild talk of freedom and just dealings owed them by their lords. The fools! To think they will be able to force the lords to do anything! *Bundschu! Bundschu!* they cry, like a pack of yapping hounds. They burn down nunneries and castles, thinking they've done something grand—but they'll get it in the end! You mark my words, they'll—you'll all get it!"

"Father, I've not come to do any such thing. Rather..."

But Johannes was not listening. "Well, you'll find you're not the first of them 'preachers' to come here—that whoreson priest, Jäcklein Ecklig, has beaten you to it. Gottfried has tried to rein him in, but he has gathered a whole pack of fools around him—including your sister's husband, that swine-fucking Eitel! *Ach!* The idiots are talking about joining with the peasants down south and away west—they're going to wash their hands in the lords' and princes' blood! Fools! It'll be their own blood they'll wallow in—and, I don't doubt, that'll not be where the bloodletting ends. Sebald and me, we'll have nothing to do with it—nothing to do with it, d'you hear?"

A swirl of emotions confused Lorenz; he felt he had to justify himself to his father—though why, he did not know. Was he not a man now? "Father," he said, "I am opposed to such doings as much as you are. God! Do you think the Marshal would have sent me here to stir up the peasants against him? I came here to hinder it."

Johannes' lips twisted into a sarcastic smile. "Well, then you might as well go back to the Marshal and tell him to make himself ready. You're not going to stop it. No one is going to stop it. The Marshal and the lords have picked the peasants' bones dry and they won't take it anymore. I don't say they're not right; I only say, you can't do nothing about it. They'll rise up and shed a lot of blood, but in the end they'll all be destroyed—and *our* gullets will be slit along with theirs."

In the confusion of his feelings, Lorenz turned to go, without taking leave of his father. It was clear he would make no headway here—his father would oppose him, and his father no doubt still had influence in the village. He would return to Weissenbrücke and there resign his charge. Then, he would go back to Nürnberg or Wittenberg.

His hand took the door latch. But then he heard his father's voice.

The old man tried to speak, then coughed. When he recovered himself, he spoke with a softer timbre.

"Boy," he said. "Hold up!" Lorenz turned. He heard almost a note of regret, in his father's tone. "I'm supposing you'll be needing lodgings," Johannes said, not looking directly at Lorenz. Then, after a pause, "Whatever you've become, you're family. You'll lodge here."

Lorenz nodded. "Thank you, father," he said. Again he turned to go, but his father bade him wait. The old man sounded tired.

"Son," he said, "do what you can. You'd best go talk with Gottfried—but, mind you, treat him with respect! He's not the man he was. Since his woman's died—well, you'll see. Some of the folks hereabouts are even calling him a saint!" Johannes snorted a laugh.

"Who would've thought?" he said.

CHAPTER 8

LORENZ LEFT HIS FATHER'S HOUSE, TOOK his way through the village, paying heed to no one nor anything. He soon found himself in the meadows outside the village, where they used to gather berries. It was still too early for berries; the trees were only just greening. And it was still cold. Would true spring never come?

From the meadows he could see the village church with its tomb yard on the small rise, girdled by the stream. Without hesitation, he betook his way there, though with lingering step.

He remembered where her tomb was, hard by the apse. Her marker was of stone—his father had seen to that.

GERTRUDE LIST
LIEBSTE WEIB
ANNO 1502

He knelt and traced the letters with his finger, as he had done at Heimrad's grave in Weissenbrücke. He thought of a day when he gathered berries in the meadow. And of the branches of the linden tree gently brushing her window.

The sound of a latch, metal grating on metal, startled him. He rose from kneeling to see the door on the north side of the church open slowly. An old man, supporting himself with a stave that looked like a gnarled branch, slowly shuffled out. He was bald. His beard, long and white, fell to below his chest. He was clad in black.

287

The old man turned to close the door, then began to make his way on the path that ran along the north wall and then wound its way about the apse. As he negotiated the turn around the apse, he hesitated, and half turned to go back, as if he had forgotten something. But he halted. He had seen Lorenz. He wavered for a moment in indecision, asquint; and then he slowly hobbled his way toward him.

* * *

Salve, magister! Tibi in his partibus similis rare videtur.

Lorenz smiled to himself. It was indeed Gottfried — but how changed! The pig's eyes were the same, only more tightly screwed for their squinting; but folds of skin hung from the shrunken face. The priest's once mighty girth had withered to gauntness.

Non cognosces me, Pater? Sed mutatus sum nimis a pueritia mea . . .

Et oculi mei infirmi crevunt, the priest said with a chuckle. *Narra mihi — quis es?*

"Lorenz List, your once student," Lorenz said, falling back into German. "How fare you, Father?"

Gottfried at first seemed confused, but then he let out another chuckle. "How I fare is very apparent," he said, passing his hand in a flourish from his head down towards his feet. "I am not the man you would remember. I am much changed — and hopefully not just in this my old ass of a body!"

Gottfried again squinted his eyes at Lorenz. "Maybe if these old eyes could still see, I could tell your looks. I recall you favored your mother, though doubtless that beard of yours obscures the likeness." Gottfried, still squinting, approached closer. "No," he said, "I doubt that, even if these eyes were hale, I would recognize you."

Lorenz smiled. "It has been a score of years or more since we last met, and I was a stripling then," he said.

288

"And without a beard," the old man nodded. Again the eyes searched for recognition. "My God! Johannes' List's boy! It hardly seems that so many years have passed—but that is the way with old age, lad. Time plods with the young; it takes wing with the old. The young hanker for the future the old folks dread."

The priest's smile had been complacent; but then it faded. "Your father's said nothing about your return," he said, his head cocked.

"He did not know of it until today."

"Is that so?" Gottfried eyed him quizzically.

Another pause followed. Gottfried seemed to be struggling with memory. "How long have you been home?" he asked at last.

"I arrived only yesterday."

"And whence came you?"

"Weissenbrücke."

"*Ach!*" Gottfried muttered and took a couple of steps closer to Lorenz. The priest's eyes were scrutinizing, searching. "I had not heard that you have been in Weissenbrücke. I thought you dwelt in—in Erfurt, wasn't it?"

"I have not lived there for some ten winters," Lorenz replied.

"But you have not been in Weissenbrücke all that time." The priest's manner had become wary.

"No," Lorenz replied. "Until this past September, I was in Wittenberg."

Gottfried slowly shook his head. But then his old face quickened and grew hard. "Hmph!" he said. "In Wittenberg? *Ach,* Wittenberg! *That* explains it." Waving his hand as if he were warding off a beggar, Gottfried turned as if to walk away. The priest's manner—so suddenly disdainful, dismissive—vexed Lorenz.

"Explains what?" he shouted after the priest.

Gottfried stopped; he glanced back at Lorenz. He growled. "Explains what I could not at first remember but do now." He turned away again and hobbled a few more steps.

"And what is that?"

Gottfried again halted; but this time he did not turn to face Lorenz. "The other reason why I wouldn't have recognized you," he grunted. "I now remember it—your father telling me that you were a monk. But it's clear you're no monk—at least one no longer."

"No, I am not." Lorenz was now thoroughly piqued at the priest's manner, but he spoke calmly.

Gottfried grasped his stave more firmly—Lorenz wondered if he would turn and cudgel him with it. Instead, the old man again shook his head and snorted. "Then you've told me all I need to know," he said and again commenced his slow retreat.

"No, I haven't—not yet."

Again the priest stopped. He half turned toward Lorenz. "What more have you to say?"

"Much," Lorenz said. "Much that is in your interest and the interest of the folk hereabouts."

"Indeed!" Gottfried snorted. "I have no interest in renegades," he gnarled, and again betook his way.

"That you may not," Lorenz replied. "But it may interest you that I come here with the warrant and at the command of the Marshal."

Gottfried halted abruptly. For a moment he moved not and bowed his head; but as he slowly turned to him, Lorenz saw that an ironic grimace played over the old man's face. "Saving the best for last, eh lad?" Gottfried said, with an icy laugh. And then, half to himself, "The Marshal! I thought this might come." But lifting his eyes to meet Lorenz's, he sneered. "So, when do you move into my parsonage? You won't find it much to your liking."

Lorenz shook his head. "It is not what you think," he said. "I have not come to displace you. But I would rather not talk of these matters here in the open. Where can we speak in private?"

Gottfried looked as if he were studying the grave at his feet. He lay his hand upon the wooden marker. "My house," he said wearily. "That's the only place. I live alone there now; no servant, no one—I admit no one, not even my daughter, now." Then Gottfried cocked his eye at Lorenz and pulled a gelid smile. "But for you I will make an exception, *Herr Magister!* Come, follow me!"

* * *

Gottfried laughed dryly. He leaned forward in his chair, resting his elbows on the table. He lifted his head and looked hard on Lorenz. "No, I think your Luther and those that follow him nothing but a pack of heretics! Just a pack of heretics!"

The priest's house was not as Lorenz remembered it. In Lorenz's childhood, it had been small and comfortable; now, it was small and austere. Most of the furniture and all of the womanly touches that once had graced it were gone. The hearth room was like an oversized monastic cell; it held now only two straight-backed wooden chairs and a small table. Over the hearth, where no fire was burning, hung a crucifix.

"But if there is anything they are right about, it's priests like me."

Lorenz sat in the chair, nearer to the dry hearth. Gottfried glowered at him from behind the table.

"I'll not tell you your motives for coming here. I figure the Marshal can provide you with better than a poor benefice and a ramshackle parsonage—so you're not come here to replace me. I remember you as a good lad, so I conclude that you're not here for self-seeking, whatever lies you'll want to preach. But I'll tell you this—you thought it no hard task to come here and do what you want with that old reprobate, Gottfried!"

He uttered the last words with some vehemence and then fell back in his chair. He closed his eyes and breathed heavily. (Lorenz heard a scratching noise. He spied a small mouse was popping its head jerkily in and out of a hole chewed into the wall where the wood met the stone of the hearth.)

"But maybe since coming back you've been told that Gottfried is a changed man," the priest said slowly and tiredly. "Maybe you've heard that, since his woman's died, he's been doing penance and living like a barefoot friar. Some of these asses' arses might even have called him 'holy' ..."

(How terrible we must look to that mouse—hence, his skittishness, Lorenz thought. There was nothing in that room, nothing...)

" ... and you might yourself have some feeling that that they speak truly, looking at this room here ... "

(Why then did he risk it? His little body had emerged entirely from the hole in the wall, though he did not venture far. Still, he must know he would find no food here, none at all...)

Gottfried laughed and shook his head. "But if this is what it takes, then holiness is mighty easy. Mighty easy!"

The priest's sudden guffaw startled Lorenz and frightened the mouse. It whisked round in a brown flash, back into its hole. Lorenz turned his attention to Gottfried; the old man still leaned back in his chair. His eyes were like two black coals, but they weren't focused on Lorenz but on something else up and behind him. There was nothing of timidity in the demeanor, but he had softened a little. His words put Lorenz in mind of another old man and just such a conversation in a small house in a field, just outside of Weissenbrücke.

"I might have thought so, too," Gottfried continued, after a short pause. "I did think so—but it isn't so. I did not do the one thing that might have counted—I might have given her up, but I didn't. I didn't give her up—God took her from me. And if he hadn't, she'd be here still, and everything would be as it was before. Just as it was before."

Lorenz did not wonder at the words. He understood.

"But that's not the worst of it—not the worst of it by far," Gottfried said, now rubbing his eyes with a bony, blue-veined hand. "The worst of it is—and I've never said this to a breathing soul—I want her now and I would storm heaven itself to get her back. I can't get myself to regret having her! I beg God's forgiveness, but I can't regret it. I can't regret it at all. God! How I miss her!"

A winter silence pervaded the house, without even the crackling of a hearth fire to relieve it. Lorenz glanced left away, but he could no longer see even a hair of the mouse.

"So, you see, whatever you've heard about Gottfried after coming back here is a lie. I'm the same whoreson priest I was when you left. I have offended God, broken my vows, and betrayed my love—*Ach!* I even gave her absolution before she died, bastard that I am! But if you think"—and here Gottfried seemed to waken; he roused himself, leaned forward in his chair, his pig's eyes shrunken to two small sparks for his squinting, staring defiance—"if you think that I'm going to allow you to preach your shit in my church—no, I will not! I can't stop you from bawling out your lies in the streets or the woods, but from my pulpit—never! I may be a whoreson sinner, but I'll not be a heretic!"

Gottfried's manner had not prepared Lorenz for this sudden arousal; but he had come prepared for some such opposition in the village, by Peter's insistence.

"Are you done?"

Gottfried nodded, and then again fell back into his chair.

"Then, this is my reply."

Lorenz pulled from inside his coat a long, leather wallet, opened it, and took from it a folded, sealed document. He stood, walked to where Gottfried sat and handed it to him. The priest eyed him doubtfully, then broke the seal (it bore the Marshal's signet) and read it. When he had done, he folded the paper and handed it back to Lorenz.

"So, our lord the Marshal has handed my pulpit over to a heretic—God! His father would not have done so!"

"And not just the pulpit," Lorenz said. "I shall lead the folk here in true evangelical worship..."

Gottfried laughed. "*Ach!* The Evangel! The Evangel!" he mocked. "D'you know who else blathers that crap? Jäcklein Ecklig, my *cura*—not only a fool but a traitor to his lord—your lord and mine, *Herr Magister!* His Evangel calls for blood sacrifice, real blood sacrifice..."

"And that is, in part, why I have come," Lorenz replied. "God commands obedience to our lords," he began sanctimoniously.

But Gottfried would not let him finish. Pounding the arm of his chair with his fist, he growled, "Is that your Luther's doctrine? Hah! If it is, he has a pretty way of proclaiming it. It is he and no one else who has whetted the peasants' thirst for blood. God! I know what they have suffered—no one better than I. But they will suffer the more because of all your Luther's preaching."

"Not if they heed it, I assure you," Lorenz said.

The priest's eyes were like two small points of wrath. His voice, however, was measured. "Yet, I shall continue my own duties, so says the Marshal," he said stolidly, slapping the paper on the chair's arm.

Lorenz nodded. "Yes, for the time being."

"Yes, for the time being," Gottfried sniffed. "Then, *for the time being*, I shall do my duty. I will defy you, lad. I will defy you!"

The two men had fixed each other in their gaze; they were sparring with their eyes. It was Lorenz who first turned away.

"So be it," he said at last. "But then you will be defying the Marshal, your lord."

Gottfried snorted. "My lord?" he said. "Humph! My lord! It seems I have no lord now but God."

CHAPTER 9

E STARTLED INTO AWAKING.
He had been lying on his bed, in his cell in Wittenberg, in the early hour before Matins awaiting the knock on the door that would call him to prayer; half-slumbering, as he ever did, before the summons, ready to spring up from his hard bed when called. It was dark, so dark that he could not see his hand before his face. He could feel the cross in his hands, on his chest; the carven body of the Crucified, entwined in his fingers.

Then, the knock. His eyes opened on nothingness. Nothing but darkness, the comforting night.

But, with the knock, the door to his cell swung open, slowly, slowly, letting in a brilliance of light. It flooded his cell with painful illumination, chasing shadows from every corner. Everything was revealed, everything. He closed his eyes, but the light burned red and seared his eyeballs. In a panic, he sat bolt upright on his bed and opened his eyes.

But this was not his cell. It was a room that he could not recognize, staring with wide eyes into a paned window of light.

This was not his cell. He was not in Wittenberg. He was in a soft bed, in his father's house, where he had slept as a child. Where he had once slept with the innocence of a child.

He rubbed his eyes and rose from the bed. He poured water from a pitcher into a basin. He laved his face and dried it.

Then he dressed. Kneeling, he prayed. Then he rose and left the room.

It was high morning—he had slept so long that he would not meet his father or his brother. That was just as well. He breakfasted on coarse bread, which he washed down with weak beer. Then he steeled himself for the task he had set for himself that day.

* * *

The courtyard outside the house was empty of people. His father and brother had gone to the fields, with the hands. Spring plowing. He passed into the street, closing the small wicket behind him.

He knew the way. He followed the road out from the village. He met no one; they were at work in the fields. The road led him into a small copse. It was colder under the spreading branches, spiked with baby points of leaf. Passing out of the wood, the road turned sharply to the right. Only a hundred yards further, he came to the bridge spanning the Tiefer Bach.

He hesitated on this side of the stream. Dared he go any farther, dared he cross it? What lay beyond it? Reconciliation? Restoration? Or the old loathing?

He had told his brother to say nothing to her of his homecoming. He would send himself as messenger. He did not want her to come to him. He hoped he could be alone with her; that none would witness their meeting, after so long a separation.

But how would he greet her? How would she meet him? He had been cruel, and he was certain she had felt the lash. She had not written him, not after that last letter.

And what if she had changed? What if she had been molded to him with whom she had become one flesh? Could he stand it? And could he hide his loathing?

He did not want to hurt her. Yet, it could not be avoided, mayhap. If he did not go to her, she would hear of his coming;

she would come to him, perhaps with *him*. If it must be a spurning, it were best done when they were alone.

Still, he nearly turned a craven back to the stream. Another day, could it not wait another day? But a flutter of longing checked his fear.

He took one, irresolute step onto the bridge.

* * *

The path followed the bank of the stream for a short way, then it meandered sinister to climb a small hill. On the hill's crest perched the Moeller house.

Other houses stood along the road, but only a very few. The *Moellerhof* was an outlier of the village, on the stream's left bank. Some folks had said that Conrad Moeller's father had been uppity when he built his house there, apart from the village. But it was said that Theobald Moeller hadn't cared what folks thought—he was a rich enough peasant; rich enough to ignore peasant scorn. His son, Conrad, had been cut from the same cloth, though he was jollier than his father had been and more given to enthusiasms. Theobald Moeller would not have walked two feet, much less two miles, to hear some vagabond preacher like Conrad did. And Conrad's son, Lorenz reflected, was twice the fool his father had been.

Set back from the road, the house was reached by a small path flanked by diminutive conifer bushes. It was a short path, and Lorenz soon found himself looking over the wicket, into the courtyard. No one seemed to be about—but then Eitel and his hands would have gone to the fields; they would not be home until dinner, some three hours away. Yes, there was time enough . . .

The wicket was closed but unlatched. As he pushed it, its hinges cried with a metallic screech. But it was not until the gate closed behind him that, without warning, they sprang at him—two huge, ugly dogs, teeth bared, the fur standing up on the scruff of their necks. They did not lunge at him, but they warned him not to pass farther into the yard.

"Räudig! Hauer! Be still! What is all this barking?"

The voice of a woman came from the direction of the house. He could see the main door stood open and someone standing just inside the portal. He could not see who it was, for the shadow of an overhanging tree — a large oak that shaded the house. But the sound of the voice stirred memory. It was the same voice, though with a fuller, darker timbre.

The command, however, had no effect on the dogs. They continued to worry him with their barking and growling. He dared not move farther into the yard, nor turn his back on them and beat a retreat. He had to wait until they tired or decided to tear him to pieces.

Again the woman's voice, with a note of exasperation — "Be still, you stupid dogs! Can't you hear me? Quiet, I say!"

As she said this, the woman passed out from under the overhanging tree limbs and into the bright day sun.

Dismay and wonder seized him — could it be? He half thought, "no, it could not. She is long dead . . . "

The woman was full of figure, but not fat. Wimpled and modestly dressed as befits a farm wife, she was a handsome woman — and so provoked the memory of her who had been taken from him. But as she drew nearer to him, he saw his fancy had deceived him. The woman's visage, though favoring the mother, bore some resemblance to the father. Two young children followed closely behind her.

"Quiet, I say! Get you gone, I say! Get you gone!"

With their mistress now close behind them, the dogs ceased their clamor and hung their tails between their legs. Though her rebuke seem to inspire them with shame for their canine abandon, they saved face by snarling a valedictory warning as they turned tail and ran back towards the house.

"Forgive us, stranger, for such an inhospitable greeting," the woman said as she raised her eyes to his.

She was smiling, but then a look of confusion, followed by astonishment passed over her face.

He found he was unable to speak.

Confusion, then a look of dawning recognition. The smile faded. Her lips parted, but she said nothing. She lowered her eyes and blushed.

Yes, it was she. Her figure was indeed fuller, her face rounder than he remembered. He glanced down at her hands; they were pudgy and red; they were, he saw, calloused by labor. The children stood close behind her — the boy had dark brown hair; the girl's, the color of barley. He looked into her face; her hazel eyes were again looking up into his, but timidly. With a pang of something like remorse, he understood — she was afraid of him. And he pitied her.

"Don't you remember me?" he said at last.

She nodded.

Though he fought it, he could feel the tears well up in his eyes. All she had ever been to him flooded his memory. He felt again the girlish arms embracing him in his childish sorrow. He pictured her as she had been so many years ago, sprightly and joyful and motherly. The intervening years contracted into a moment. They stood before each other, as they had once been to one another — though, now, she was blushing with what seemed like shame. She had nothing for which she need feel shame.

"Inge," he said. And he held out his hands to her.

The touch of her hands — they were rough and dry, not as he remembered them. But they were her hands, and he rejoiced to hold them again in his.

"Dearest sister," he murmured.

She answered him with a smile through her tears.

299

* * *

It was a warmish spring day. She had a table set out under the spreading oak that shaded the house portal. She had set out bread and cheese and ale. She said she had brewed the ale. He told her it was very good. She had asked him to stay for dinner, but he said he couldn't, not that day.

The children sat with them at table. She had made to send them away, but he forbade it. The elder, the girl, was named Gertrude. She was ten years old. The boy, two years younger than she, was called Conrad. Neither looked much like the father. Her two older sons, Johannes, age 13, and Lorenz, age 15, were with their father in the fields. He pulled from his satchel a sweet bread he had bought at the baker's that morning and fed it to the children. "Lori, you'll spoil them," Inge said. He smiled. For their part, the children seemed well pleased with their uncle.

They fell to talking about the intervening years. Her talk was of the details of housewifery and motherhood. She had lost one child, she told him; it had been a boy. "He was born sickly," she said. She was now expecting a child.

Farming was none too good, she said. It wasn't as if the crops hadn't been good, only that the prices were so low—Eitel, she said, complained about grafters in the cities. Eitel was master of the farm, his father having died some three years back.

"But none of this must seem interesting to you, brother," she said with a self-deprecating smile.

"On the contrary," he said, "I find it most engaging." It was not so much her words but their simplicity. She was his Inge still.

"But you have seen so much—been to such lordly places, like Nürnberg and I don't know where else . . . ." Her eyes widened and a playful expression came over her. "Compared to us you are like a king, brother—King Thrushbeard!" Her laugh was musical.

"King Thrushbeard!" he said. "You then remember our games?"

"I can't forget them — King Thrushbeard, and then there was Briar Rose . . ."

"And the Maiden in the Tower . . ."

"Kings and Queens, and the one you used to like to play, Robber Knight . . ."

"But there was one I didn't like," he said. "I think you remember."

"Yes, I remember it well" — and she laughed. "You were such a little wicked one! But I know now that you were just being a boy."

He wondered at her buoyancy. For their entire conversation, he had asked himself why she did not broach the question. She knew, but yet she said nothing.

"Womenfolk," she said, "don't always know what boys are like — but I was lucky, because I had you to teach me. I try to get my boys to pray, but I don't worry them over it. You can't make 'em girls. They just have different ways."

"Inge," he said, and she must have noticed the altered tone of his voice, for her countenance changed from joyous recollection to mild puzzlement.

After a little hesitance, he continued, "Do you remember one day when you said to me, 'sometimes I think all I want to do is pray?'"

Her eyes warmed to serious wonder. She nodded.

He continued. "I do not know why I feel I must say this to you — but I feel I cannot hide myself from you any longer. I, I, too, once thought all I wanted to do is pray; at least, that is what I told myself. I found I wanted something very different. That is why you see me as you do now. I am no longer what you may have thought I was."

Both were silent for a few moments. Then she spoke.

"Lori," she said. The mood of her voice was soft and caressing, but she blushed. "Yes, I did wonder, but not enough to ask you. You will tell me, if you wish—but it is well if you do not want to tell me. I will not ask you."

"I cannot tell you, dearest sister," he said. He felt his love for her stirring strongly. "But I must ask you—can you trust me, that I had good reasons for it? I cannot bear the thought that you would think ill of me."

How her eyes bespoke compassion, tender compassion. "I do not feel that way about you, Lori," she said. "I know I can't understand; I am only a simple *Hausfrau*. I am happy—yes, just happy—that you have come back to me, dearest brother."

THE SACRIFICE

CHAPTER 1

THE SUN WAS ALREADY HIGH IN THE
east when he awoke. He had dreamed that his father,
wrathful glaring, had stood over his bed, commanding
him to shake off slumber. It was already late—the pigs needed
feeding; and then there was school and Gottfried! "Don't you
want to be a great man?" his father mocked. "You can't if you
tell your beads all the day! The Marshal can't help you here,
lad! I'll thrash you to within an inch of your life if you don't
take your hands off the lass ..."

He started up in his bed. My God, it *was* late! They must
have gone to the fields long ago—but his father; why was he
still here? He turned to where his father had stood—but saw
no one. He was alone. Then, after rubbing his eyes, he laughed.
It had been only a dream.

He looked about the room. Naught had changed in it since
he was a boy. No wonder he dreamed such dreams, sleeping
in that room! He stood, yawned, and then made the bed. He
had not lost all monastic discipline.

He dressed himself in leisurely fashion—for he had really
nowhere to go, nothing important to do, that day. As he poured
water from a pitcher into the basin, he thought about how
he would pass the day. The water was cold and bracing; he
shivered as he laved his face and neck. It was only when he
had dried himself and hung the towel on the rack, that he

noticed it—someone had changed the basin! The old basin had been chipped along the rim and gray, but this one was flawless and white. It was, moreover, just like the basin in his room at *Auerhaus* in Nürnberg. And the pitcher—painted with depictions of birds on a linden branch—it too was the exact image of the pitcher he used in his room in Nürnberg.

Who had brought them here, he wondered?

He passed out of his room and, again, he was puzzled. The hallway that morning looked strangely elongated; the verge of the stairway that climbed down into the hearth room seemed very far away. To left and right he passed closed doors—far more in number than he remembered—until he came, on his right, to the door of the room, whose window the linden leaves gently brushed. It stood ajar.

All the other doors were fast shut; this one, alone, stood open, though only barely, like lips tempting to a kiss. Ever since his return to his father's house, he had wanted to enter this room; but he dared not. His father himself never entered it, nor did anyone else. It had remained unchanged, it was said, since the day *she* died.

But the open door called him in. Hesitantly, he pushed on it and crossed the threshold.

It was just as he remembered it.

The crucifix above the bed.

The wash basin to the right of the bed.

The chest of drawers directly across from the bed.

Curtains were pulled across the window on the far side of the room. Closing the door behind him, he walked over to draw them aside. Bright light streamed into the room, hurting his eyes.

He heard strange noises coming from the courtyard below, the rumbling of human voices. He could not see at first what was below, for the brightness of the light. Then, as if a cloud had passed over the sun, the light softened, and he could see.

306

A horde of peasants armed with halberds, old longswords, axes, and fowling pieces, some carrying pitchforks, clamored in the courtyard. Their number stretched beyond the courtyard into the road. They had an antic manner, and he knew that they were preparing themselves for war.

At first the sight of the peasant host frightened him. But then, its spirit began to infect him. It was as when he had passed into the wood at Lenzgrab and bathed himself in the mere. The spirit of his Folk! They sang songs of vengeance and bloodletting; of freedom and the planting of a new age. A longing to join them, to march shoulder to shoulder with them, began to flicker in his soul; and biting into his dryness, it set his heart afire...

But then he heard a woman's voice.

As he turned toward the bed, the room darkened — as if evening suddenly had fallen. The bed, however, was surrounded by a phosphorescence of light, so that he could see who lay in it. At first he did not recognize her. Fair she was. Her rich, dark hair fell over her naked shoulders — for naked she was, though the coverlet she had pulled over her young, round breasts. Her white arms lay on the coverlet.

She spoke his name again — and as she did so, he recognized her.

"Pray, Lorenz," she said, "draw that curtain, and come to me! What we would do is best done in the dark."

He could still hear the clamor from outside. He turned his eyes to the window, where the room was light. Irresolute, he turned to her again.

"Draw the curtain! We will not hear them, and then we can play! We will make good sport together."

"But you refused me, at Pillenreuth," he said.

"Silly boy!" she said, and laughed wantonly. "Don't you know when a woman is teasing you? I was only stoking the fire . . ."

Lorenz smiled. "I suppose I was too long a monk," he said.

307

"You named me there—do you remember?" she said. "Come to me, and name me again. We will make good sport together."

He felt the tug of the peasant horde outside, but the allure of her was greater. He could not have both. With slow step, he approached the bed.

How beautiful she was! The monastery had not dimmed her loveliness. She seemed as young as when first he lay with her. He reached out his hand to touch her cheek; as he did so, she smiled.

But the smile was wanton. As if he had touched a fiery surface, he whipped back his hand. He stepped backwards. He could not do this thing.

"Name me, name me again!" she laughed. "Name me! I will pleasure you! Call me the name by which you will be mine!"

How could he violate so sacred a thing? He longed to, but desire had to strive with compunction. He could not do this thing—not to her.

It took his entire resolve; longing for her engulfed him; but fear and reverence goaded him from within. "I will not call you that," he said at last. "You are Agnes. Only Agnes!"

He turned toward the window—but a blinding light streamed in through it, forcing him back toward the bed. He reached out a hand to steady himself, and touched something cold and clammy. It lay, stretched out where she had lain. Fear and horror drove him toward the doorway. He ran toward it, opened it and plunged through it into the darkness waiting for him without.

* * *

When he awoke, he was lying in his bed, in his own room. Through the window, the sky shone gray with early morning light. It must be half-past terce, he thought.

He went to the window, opened it, and breathed in the morning air. It smelt of rain. And as if in confirmation of this surmise, he heard, in the distance, the rumbling of thunder.

308

Chapter 1

It came from the west, that thunder—just as would come the storm that would sweep them all away. Where injustice held sway, violence would spawn, and terror, with the loss of all one loves and holds dear. It was this that held him back (for was not their cause just?) and only this. Or was it?

He remembered his dream and pondered.

CHAPTER 2

H E WAS AT FIRST DISPOSED TO DESPISE
Jäcklein Ecklig. The priest was small of stature and
had a sickly hue. The cheeks of the man's ferret-like
face (recalling for him Melanchthon's) were pock marked. From
his chin sprouted a thin beard, of the same color as the strands
of hair that fell pale red to his shoulders. His lips were set in
a kind of imbecile smile that Lorenz found unsettling.

Jäcklein Ecklig was the type of priest that Lorenz and his
party so deplored but yet pitied. Without Latin, they muttered
the Mass like an incantation to call down Mammon. (They
were so poor they could scarcely provide a living for themselves.) Ignorant, they infected the people with superstition,
all the easier to draw money from them by. Without regard to
their vows, they more often than not kept a woman and, soon,
children. For all this, folk scorned them but shrugged their
shoulders: can any man but a saint live without a woman?

Priests like Ecklig were coarse in the extreme. Their conversation wallowed in excrement and lewdness. Ecklig himself
was fond of ribald jests; and he would utter them before men
and women both, even children. His own bastard—a filthy
brat of some eight years—was conversant beyond his years
in carnal lore. The child's mother, a pale-faced, yellow-haired
drudge—thin, flat-chested, and ugly—took no charge of the
boy but let him run about wild.

It was a wonder, then, that Jäcklein could draw such a following among the peasants. Lorenz, hearing only report of the man, could scarcely credit it. It was only when, at last, he heard Ecklig address a crowd that he understood.

For Jäcklein Ecklig, though in the coarsest peasant way, was eloquent. Banned by Gottfried from the pulpit, Jäcklein had taken to the streets, or the recesses of the woods, to preach his gospel. His burning words stoked the indignation smoldering in the peasants' hearts into a small conflagration. Not all the peasants heeded him, but a growing number did. Ecklig knew how to speak to these people, his Folk.

"How long will ye spread your legs for the lords and their flesh peddlers, the foul, fuckin' priests? They rob ye of your honor and then make ye pay the fee for it! Time was when decent men paid the whore her wage . . .

" . . . the forest was yours to hunt whatever ye damn well pleased. Ye could fish the streams to feed your families — no more! Even the conies is kept for their lordships. They can't even spare ye one wee rabbit! Our Lord God gave every man the birds of the air, the fishes of the streams, and the beasts of the field for their provender — where do the lords get off taking all for themselves what God has given to all? . . .

" . . . and they seize your cattle, calling it *holy tithes*. When one of ye dies, the lord takes the best of your boves, as a 'death tax'! As if they're not already taxing ye to death! And they work ye like beasts, building their roads, plowing their fields, while your own lands go untilled, and your children starve for lack of bread . . .

" . . . And where be the woods, that was owned by all? Our grandfathers and our fathers could gather wood in the commons — and not just for fires but to build them houses and barns. This wood now only goes to warm the manors and castles of their all-mighty highnesses, while our folk shiver in their huts and our children die of cold . . .

" . . . And don't I know it — don't I? Behind the lords are the priests. Nay, the priests stand over the lords and clap a dance and song for them! The lords dance the jig — don't I know it? Ain't I one of those whoreson man-fuckers? Or I was, until the Almighty saved me by the Holy Evangel. The priests feign that they hold salvation in their hands — and make ye pay them dear for it! Your children eat gruel so that the priests can scarf up capons and wax drunken on wine. Your wives' dugs hang to their bellies without milk to feed the bairns! The children cry, but the priests laugh — laugh at ye fools. Laugh, laugh, laugh at ye . . .

" . . . And ye are free men — free sons of the king! It is the humble that be his heirs, not the proud and lofty! Christ died to save ye from sin and slavery — and knavery! Ye need not obey the proud priests, the bishops, and that antichrist, the pope! Ye are all priests and kings and popes! If they rule over you, 'tis only by your sufferance! If they no longer serve ye; if they play the tyrant to ye, ye can pull them from their thrones. But I'd say, do more than that! Overturn the thrones even if it means bathing the earth in blood! . . .

"*Ach!* Do I not see that some of ye peasants are fat and well fed? Well do I know it — but do ye well dressed, ermine-lined peasant asses not see that where poor folk are now, ye soon will be? With the help of priests and the accursed race of *lawyers*, the lords write laws ye cannot read and can never know, to trip ye up when ye dare, peaceful-wise, to claim your rights ....

" . . . don't ye see our brothers in the south and west, in the Schwarzwald, in Schwaben, in Schwyz casting it all off? The lads are up! They are up, ye Frankish sluggards! They are bringing all this devil's work to light — the light of burning castles and cloisters! Our brothers are marching here to us and calling on us — yes, us! — to play the man! Will ye join them? Or will ye play the whore for this devil's spawn forever? It's bad enough to be fucked by a man — but by a gelding too? Light a fire, brothers! Light a fire to cleanse the earth of this sin!"

* * *

Lorenz knew he could not preach like Ecklig. Though born a peasant, his years in Nürnberg, the university, and the cloister had gentled him. Nor could he speak with such ease as the peasant priest. Ecklig was a born orator, while Lorenz was more of a plodding scholar. When he wrote his sermons, he could hit a note of grandeur; but he soon found it was not the sort of eloquence that readily spoke to the peasant heart. Gottfried, with his rough-hewn, work-a-day, moralizing and saint-mongering had the greater appeal among the not-insignificant number of peasants who continued to hear Mass at the parish church—among whom were his father, Sebald, and Inge.

Inge, however, would attend the Evangelical service Lorenz led, and listen intently to his sermons. She would ask questions of him afterwards, though, he could see, his explanations left her confused. Eitel, too, frequented the Evangelical service, but it was obvious he had little interest in what his brother-in-law had to say about sin, redemption, and the hope of eternal life. For Eitel was a deep-dyed Ecklig man.

As were most of those peasants who had abandoned the Mass. Some few attended the Evangelical service, but most scurried off to hear Jäcklein declaim in the forest. Lorenz's tactic was not to attack Ecklig directly but to prepare the ground with the preaching of the Pure Word.

"My brothers, look not to salvation in this life! The world belongs to the Devil, and we can't overthrow his kingdom. Not in a day, nor in a year, nor over centuries. God has chosen his elect, but not to free them from the sorrows and hardships of life. Indeed, for who can overcome death, the greatest of sorrows and hardships? And if we cannot overcome death, can we overcome all suffering? Christ himself hung on the cross, he accepted the cross, to give us Paradise. But he had not Paradise as he hung broken and bloody. Only in his Resurrection—which we will celebrate in little more than a fortnight—did he attain victory. A victory he will grant us if we have the faith that will carry the cross to the end.

" . . . Christ has set us free by his voluntary bondage. He has given his life by his voluntary death. Freedom and life, brethren! We hear much talk of freedom—but from what have we been freed? From sin, yes! From the tyranny the priests and popes have laid on us, yes! They would have us work for our salvation—in part by paying them tithes and by receiving, as they say, Christ from their very hands. But, if we are baptized, we all, all we Christian folk, hold God in our hands! We are all priests! But as priests, we are the servants of all . . .

"Do not seek freedom in this life, just like Christ didn't seek it when he walked the earth. Do not hope to be delivered from suffering or even injustice—for Christ was the victim of injustice and delivered himself over to suffering. A kingdom is not to be won in this world; it has been given to us . . . "

Only a little over a year ago, such talk was revolutionary. But it had come to seem, to Lorenz, as dry and as lifeless as the scholastic logic-chopping he had cast aside with loathing at the university. What once he thought the well-spring of life was now a dry cistern. No, that was not the right analogy. No, for though the words no longer stirred the heart, they hid, like a marble sepulcher, a horror within. But this horror was not a rotting corpse; nor was it a living thing. *It* was a coiling terror, eyeless and breathless, but resolute and intent. *It* lured him on to open the tomb, pull back the shroud, and fix *It* in his gaze—like Moses longed to do on Sinai. *Ostende mihi gloriam tuam.*

Ecklig's words resonated with this terror. They were probing and deep rooting into the mold. Lorenz's were like last autumn's leaves, sere and rotting, covering the life that stirred in the soil that lay beneath.

CHAPTER 3

THOUGH HE HAD ABANDONED SO MUCH else, Lorenz still kept Lent. Thus he approved Inge's resolve to forestall a family celebration of his return until Easter. She had been somewhat shamefaced when she told him this, but he assured her he did not take it amiss.

But though it was Lent, Lorenz did not forgo the pleasure of visiting his sister as frequently as he may. To his joy, he found she was as she had been in youth—except that she had mellowed and attained greater balance. And, if it were possible, her love was even less self-regarding than it had been when she was a girl. If any could win heaven by works, it was his sister, Inge.

Lorenz marveled at Inge's patience with their father. Johannes' changes of mood had grown the more fickle with age. He could be kind to Lorenz, but suddenly cutting and cruel—so much so that Lorenz a few times resolved to leave his father's house. Inge the old man seemed to take for granted. She would come with her children to the house, tend to her father, drawing his beer for him or cooking some dish he liked. But no word of thanks would she receive. Instead, she at times had to endure Johannes' sneers at her husband. He would say, "Why is that husband of yours not with you today? Working? Hah! Probably slinking about the tavern." Or, "I hear tell that your husband's affairs are none too good. Just like a Moeller! Neglecting his fields and livestock to run after

315

wandering monks who can't keep their dicks in their skirts!"

Once, though, Inge did lose patience with her father. It was upon a warmish afternoon (rare for that time of year), on a Sunday; following dinner, they had moved outside to enjoy the light of the sun. Eitel, who had eaten with them, had just left, saying he had some business to attend to. As the gate to the *Hof* closed behind Eitel, Johannes shook his head and snorted. "I marvel, daughter," he said, "that you give your husband such liberty. What *business* has he to attend to on a Sunday? A deft bit of plowing, no doubt, of some other man's acre!" And Johannes laughed, seemingly well pleased with his jest.

But Inge reddened; her eyes set hard. (More than ever, in her looks she favored her father.) Her sudden swing of mood did not go unnoticed; Johannes' laughter ended abruptly. Half smiling, he said, "what ails you, daughter? Have my words touched a sore spot? Have they laid bare a wound?"

She did not answer immediately; and when finally she did speak, her tone was calm, bitter cold. "You may think it a small matter, father," she said, "to insult my husband. But this jest doesn't just drag him but your daughter, too, through the mire. You would make me a dishonored woman just to enjoy throwing scorn on my husband, who doesn't deserve it. But think—by dishonoring me, you dishonor your grandchildren, and even yourself."

Lorenz expected his father to erupt in anger at this impertinence. But, he didn't. Instead, Johannes' eyes evinced confusion; he sucked in his lips and then nodded. At last, "daughter, I beg pardon," he muttered, and took a long draw from his great stein.

* * *

But Lorenz soon learned that, though his sister would defend her husband if forced to it, she suffered great anxiety on his account.

He had spoken little with Eitel since returning to the village — until the Sunday before *Laetare*, when he and Sebald
came to supper at *Moellerhaus*, following the morning service.

"Father is not with you?" Inge asked them at her greeting.
There was sadness and disappointment in her voice.

"*Ach*, sister," Sebald replied. "You know it is for the best!"

When she had left them alone, Sebald whispered to Lorenz.
"Poor Inge, she is always so disquieted because of Father. But
she knows 'tisn't good when he and Eitel share the board. They
get to drinking and then bickering, like two cocks in a cage.
'Tis better this way."

Sebald smiled and gave Lorenz an arch look. "But you better
prepare yourself," he said.

It wasn't until shortly before they were to sit down to eat
that Eitel entered the house, with his two eldest sons, Lorenz
and Johannes. Eitel had the same fatuous look on his face
that Lorenz remembered; he was fuller in girth, however, and
no longer pimply. His red hair had receded back across his
forehead. His face was bloated and somewhat livid. His eyes,
under pale eyelashes, were a watery blue.

As he entered the house, he cried out, "Wife! Is our supper
ready?" Lorenz noticed that the man spoke with almost the
same piping treble of the boy. Eitel then turned and nodded
to Sebald and Lorenz. "Brothers," he said with a sneer. "Ye're
welcome to our table." He shouted again, "wife, call me when
all is ready," and went outside.

The two brothers did not follow their father, and Lorenz
for the first time had a chance to observe them up close. The
elder, his namesake, favored Inge in looks, while the younger,
Johannes, took after Eitel. Yet, it was not the younger Lorenz
who graciously greeted the uncles, but Johannes. The elder
stood aloof, while in the younger (a rather ugly boy) Lorenz
perceived the spirit and grace of his sister. Lorenz wished he

could close his eyes and just listen to his nephew Johannes — to look at him disposed him to dislike; but to hear him kindled affection. The effect was a kind of vertigo of feeling.

Eitel for a time said little at table; Lorenz, Sebald, and Inge (who served the menfolk) carried on the conversation. Whenever, it seemed, she would sit down, Eitel would demand something of her. The man's manner toward his sister irked Lorenz — and, he perceived, Sebald as well. His brother, Lorenz saw, strove to be blithe, but his eyes kindled fire. ("Yes, he is very much like Father," Lorenz thought.) At last, when Eitel demanded the beer pitcher be refilled, Sebald interposed: "Sit, sister," he said, "I am sure your Gertrude would wish to do it, so her mother can rest." The ten-year old Gertrude looked to her mother, then (with a flash of fear) to her father. Eitel was peeved; but he did not gainsay his brother-in-law. Instead, he grunted for Gertrude to go.

This was not the last time Gertrude refilled the pitcher. All partook freely of the beer, but Eitel more than anyone else. And as he drank, the more talkative he grew. He began to tell tales of folk in the village — and laughed at the foibles he related. The young Lorenz listened with a scant smile to his father's stories — and, after a time, it seemed Eitel was speaking to no one else but the boy. Eitel's stories soon turned ribald — and when Inge interposed to send the children from the table, he lashed out at her. "*Ach*, leave them be, wife," he snarled. "They must know what manner of neighbors they live among!"

Cup followed cup, and Eitel was slurring his speech.

" . . . that fool of an Ulrich! Taking a young wench like that for a wife — he should have known she'd cuckold him. But she'd been carrying on with that young hand of theirs for a twelvemonth before he'd figured it out: and I know he has, though he won't fess up to it. But no matter how he tries, he can't hide the horns. Why, just the other day. . . "

Chapter 3

Sebald rose from the table. Eitel stopped short in his story. "What ails you, kinsman?" he said.

"Nothing ails me," Sebald said, like a man reining himself in. "But I remembered me—I had promised Father to do a task before sunset, and if I am to do it, I must go."

Eitel's eyes stared out as if through a mist. He smiled stupidly. "Must be a pressing matter indeed if it takes ye from such good drink and fellowship," he said. "But if ye must—Lorenz, I am sure, can stay. Eh, cousin?"

Lorenz felt the fool's eyes fixed on him. He longed to be gone, but he looked first to Inge. Her countenance was pale and her eyes cast down. He felt deep pity for her. "Perhaps if I go," he thought, "Eitel will leave her in peace."

"No, brother," he said, turning to Eitel. "I had best go with Sebald. He may need a hand . . . "

A look of cruelty distorted Eitel's coarse features. He laughed. "Your brother need a hand?" he said, with an edge of mockery. "What? A priestling help a peasant? 'Twould be a new thing, to my ken."

"Husband!"

Inge's voice rang with a tone Lorenz had never heard in it before. Her eyes flashed with something like anger at her husband.

"Lorenz is my brother and our guest," she said. "Such language—it has never been used toward a guest in our house!"

It was as if he had been struck in the face. Eitel seemed confused, as if he did not know what hit him. But when it seemed his slow mind at last understood, his face turned livid. He half rose from his chair. "Shut up, woman!" he shouted. "*Such language?* Why, we've never had such a guest at our table! I didn't want him here—'twas ye that wanted it!"

"What's he come back here for? Hah, don't I know? He's a fuckin' marshal's man, working against his own folk. All the shit he spews—nothing but heaven, nothing about how his own are suffering—us, his kinsmen! He don't care, because the Marshal pays him well, I don't doubt. He's no better than that whore-ruttin' Gottfried, except he pretends he ain't the old church—but he'll flay our hides like they've done!"

"Husband, I pray you—be silent!" Inge's tone was calm, but her face was pale—with anger or with fear, Lorenz could not say.

"No, I'll not be silent!" Eitel spluttered. "This is my table, my house, and ye're my wife, who should stand with her husband, not against him like some bitch of a whore!"

Eitel would have said more, but Inge rose from her seat. Tears stood in her eyes, but she was not weeping. There was no bending in her mien; her shoulders were thrown back. Her eyes were fixed on her husband's. "You will not speak so to me," she said, with a proud but even confidence. Lorenz had rarely seen such dignity, even among the rich women of Nürnberg. "I am not one of your chattels! I am your...."

"What ye are," Eitel screamed, "is a bitch of a whore! A bitch of a whore!" And he rose from his chair.

It all happened in what seemed an instant. Eitel had raised his mug to throw at her, but he cried out with pain. The mug fell to the floor, and broke. Sebald had grabbed Eitel's wrist with one hand and had him by the collar with the other. The drunken man struggled and spat in the other's face; Sebald thrust him from himself, and Eitel fell backwards, over his chair, and sprawled on the floor. He lay there stunned for a moment, but then rose—he held a knife is his left hand. Sebald grabbed that hand, and with a moan, the knife clattered on the wood floor. Sebald slammed Eitel against the wall and with his free hand grabbed his neck. Eitel's eyes bulged with terror. He gurgled and hacked. The boys, Lorenz and Johannes, sat stock still with terror. Gertrude wept uncontrollably.

"You will grovel before her, dog! Grovel before her! Beg her forgiveness—or she'll soon be widow!"

Eitel grabbed at Sebald's hands, both of which now throttled him. Lorenz rose to stop his brother, but Inge was already upon the struggling men. "Sebald, brother!" she cried with fear and horror. "Sebald! Leave him be, I beg you! For me—he's my husband! Let him be!"

Sebald relaxed his hold, and Eitel collapsed at his feet, breathing heavily and hacking. But for the coughing and Gertrude's weeping, the room was silent.

When at last Eitel recovered himself, he sat on the floor, his back against the wall, and stared up at Inge, who the while had been watching him. He snarled; his voice was hoarse. "You're a bitch and a whore!" he said.

Lorenz feared that Sebald would again lunge at the man. He took his brother by the shoulder, to lead him away, but Sebald shook him off. "Fear not, Lorenz," he said. "I will not dirty my hands with that mess of shit again. But I say this," and he fixed his eyes on Eitel, "if I ever hear that he has raised his hand to my sister or I see aught of a bruise on her fair skin, I will change my mind. He will not live to see the morn. I swear it before God and the saints!"

A look as of fear passed over Eitel's freckled face, but then his lips twisted sardonically. "I hear ye, kinsman," he croaked. "I'll leave the bitch alone—nay, don't start at me! You'll sorrow your dear sister," he sneered.

"No, ye needn't fear for your sister," Eitel continued, hoarsely. "It's for yourself ye should fear. Remember this, that it has been me that has been staying the hand of the Brethren against ye and your old man. Now, no more! Nothing will stand between ye and them. Ye'll soon need to make your choice between us and our enemies."

Eitel pushed himself up painfully. "I'll not stay any longer among ye," he said. He stood, swayed on his feet for a moment, and then stumbled toward the door. He opened it, and stood looking at them all and breathing heavily.

"Lorenz, Hans—go ye with your father?"

But the boys did not move. It was if they were fixed to their chairs.

"*Ach!* You've turned even my boys against me," he said, coughing. "To hell with ye all!" Eitel spat into the room and went out, slamming the door behind him.

Inge merely stood stock still and stared at the door. Lorenz laid his hand gently on her shoulder. "Inge," he said.

But she interrupted him. "He is gone," she said, without sorrow and without anger, it seemed. "He has gone to them.

"And now we're all lost," she said.

CHAPTER 4

THAT NIGHT, LORENZ SPOKE LONG WITH his brother. Sebald felt remorse for his treatment of Eitel, though, he said, "'twould have been better had I killed him. He has always treated Inge ill—though, until today, I think, he has not raised a hand to her."

"Really," Lorenz said, "I would have thought . . ."

Sebald smiled. "Yes, so would anyone who did not know Inge well. Most judge her as meek, thinking that means she is weak, too. But they don't reckon that her father is Johannes List." Sebald smiled with fond recollection. "She has imbibed much of his spirit, I trow.

"You see, brother, Eitel is a weak man—oh, he is a hard enough worker and tends his farm well. But he is given to drunkenness and whoring. He is often in ill humor with Inge—but, he fears her spirit. Only drink emboldens him, and when he is in his cups, she lets him be. Today was different."

Indeed it was, Lorenz thought. And the difference was his presence—that of the brother she loved and for whose honor she would tempt the violence of her husband. And how he had neglected her these many years.

"Eitel," Sebald continued, "has been cozened by the violent peasants—they call themselves the 'Christian Brotherhood.' Since the summer, they have been meeting in the forest with that worthless Jäcklein Ecklig, hatching plots. By themselves, they are of no account; but I hear they have been in contact with the peasants in the south — which is why they have gone from trying to convince those of us who haven't gone along with them to threatening us if we don't."

"Threatening you, how?"

"Those of us as won't join them, they give a choice: join, or have your property set afire. It hasn't happened here, yet; but I hear that in the south they drive in a stake on a man's property as a final warning. Many a good man has joined their ranks out of sheer fear of losing all he owns — maybe even his life."

Sebald paused, as if contemplating his own words. A sad smile played about his lips.

"It seems Father and I have Eitel to thank for the Brethren's ignoring of us. Inge had told me that she had gotten Eitel to swear that he would have nothing to do with them — but oaths mean nothing to that fool. It seems he has been meeting with them all along — and because of me, he will turn them against us. I may now have no other choice."

"No other choice?"

"But to join them," Sebald said simply. "How else am I going to save our property, and Father? Though it won't save us in the end. The princes won't let us prevail.

"Inge is right, we are all lost now," Sebald said.

* * *

The incident with Eitel and what Sebald told him chilled Lorenz to the core. A revolution, relentless and cruel — a response, yes, to relentless cruelty, but for all that, dreadful still — had sprung up from the mold of the forests, the rivers, meres, and wells, the ancient haunts of the Folk. It was as if something that had long lain asleep, charmed into oblivion by the ringing of bells and the chanting of prayers, had been stirred to wakening. The horror of the days when the gods ruled the earth.

It had never been fully asleep—that Lorenz knew well. There had ever been those who had consulted witches to stir the ancient powers from deep within the earth. And well he remembered Bruder Thaddeus. But these had been as flickers of light on a mere; faded memories from an age long since passed. What was stirring now was different; or, rather, it was the fulfillment of the premonitions of terror that all his life had danced on the edge of consciousness.

And the Gospel he preached seemed powerless against it. How little men cared for the things of God! Their thought was ever on the chances of this life. What does it matter, he had told them, if you gain the wealth of princes but lose your soul in the bargain? Did they not know that he who resists the prince resists God? Did they not wish to die with Christ, to suffer for justice's sake, rather than do injustice? The unjust prince, he had declaimed, will be judged of God, who alone has the right of judgment and of rectifying wrong. It is the Christian's task only to take up his cross, as his Lord did, and suffer.

Such words had little effect on his neighbors, he saw. And well he knew why—they had long felt the lash; they longed for revenge. But this was not all, he knew. This was not all. They not only smarted under the strokes, but dreamed. Their thoughts were not all of blood and spoliation; they had conceived of a new heaven and a new earth, where the peasant could sit under his spreading shade tree and enjoy the fruits of his labor. Lord and priest would no more tear from the hand what, in sweat, in blood, it had labored for; for all would be brothers in Christ, and servants one of another.

Yet, Lorenz knew the power and relentlessness of the peasant's foes—the Church and the princes. The peasants may have driven them back for the nonce—with, alas, much bloodshed, rapine, and destruction. But the hand bedecked with rings, clasping the crosier, could not be stayed for long. The powers had, only for the moment, been blindsided. When at last they joined together—and they would join, Catholic prelate and Evangelical prince—they would trample on the peasants in the onrush of their implacable wrath. No mercy. They would not tempt such an uprising ever again.

And what were his feeble words against such forces, on both sides? Feeble words! Only a few years since these *feeble words* had stirred Germany to her depths. They, like sparks in dry straw, had kindled a conflagration. Now they seemed like dead embers, cold and black. There was no life in them—not for his people, the Folk. Not for himself.

* * *

"'Twould have been better had you throttled the bastard!" Johannes List was in his cups and raging—though his eyes sparkled with something like mirth. "God! I would that I had never given her in marriage to the swine!"

Lorenz had advised his brother to keep the incident with Eitel secret from their father—"It would do little good for him to know of it," he had said. But Sebald's resolve was stony. "No," he said, "Father should know what manner of husband he has given his daughter—and what danger may threaten all of us."

Sebald, at least, Lorenz thought, should wait to find a time when his father wasn't drinking. But such times were rare, save in early morning—and then, when work was awaiting, Johannes would not tolerate conversation. "And it doesn't matter if Father is somewhat drunk," Sebald added. "He will recall it all the next day and, sober, give thought to it."

That night, however, though Johannes wasn't drunk, he wasn't entirely sober, either. "*Ach!* I am sure I would have killed him if I was there," he bellowed. "I never lifted a hand to your mother, God rest her," and, for a moment, Johannes grew wistful. "And she—she is the spit of your mother! The very spit!"

Johannes, however, dismissed Eitel's threats. "The *Christian*

326

Brotherhood!" he snorted. "I know who they're made up of—Balthas Hecht and his tavern tipplers. The cottagers and some middling farmers and tenants. Eitel is the only one of the bigger farmers fool enough to join ranks with them. They wouldn't have the balls to do anything to us—the whoreson geldings!"

But Sebald slowly shook his head. "If 'twas only them, you'd be right. But it's not, not anymore. Others from outside are coming in, connected with the uprisings toward the south."

Johannes' mirth seemed to dissipate at these words. With knit brows, but glazed-over eyes, he focused on Sebald. "And how do you know that, boy?" he said.

"I know it," Sebald replied with decision. "I keep my eyes and ears open. I see and hear things."

Lorenz could not help marveling at this brother of his. He was a man of strong spirit and resolve—probably something of what their father must have been in his youth, before sorrow had become his daily bread and disappointment the cup he had drained to the dregs.

Compared to the man his brother was, Lorenz felt like a mere boy.

CHAPTER 5

IN THE DAYS FOLLOWING THE INCIDENT with Eitel, Lorenz noted a marked change in the villagers' attitude toward him. He had known that he had failed to move them with his preaching, but he had felt no hostility from them. At the worst he figured they laughed at him behind his back—that he was the butt of many of their jokes. Yet, they had extended him kindnesses, as folks often will to one who affords them pleasure, even if they despise him.

But now, whatever he had felt of good humor had given way to a sullenness. It was as if folks were avoiding him. They would speak to him, but only with the fewest of words, and acted as if they wished soon to make their escape from him. Even Balthas Hecht now treated him with the barest civility when he went to drink in the tavern.

"It is Eitel's doing," Sebald said. "This is the womanish way he takes his revenge."

"Have you experienced aught of it?" Lorenz asked him.

Sebald laughed. "No, not the shunning or the dark looks," he said. "You see, most of the folk around here like me a heap better than they like Eitel. And they've always had a respect for Father. But, I fear, not much longer."

Sebald's countenance darkened.

He grimaced and sighed. "Just this morning," he said, "I was visited by three of our neighbors . . . "

"Who were they?"

Sebald shook his head. "I'd rather not say," he muttered. "But I can tell you, they didn't like the task they were set to."

Sebald paused, breathed deeply, then continued.

"They came, they said, by the command of the Christian Brotherhood. The Brethren, they said, have till now ignored our refusal to join them. They said they wouldn't bear with it any longer."

Sebald laughed. "You should've seen them, Lorenz! They've been honest neighbors, but none too smart. They never in their lives had any thought save for getting in a good harvest and wasting it at the tavern. They threatened me, but with shuffles and shaking. God! What fools they made of themselves!"

"But they threatened you. With what?"

"They told me to join the Brotherhood. And if I didn't, they said, Father and me would pay. 'There's no room around here,' they said, 'for folk that won't stick with their kind.'"

"And you said . . . "

"I said nothing," Sebald said, simply. "You see, Lorenz, I didn't know what to say. I don't know what to say now."

Lorenz thought he could detect in his brother's strong features the faintest outlines of worry.

"But I reckon I shall have to say something soon," Sebald said.

* * *

Two days later, Lorenz was following a path into the woods that lay to the south of the village. He remembered the path well—it was one he and his mother had followed, long ago, to go a berry gathering. He followed it today because he could not bear to pass along the village's main street. He did not want to meet any of his neighbors.

He had no clear destination in mind. He knew only that he wished to be away from the village and alone. To think and to consider. To deliberate—what? He did not know. He could see that his sojourn in his home village had been a failure, and worse than a failure. Hadn't he been the cause of Eitel and Sebald's altercation? If he hadn't been here, where it was clear he no longer belonged, Eitel had not have stung Inge to indignation, and all would not have fallen out as it did. And now his father and Sebald were threatened with "there's no room around here for folk that won't stick with their kind."

Lorenz wondered what Sebald would do. Would he stand firm in his resolve and so risk reprisals from the Brotherhood? Or would he join them? Lorenz knew what the Brethren did to the intransigent in other places—destroyed their property and, sometimes, far worse. And if the worse should befall, what, Lorenz thought, would become of Inge? Without father or brother to protect her, she would be at the mercy of petty, cruel Eitel. "For," thought Lorenz, "if Sebald and my father fall, so shall I."

No, it had been best had he never come here. All might have been very different had he not. He should have known he was not the man to move a peasant's heart—peasant though he himself was. Could he not have found a preacher better suited to counter the likes of Jäcklein Ecklig? Yet, who? He himself might not be the best and most moving of speakers; still, he was one of *them*. He could understand his people like no one else could—or so he had thought.

Yet it seemed that his years away—first at the *schola*, then in Nürnberg, the university, the monastery, Wittenberg—had changed him to the heart. He was a peasant, yes, in ancestry and rearing; but he had, it seemed, risen beyond his estate—or, fallen below it. It was hard to say which. He didn't want to admit it, but he had felt himself superior to these old neighbors of his, even his family. Oh, he had rediscovered his love for Inge, but his affection for her, he knew, dripped with a lofty condescension. He had felt so for Sebald, until the last few days. Now he saw that his younger brother possessed a strength of resolve that he himself lacked. Sebald was a man, while he felt himself a vacillating child.

And now where would Sebald's resolution lead him? Both courses were fraught with perils. Sebald, he knew, would not decide according to his own advantage but of that of his father, sister, and (Lorenz sadly confessed it) his brother.

The path now opened up into a meadow. Beyond the meadow, to the north, at the crest of a slope covered with leaf-budding trees, rose the village church. The path did not cross the field but here forked; one branch of it—winding off to his left, skirting the meadow under the eaves of the wood, and then, running along the base of the chapel hill, and turning sharply to the north—climbed up the hill's western side. The other path followed the forest's edge toward the east and then, about a furlong's distance, turned abruptly south and was hidden by the wood.

As Lorenz stood undecided at this crossroads, he thought again—what would Sebald decide? What *should* he decide? Then, Lorenz thought—*what would I decide for him, had I power over his destiny?* And then the thought struck him, like a drenching of cold water, "what would I decide for my himself, if his choice were mine?"

This thought shook him—shouldn't it be certain what course *he* would choose? Wasn't his choice, his duty, clear? Though a poor one, he was a servant of the Gospel; to act otherwise would be to deny the cross. Had he not preached now for weeks what man's duty demanded? And hadn't he come here under the warrant and in the trust of his lord, the Marshal? To choose otherwise would be to betray the fidelity he owed to Herr Sigismund and to God. Would it not be so? Would it not?

But, perhaps, it would not. To his horror he felt, deep in the unturned loam of his flesh, a stirring. He had felt so when he had listened to Jäcklein Ecklig's preaching. It was the same when, long ago, a boy, he had felt the terrible allure of Bruder Thaddeus in the depths of the wood — and on the edge of the mere, in the storm, and when he had lain with her under the forest trees...

The Gospel he had learned, that he had preached — what was it in power ranged against *this*? Oh, it had given him hope and once had joyed him so that he had thought he could ascend the clouds *in jubilo*. But how soon that euphoria had dissipated — like dew under the hot rays of the morning sun! A malaise of spirit had succeeded the primal joy and hung about him, like a wet woolen cloak. And then to have been admitted into the mystery of the faceless One, who vests himself in guise and mask only to cheat us with seeming, in accord with his "hidden will" — this did not plunge him into the old terrors; rather, the old malaise blanched into a hue very near to despair.

In compare, the uprising was a stirring to life. If it lasted but a moment, it would be a moment well bought, even at the steep price of eternity.

And wasn't the cause just? Weren't the peasants' grievances such that only blood could wash and fire scour away?

Who could say? Mayhap it was the revealing of the hidden will.

He had been following the path toward the church and now crested the hill; before him, the cylindrical apse of whitewashed stone. As he approached it, it seemed to swell and expand. He threaded his way among the grave markers — most of wood, but some of stone. Grass and weeds grew rank on many of the grave plots — the oblivion of the dead. He halted before one plot, marked by a small monument of stone. She who lay here had not been forgotten. He knelt before the grave.

"Mama," he whispered. "Forget not your child." He felt no compunction in the prayer—nor in the cross with which he signed himself.

*   *   *

He rose and entered the church through the main portal that faced the West. Just inside the doors, the holy water stoup. Out of habit his hand moved toward it; but then realizing what he did, he let his hand drop to his side.

He walked slowly through the nave; he heard the scuffling of his boots on the flagstones as if they came from another. He stopped before the altar rail and studied the simple wooden altar, the crucifix hanging above it, and the small wooden house with the locked door, wherein he had once believed *It* dwelt. A small, flickering lamp, betokened *Its* presence. To his left he knew the Mother stood, gazing with love and adoration into the face of her Babe. To his right, against the north wall, the image of Sankt Lorenz with the reliquary. But he looked neither to him nor to her. They, he thought, would not help him.

He sought to pray, to say something to his God. Yet, he could not. His lips would not form the words.

Then, as if rising up from a place in his soul long buried, a sudden fear seized on him—*It* beheld him from this *Its* humble throne. *It* scowled at him with disgust and wrath! Terror filled his heart—he had to leave this place, but he dared not turn his back on *It*! He wanted to say, "What do you want of me?" But he could not. Slowly he walked backward, step by faltering step down the nave, his eyes fixed on the door of the little box. Though the church was small, the distance seemed long; he felt he could never traverse it.

He ran up against, bumped into something soft. Hands clutched him from behind; but they did not hold him. They thrust him forward. He almost lost his balance and fell, but he saved himself; and, turning round abruptly, he gave out a little yelp of fear. Before him, a black-clad figure, a long white beard. His first impulse was to flee; but when the initial fear had passed, he saw he had nothing to fear.

It was no one or nothing else than the old priest, Gottfried.

* * *

The old man smiled derisively. "What, did I spook you, lad?" he sneered.

Lorenz tried to recover himself. But he could find nothing to say.

"Hah! Cat got your tongue?" Gottfried laughed dryly. "But it isn't me you need fear—but I think you know that!"

Gottfried cocked his head and leered slyly at Lorenz.

"*Ach!* Leave me be!"

Lorenz turned to go, but Gottfried's bird-claw hand caught him by the arm.

"No, I'll not let you be!" Gottfried's countenance now betrayed no signs of mockery. Lorenz looked him dead in the eye. The old man was in earnest.

"I'll not let you go until I tell what I deem is eating at you—for your blanching shows that something is! You've heard, lad, you've heard! The harvest is going to be brought in, what's been sown by your Luther and his cat's paws—yourself, Melanchthon, and only God knows how many others. They've come!" And Gottfried wagged his shaggy head.

Lorenz felt sick. He understood the old man's meaning, but he would dissemble. "Who's come?" he said.

"The very devils you and your ilk have conjured up!" Gottfried growled. "Schwaben, the South, have vomited into Franken—all the dregs of the peasant folk who have been seduced by your 'holy Evangel!'"

"We have seduced no one . . ." Lorenz spoke with an assurance he did not feel. He knew he could not really dispute with the priest. He could say that Luther waved the sword of God, not man; but he knew it would fall flat. What Luther might mean was often not what his words betokened. Instead of defending Luther, then, he defended himself. "You know," he said (he would not look Gottfried in the eye), "that is not what I have taught."

"What you have taught? I have not given ear to what *you have taught*. I have heard" — and here Gottfried's manner softened a little — "that you have tried to dissuade our folk from insurrection. But do you think that is enough? You have preached heresy, boy, and heresy is revolution! And now it's come to roost here — even here!"

Gottfried paused, then said, "I have been told about the meeting." He gave Lorenz a look that said, *you know whereof I speak.*

A wave of dread passed over Lorenz. "The meeting?" he said quietly. "What meeting?"

Gottfried eyed him doubtfully. "You don't know?" The old man peered at him more intently. "No," he said at last, "could it be you don't? I speak of the meeting in the forest, an hour before sunrise, upon this Sunday of the Passion."

"I know nothing of this," Lorenz said. "How do you know of it?"

Gottfried's manner was wary. Then, he erupted, "*Ach!* Do not play the innocent with me! Your own brother will be there!"

"Sebald?" Lorenz muttered. The news had struck him hard. "God, no! How do you know this? Tell, how do you know?"

Lorenz's incredulity seemed to confuse the old priest. His eyes widened; he stared at Lorenz. "I will not tell you who told me this," he said, like one treading upon ice, testing whether it would hold his weight. "But he who told me is faithful and sure. Firebrands from the South and Schwaben will be here. They will raise the *Bundschu*. God only knows what will follow." Gottfried's eyes softened. They fell.

Dismay, fear, and horror. Lorenz raised his hand to push the priest aside — he must not stay here longer! But Gottfried grabbed Lorenz's hand. "But one word more," he said in a low, husky voice.

"What?"

The old priest's eyes no longer shone with wrath. They looked intently on Lorenz. They were wide and moist. He still clasped Lorenz's hand. "Only this," he said. "I despise everything you stand for. I could wish you had died when your mother bore you. I should have defied you and the Marshal when you came here to spread your poison among my flock, but I was a coward. I allowed the wolf into my master's sheepfold. But I will not be guilty of your blood, so I warn you — flee from here! If you remain, your life is forfeit. Whatever part you've played in this, it has gone beyond you. They will trample you. They will destroy you."

The two men stood stock still, studying each other. Lorenz saw the old man spoke the truth.

"And you, what will you do?" Lorenz said.

"I?" Gottfried's smile contended with the fear in his eyes. "I shall remain here, in my church, for when they will come for me."

Gottfried dropped Lorenz's hand and stood aside. Without another look at the priest, Lorenz plunged into the warm sunlight outside.

CHAPTER 6

THE GIBBOUS MOON HUNG IN THE WEST-ern sky. It would be another hour at least before moon-set. The air coming through the open window was chill; still, he had cast aside his coat. Anxiety had pricked him impatient of the garment's confinement. A single candle by his bed lit the room, casting his shadow across the two walls' joining. He sat by the window, looking out into the yard below.

Would he stay here all night, waiting to see if or when his brother would steal out into the raw air? His body felt drawn and wrung out like an old rag. Following his last talk with Gottfried, he had hardly slept at night, and now he was exhausted. Even so, he wondered, if he lay down, whether or not he would sleep; would not the pricking anxiety of his mind keep him awake, even now? Would not the fears of what this day held banish slumber?

He awoke with a start—he had nodded to sleep in his chair. He stood up and began pacing the room. It was only two hours past midnight; it would be another hour and a half before his brother stirred, he knew. He could not fall asleep, lest he oversleep. He had to stay awake, to follow Sebald, if he rose. *If he rose*—perhaps Gottfried had been wrong about his brother keeping tryst with those folk.

But whether Sebald stirred or no, Lorenz was determined that he himself would not wait here for them. He would go to them, brave the horror of the woods and the magic of the clearing, that place where a child, many years since, had felt the terror of the deflowered Angel Man. He had to see for himself what would befall that night, despite the danger to himself. For of this, at least, he was convinced; Gottfried was right—if they caught him, his life was forfeit.

The candle's light fell across the pile of clothing on his bed—"yes," he thought, "I had better change into those things. There is not much time." He pulled off his shirt and slipped out of his pants. He was already barefoot. He sat on the bed, took up the pair of hose, and pushed his legs, first one, then the other, into them. He had forgotten how coarse the fabric could be; it made his legs itch. He took the shirt, thrust his head through the hole and his arms into the sleeves. He then donned the tunic and the hood that he would pull over his head so that, he hoped, no one would recognize him in the dark. He would wait until he went out into the courtyard to pull on the high boots. He feared that they would be heard, striking on the wood floor of the house.

Again, he paced the room. He both dreaded the event and wished for its hastening; at least *then* all doubt would be removed. He would *know* and could choose his course accordingly. But certainty, he knew, is double-edged. Certainty, he had found, is oft the death of hope.

It was only after he had strode several times, back and forth, back and forth, that he heard the groaning of the wood floor beneath his feet. He did not want anyone in the house to know he was awake; and moreover, he felt so very weary. He sat down in the chair, close to the window. The chill air would keep him awake, he thought. And the chair was hard and uncomfortable. He had only an hour or so to wait—surely he could keep vigil for so short a space...

* * *

338

He shivered and opened his eyes; at first, he did not know where he was. But as recognition dawned, he wondered why he was sitting in this uncomfortable chair, with the cold air coming in from the open window. Rising, he remembered. Hastening toward the window, he looked out. It was still dark outside, but he knew he had overslept. If his brother was trysting in the wood, he would have already gone.

Lorenz grabbed the boots and a coat, and with care, but in haste, he passed from his room into the hall, and from the hall down the staircase into the hearth room, below. Coals under the ashes still would give off heat, he knew, but he did not stop to warm himself, though he shivered with cold. Carefully, he opened the main door to the house; it screeched slightly on its hinges. He knew the sound would stir the dogs—and the two bitch hounds came running toward him, barking. "Zahn and Grausig," he whispered. "Be silent—it is I." The dogs recognizing him, gamboled about his legs and wagged their tails. He patted them and commanded, "be off, out!" He sat down on the bench at the base of the linden and pulled on his boots. In a moment he was up, hurrying across the yard, and out through the gate.

Gottfried did not know, or did not tell him, where the gathering would be; but he was sure it would be in the Hunters' Clearing. He could see a little blue-gray gleaming in the east, but it was still quite dark; yet he knew the way so well—along the stream side, around and up the small hill, and down into the dell, harvested naked of trees. He wrapped his coat more closely about him—he felt cold; but with each step forward he reckoned less of the cold, for fear began to grab at his heart. It was not for his own safety that he trembled, but for what he would see in the clearing, once he got there.

Once again, he felt as if he were shrinking into his childhood. He could almost feel that Gerd was beside him and it was the morning of Sankt Stephanus. Did the dead preacher await him in the wood, his beard singed away, his body burned to a crisp charcoal blackness? Was he returned, seeking vengeance? Though at first he had hastened, his steps began to flag. When at length he reached the foot of the small hill, he hesitated—should he turn back? He stood stock still, uncertain of what he should do. If he took one more step, he felt he should plunge into the abyss. He would fall, perhaps never to find bottom.

When at last he took the next tentative step, and another, and another; and when he found that he was what he had been, not the child he once was, that he was not plunging into a dark hole, he felt his courage rise. With each new step, he grew more determined. He knew not what he would do when he reached the other side, but now he felt he need not concern himself with it. What would happen, would happen. He knew only this—that he must push onward.

The path wound up and around the small hill. Now, with determined step, he climbed the last few feet to the crest. When at last he reached it, he could look down into the clearing, below. He nodded. The clearing was bright with a myriad of torches. Like a lurid crescent moon glimmering they stretched along the curve of the forest. At the far end of the clearing, where a single boulder jutted from the soil, stood the squat figure of a man, flanked to left and right by men holding flaming brands. Lorenz pulled his hood forward over his head and began his descent into the dell.

CHAPTER 7

L ORENZ INSINUATED HIS WAY TO WHERE
the crowd was thinnest. Carefully, lest he discover
himself, he glanced from side to side to see if he could
find Sebald in the throng. He noted some villagers he knew,
though many of the faces were strange to him. Folk must have
gathered here from other villages, he thought. Still, it was yet
too dark, the flaming brands too flickering, to allow for too
firm a recognition. Sebald, thus, he could not find.

At first his mind had been too occupied with distress for his
brother and anxiety lest he himself be recognized. But it was
not long before he saw that there was little fear of that. No
one in the crowd seemed to care a wit for those around him;
everyone's eyes were set on the man standing by the boulder.
He was not tall, but, from what Lorenz could see of him in the
torchlight, he was powerfully built. He was dressed as any peasant, except that he wore a long cloak and a wide-brimmed hat,
alive with curving pheasants' feathers. His beard was long—it
hung down to his rather round belly; and his hair fell, thick,
to his chest, below the level of his shoulders. Lorenz reckoned
that the man was well nigh on to middle age.

The man's voice was a deep bass. At first it sounded like
an inarticulate rumbling in Lorenz's ears; but gradually the
rumbling took on the contour of words—

"Nay, nay! Is it to be said that the folk hereabout will not join with their brethren in the great struggle? God forfend, friends! God forfend!"

"And what assurances can ye give us?" A voice, which Lorenz recognized but was unable to name, issued this challenge.

"What assurance?" boomed the man in the cloak and hat. "What assurance do bold men need, save their own firmness and stoutness? What! Are the folk of the Altmühl lands fearful to touch what the men of Schweiz, the Schwarzwald, and Schwaben have seized with both hands? We have been no better equipped than you folk—not in arms, not in money—though maybe in boldness and courage!"

A roar went up from the crowd. "Watch your words, Hubmaier!" someone cried, "or you'll discover what payment we can make from our boldness!"

But the man, Hubmaier, was undaunted. "Well, if you be *bold* men," he shouted back, "why don't you show it? Why hang you back? What signs do you need?"

"Aye, 'tis as I've been declaring to ye now for well over a year!" cried a voice that, after Hubmaier's, sounded like childish treble. From the shadows, Jäcklein Ecklig stepped into the light. His lips, twisted as they ever were in an imbecile smile, belied the scolding words they uttered.

"I have told ye, have I not—that it is *men* that seize what belongs to them, with full fists?" Jäcklein's tone was bitter with scorn. "I have proved to ye from Scripture that it is God who wishes your freedom—that it is God who pulls down the mighty from their thrones and exalts the lowly, who is calling—nay, prodding—ye forward. But ye are stubborn oxen and too stupid to see the sweet pastures what God has set before ye!"

A roar of indignation went up from the crowd, but Jäcklein was undeterred.

"Ye may cry out as ye will!" he nearly screamed, "but ye'll not daunt me. I have a power that ye cannot fight against—and

342

it walks with this man, this Hubmaier, who has, not once, not twice, but over and over again reddened his hands with the blood of tyrants! And see—this silken cape he wears, and this"—Jäcklein reached over to Hubmaier and took hold of a great chain he had hung around his neck, and lifted it so all could see. In the firelight, Lorenz could see a great, gold cross hanging from the chain; jewels sparkled in the lurid light. "This is but one of the treasures he has seized, as a down payment for what the shaved-pates owe him! 'Twas from the sack of—whence, brother, did ye take it?"

"The sack of the monastery of Roth," Hubmaier boomed, with a savage chuckle.

"Aye, Roth! No doubt the Black Robes now know what 'tis like to be peasant! And this is not all that he has gained, nor those as followed him—not by an ell it isn't! But if he has done it and his Christian Brethren, cannot ye all do it as well? Or shall we say that the folk of Franken have not the stout-heartedness to do the like?"

Jäcklein paused. No cry or word of protest came from the crowd. Except for some shuffling of feet and queer sounds high in the trees, all was silent. Jäcklein seemed to relish the silence. When at last he broke it, his tone was even and timbred with solemnity.

"And do ye not know, my neighbors—*Christian Brethren*, as ye here call yourselves, hah!—what signs God has vouchsafed ye? Need I tell ye, what all ye wot of? Shall I tell ye again of the cow at Waltersdorf's hideous abortion? Yea! I myself saw it, with these very eyes! 'Twas horrible, it was—half calf and half monk! *Ach!* I saw it, indeed, and it struck terror into my heart! God, my brothers, has declared by it, and by many other signs, that the end of the reign of Antichrist draws nigh, that the shaved pates and all their works will be cast into the burning lake! Only them as fight with Christ shall enjoy the Kingdom

343

he has prepared. Ye are either with him or against him!"

Jäcklein now bent himself slightly forward, and scanned the length of the throng, slowly, beginning from the left and moving toward the right, to where the sky, seen partly through the trees, was now glowing with the earnest of the dawn. The crowd stood silent, as if enchanted; those nearest to him, Lorenz saw, followed the movement of Jäcklein's eyes. Lorenz felt an awe and wonder welling up within him; though he struggled to suppress it, he could not force it down. He could not smother it.

It seemed an age before Jäcklein again spoke. But when he did, it was no loud harangue, only a whispering that seemed to suffuse the chill, damp air. Though he stood afar off, it was as if he was at one's elbow and spoke into the ear.

"Comes the morning, my brothers—it comes!" (Was it Jäcklein who spoke, or the sibilant air?) "Ye cannot stay it! And when it comes, ye must be decided; there will then be no turning back! The pact, my brothers, must be forged in the dark, for 'tis of faith. Once your eyes can see, 'twill be too late—for faith knows only blindness. Ye may wonder at my words—for I tell ye a mystery, before hidden from all but a few. The trees know it, the grass knows it; they have sucked it from the mold that man stupidly treads upon but has never kenned—save for a very few. The priests have tried to conjure it away, but in vain; for they speak Christ against Christ."

Lorenz had heard such words before and felt a wriggle of the old terror. Would he never be free from it?

Jäcklein again paused and folded his arms across his breast. Then raising his eyes toward the sky, he stretched forth his hands as if he were offering an oration. "O God of all the earth, water, air, and fire!" he cried. "Reveal yourself to these blind ones! Speak to them—tell them that ye dwell not in little houses made by man, that ye are not commanded by bell and book! Show them ye fill all things—that the spirit of the fire is yours, the life-giving earth, and the powers that dwell in stream and tree and herb and stone. Thousands upon thousands serve ye—the lowly and the weak, the powerful and despised.

"And let them now give heed to the word of your hand-maiden, one among your servants hidden and despised!"

* * *

Jäcklein's hands fell to his sides. His head and Hubmaier's (who had been at his side the while) together nodded as if in sudden slumber, chin to chest. Each now turned his back to the other and parted, one to the right and the other to the left. Where they had stood, before the great jutting stone, swelled a small gray mound. Was it a stone? No, for it wiggled and twitched, like a cocoon with living worm. What hideous creature was there? Lorenz felt he had awakened in nightmare; there, before him, soon to emerge, some loathsome monster, a giant cater-pillar or maggot creature. He thought to cross himself, but he could not command arm and hand. They hung limp at his side.

More agitated, it twitched, that gray mound, while the torch flames seemed to grow brighter in the still, early morning air. Then, of a sudden, the gray mound was stilled; one could hear only the crackle of flames and the breathing of his fellows.

Then, it spoke, as if from the depths of the earth—

"Command me!"

And, together, Jäcklein and Hubmaier, their heads still bowed, muttered, as if in sleep: "Come forth!"

A fissure, seemed to split the gray mass in twain. Slowly it parted, revealing an embowered human figure, crouching, its head bowed, its arms extending to left and right under the covering. Long, dark hair cascaded from the crown of the head and washed the ground before it. Then, slowly the figure rose beneath the gray veil. The legs, from kneeling, straightened, hidden by the skirt of a gown, black against the cloudy gray,

345

the head still face down toward the earth, the hair hanging, sweeping the mold, the arms outstretched like the wings of a great bird. Then, as if from under the earth, a low moan, swelling in volume as the torso of the figure, pivoted at the hips, drew upward — a howling that at last shattered the gloaming, ululating as with unslaked desire mixed with anguish. Lorenz beheld the tall figure of a woman, draped in night, her hair hanging to almost below the calves of her legs. Her gray veil slipped from her head to her shoulders.

Shapely she was and seeming fair, though one could not tell her age. She seemed both old and young, like the corpse of some fair maid or an old dame pickled in beauty by arcane art. Her face was a ghastly white, death pallor, but without wrinkle or blemish of age. Her lips were slightly parted. Her eyes stared into vacancy. Lorenz felt as if he were gazing into a deep water at a body drowned. He longed to plunge his hand into the water, touch the face, though he knew he could never reach to its depths.

Frau Berthe! Heulandweib!

Lorenz felt rather than heard the mutterings of the bystanders. That it was she, he did not doubt — she, who wandered the woods, dwelling in their depths, luring lads and maidens to their destruction. She, who, 'twas said, held commerce with elves and the fairy-folk; who cast blight on crops and could conjure a storm and inflict the murrain on cattle. She, whom women sought for love potions; men, for power over enemies; who by one glance of her eyes could enchain a soul to her will, or drive it into madness.

It seemed an age she stood thus, as if changed to stone, gazing into nothingness, her arms extended, her lips slightly parted. Then her arms fell to her sides. She sank onto her knees, groaning deeply. Slowly then, ever so slowly, she lifted her hands to the level of her face, palm facing palm, as if she were clasping something between them. She bent her head forward and made as if she were kissing.

Then, she spoke in a lilting monotone:

"From the depths of the earth, deep beneath the mold and loam of earth, I hear it—the clash of weapons and groans of death, wound inflicted!"

Her voice was unusually deep for a woman's. It was melodious, yet unsettling, like a fair song that speaks despair.

"They rise, the sons of earth, too long trampled by tread of the mighty, haughty-hearted. The great ones on their thrones tremble with fear. They quake. Their power is shaken by the earth-tillers, bloody pated."

Again she fell silent. Her hands moved downward, delineating in their motion the form of a man. Now they made as if they caressed an unseen figure, and again she leaned forward and kissed.

"Hear me!" Her voice swelled at the entreaty. "Give heed to my prayer, thou who hath schooled me in the ancient lore—the lore of growing things and of stones, of the teeming things and of the cold and lifeless beings underground! Fill me with thy power, the power that burgeons forth in branch and leaf, and tunnels into the soil-deeps, sucking at the abundant breasts of Erde! Fill me with thyself, that I might fill these here with resolve, the resolve to carry out thy will in the long-awaited Vengeance!"

The woman's words filled Lorenz with dread, but yet with palpitating desire. His flesh was tingling with yearning, the yearning to merge himself with those standing round him, to be ruled, with them, by arcane power. All his life he had heard of the Body of Christ; but only now did it seem a reality. Christ the head, and they the members. Christ reborn on earth in a second coming, to wreak vengeance on their enemies. And she the furtive birth giver of a new incarnation.

The woman rose to her full height—and it seemed to Lorenz that her head would touch the fading stars. With her right arm outstretched, she described an arc, passing from the extreme verge of the crowd to its furthest end, and then back again until it halted at the apogee. She stood thus, arm outstretched, her countenance now charged with an ecstasy. When at last she spoke, her voice seemed to echo through the forest.

"Ye must decide!" she cried. "No more can ye waiver! Will ye stand with us or with our enemies? There is no other way!"

And as with one voice, the crowd cried out, "we will follow!" Lorenz heard himself crying out, "we will follow!" His lips formed the words, but it seemed as if another spoke from within him.

"Then, prove your resolve!" the woman cried. "Perform what has been commanded!"

As one man, the numerous crowd fell back, as if struck by a sudden, mighty wind. Then it churned in confusion, as each member groped to find its place in the procession. Now moving as one creature, it squeezed its ungainly bulk into the narrow compass of the path that snaked back to the village. As it wound its way along the path, first one voice, then more, then, running along the serpentine procession, nearly all hymned the song—of bloodletting and vengeance, punctuated by *kyrieleis—Kyrieeleis!*

Lorenz felt as if he walked in a cloud. He passed by familiar landmarks and sights, but they seemed warped, as if in dream. Thoughts of his father, sister, and brother flitted through his fevered brain, but they no longer seemed real. Only the long, serpentine body of which he felt himself merely an appendage—this alone was being and truth, mind and will. His heart throbbed with its heart; he had tasted blood, and he savored the salty bitterness of it with his tongue. He knew vaguely where they were to go, but it did not matter. *He* need not ken it; for did the hand need know the intent of the mind that commanded it?

Kyrieeleis!

It had passed over the bridge spanning the Tiefer Bach. *It* was now ascending the hill. The sun's rays, filtered through the still-too-barren branches of the trees, splashed their radiance on the curved apse. Stones and wooden markers, jutting out in wild angles from the loam, cast weird shadows to north and west. "They will rise with us," he felt and half thought. "The day of judgment is at hand." The graves would spew forth their dead.

The creature slithered along the northern wall and then, swinging suddenly to the left, turning in a tight arc, moved directly against the western portal. The two, iron hinged oaken doors stood shut, but this alone did not confuse the mind that had mastered him. But a tremor rippled along the line of the serpentine body. *It* had halted in indecision. A roar went up from *Its* mouth, but it was an impotent complaint.

For before the doors stood a man, swathed all in black, bent, leaning on a wooden staff. Lorenz thought he knew him; but his mind, drugged as if with sleep, could trace no delineation. He could not recognize him; yet, he knew him. He knew him! The figure's voice cried out feebly. The Mind was shaken with indecision. Lorenz felt it. A ripple shuddered the long line of men, tearing at its sinews with excruciating pain.

Then a voice, one that he had heard in the forest, haranguing.

A clamor, the voices joined in a savage cry. Something struck the black-swathed figure at the doors, and he fell. The great doors were tugged, pulled on, and then wrenched open, and the great mass poured through them into what lay within. Lorenz stood, as if rooted to the earth, gripped by confusion and terror, while bodies rushed past him, and onward, toward the gaping portal. The man had fallen, and Lorenz could not move. He would not move, though all the tide of them thrust against him. "God help him!" Lorenz heard himself cry. "I cannot do this thing!"

Louder swelled the clamor that washed about him, like the current of a mighty river—he a stone, unmoving; *It,* a relentless force, unthinking and unfeeling, obeying the inner compulsion of its nature. Over the crest of the distant hills, the eastern light was now streaming with greater vehemence, splashing over the ground at his feet, though a long shadow stretched over the place where the black-clothed figure had fallen. Men continued to pour through the doors, wrenched back on their hinges; scarcely human voices echoed forth from the dark interior. Ever and anon he could just detect the singing—*kyrieeleis!*

There seemed to be a struggle at the portal. The throngs pushing in, were being thrust back. They were cursing, and fists were flailing; but, at last, they were pushed back. Those emerging, bearing burdens—a savage cry rose up, not of wrath nor of joy, but of a passion more violent and bestial. "God, no!" Lorenz heard himself say, though whether he shouted the words or whispered them, he could not tell. The figures were, one, of a man; the other, a woman with a child. They were cast to the ground, and a wielded ax, rising and falling, bludgeoned the bodies. "No! Stop this! Stop!" Lorenz heard a voice cry—was it his? Then he felt something crash against the back of his head, and he knew no more.

* * *

His eyes opened to a world of light. He lifted himself from the ground, slowly, pushing himself up, first onto his hands and knees; the back of his head throbbed with a dull pain. He rose onto his knees and looked around, confused at first as to where he was. From where the pain came, the back of his head, he felt a slight swelling. He looked around him—he seemed to be alone. Where was he?

It was then he espied the bodies, lying only a few yards from where he knelt; and he remembered. "*Ach, Gott!*" he muttered. "God, no." He rose slowly to his feet, feeling dizzy; but he managed to walk to where the bodies lay. He knew them. He recalled, as if from a distant age, how a woman had led her child to one and bade him say his *Ave* at her feet. The carven head lay a few feet from the hacked torso. To her right, stretched the male form — to whom the child he remembered had once been dedicate — still whole, except that the hand that had been raised in blessing was broken off at the wrist. "God, no," he muttered.

His eyes moved slowly up from the figures, across the expanse of grass. The doors, hanging crazily from their hinges; before them, on the stone pavement before the gaping portal, the body of a man, clad in black, a long, white beard flowing from the twisted head, over the breast, brushing the stone. And beside it, another figure, kneeling.

Slowly he approached the figures — the one lying, the other kneeling. The kneeling man did not move until Lorenz halted at the feet of the recumbent one. Then, slowly, he raised his head, and their eyes met.

"Sebald!"

"He is dead, Lorenz. He is dead."

Lorenz knelt by the side of the body. The old priest still clutched, with his right hand, the simple wooden cross that had hung from a rope around his neck. The eyes were shut, and he appeared to sleep, like a child when the long day of his playing is done.

"I could not come to him, in time," Sebald said, slowly shaking his head. "I should have fallen with him."

"Do not trouble yourself, brother," Lorenz whispered. "It is better, thus, for him."

Both men now rose to their feet, and Lorenz saw wonder and confusion pass over his brother's countenance. He felt himself smile feebly. "Do not fear, brother," he said. "I was not—no, I was no party to this thing, I . . . " And though he struggled to repress them, he felt the tears stream from his eyes, over his cheeks.

"We cannot let him lie here," he said. "Come, I will help you bear him away." And he bent forward as if to lift the body.

But Sebald grabbed his brother's arm and pulled him forward. "No," he said, vehemently. "*You* will do no such thing. You must leave this place! If they find you, they will kill you." And Sebald glanced down at the body and shuddered.

Lorenz considered the body lying at his feet. He shook his head. He felt it mattered nothing what they did to him now. "We cannot leave him lying here," he said as calmly as if he were speaking of a daily chore. "Let us bear him away."

But Sebald, who had not loosened his hold on his brother, shook him. "Can't you see that you must not stay here?" he almost shouted. "You can do nothing here. It has gone beyond you!"

Lorenz recalled hearing the same words from another.

"Don't you see? You would be casting your life away, and . . . and we will have sorrow enow ere long."

He felt his brother's eyes scrutinizing him; Sebald was not convinced, he saw, that he had moved him.

"If you think nothing of your life," Sebald pleaded, "think of our father . . . "

"He will not care if I live or die," Lorenz said.

"Then think of our sister! Think of Inge!"

The evoking of his sister's name struck Lorenz to the quick. He shuddered.

"And think of your duty! Who will bring warning to the Marshal, if not you?" And, after a pause, "mayhap, you might stay his vengeance against us."

Lorenz pondered. He cared nothing for his own life, he felt.

And as for the Marshal; well, he had made his bed. But for Inge, and his brother and, yes, even his father, he would offer up his life. And now, he saw, for them he would sacrifice even his death.

He breathed deeply and sighed. "Your words, brother, are a talisman of great proof," he said. "I will obey."

"Christ and his Mother be praised!"

* * *

Lorenz wondered at this brother of his—he was a man that he himself could never become. But as he thought of Sebald, apprehension seized him. What would *he* do now?

"What will I do?" Sebald replied with a faint smile. "I will remain here. I will not now follow this rabble. I feel already that I am almost guilty of this man's blood," he added in a whisper.

"But they will take vengeance on *you*—you see that, don't you?"

Sebald shrugged. "Mayhap they will," he said. "But this old whoreson priest has taught me my duty. I will take what comes—as will Father. As he always would. Maybe I'll prove myself worthy to be his son." And when he said this, Sebald was looking down at the body at his feet.

Lorenz grabbed Sebald's shoulders. He pulled his brother to him, and the two men embraced. He released him and, without a further word or a backward glance, he left him, following the path that descended the hill on its northern side and crossed the stream of the Tiefer Bach over a little bridge.

The morning sun was riding high, undimmed by any cloud, in the east.

HOLY
WEEK

CHAPTER 1

"I WOULD LIKE TO ACCOMMODATE YOU, but I simply cannot. I cannot get you in to see him today. It is just not possible!"

Peter's insistence, his intransigence, dumbfounded Lorenz. As did the nonchalance with which he had received his news. Did Peter not see the danger threatening?

"Then, perhaps, you could report to him what I told you—it is of the utmost importance!"

Peter shook his head and chuckled. "*Ach,* Lorenz!" he said, though with some annoyance in his tone. "A handful of peasants storming a church is hardly the dire threat you make it out to be."

"They killed a priest . . . "

"Yes, they killed a priest." All semblance of humor fell from Peter's countenance. "But, don't you know this is nothing compared what has been happening all around us? What of Rothenberg—an entire city seized by the rabble? Compared to this, the violence on the Tiefer Bach is but a gnat's bite."

"But I have described for you the numbers I saw . . . "

"They are a trifle, a mere trifle." Peter took up the quill that lay before him and ran its feather through his fingers. "Other regions have seen thousands—thousands, Lorenz—take up arms. It is these troubles that occupy the brains of His Lordship, not a few hundred (if even that) irate farmers in an obscure hamlet in the hinterlands. I know they are important to you, your people; but Herr Sigismund will hardly find them significant."

Lorenz pounded his hand on the arm of his chair. "I have told you," he fairly shouted, "that it is not just my people, as you call them, that were there, but others I did not know. That man, Hubmaier, came from the south; and there were others."

"Still, you have not demonstrated that very many were there." Peter's tone bore the icy tone of finality. "You have told me of a crazed goodwife, a derelict priest, and a small cadre of peasants—these will not impress His Lordship. You will only anger him if he receives you and if this is all you can relate."

"Yet, he should know," Lorenz said, with a feeling of despair.

"Indeed he should," Peter admitted. "And he shall, but not today." He rose and smiled coldly. "I will see if I can get you an audience tomorrow. But it shall probably not be until the next day."

"I shall come tomorrow then," Lorenz said.

Peter sat down again, took up his quill, dipped it in the ink, and began to write. The audience was ended.

*　*　*

"When I heard you were returned to the city, I knew I should speak to you. I know you've got the ear of the Marshal . . ."

"Well, Aunt," he said, reluctantly, "I don't know if that's ever been the case, but now . . . "

"Well, then you've got to get it—you're the closest thing I have to getting it," she said, with an imperious nod. "You'll see this is so, when I've told you all."

Lorenz had only been back in the city a day before he received the note that Tante Ursula wanted to speak to him, without delay, "on a most important matter." How she knew so quickly that he had returned, he could not say. But then he recalled that, through her network of gossips, Tante Ursula had always been one of the best-informed persons in the city.

Thus, he found himself on the afternoon of the day of his meeting with Peter Schwach, sitting with his aunt, in her drawing room—which, that day, was stifling for the fervent fire on the hearth. As ever, she occupied her cushioned throne, from whence she, ever and anon, would issue orders to members of the household. Sometimes Lorenz wondered if she ever moved from there.

"As you know, lad," she said, after she had vigorously blown her nose and wiped it, "even though I'm bound to this chair most days, I still hear things. But this news as I'm about to tell you I had heard nothing of until last week — 'twas last Monday, or was it Tuesday? I can't recollect — how feeble my old head has become! Can't hardly keep anything in it these days. 'Tis the scourge of old age, my boy! Time was when I could remember what happened most days, down to the hour; 'twas my pride, and a great help to your deceased Onkel Georg — *he* had no mind for details, at least as to when things happened and all. But now I'm of no use to anyone, at least in that way — though your cousin Adolf still can't get along without me in matters havin' to do with the shop. His wife, that slatternly Ännchen, is of no use at all!"

Lorenz knew his aunt could rattle on in this fashion for some time, especially about the "slatternly Ännchen," so he interposed as she came up for air — "I am most sorry to hear that about Ännchen; but the news you were to tell me . . ."

"*Ach!* Thought of that girl almost drove it from my mind! She's a pretty one, no doubt; but, as I told Adolf, pretty don't get the food on the table! 'Twasn't the lass I wanted him to marry, but your uncle was so softhearted, and he gave in to the boy — I couldn't move him at all!"

Lorenz looked down at his feet and smiled. He doubted that Onkel Georg could ever have withstood his wife's importunity in this or in any matter. She must have thought it a good match. And as to her judgment of the girl who had married her darling Adolf — well, it was not wholly to be trusted, he knew.

But he was not interested in his kinsfolk's domestic affairs. He would have the news and then escape as soon as he may.

"*Ach!* You are right, lad—forgive an old lady for talking too much! 'Tis all I can do these days, mostly. But, that girl—no, no, I'll not speak of her more! The news—" Tante Ursula shook her massive head. "Such times we're living through! No one, it seems, remembers his duty no more! *We* do, for the marshals have been good to us, mostly. And though 'twas from Adolf I heard the news, he'll have nothing to do with these scabby folk. He's a marshal's man, through and through . . . "

"What did he tell you, Aunt?"

Tante Ursula looked hard on her nephew. "Naught but that there's rebellion in the city." She paused, as if to let the news sink in. "Yes, rebellion!" she continued, with emphasis. "The tanner's guild is what started the whole business, but it's spread to others. Even some of the carpenters have joined, God help us! They've cozened some of the council and are in contact with those accursed, thieving peasants that are kicking up such a row. Word is that they want to turn the city over to that bunch."

"What bunch?"

"The farmers, the peasants, lad! You're not a stupid one, so don't act like it!" Tante Ursula was working herself into a fever of indignation. "Why, the marshals have been our bread and butter! Our bread and butter! Such rebellion will ruin us, entirely! I can see tanners and wheelwrights going along with this; and them blacksmiths are a surly lot, all of them. But it's even respectable folk as tailors and masons—carpenters, by God! Carpenters! Times are a-changin', and not for the better!"

His aunt's news distressed Lorenz, though it was not all unlooked for. Other towns had followed this course—their tradesmen in league with the peasants. Rothenberg, he had heard, had fallen to a combination of peasants and townsmen. He thought of Karlstadt and wondered what part he had played, if any, in the capitulation of that town.

In his agitation, Lorenz abruptly rose from his chair. "God's blessing on you, Aunt," he said. "What you have told me—the

Marshal shall hear of it! But I need more information—does Adolf know the names of the ringleaders?"

"*Ach!* He acted as if he didn't know at first—I reckon he didn't want trouble for his cronies; that's my Adolf, a fast friend, he is. But"—here she pointed a crooked, jabbing finger at Lorenz—"I got it out of him. I made him write down the names. Here they are." From under the blanket on her lap she produced a folded piece of paper and handed it to Lorenz. "Take this to the Marshal, lad, and don't delay!"

Lorenz thanked her, and turned to leave.

"One word more, before you leave," the old woman growled. Lorenz, his hand on the latch looked back at Tante Ursula over his shoulder.

"Tell the Marshal of what my Adolf has done for him, will you?"

Lorenz paused. "Yes, Aunt, I will." He lifted the latch.

"Your father and brother—they ain't mixed up in this, are they?"

Without looking at her, "Thank God, no. They are not," he said.

"The saints be praised for it." Tante Ursula's tone suggested doubt. "Hmph! 'Tis good to see that your father has some of your late uncle's sense, God rest his soul."

CHAPTER 2

REBELLION—THE WORD CHILLED Lorenz to the quick. He had seen rebellion, and it had been terrifying, ugly. The body of the old priest, lying on the grass, its head twisted; the doors swinging askew, the temple pillaged, the hand held in blessing broken off at the wrist. That was the face of rebellion. Could he stand by while it threatened *this* place, as he had where a greater duty and debt had lain upon him? Or should he flee again to where rebellion could not touch him?

But was there any place raised on ground high enough to escape the flood?

He might flee, he had thought, *if* it would mean he would not be playing the coward. He would not be coward again.

His brother had not thought his flight cowardly; indeed, he had urged him to it. "I had opposed it, I had resolved to stay!" But, for all that, had he not given in too easily? He had thought he would offer himself up for his sister, father, and brother—but, in the end, what course had he taken? One that seemed to assure only his own safety.

Yes, Inge had urged Sebald's counsel during that half hour stolen from his flight. He could not depart without a farewell and word of explanation. She had wept, but her resolve was firm. "You must not stay here, Lorenz. You cannot help us more, and your death would only heap sorrow on sorrow." He had urged his remaining, but all the while, he knew he would leave . . .

"... And run with your tail between your legs to Weissenbrücke ... 'Tis about all you've ever had between your legs!"

So his father had said. He had gone home to collect his
few belongings, hoping not to meet Johannes; but he could
not avoid him.

"So, you're abandoning your charge, here, that the Marshal
laid on you—just to save your skin?

"*Ach, ja!* The Marshal needs forewarning—from you? As if
he don't already know all about it.

"And you'll be betraying your own folk ...

"It's Gottfried's death, is it, that troubles you? But it seems
you did nothing to hinder it. You could have, you know. You
could have tried. I would have been sorry at your death—not
ashamed as I am now at your hightailing it out of here ...

"But you're constant in nothing ... "

Constant in nothing—was it not so? Wasn't his father right?
Beatrice. Her father. The monastery—had he not, there, made
a vow, like that one he had made to her? And had he not broken
it? Oh, he could justify *that* abandonment; it were no betrayal to
follow Christ wherever he leads, to obey the Gospel, to cast off
pretense and falsehood. But, if it were so, why could he not but *feel*
that it had been really and truly nothing but a most foul betrayal?

And had he not a duty to the Marshal? But what of the duty he
owed his folk—for he knew that far more than the guilty would
suffer from Herr Sigismund's vengeance? If he had remained,
had cried out against the rebellion, he would have been killed.
Yet, he would never have stained his hands with his own people's
blood. With or without him, the Marshal could save himself; but
his folk, his own, were, if even victorious for an hour, dedicated
in the end to destruction.

And that promise he had made to Inge, that he would try to
save her husband in the hour of defeat—would he risk the Marshal's displeasure for the likes of Eitel Moeller? Would he not in
the end betray even Inge?

His mind was in a turmoil of confusion as he climbed the stairs to his room. Locking the door behind him, he threw himself down on the bed. Yes, he would meet with Herr Sigismund tomorrow—if he could gain an audience. It would be his duty to tell the Marshal all that he knew, including the conspiracy in the city. And he must hand him the list of names, though he was loath to do so. After all, he didn't know if those listed *were* conspirators; they could have been named so by their enemies. But if he didn't give the names over, and it proved that they were guilty as alleged, the burden of the result would weigh on his shoulders. And if it should be discovered that he had the names, but hid them . . .

Rising from his bed, he crossed the room to the south-facing window, and swung open the casements. He looked out on the expanse of the *Marktplatz*, on the far side of which rose the city church.

No sooner had he opened his window, than the bells took to ringing; and over the plaza folk began to hasten their steps toward the church. It was the hour of Vespers; and this day, he now recalled, was the Thursday in Passion Week. Sunday would see Christ's entry into the city, hailed by waving palms and singing children—*Pueri Hebraeorm portantes ramos olivarum, obviaverunt Domino . . .*

But no such praise and adulation would greet the Lord this year, he thought. It was not the humble Christ who drew near the city a-donkey back, but a wrath (whether God's or Satan's, who could say?) that threatened overthrow and destruction. The cobblestones of the *Markplatz* below would be slippery with blood, the gutters run freely with it. The bodies of defenders and assailants, common tradesmen and women, would lie strewn over the plaza, like dead fish cast up on shore after a storm. With the great bronze doors of the church flung open, almost torn from their hinges, the mob would enter, smashing windows, pulling down statues, slashing pictures.

The canons would be driven out, or murdered in cold blood. And Heimrad's bones — they would not spare even the dead.

Every moment brought the terror nearer the city. How long could he delay before any intervention would be too late? The Marshal did not keep a large body of armed men at the castle, not enough to counter hordes of vengeance-thirsty peasants. He would have to gather troops from outside. Would there be time enough, if he delayed till tomorrow? And what if, again tomorrow, he could not gain an audience with the Marshal?

* * *

But why need he to wait on Peter? The question at first startled him but then clarified everything. Despite himself, he laughed. He need not wait on Peter! After all, who was Peter? A mere adviser! "If I beg an audience by myself, making clear that I would treat of dire matters, surely I will not be turned away." He paused and pondered. The matter was simple. "I will go to the castle as soon as the gates open in the morning."

But why wait until morning? He looked out on the *Marktplatz* again. Two hours were still left of day; he could make it to the castle before the city and castle gates closed, though he might not make it back. "Still, I must risk it," he said to himself.

He took up his coat and hat and strode to the door. Opening it, he paused, irresolute. But, struck by the absurdity of his fear, he shook his head and laughed. "There *is* no other course," he thought, closing the door behind him.

* * *

He was ushered into a dark-paneled room. Against the far wall, between two windows, stood the hearth, ablaze with a lively fire. The windows of stained glass, bearing the armorial devices of the House of Weissenbrücke, faced west; the rays of the setting sun streamed through them, casting light on the carpeted wood floors. Between Lorenz and the hearth stood a long, rectangular table, with a row of smaller chairs hearthside and two larger, high-backed chairs, carven with intricate designs, on the far ends. On the table stood two candelabra, each holding multiple tapers. The servants who brought him into the room lighted the tapers; then, with a slight nod of the head, exited the room by the door through which they had come, closing it with a click behind them.

Lorenz was bemused. It had not been hard at all to obtain an audience with the prince. The porter, learning that Lorenz came with news "touching the safety of the Marshal and his family," questioned him little, allowed him to pass through the great doors into the castle, and then went quickly to deliver the message. It was not a quarter of an hour before the porter returned with another servant, who bade Lorenz follow him.

He was not bidden to sit, but he reckoned little of it. His heart was too agitated. He went over in his mind, again, what he would say to Herr Sigismund; he had practiced it on his walk to the castle. He had to take care, he thought, lest he stir up in the Marshal a fear that would lash out in vengeance against the peasants and the townsmen. After all, did they not have *some* just grievances? At least the peasants did; the townsmen — what hardships had they suffered that remotely compared with all the peasants had had to endure? Yet, he so loathed the thought of the cruelty the Marshal's fear might inspire that he thought he must choose his words carefully when he spoke either of peasant or burgher.

A clicking sound — the turning of a latch — he glanced to his right where a door, communicating with some other room or passageway, opened. An older man entered the room; he was garbed in a long, dark coat, ermine-lined about the collar. His hair, a silver gray, grew thick upon his head, and his gray beard fell to just below his broad chest. This, Lorenz knew, was Herr Bertold, the Marshal's uncle and chief counselor. Behind him followed a tall, young man and a woman. The man Lorenz recognized immediately from their last meeting, but he scarcely noticed him for the woman's great beauty. She was tall, lithe, and shapely. Her skin was of a marble whiteness, though rose colored in the cheeks. Her eyes were large and round under dark brows. She wore a snow-white wimple over her hair. He had not thought that both the Marshal and the Countess would hold audience with him.

Herr Sigismund and Countess Mechtilde took the high seats at the extreme ends of the long table, while Bertold stood behind the table between them. The old lord's grave demeanor was emphasized by his bushy eyebrows overhanging deep-set eyes. It was he that first addressed Lorenz. "Magister List," he said in a deep-toned though melodious voice, "Greetings. You bring us important tidings?"

Lorenz bowed. "Indeed I do, my lord," he said. "I have just returned from the Tiefer Bach, where I had gone at my lord's bidding to preach and bring the people to submission to my lord's just rule. I return in regret with sad tidings. I failed in my charge."

Bertold grunted. "You failed, you say? Do you accuse yourself of negligence, then?"

Lorenz lifted his eyes and fixed them on those of the old counselor. "I deem not that I was negligent, my lord," he said, with more confidence than he felt. "If I failed, it was not for lack of loyalty or application, though it may have been for want of skill."

"Certainly, his assiduity is not the subject of his visit—for no man would seek an audience to accuse himself of ill-doing—eh, uncle?" It was Herr Sigismund who spoke. Then, addressing Lorenz, he said, "There is something more, doubtless, that you wish to say to us."

The Marshal was as Lorenz had remembered him, except that today he squinted, as if he suffered from headache. But Herr Sigismund's eyes widened when Lorenz said, "I have come to warn you, my lord—your realm and, indeed, yourself and yours face grave danger. Many of the peasants of the Tiefer

Bach have joined forces with rebels from the south and west. They are probably, even now, moving against Weissenbrücke."

Herr Sigismund blanched, but his tone was even as he spoke: "A force of peasants, you say? How many—can you say how many?"

"I cannot say just how many, but I fear a great number of them have bound themselves to war against your lordship. They have already shed blood." Lorenz then told of the meeting in the wood, of Hubmaier and Ecklig, and Frau Berthe. He described the attack on the village church, and the murder of Gottfried. As he spoke, he studied the three sitting before him. The Marshal was agitated, he saw, and frightened. Bertold listened with the demeanor of a man who wants to absorb every word. Only the Countess—she alone seemed calm, even peaceful. She sat, her hands folded on her lap, her eyes cast down. She was listening to him, he was certain, but she was also taking counsel with her own mind.

"I saw that I could do nothing more. I returned here, to warn you." So Lorenz ended his tale and fell silent.

All were silent for some moments. Then Bertold, with knit brows, shot him a glance—"Do you know when they would have set out?"

"I do not," Lorenz replied softly. "But I do not doubt that they have already."

And Bertold, "Are you done?"

"No," Lorenz replied, in the same even tone. He dreaded what came next; he had half a mind not to carry through with it. He pulled from a pocket in his coat the list of names and handed them to Bertold.

The old counselor, with a puzzled look, unfolded the paper. "A list of names?" he said, with what seemed an angry look at Lorenz.

"Yes, the names of conspirators in the city. I have been assured that they are in league with the peasants."

"And who told you this?"

Lorenz paused. "I'd rather not say, if it please my lord," he muttered.

"But you must!" said Bertold, striking his hand on the table. "How can we judge the truth of this, if you do not?"

Lorenz hesitated, then said, "Please be assured, my lord, that those who gave me the names are faithful to . . . "

"No dallying, man!" Bertold nearly shouted. "We don't have time for this! Who gave you these names?"

The old count's peremptory manner irked Lorenz. He raised his eyes to meet Bertold's "May I, my lord, have assurance that their names will not be noised outside this room? Those who gave them to me are innocent of any treachery."

"Yes, you may be so assured, Magister List."

It was not Bertold nor the Marshal who answered him. It was the Countess. Her head was raised, her eyes—they were gray, he now saw—regarded him. "My husband will punish no one who is not deserving of it. Do not fear."

The Countess, he saw, was no mere ornament to the court, beautiful though she was. Her whole demeanor radiated grace mingled with a strength of spirit and courage that one might think no woman could possess. He both trusted her word and was confident that neither her husband nor his uncle would dare gainsay her in this matter.

He bowed. "I give you thanks, my lady," he said. Then looking on Bertold: "It was my aunt, the widow of Meister Georg List, who gave them to me. She had gotten them from her son, Adolf."

Bertold nodded. "*Ach*, I knew your uncle well—I had not known he was kin to you," he said. "The Lists are faithful, of that I have no doubt." Then, turning to the Marshal, "nephew," he said, "we must study this matter and then hold counsel. I suggest we do so immediately."

Herr Sigismund rose. His face was pale, and his pouting lips suggested irresolution; but when he spoke, his voice was even and strong. "Indeed, we must, uncle," he said. Then, addressing Lorenz: "you have served us well, *magister*. You may go now."

Lorenz bowed and turned to go, but then he heard the Countess' voice. "No, go not yet, I pray," she said to him. Then she, too, rose from her chair and said to her husband, "my lord, we cannot let Magister List go from us like this. It is now night and the city gates are locked. Surely we can find a room for him here."

The Marshal nodded. "You may do as you will, my lady," he said. A small smile then passed over his face. "You see, Herr Magister, my wife's solicitude? She can ponder secrets of state and yet give heed to domestic trifles. She is my best counselor."

Lorenz again bowed and turned to depart; but again, he was arrested by the Countess.

Now her expression was grave; the tone of her voice resolute but without rancor. "I would be remiss," she said, "if I did not tell you, Magister List, how much I loathe all that you stand for and what you would do to our realm. I deem you an enemy of Christ's Church. I would be equally remiss, however, if I did not thank you for your fidelity to my lord and his people. In sign of my gratitude, what boon would you ask of us?"

"I ask naught for myself, my lady, but for my people." Lady Mechtilde's question had surprised Lorenz, but now it buoyed up his heart. This one thing, he felt, would not be laid to his charge. "My people, the peasants of the Tiefer Bach, my lady—they are not all guilty; many of them will not put on the *Bundschu*, and some of those who do, do so only out of fear. I would beg this boon: that His Lordship go gently with my people, hear their grievances, and if he can, redress them. So many are faithful, though they have suffered much."

"Your boon is granted, Magister List."

These words the Marshal had spoken. His lordship was still pale in the face, but a new resolution seemed to have descended on him. Lorenz saw that this man was indeed lordly.

"I thank you, my lord," and he bowed

"Thank not me," Herr Sigismund replied, with a slight smile. "It is my lady you should thank."

Lorenz turned to the Countess. "My lady is most kind," he said.

"Kind?" she replied, glancing at the Marshal. "No, not kind. But we do try to be just."

And the Countess Mechtilde smiled on her husband.

CHAPTER 3

L ORENZ WAS AWAKENED BY A RAPPING
on his door. At first, he was confused—was he in his
room in the city? A quick look around the room—no,
he was not. Then he remembered. He was in the castle.

The rapping continued. It grew more insistent. Lorenz rose,
wrapped his cloak around him, and opened the door a crack.
Outside a servant stood, his hand raised as if he were in the
middle of a knock. With a look of annoyance, he let it drop to
his side. "Meister List," he said, "dress yourself. The Marshal
would speak with you."

He found himself following the servant along a hallway,
down a flight of steps, and along another passageway. They
stopped before a large oaken door. The servant knocked.
Lorenz was admitted into the room of the night before.

Herr Sigismund sat where his uncle, Bertold, had stood
the previous evening. The Marshal looked haggard—he had
probably been awake all night, Lorenz thought. Bertold sat
directly to the Marshal's right; to his left, the commander
of the castle guard, Gottfried von Eisenbronn. Several other
counselors were present, as well as the abbot of the *Marienkirche* canons, Pater Adrian Kurz. Sitting against the wall on
the Marshal's left, was Peter Schwach. He gave Lorenz a blank
look, as if he did not know him.

Lorenz bowed. "Magister List," the Marshal began, in a
weary voice, "God's greetings! We have been able to gather our

counselors to us, though it is early morning. I want them to hear from you what you related to us last night. And I am certain that they will have questions for you when you have done."

Herr Sigismund directed Lorenz to sit. And Lorenz began his tale.

He felt like a beast on display to a crowd of gawkers. All eyes were fixed on him, some with no expression; others, like the abbot's, betraying a mild hostility. Gottfried von Eisenbronn did not look at him once; instead, with arms folded and pursed lips, he appeared to be studying the ceiling of the room. From where Lorenz sat, he could not see Peter.

"How long has it been since the attack on the church?" Lorenz had just finished describing Gottfried's murder when an old man with a long neck and prominent Adam's apple, sitting just to the side of the abbot, asked him this. This was Ludwig Storr, Lorenz knew, the castle's seneschal.

"Three days," Lorenz replied. "I departed for the city soon after."

"And when did you arrive in the city?"

Lorenz paused. It occurred to him that if he said, yesterday morning, he would be asked why he did not come to the Marshal directly. Though he could not see him, he felt Peter's eyes on him.

"Yesterday afternoon."

"Very good," Storr replied. "And you came right over to the castle. Very good."

"Can you tell us where the peasant mob was going—that is, were they to move on the city directly?" It was Herr Bertold who asked him this.

"I cannot say. I knew they had designs on the city, but when they would move against it, I don't know."

Herr Bertold nodded. For a time, the room was silent. Lorenz wondered what would come next—would he be peppered with questions? He feared his lie would be exposed—and then what would happen to him? He was angry with himself—why did he feel that he had to spare Peter? It had struck him as queer that, yesterday, Peter had not taken him directly to the Marshal. Yet, he was reluctant to expose Peter. Why?

It was Herr Sigismund who, at last, broke the silence. "Our course is clear," he said. "We must send out scouts to discover what the peasants are up to. As for what else we should do—we will discuss that anon."

Then, turning to Lorenz, he said. "Again, I thank you for your faithfulness to us. I will not keep you longer. You may depart now, back to the city."

Herr Sigismund now rose. "We will now meet, alone, with our uncle and you, Herr Gottfried. As for the rest, God's blessings on you."

Everyone rose. As Lorenz turned to go, he caught sight of Herr Sigismund whispering something in the abbot's ear.

*　*　*

It was late morning when at last he climbed the staircase of the boarding house. He was weary; he had not slept well that night. And then to have been wakened so early in the morning...

He reached the third floor, turned down the hallway and came at last to the entrance of his room. As he opened the door, he noticed something white on the floor. He picked it up; it was a folded piece of paper. Opening, he saw it was from the preacher, Wohlgemut Kraft. It was a short note. Kraft had come down sick; he did not think he could lead the service or preach on Sunday. Would the Herr Magister...

Lorenz closed the door behind him. He threw himself onto his bed. *Ach!* Why this, now? He was so very weary. Of course, if Kraft were sick, he could not refuse; but his whole soul revolted at the thought of it.

It would be Palm Sunday, the beginning of Holy Week. They would celebrate it right evangelically. No papist frippery for them, by God! They would set up the makeshift altar in the

Butchers' Guildhall, for the Marshal, though he allowed them their German mass, would turn over no churches to them. Not yet, at any rate. No images draped in somber purple. They would sing the *Pueri Hebraeorum,* in German, no doubt; but there would be no palm branches and no procession. He would sing the Passion, in German, and he would preach about the grace of God and how we must receive Christ in faith—not like the Jews, who greeted Christ with palms though they would in a few short days betray him.

Betrayal! He thought back on the meeting in the castle that morning. He could not but think that he himself had betrayed, that he was a Judas with the Marshal's thirty pieces of silver jingling in his purse. The Marshal, the Countess, Herr Bertold, the abbot—were they not like the Jewish priests? And was he not like Judas—no, worse than Judas; for Judas at least repented of his treachery, flinging the silver at the high priest's feet. He knew, however, that he would cling to his money bag. He would hold fast to it. He was too afraid to cast it away.

For he knew in his heart—though he sought to deny it with his mind—that, in the end, his people, guilty or innocent, would not be spared. The fear that clutched at the hearts of the counselors and, though he put on a brave face, the Marshal himself, could be purged only by blood vengeance. Once the peasants were routed, the nobles would make sure that such an uprising could never happen again.

And then that lie he had told—oh yes, it was but a small lie, and truth telling then could have done no good. Yet, for reasons he could not fathom yet, he felt that, by telling that lie, he had compounded the betrayal. Whom he had betrayed with the lie—for it *was* but a small lie and of no bearing on events—he could not say. He had perhaps saved Peter some uncomfortable moments and, himself, some vexation—but these did not add up to a betrayal or even anything remotely near one. Why did he bother himself over such gossamer-light peccadilloes?

From what was he sparing Peter? If the Marshal could grant no audience that morning, surely Peter would be in the clear. Yet, Peter had treated his tale like it was a small matter, but the Marshal did not treat it so. The convening of the counselors proved that his news was of great import. And then the fact that Peter did not acknowledge him, even with one of his side-long looks, as he entered the room, puzzled him. Perhaps Peter knew he had erred in judgment and was ashamed, did not want to be exposed. That, Lorenz thought, must be the clue.

Yet, the thought of it all still troubled him.

* * *

Why could he not warm to the German mass? It was the Gospel prayed, of that he had been assured. Yet, it did not stir his heart as the old papist Mass had. It was like a church, still having the form of a church, but gutted of all that had made it fair. A church without images, stained-glass windows, altar piece and lamp, was really rather like a barn; no place for men. So was the German mass.

He sang the mass, that Palm Sunday, in the guild hall—a stately enough building, to be sure, but no church. Not so many attended the mass as on other Sundays—probably because the display was not so magnificent, or sublime, as what they would get at the *Marienkirche*. He was vested in a purple chasuble, for Kraft had thought "such frippery" advisable for the time being, given the Marshal's diffidence. He sang the service entire, read the Passion from the Gospel of Matthew, and distributed the sacrament. The choir, such as it was, sang German hymns. He preached a dull, uninspiring sermon. No palms were passed out. No procession.

When freed from his duty, he dined at a tavern. His fellow diners were strangely quiet. A tension of expectation, he felt, had fallen on the city. For him it was a barely perceptible sense of dread. Christ had entered the city amid children's praises. But joy would be turned to weeping in the end.

376

Leaving the tavern, he wrapped his cloak tightly about him, for it was cold outside. The thought of calling on his aunt and cousin Adolf repulsed him. He returned to his room and read the Scriptures until night—surely, he could stir up some feeling for the sacred within him! But the thrumming, thrumming, thrumming of dread barely allowed him to attend to the words he muttered.

And sleep with its visions afforded him no rest.

* * *

Judica, Domine, nocentes me, expugna impugnantes me: apprehende arma et scutum, et exsurge in adiutorium meum, Domine, virtus salutis meae . . .

The introit of the old Mass flickered through his memory as he led the service the next day, Monday of Holy Week. "Judge those who would harm me, O Lord . . . take up arms and a shield, and rise to help me, O Lord, strength of my salvation." The Gospel appointed for that day told of Mary, how she poured precious ointment on His feet and wiped them with her hair.

"Why was not this ointment sold for three hundred pence and given to the poor?"

". . . the poor you have always with you . . . "

Yes, the poor.

It was the poor who had risen, because they were poor and would be poor no longer. They had been crushed down, ground between mortar and pestle, and would suffer it no longer. They cried with the psalm, *apprehende arma et scutum, et exsurge in adiutorium meum, Domine.* Herr Sigismund doubtless prayed the same prayer, against *his* enemies. Both called on him, who was the strength of their salvation. Who would be heard?

* * *

"'Tis said the Marshal (God save him!) has sent to Strassburg for help from the Austrians."

"Where did you learn this, Aunt?"

"From Berta Stimmlose! She says 'tis all over the city."

(How fast the news travels, he thought.)

"And 'tis said he has only a handful of mounted men — some three score and ten, three score and fifteen, something like that. But there is the militia . . . He has called them up, 'tis said. . . .

" . . . why he don't do something about that pack of traitors in the city, I can't say." Here she lowered her voice. "You gave him the list?"

"I did, Aunt. But you mustn't speak of it, not to anyone."

"*Ach!* Don't worry about me, lad! It's been mum with me — and with Adolf too, I can assure you . . ."

* * *

"And I was as a meek lamb . . . a victim . . ."

Again, the next day, he read the service. The first reading from the Prophet Jeremias.

" . . . and I knew not that they had devised counsels against me, saying: Let us put wood on his bread, and cut him off from the land of the living, and let his name be remembered no more."

A great silence hung over the city. The clouds threatened a storm.

"But thou, O Lord of Sabaoth, who judgest justly and triest the reins and hearts, let me see thy revenge on them: for to thee I have revealed my cause."

Then, the gradual and tract. Then, the Passion according to St. Mark.

He felt nothing. He read it, for duty bade him to. He was like a bystander from a distant country — like that Simon the Cyrenian, forced to carry the cross, but unconcerned with it all. He stood neither with the victim nor the persecutors. He had not fled, for fear or any other cause; for it all touched him not. He was a sojourner in a foreign land.

Of course, he had played a part in the drama — though not an important one. He doubted whether he had affected the

378

course of events in the least. He had cast in his lot, but not his heart. He had done what he thought was his duty. That was all.

He was an unworthy and profitless servant, without remorse and without pity. Like a bystander from a foreign land.

*   *   *

The talk in the tavern that day was of the rumors. Some said they were coming; others said, no, they had turned aside and were moving on Heilbronn. The Marshal had sent agents to pay them off; no, he had sent agents to Strassburg, to enlist the Austrians. He had alerted the militia; no, he was preparing to flee the city. The peasants would fire the city; no, they would free us from oppression . . .

And he, did he care what would befall? The Countess — she had been grateful to him, whom she despised. He had been moved by her beauty and her devotion. But now, now — in his mind's eye he could not conjure up an image of her face.

*   *   *

Who is this that cometh from Edom, with dyed garments from Bosra, this beautiful one in his robe, walking in the greatness of his strength?

He could hardly fix his mind on the reading. He prayed it perfunctorily, for the sake of the people.

Why then is thine apparel red, and thy garments like theirs that tread in the winepress?

The city was abuzz with the news. One of the scouts sent out by the Marshal had returned. A host of peasants, many of them armed with guns, it was reported. Thousands upon thousands of them, moving against the city.

. . . I have trampled on them in my indignation and have trodden them down in my wrath, and their blood is sprinkled upon my garments, and I have stained all my apparel . . .

"Thousands upon thousands" — the words were repeated, passed from street to street. Some spoke in fear; others, with ill-concealed delight. He was certain many praying the service

with him were praying for the *Bundschu*. Few, if any, he was
sure, for the Marshal.

I looked about, and there was none to help.

Where had the peasants gotten the guns? They had many
guns, it was said. "The Counts von Hohenlöwe had gone over
to them, signed the Twelve Articles. They were arming them."

Betrayal.

*At that time the feast of unleavened bread, which is called the
Pasch, was at hand; and the chief priests and the scribes sought
how they might put Jesus to death; but they feared the people . . . "*

To save their wretched hides, the Counts von Hohenlöwe
were arming the peasants. They had turned against their own,
to salvage a little power. What will men not give for power, or
the show of it?

*And Satan entered into Judas, who was surnamed Iscariot, one
of the Twelve . . .*

And were he and his comrades much better? Both he and
Wohlgemut Kraft had agreed—their masses, though said in
German, would keep to the main lines of the Old Mass, so as
not to turn the Marshal needlessly against them. They wanted
power, sacred power—but that were not degrading, if it were
done for the sake of the truth.

If indeed it were.

Wednesday in Holy Week—the day Judas betrayed his Lord.
How many traitors did the city hold? As he left the guild hall
after the service, he saw the militia, a few hundred men, gathered in the *Marktplatz*. They were well armed, but they were
only a few hundred against the thousands bearing down on
the city. And how many Judases were in their number?

And was he, too, Judas?

* * *

He was awakened the next morning by a pounding on his
door. He rose, grabbed his cloak, and wrapped it round him.
He opened the door. Wohlgemut Kraft stood without.

Kraft, he had heard, was on the mend, but his face was pale. He was agitated.

"Come in, man—what are you doing out? You are still not well, I think."

"Don't mind that," Kraft said hoarsely, as he entered. "Close the door!"

"Here, read this!" Kraft handed him a large sheet of paper, affixed with a wax seal.

Reading it, he knew it should have dismayed him, but it did not.

"It was posted on the guild hall door . . . "

Even before he read it, Lorenz knew its purport.

From henceforth, Evangelical worship was banned in the city.

None can expect God's favor, if he ignore what God has appointed . . . From this day forth, any who dares to teach or foster heresy shall be imprisoned . . . By order of Sigismund, Markgraf von Weissenbrücke.

Kraft was livid. He cursed the Marshal, the Countess—"for it was she," he spluttered, "who has moved him to this! She has worked on his fears, the coward!"

Lorenz, however, said nothing. Handing the paper back to Kraft, he walked to his window. Opening it, he looked out on the *Marktplatz*.

He could not say why, but he felt a strange relief. And, for the first time in many months, an earnest of hope.

CHAPTER 4

THE NEXT DAY, GOOD FRIDAY, HE SPENT in his room. For food, he had bought a small loaf; and for drink he had water. All the day, he read the Scriptures, prayed some, and waited. It was a dark and cloudy day, but without rain. A storm threatened; but as of yet, there was no rain.

Through his window, he could see folk streaming into the *Marienkirche.* He recalled — it seemed so many years ago, now — how the prayers, chanted solemnly, the singing of the Passion, and the veneration of the Cross had once moved him. Then, he would kiss Christ's feet, though he knew he was unworthy. Now, he was convinced that, whatever the ritual betokened for others, it meant nothing to him. He was cast off.

He knew not where God was. If he was in the *Marienkirche,* why the destruction that threatened it? If he stood with the Marshal, why his almost certain demise? Was God with the peasants? He thought back on that night in the forest: of that loathsome Jäcklein Ecklig, Frau Berthe, the bestial passions of the mob. Bruder Thaddeus. The burning but yet unconsumed Angel Man. And could *this* be God?

A noise from without jogged him from his reverie. He rose and moved toward the window. He flung open the casement — why the commotion? His nerves were on edge; he expected to see blood-frenzied peasants rushing into the *Markplatz.* But the cries were not of fear and dismay, but of joy! The people in the square were crying out in jubilation! And then he saw it—a body of armed men, and in their midst, on foot and clad in black, the Marshal and the Countess. The people were cheering them—like the Jews did Christ. Yet, this sounding of devotion, even if from many mouths feigned, strangely moved him. He longed, too, to cry out.

The crowds parted before the church portal. The guards formed two lines on either side of Herr Sigismund and Countess Mechtilde. Together, side by side, they climbed the steps towards the doors that opened to the mystery.

* * *

Church bells pealed lustily throughout the city the next morning. The long expectation was over. They had lit the *tricereo* from the bonfire. To the chant of *Lumen Christi! Lumen Christi!* it had been carried through the darkened nave of the church. They had lighted the Paschal candle, and the deacon intoned the joyous sequence,

> *Exultet, iam Angelica turba caelorum,*
> *Exultet, divina mysteria . . .*

Then the readings, like steps of the mystical ladder in the ascent to the culmination and assuaging of all longing:

> *Una autem sabbati valde diluculo venerunt ad*
> *monumentum, portantes quae paraverant aromata:*
> *et invenerunt lapidem revolutum a monumento . . .*

Then the offering of bread and wine, the consecration, and the return to his altar throne of the God-man who had lain in the cold, dark tomb. It was this the bells greeted in raucous jubilation.

Lorenz heard the bells from his room, and he remembered. As a boy he had heard these same bells ring out his first paschal vigil in the city. And over the years he had heard other bells, more keenly musical than these, in Nürnberg and Erfurt. But no bells could ever, he thought, sound as sweet to him as the bells of Weissenbrücke, which spoke to him of youth—his youth, now long lost.

Then the bells ceased their ringing. The Mass would soon be ended, and the city would return to that queer Lenten silence that lay between the vigil of Holy Saturday and the first Mass of Easter morn. It would be as if Christ had not risen. It must be what the disciples felt, seeing only a glimpse of Christ on the way and then his vanishing from their sight.

This Holy Saturday morning, however, a strange commotion stirred the crowd. Instead of dispersing to their homes to await the morning, they gathered in the plaza before the church. A line of knights, mounted, formed up between the crowd and the church steps. Then, from the great church portal, flanked by vested clergy and the white robed canons, came the Marshal with his lady, the Countess, on his right arm. They halted at the edge of the topmost step and motioned for silence from the murmuring throng below them.

Herr Sigismund began to speak. Lorenz grabbed his coat and hat; he left his room, hurried down the steps and out the door, into the plaza. He came to the edge of the crowd; he looked for some way to push himself in among them, but he could find no opening. Still, though only barely, he could hear the Marshal's voice enough to make out the purport of his words.

A large force of peasants was moving on the city, but no one need fear—he had sent for reinforcements from Strassburg. They would doubtless arrive soon. In the interim, the city's defenses were stout enough to hold off an enemy who had no siege engines and sappers. The city's forces were small, but large enough to hold off the enemy, even if the Austrian forces delayed. He was confident, however, they would come very soon—perhaps even this very day!

"And though I have asked my lady, the Countess, to retire to the castle, I myself will remain with you in the city, and, if need be, man the walls myself, doing duty with the humblest of my soldiers."

At these words, cheers went up from the knights, and from the crowd. (Though, thought Lorenz, the crowd's response sounded feeble and diffident.) He wondered if many at all among them would, in the press, stand with Herr Sigismund or gladly throw off his livery and join the ranks of the bloody peasants.

* * *

That evening, an hour before sunset, the peasant army made camp before the walls of Weissenbrücke. Lorenz was certain that the Marshal had intended to send the Countess and their son away, far from the city; but events had overtaken them. He was certain that she had not left the castle. And now she was trapped inside its walls. Herr Sigismund's scouts had misinformed him of the peasant mob's whereabouts.

When he had heard the news, Lorenz betook himself to the western gate. It was closed and blocked, of course; but he had not thought of passing through. He turned, rather, down a side street, and then along another lateral. He climbed the stone steps to the catwalk. No one hindered him — and, indeed, the militiamen on the walls were few and seeming listless. One young man glanced at Lorenz and then looked out again over the wall. Lorenz's eyes followed his.

There, below, encamped on the fields but newly plowed and sewn, spread an immense host of men. Already they had lit their campfires; the tongues of flame flickering in the early dusk were innumerable. Thousands upon thousands there were, it seemed.

* * *

The bells of the city's churches greeted the morning. In the plaza, the cool of night radiated from the flagstones. Lorenz stood by the octagonal fountain, but without diffidence. He had, in the dark throes of night, settled his mind. As the Marshal and his men entered the *Marienkirche*, Lorenz followed them. He would, this Easter morning, hear Mass.

Resurrexi, et adhuc tecum sum, Alleluia . . .

The music of the introit, sung by the strong male voices of
the choir, flowed over him like a refreshing water. It was this,
this that he had longed for all these long, barren years. His
heart had been like a land parched dry and waterless. He felt
no quickening of life within himself—not yet. But he felt
thoroughly and utterly drenched. The wetness would moisten
the dry husks; the new life had to burst forth from the dead
seed corn, sending up its green shoots toward the sun.

. . . posuisti super me manum tuam . . .
Domine, probasti me et cognovisti me,
tu cognovisti sessionem meam et resurrectionem meam

"You have laid on me your hand, you have known me—
but I have hidden in the tomb, fearful of resurrection.
Grant me, oh, grant me your resurrection!"

The words of the Epistle—*Expurgate vetus fermentum*—commanded him, but coaxingly, in the sweetest tones of blandish-
ment: *Purge out the old leaven; be you a new dough, for Christ
our Pasch is sacrificed.*

"Grant it, O Lord, grant it; for I am unable!"

He stood at the back of the church, in the shadow of a pillar.
The nave was packed with townsmen, rich and poor, young and
old. And at the farthest end, nearest the sanctuary, the Marshal and his retinue. All these, he knew, belonged there, but
not he. He was Judas, still clutching his bag of silver. Would
he cast it at the feet of his Lord or hurry away and squander
it, the price of his betrayal, like a prodigal, on the cheap and
tawdry blandishments of the world?

Mors et vita duello,
Conflixere mirando . . .

Ach! Glorious God! In his reverie he had not heard the inton-
ing of the sequence. Life and death, struggling in wondrous

conflict—here, in this church, in the fields outside the city, in the universe entire, but not least in himself. What would be the issue of that contention?

> *Surrexit Christus, spes mea,*
> *Praecedet suos in Galilaeam . . .*

But would he, even he, follow?

> *Sequentia Sancti Evangelii secundum Marcum . . .*
> *In illo tempore, Maria Magadalena et Maria Iacobi, et*
> *Salome emerunt aromata ut venientes ungerent Iesum . . .*
> *fugerunt de monumento: invaserant enim eas tremor et*
> *pavor . . .*

Like the women—*Ach, Gott!* Like the women he had been running, fleeing, fearful of what he would see when the stone of his own tomb was rolled away. No young man clothed in white would greet him with words of peace and hope; for if Christ had lain there, he had been absent for many a long day. But as he, alone, wandered outside the tomb in the wasted garden of his soul—if he could but hear the voice, speaking commonplace-wise, "Why do you weep? Whom do you seek?" he would cast himself at the feet of him who spoke, without presumptuous hand. He would only wait until the Other, father-like, lifted him from the dust and enfolded him in a close embrace.

> *Cito proferte stolam primam, et induite eum . . .*

* * *

Oremus!

The priest had turned and was facing the altar. The choir had intoned the chant. All else was quiet.

> *Terra tremuit et quievit, dum*
> *resurgeret in iudicio Deus . . .*

One great door of the church flew open. Clear sunlight washed the flagstones with their radiance. The man stopped just inside the portal. He was pale with terror. Song reverberated in groined vaults. His voice echoed, resounded—

"Betrayed! God help us, they are through the walls! The city has been taken!" His words were taken up and rippled like a wave through the church.

The voices that had just sung alleluia faltered. A roar of dismay rippled in a black wave through the nave. Three knights, who had been standing at the back but whom heretofore Lorenz had not noticed, rushed to the open door, shoved the man aside, and pulled it closed. Then, hoisting the large, heavy beam, they barred it shut.

The crowd swayed like corn blown by a gust of wind. It parted to right and left as knights, with swords drawn, forced their way down the center aisle. At their head strode the Marshal, his sword yet sheathed.

A roar and a clamor surrounded Lorenz on all sides. He saw everything that was happening, like one walking in a dream. The grim-visaged knights, the Marshal issuing commands, but coolly, without a glimmer of fear in his countenance. The knights flanked him on left and right and stood in two ranks behind him. And behind them, behind the people, at the far end of the church, the priest stood at the altar, facing the East. He was continuing the prayers of the Mass.

A silence descended on the church. Waiting. Expectation. Then, from outside, a roar of voices, faint at first but growing louder and louder, drawing ever closer. The great doors shook against the beam barring them fast. A clamor of anger and rage from without; then a loud banging, striking at the door, and a voice, muffled by the thick wood planks, demanding entrance. The Marshal, his right hand grasping the hilt of his still sheathed sword, cried out, "You shall not enter! Go back from whence you came, in the name of God!"

The doors shook, the thick beam barring them rattled in its iron braces. Lorenz glanced toward the sanctuary; the priest was still saying the Mass. He had just intoned the *prefatio.* Though Lorenz could not clearly make out the words for all the racket from outside, he knew them well—

> *Te quidem, Domine, omni tempore, sed in hac potissimum die gloriosius praedicare, cum Pascha nostra immolatus est Christus. Ipse enim verus est Agnus, qui abstulit peccata mundi . . .*

> "The true Lamb, who has taken away the sins of the world . . ."

The choir—they still kept their place in the sanctuary!— chanted, *Sanctus, Sanctus, Sanctus, Dominus Deus Sabaoth!*

A great boom and a crash! The doors jarred, groaned from the force of the blow, as if by the hand of a giant. Again, another crash. Voices from behind him cried out in dismay, "a ram, they have a ram! Christus, Maria, save us!" And the Marshal stood there, still as a statue, his hand on his sword's hilt, his eyes fixed on the doors. Another crash, and yet another—the giant was pummeling the doors, but the beam still held them fast. But it would not be long before all gave way—Lorenz could see that the wood at the center was beginning to splinter. Another slam; the metal braces cried out their anguish as they were bent back against the force—but then—ah, the piercing beauty of it!—the church bells began to ring. Their resonance reverberated throughout the church, drowning out the cries of anger from without.

Lorenz turned his eyes to the sanctuary. Raised on high, a pin-prick of white in the hands of the priest. A tiny sun of purest light, illumining the world. Then, it descended, and the priest fell to his knees.

Another crash, and then another. The wood was splitting—but, again, the bells in the steeple rang as the chalice rose, its gold and jewels glittering in flames of candle light.

Another slam. Another crash. A groan and a snapping crack. The head of the ram broke through into the church. The beam leaped from its metal braces and fell with a thud onto the stone. The broken doors were shoved in. The Marshal cried out and drew his sword. With a roar, the peasant mob — some armed with pikes, others with swords, still others with pitch forks and a few with guns — rushed into the church. The Marshal and his knights advanced, the sunlight streaming into the nave flashed from their naked blades. With shrieks and cries and cursing, the first line of peasants fell before the onslaught of the Marshal's grim soldiery. Like a wall of steel, Herr Sigismund and his henchmen drove the peasants back over the threshold and down the steps. Some of the knights sang as they plied their brands, striking at their foes. A shout rose from within the church — the attack had been turned to a rout! Lorenz felt himself being pushed forward by the press from behind. He stumbled, but fell against a shattered door. He stepped over a body at his feet and found himself outside.

Then he raised his eyes, and his heart quailed, and sank. The Marshal and his men fought on, still driving the foe before them; but below them, in the plaza, churned a sea of men — hundreds upon hundreds of them. Terror, perhaps, of the Marshal's first assault had driven them back; but now that the paltry number of their foe was apparent, like a wave, they surged forward again. There was no order in their attack; and like a flood water that rushes and breaks against an obstacle in its path, so the peasants' frontal assault slammed into and fell before the Marshal and his men. But it was not long before the peasant deluge swept the flanks of the small band, pressing in on it from the sides. The insulated cohort of knights reformed and now fought back-to-back, with their lord in their midst. Pikes rose and fell, or were driven in like spears. Knights fell, struck in the head or neck, or bludgeoned in the gut. Herr Sigismund pushed through the curtain of his men, parried a pike thrust, and with one deft upper cut, struck his foe in the neck, severing the head from the body...

Chapter 4

A blow to the side—

Lorenz lost his balance, and fell, knocking his head against the carven stone. Reeling, he glanced round to see what struck him. He felt a hand grab him by the collar of his coat, and again losing his balance, he tumbled down the steps. In a trice, his assailant was upon him. With what was left of his strength, he fought back; but the other man struck him in the stomach. He gasped for breath, tried to roll away, but the other had him by his collar. He felt a point of cold steel press against his throat. He fell limp, and waited for the final thrust.

But it did not come.

Instead, through the churning confusion like a roar in his head, he heard a high-pitched laugh; then, a snarl—

"God's greetings, brother! I'd hoped I'd find ye here!"

And Lorenz found himself staring up into the face of Eitel Moeller.

391

CHAPTER 5

ITEL DID NOT REMOVE THE BLADE from Lorenz's throat. "Heh, heh! My preacher kinsman!" Eitel's freckled face contorted into a grin. "God, 'tis good to see ye again!" And Eitel laughed

Eitel mocked him. "Ye high-tailed it out of the village fast enough. Ye thought ye'd find safety with your marshal, didn't ye! As ye see today, 'twas not to be so!"

Eitel gloated. "And now look at ye — ye're not the great man you thought ye were! And here ye are, at the mercy of that Eitel Moeller that all of ye looked down on — even that bitch of a wife of mine."

Lorenz, though he could not understand why, felt at peace with what he was certain would be his fate — Eitel would slit his gullet, he was sure. He almost hoped that the man would just get it over with. But to speak thus of Inge — *that,* at least, could still stir his blood.

"Hold your tongue, dog! How dare you . . . "

Eitel's face screwed itself into a mask of imbecile rage. His voice shrieked — "how do ye dare! I can slit your goddamn throat!" He pressed the knife blade in more firmly.

Again, Lorenz felt a calm enfold him. He looked directly into Eitel's eyes. "Then do it and leave me at peace," he said.

This was not the response Eitel had expected. His rage dissipated in a moment. An idiotic expression of wonder passed over his countenance. A feeling of disgust overwhelmed Lorenz.

"To think, I must die at the hands of this fool!" he thought.

But Eitel's confusion was fleeting. Cruelty now twisted his features. "Ye don't understand me, Inge's brother—ye don't ken my family feeling! Ye thought, didn't ye," he said, bobbing his head, "that I'd kill my own kinsman? No, brother, ye'll not die at *my* hands—there's others who can tickle ye better than me. Now pick your fuckin' carcass off the ground. Don't try to fight me, or I'll forget ye're my dear wife's brother and skewer ye!"

Slowly, Lorenz, his head throbbing, lifted himself up from the ground, while Eitel, with his left hand, kept hold of his collar and with his right pressed the point of the knife against his throat. When both were standing, Eitel quickly glanced to his right. He smiled cruelly and laughed in Lorenz's face. He called out, "brothers! Come here! 'Tis me, Eitel Moeller! Come see the rat I've caught!"

Lorenz saw three men separate themselves from the roiling mob of peasants and approach them. He recognized them—they were men from the village. A savage cry tore from their throats when they saw Lorenz.

"'Tis my kinsman, the preacher!" Eitel laughed. "What say ye? Shall we make him feel what it means to betray his folk?" One of the men—Lorenz recalled his name, Klaus Niederauer—gnarled, "*Ach!* Let's play with him, Eitel!"

"No, brother, no," Eitel said, his eyes searching Lorenz's face, as if he were gauging the effect of his words. "We'll do nothin' to him. 'Tisn't our place now, is it? And he is my kinsman. No, we'll take him to the Lady—she'll tickle him good, I'll warrant ye."

Eitel directed Klaus to grasp Lorenz's left arm while he held onto his right. One of them walked behind while the other led the way before Lorenz. As they walked along the base of the *Marienkirche's* steps, Eitel halted them and pointed upward. There a remnant of the knights was making a last, desperate stand against the mob of peasants, pressing on them from all sides. He could not see the Marshal. The battle would soon be over. All was lost.

With a thrust of his hand, Eitel shoved Lorenz forward. The four men, with their prisoner, pushed their way across the *Marktplatz.*

* * *

The street was thick with people, mostly men, clamoring, shouting. Some were singing—Lorenz could catch snatches of hymns garbled with ribald songs. Men laughed aloud, others cursed, as they collided with one another. Some were moving toward the *Marktplatz*, others were heading away from it. Still others dashed from one side of the street to the other, or turned down laterals. Nearly all were armed with long knives, swords, pikes; some, with guns. A wine merchant's shop had been broken into, and several men were emerging from it equipped with bottles.

The cacophony in the street was deafening; Eitel shouted for people to make way, but he could not be heard. Their progress was very slow. Lorenz scarcely wondered where he was being taken—they were on the street that led to the western gate; but he thought little more about the direction they were going. He was certain that, whatever path they took, it would end in his death. The prospect did not frighten him. It left him numb.

He marveled that, scarcely an hour before, he had been hearing Mass in the *Marienkirche.* The thoughts that had agitated him then had flitted away. He had awakened from a dream, he felt, into the cold light of day; he had passed from a beauty clouded by incense, pungently sweet, alluring, into a damp greyness that chilled him to the marrow and left him feeling dead. The world—the real world—was drab; it was soaking into him with its ineluctable gloom.

A peasant with a long knife thrust into his belt and grasping a bottle haled Eitel. They shouted something to each other and then the peasant offered Eitel the bottle. He tilted it to his mouth, spilling some of liquor onto his beard and doublet. "Have a care, whoreson!" the other shouted; and both laughed. Eitel turned and thrust the bottle into Lorenz's face—

"Drink, kinsman!"

Lorenz shook his head.

"Drink, for 'twill likely be your last!"

"By God, don't waste it on him!" Klaus Niederauer tore the bottle from Eitel's hands and took a long draw. They passed it around until the first peasant grabbed it back. He had torn it from Eitel, and cursing him, stumbled away in the direction of the *Marktplatz.*

A blow landed between his shoulder blades, and Lorenz, losing his balance, fell to the cobblestones. Niederauer and another of the peasants pulled him up roughly and forced him to move on. Lorenz's head was throbbing, and he was beginning to feel sick. Whatever would happen to him, he hoped it would happen quickly.

* * *

Shouting and cursing—and a voice booming out over the din. They had come to a halt. Looking up, Lorenz saw they were only a few yards from the western gate. It was closed, and men, armed with guns and pikes, were lined up before it. Some also carrying guns were posted on the parapet of the city wall. They were members of the city militia.

With the throbbing in his head, Lorenz could not make out what the voice was saying. It came from a man posted on the parapet just to the left of the gate.

Eitel swore a round oath and accosted a peasant standing nearby. "What in the name of hell is going on?"

The other turned—he was a man of some two-score years and ten, Lorenz thought, with a thick mop of hair and a long beard, both grizzled. "They won't let us through," he said, with a Swabian accent. "The town rats say 'tis by orders of Hubmaier. *I* say they're liars!"

"We're more than they are," Eitel replied. "Can't we rush the bastards?"

"If ye want to stop lead," the other said. "Look, them on the walls have guns."

Eitel swore again. He turned and motioned to Niederauer and the others to follow him, and then began pushing through the crowd. "We're here on business for Hubmaier and Jäcklein Ecklig. We've got a prisoner!" he cried. And though curses flew at him, people moved aside. Pushed and prodded by his captors, Lorenz stumbled on. He fixed his eyes on the ground before him.

When at last they halted again, Lorenz knew they were close to the gate. He felt dizzy, and he screwed his eyes shut, hoping he wouldn't collapse.

"We've got to be let through—we've got a prisoner for Jäcklein!" It was Eitel who spoke. A voice—it must have been a guard's—answered, "No one's to be let through yet."

"But Jäcklein—and Hubmaier—want this man. We have to get through!"

The other growled, "tell it in the guardhouse yonder!"

Eitel must have done as the man said, for Lorenz heard nothing more than the general clamor around him. He bit his lower lip, clenched his fingernails into the palms of his hands. He felt his head spinning. He had to keep from collapsing.

After what seemed an age of pain and apprehension, he heard someone shouting, "make way!" Then, he heard a voice say, "Is this your prisoner?"

"Yes, and Hubmaier and Jäcklein are waiting for him!" It was Eitel who spoke.

Then, he heard another man chuckle. "That is no prisoner," he said. "You'll have to let him go."

With a shock of recognition, Lorenz opened his eyes and looked to whence the voice came.

"We will not!" Eitel cried. "He's ours! He's a traitor!"

"No, he is not yours," the other said. "He belongs to the city. He is our preacher of the Holy Evangel." The last words were tinged with mockery.

Eitel cursed, but he did not resist—he was surrounded by well-armed men. With a nod of his head, he directed Niederauer and the others to let go their hold. Lorenz stumbled forward until he stood face to face with his deliverer.

"Peter Schwach," he managed to say in his bewilderment. "It is you! I . . . I don't understand."

"Nor can you for the nonce," the other said. "Here, come with me."

And taking Lorenz by the arm, Peter led him with slow steps to the guardhouse.

CHAPTER 6

LORENZ AWOKE, CONFUSED. HE SWUNG himself on the cot, sat up—and the pain in his head recalled to him all that had happened that day.

What he last remembered was entering the guardhouse and then laying himself down on a cot on the far side of the small room. "I must then have fallen asleep," he thought to himself. He leaned forward, his elbows resting on his knees and his head in his hands. He sighed.

"I trust you are feeling better?"

Without moving, Lorenz answered that he was—"though my head still aches."

Peter rose from where he was sitting behind a simple wood table. From a clay pitcher on the table, he poured out a cup of water. He offered it to Lorenz, who accepted it gladly, for he was parched.

"What time is it?"

"About an hour past noon. You have slept some time. I think you are probably hungry?"

"I am."

Peter tore a piece from a loaf on the table and handed it to Lorenz. The bread was rather stale, but his hunger made him scarcely notice it. When he had finished the bread, he was still hungry. But he did not ask for more.

"I owe you thanks, Peter," he said.

"You owe me nothing. 'Tis only my repayment for your

398

keeping mum with the Marshal. It probably saved my skin."

Lorenz ignored the last words. "Well, if you hadn't stepped in, those men—well, I have probably never been closer to death."

"I was an agent of divine providence, then, my dear preacher, eh?"

"We all are, Peter."

Yes, we all are, Lorenz thought—and what sense does it all make in the end? His failure to save the Marshal, his journey to his home, his reticence to reveal his friend's guilt, his repentance in the church—all mere gestures without meaning, cankered buds, no hope of burgeoning fruit. Did anything have meaning?

Peter sat down again behind the table. Lorenz could feel his eyes on him.

"Those peasants—they bore you no friendship," Peter said matter-of-factly.

Lorenz sighed. "One bore me great friendship," he said. "He is my kinsman."

Peter laughed. "Ah, the blessings of family! Don't I know it well." There was bitterness in Peter's voice. Then, he added, "friendship can be near as treacherous . . . "

"And sworn fealty."

Silence. Lorenz knew his words had struck home. He had not meant to say it—his best chance of saving himself rested, he knew, in Peter's good pleasure. He could have kept silent, pretended gratitude, friendship, and at the first opportunity, fled back to Nürnberg. Ah, Nürnberg! But what would he find, even there? Memories of her, longings unappeased. And Wittenberg—a prospect of long, dreary years of pretense. Was he capable of such a pantomime? No, perhaps it were better if he died here and now. God's providence . . .

"Ah, yes, *fealty*," Peter's chuckle broke the silence. "The sentiment by which they bind us. A tawdry bit of goods purchased at a paltry price. To be kicked aside, like a piece of trash in one's path. You know that's true . . ."

Lorenz massaged his head. "I do not know that," he said.

Again, silence. He could hear Peter pour himself a cup of water. The cup slammed down on the table with a dull thud. The chair creaked.

"I saved your life, Lorenz." There was petulance in Peter's tone, but also a note of warning.

"But not the Marshal's." Lorenz straightened himself, but he did not look at Peter. "I wondered at it, but now it all fits," he said—"why you sent me away."

"And why was that?"

"Why else? I could have ruined your plot."

Peter forced a laugh. "Oh, there was little fear of that," he said. "I knew the peasants were but a few days away, and there would be little hope that the Austrians would come in time—if they came at all. That was the Marshal's only hope—his overlord and protector, the man to whom he had sworn *fealty*—Herr Markgraf Casimir—was too preoccupied with his own peasant troubles to concern himself with his little Weissenbrücke. No, your news could have made no difference to the outcome."

"Then, why didn't you let me in to Herr Sigismund?"

"Superstition, perhaps?" Peter jeered. "I was going to take no chances."

Lorenz leaned forward and rested his head in his hands. Again, a lingering silence.

Then Peter continued in a calm recital. "The militia commander was with us," he said. "Most of the men supported us. Even if the Marshal had known the names of the ringleaders, he could have done nothing—there were too many of us, and he knew it. The city would not have held out until help came, if help would have come, for its defenses were weak. The gates would just not stay shut . . ."

"And the castle?"

"Its defenses were strangely weak, too. It scarcely resisted."

Lorenz thought of the Countess and her child and winced. The ruffianly mob, what had they done to her? She was beautiful. And what had *she* done to them? The lords, the priests—*they* were guilty; but the womenfolk, the children . . . of course, peasant women and children had suffered, and were suffering. Vengeance knew no pity.

"Why did you do it, Peter?"

He heard Peter's chair scrape against the stone floor. He had risen. "*Why did you do it!*" Peter's tone was scornful. "*Ach,* Lorenz! Don't give me that unctuous flap! After all, you—did not you have a hand in all this . . . "

Peter's words stung him. He sat up and for the first time turned and looked at Peter. "I had a hand in this? By God, Peter! I tried to stop it . . . " His weary tone could scarcely mask the sudden jab of pain he felt at Peter's blow.

Peter smiled derisively. Lorenz knew that he saw right through him. "Oh, Lorenz, you little, carping innocent," he sneered. "You believe none of that. If anything, you have done more than anyone to bring this all to pass."

"I?"

Peter now was pacing the small room. Back and forth, back and forth. "Yes, you," he said, "though not you alone. You and your Luther and your Karlstadt—oh, yes, I know he was in the city—and all your pack of petty preachers!"

"I scarcely understand you . . . "

"Do you?" Peter wagged his head. "Your *Evangel.* It and nothing else has ignited the dry kindling of discontent in Germany. You did not lay the piles—it was the princes and priests who did that. They have heaped hardships on the peasants blithely—you, a peasant, I shouldn't need tell you that. But this conflagration had not started or at least have grown so terrible if you had not fired it with your preaching. You and

Luther have preached a gospel of blood-letting. You cannot pretend that it isn't so!"

The cold pain of recognition—wasn't this devil speaking the truth? Oh, yes, yes—hadn't he, many a time, winced at the brutality and violence of Luther's calls for liberation? Hadn't he himself doubted, wrestled with his doubt? And wasn't he, just a few hours since, ready to cast it to the ground in a paroxysm of repentance?

"Oh, you offered it all up on a golden platter to us! And can you blame me, or the townsmen here, for taking advantage of the splendid opportunity you presented us? A league with the peasants under the banner of the new Gospel could only give us what we hankered for—the townsmen, the coffers of the Church, and I . . . ."

A dull nausea passed over Lorenz. Was it for this, *this* that he had labored, sweated blood in his secret chamber? And this man—"have I been the agent of his ruin?" Could such a man—could such men as this Peter Schwach resist the bauble of gold he and the likes of him had held out to them? And now, in this place, to see it all for the first time! God's hidden will...

Peter halted, looking down on Lorenz. The man's eyes flickered with a cruel gleam. He and Lorenz stared in silence at each other. He scarcely dared ask the question, but his reluctance could not command his lips—

"And you? What could you gain from this, Peter?"

The answer was what he had expected.

"Vengeance, Lorenz."

The mist that had partly obscured the man's features in a silhouette of darkness—it was if a sudden wind had blown it away. He now saw the man whom he once thought a friend for what he was, and always had been. The boy's boasting and petty cruelty; the mockery and raillery; the scorn of the man, heaped on all whose abilities and accomplishments he had envied; the cringing cowardice masked by a strutting arrogance.

He had found, at last, the way to pay them all back for all the disdain and condescension they had heaped on him, a petty servant of a petty lord, a lackey clad in threadbare finery.

A loud knocking on the door jolted Lorenz from his reverie. Peter, turned, opened the door and exchanged words with someone without. Then, closing the door, he turned to Lorenz.

"You scorn me? Pity me, perhaps?" he said, with his old, self-assured smile. "Do not. Save it for those who don't want it."

He opened the door. Outside, a large, boisterous crowd was moving about.

"Come, Lorenz. Our interview is ended. You will now accompany me to witness the final drama. With your own eyes you will see what you and I have wrought."

403

CHAPTER 7

I N THE MEADOW, THE NEW GRASS, A FIR-
mament for infant blossoms, had been trampled underfoot. A space had been cleared amid the green expanse
of bobbing white and yellow flowers (here and there a splash
of purple) where stood but three—two men and a woman.

When Lorenz had stepped from the guardhouse, he had
been accosted by two militiamen. Peter commanded them to
bind his hands behind his back—"though none too roughly."
Still, the rope bit into the flesh of his wrists.

The meadow lay just outside the city gate. The road leading to the castle skirted it along its northern edge. Astride
the road and spilling into the meadow, a confusion of men,
women, and children—townsfolk and peasants, many of
them armed. They sang and a few danced; there were musicians among them, playing on the sackbut, the pipes, and
the drum. They laughed boisterously, swore oaths, and jeered.
Some wore priests' vestments. A woman wielding a knife—a
rouged whore—had decked herself out in a gold chasuble. It
was stained with blood.

Peter led the way; the militiamen, one on either side of
Lorenz, thrust him forward. The city gates now stood wide
open; a raucous, drunken crowd of peasants blocked the
way. Peter commanded several militiamen to clear a path for
them. The peasants cursed and swore—"what do ye think ye
be—bloody lords?" But they moved aside nevertheless.

Chapter 7

Though more and more folk flowed out of the gate, along the road and onto the meadow, none dared step into the open space amid the green. There flowers—white, yellow, and purple—still swayed in a gentle breeze. The crowd pressed closer and closer on the clearing, like a noose being slowly tightened, but they never crossed into the magic circle in which stood two men and a woman.

The armed militiamen preceding him punched a path for Peter through the pressing crowd. Lorenz, flanked by the two militiamen, followed. Seeing him bound, several of the bystanders must have thought him a prisoner. They jeered and spat at him; they cursed him with round oaths.

"Jäcklein will know how to carve ye up good!"

"More shit'll be pouring out of your ass than your mouth when you've seen the Lady!"

"She'll have ye pricked like a pincushion!"

"She'll have your neck stretched on the gallows!"

"She'll castrate ye like the pig ye are!"

Lorenz half remembered that Eitel had spoken of a lady. What did it mean?

When they had reached the edge of the crowd, Lorenz was pulled up with a jerk. He now stood on the very verge of the great empty space in the midst of the meadow—empty now except for four figures, for Peter had joined the three. He was speaking to a thin, shortish man, clean shaven but with long, unkempt locks. Jäcklein Ecklig. The woman—he now recognized her, but she did not appear so young or fair as she had in the grayness of the forest's early dawn. Under her coarse woolen gown, her form was thin and slightly bent. Her hair, streaked with gray, enhaloed an ashen-white face. She was wringing her white, skeletal hands as her pale lips muttered words he could not hear. With her eyes she scanned the crowds; once they touched on him, and he shuddered; but as quickly they flitted away. It was not him she sought.

The terror of her — Frau Berthe — "the Lady," doubtless — had held him; but now he forced his eyes away, lest she hex him. They fell on the fourth among the small throng. Clad in a dirty doublet and hose he stood. He was bound round with ropes. His bare head was bowed; strands of his long, yellow-brown hair hung about his face, obscuring it. Though his demeanor suggested dejection, his hands, bound to his sides by ropes, were clenched. He was unbroken.

* * *

Like a storm rising suddenly from afar, bellowing with an ever-increasing roar through stands of forest trees, a savage clamor and shouting stirred through the ranks of the host girdling the clearing. Pressed by the crowd, Lorenz and his guards were pushed and shoved several feet to their left; bound as he was, he almost lost his footing All around him, men were emitting full-throated cries; his guards took up the shout. In confusion and fear, Lorenz looked round from right to left, and then into the clearing.

There, the bound man — he had raised his head at the voice of the shouting. His face was pale with fear and sorrow. He cried out and plunged forward toward the crowd; but several men, carrying long knives, ran into the clearing and restrained him. He struggled, but they held him fast. He slammed his body against one of them, but one of the men struck him in the face, while a third pressed the point of a knife to his throat. The man gave up the fight and stared before him with dumb horror.

Now Lorenz recognized him, and fear and pity pierced him through. The man in the clearing, bound and now utterly humiliated, was Herr Sigismund von Weissenbrücke. The Marshal.

* * *

But what had drawn the Marshal's gaze and stirred his desperation? It was a simple dung cart, pulled by a mule led by a peasant. It was against this simple conveyance that the shouting and cursing had been directed. Sitting on the edge of the cart,

406

his back to the mule, a man clad in the Marshal's livery played on a cornet. Lorenz recognized him—it was Melchior Nonnenmacher, the Marshal's piper. The tune he played was loud and lusty—a song one piped at a festival or wedding. But it was not this simple man that drew the boisterous shouts and catcalls. It was she who sat before him in the cart. "God, no!" Lorenz muttered. It was the Countess. In her arms she held a young boy.

When the cart halted amid the clearing, Nonnenmacher rose and, bowing to the crowd (who answered with wild cheering), blared a new tune—one redolent of triumph; and while he played, Frau Berthe, laughing, danced with slow, grotesque steps around the cart. Then, laying aside his instrument, Nonnenmacher tore off his livery and threw it to the ground. The crowds again cheered their approval.

Lorenz paid little heed to the piper; it was on the Countess that he fixed his eyes. He saw her rise—she was not clad in finery but in a simple, brown serge gown. Her fair hair hung unbound over her shoulders and to the small of her back, as if she were a maid. She placed the boy on the floor of the cart and made as if she would climb out. Nonnenmacher leaped from the cart, and bowing to her with mock gallantry, opened the tail gate to help her down. He held out his hand, but she disdained it. Instead, climbing down clumsily from the cart by herself, she took her son in her arms. She strode over the greensward to where her husband stood.

Lorenz could not see the lady's face, but he saw a spasm of sorrow pass over the Marshal's countenance. Bound as he was, he could not take her or their son into his embrace; but the Countess brought the boy close to his father, who kissed him on the forehead. She then turned from her husband and crossed the few feet to where Peter stood with Jäcklein. For a moment she stood, straight and proud as a fair young tree, looking Peter directly in the eye. Then, she fell to her knees before him.

Lorenz could not interpret the expression that now passed over Peter's face. He could not understand it—this must have been just the sort of thing Peter had longed for: he had humbled those who had despised him. *She* was begging *him* for her husband's life! From the convulsive heaving of her body, Lorenz could see she was weeping; her head bowed, her fair locks were sweeping the grass. Only a heart of stone, Lorenz thought, could resist so piteous an appeal.

But it was not pity that Lorenz saw in Peter's countenance; it was consternation. The man was struggling within his own soul; but what passion had bewildered him, Lorenz could not tell. "Peter," he said under his breath, "have mercy, man! Have mercy!"

And, as if in in response to this entreaty, he saw Peter lean over slightly and speak to her. She raised herself upright on her knees and lifted her face to him. He held out his hands, and taking hers, drew her up onto her feet. And with her and the child he walked over to where the Marshal stood, and in a voice loud enough so that Lorenz could hear it, commanded the guards to unbind him.

The guards, confused, glanced over at Jäcklein. The priest said nothing but nodded his approval. As they began to untie the rope, Peter said, in a voice that could be heard in the first ranks of the crowd, "you are free! You will go hence from this land; and if ever you return, your life will be forfeit!"

A cry of dismay and anger arose from the crowd when it understood what was happening. The Marshal, now freed from his bonds, took a few tentative steps forward; Peter stopped him, and pointed toward the dung cart. Herr Sigismund drew himself up proudly, hesitated, but then turned his steps toward the cart, holding the Countess' hand in his.

They had taken only a few steps when a wild cry leaped over the clamoring of the crowd. It was Jäcklein who had cried out, and his voice had barely fallen silent when five or six men ran out from the crowd. Shoving the Countess and her son aside, they fell on the Marshal. They plunged sharpened spikes into his body. He fell to the grass, alive with white, yellow, and purple blossoms, but they would not let up. Up and down, up and down, the spikes rose and fell until Herr Sigismund's body was left a bleeding pulp.

Last to pierce the dead flesh was Frau Berthe. When she pulled her long knife from the corpse, she squatted on her haunches beside it.

She smeared her shoes with the gore and fat.

LENZGRAB

CHAPTER 1

"SHE DID NOT WEEP. IT IS ODD, BUT IT would have disappointed me if she had. It would have cheapened his death somehow, if she had."

"And they spared her?"

"Yes, and the child, too. They loaded the two of them onto the dung cart. When some of the women mocked her, she spoke only of the Friday, the passion . . . "

She fell silent and pensive.

"And where did they take them?" she said at last.

"To Heilbronn, I learned."

He was relieved she did not ask him about himself. Even now he could not express, even to himself, what he had then felt.

She shook her head. Her eyes grew hard. "That man, Peter Schwach . . . "

"I do not think he was treacherous, not then," he hastened to say. "He hated himself for it, I think; but he had not betrayed her. He who did suffered bitterly for it." He would say no more to her about it—the brutality at Böblingen. Ecklig, Nonnen-macher the piper, bound to trees, the fire kindled at their feet. The roasting. How they must have howled!

"It was the beginning of his downfall, his pity. He had wanted to be a great man, one of the leaders—but his lapse (as he must have thought it) lost him the confidence of the revolutionists. Oh, they did not entirely rebuff him; they needed Peter's cunning and knowledge of affairs. But at last,

413

he was not admitted to the inner circle. He was treated as a servant—a useful servant, but still a servant. As he had been with the Marshal."

Her eyebrows, under her high, white forehead, were knit. Again, she shook her head.

"*Quid enim prodest homini*," she said.

* * *

But, he thought, "he was powerful to pay me back."

That day on the meadow, he had watched the ox cart lumber away until it was lost to view. Why, he couldn't say; but he had felt nothing when they had struck down the Marshal; not even shock. It had seemed that it had been part of a pattern, a plan. It had to have been thus. But the Countess, loaded onto the dung cart, proud, brave, clasping her little son to her bosom; for her, he had felt pity—all the more so because she let not fall a single tear. Pale she was, but impassive. Only her long-fingered hand, shorn of rings, gently stroking her son's fair hair, betrayed the anguish she felt.

Peter said nothing to him as they passed again, back through the western gate, into the city. When the door of the guard house shut with a click, Peter unbound his hands and said coldly, "you will return to your room."

"I am not a prisoner, then?"

"God, no!" Peter forced a laugh.

"Then, Peter, I would not remain here longer . . . ."

Peter swung round on him savagely. "Not you, not anyone, will leave the city!" he fairly shouted. "You will stay here, do you understand? You will wait until you are sent for!"

The man's eyes were those of a soul in torment. For that moment, Lorenz could feel all the hate in the man focused on himself. He knew he dared not gainsay him. He merely nodded his assent, brushed past him, and, opening the door himself, passed from the guardhouse into the street.

* * *

"I only learned later that they had slain everyone they could get their hands on. Some may have escaped."

She said nothing in reply. He could not read the feeling in her eyes, for they were cast down.

"It must have been after we had returned into the city. The abbot they had dragged from the church. In the meadow, where they had slain the Marshal, they cut him down. I myself found Pater Hilarius in the *Markplatz*..."

He had been strangled. Should he speak of such matters to her? Was it right? Yet, he felt he needed to unburden himself; he had not been able to tell Veit of these things; his friend's stern censure, though it was obvious that he tried to suppress any expression of it, had made him reticent. He knew Veit blamed the Evangel for such goings on. Yet, hadn't Veit urged him to come to her?

Still, he turned his tale from any account of the fate of the nobles—of Herr Bertold's torture and death, of the destruction and burning of the castle, of the lopping off of limbs and heads. But surely the slaying of the canons would be more bitter to her than aught else. He would say no more of it.

"The city was a writhing mass of orgy and violence—I was certain, then, that the last day had come. I scarcely feared for my own life; I would rather have died that day, even if death were cruel, as it doubtless would have been. But it was if I was charmed—it seemed no one paid me any heed. I walked, as it were, unseen."

A silence fell between them. Then, she said, "I thank God for it."

"It was when I had passed through the door to my lodging that I remembered my aunt." He smiled. "I suppose I scarcely needed to fear for her—I think she could have held off the entire peasant army with one decisive nod of her head! But, worry I did. Going out again, I pushed my way through the *Marktplatz* toward the *Farbestrasse*. I was surprised, but also relieved, to find the street empty. It appeared nothing had occurred there that day—but then I remembered that the guilds had cast in their lot with the peasants."

"So your family were not hurt?" She turned to him; her eyes were warm with compassion and alive with a tentative hope.

For the first time, Lorenz laughed. "No, they were not hurt," he said. "I was admitted into the sitting room where Tante Ursula sat enthroned in all her splendor. There was a look of displeasure on her face. She shook her head and growled at me. "Them damn peasants!' she said. "Tearin' around the city like they do! Well, they'll get theirs in the end! The Marshal will see to it that they're soundly whipped, he will!"

"I saw she had heard nothing much of what had happened. I had not the heart, then, to tell her anything."

*　*　*

It was not long, however, before Tante Ursula had learned all; but, even then, she did not blanch. She was fighting mad. "God's curse on those wretched clodhoppers!" she snarled. "How dared they raise their hand against our good Marshal! And the good canons and priests—God's wrath will fall on them bloody peasants, as sure as I sit here!" She did wipe a tear from her eye. "He was a kindly master—always so good to your uncle and us!"

Lorenz remained at his aunt's house for the next few days, until the peasant army left the city. They had gone, he heard, toward Heilbronn. The city was left in the control of the council and the guilds.

Lorenz left his aunt's house on the fifth day of Easter. Crossing the bridge over the river, he saw the devastation wrought on the *Markplatz*. Carts, scattered over the plaza, were being loaded with the dead bodies of knights, priests, and common burghers. The air was heavy with a fetid stench. The great doors of the *Marienkirche* hung crazily on their hinges, partially wrenched from the portal. Above them, the great rose window had been smashed; the great hole, like a Cyclops' eye, gazed in mute surprise over the plaza.

Lorenz picked his way among the debris on the church steps—broken statues, torn books, scattered altar linens, pictures riven in their frames. Bright sunlight, passing through the shattered stained glass, illumined the nave with a violent splendor. The great crucifix in the sanctuary lay prone in the center of the nave; the head, broken from the body, had rolled a few feet to the right of the cross beam. Lorenz mounted the steps leading into the sanctuary. To left and right, the choir stalls had been overturned; some had been smashed by ax blades. The high altar stood solitary among the debris, though its stone, too, had been struck and broken by hammers. Contemplating the desolation, Lorenz wept.

But then he raised his eyes. He beheld the tabernacle. Its door had been torn off. The *ciborium* was gone—doubtless, it had been stolen for its gold and jewels. But scattered over the altar and on the stone floor below it, like a white frost of manna, lay dozens of white discs. Some had been trampled and ground into the stone; but others seemed untouched, as pure, white, and lovely as when they had been enclosed in gold.

He had not expected it. He hesitated, but then with a yelp of anguish, he rushed to the altar, knelt and hastily began gathering what he could of the hosts. Rising, he placed them on the altar, then stepped back. He quailed at the thought of what he must do—but what else could he do? Steeling his resolution, he approached the altar, and gathering all the discs into a pile, he began to consume them. One by one he ate them until all of them were gone.

CHAPTER 2

E HAD RETURNED IN SICKNESS TO Nürnberg. Through the last miles, he had walked in a misery of exhaustion. He had longed to go off from the road and collapse in the grass; what did it matter if he lived or died? He must not have appeared too sick, for the watch let him into the city, just before the gates closed. Following the familiar streets, he came at last, though without intending it (his mind and will had been engulfed in pain), to the doors of *Auerhaus*. Veit's servant, Clemens, drew him into the house and called for the master.

* * *

"We thought we had lost you."

This was the first time Veit had visited him that day. Lorenz lay in bed, exhausted but feeling, for the first time, at peace. That morning, he had awakened, drenched with sweat.

"I hardly remember coming to the house," he said. "I remember Clemens, and then standing within the doorway; but, nothing more."

"Yes, Clemens led you to a seat in the entrance hall and then ran to fetch me. When I came, you had collapsed. We carried you to your bed. For two days, you lay in a fever, unconscious. Only this morning, it broke. *Ach*, Lorenz! I thank God for it!"

Lorenz nodded. He too felt strangely grateful—for had he not abandoned all hope of life when he departed Weissenbrücke? "Yes, I longed to die," he thought to himself. But

418

now, he felt something he had not felt for many a year—an earnest of hope.

He even laughed—feeble though the laugh was. He was still very weak. "You know," he said, with a smile, "I am even hungry!"

"No doubt." Veit too laughed. "You have eaten nothing for nearly three days."

"Four days," Lorenz interposed. "I could not tolerate even the thought of food, then."

"Well, my friend," Veit nodded, "we will get some food into you—but nothing too strong. No capons, no bacon . . . "

"*Ach!* I feel as if I could eat a whole pig!"

"You will not get even a hoof, my friend—physician's orders! Herr Arzt Braunbein has prescribed broth for you, nothing more."

"But at least I can have some beer?"

"No beer! Mulled wine, yes—well watered."

Lorenz snuggled himself down further into his bed. "Well, I suppose I must be content with such fare!"

"You will soon learn how delectable broth can be, my friend." Veit rose. "I shall serve you your feast shortly. In the meantime, I would suggest that you nap before dinner."

Veit stood by the bed for a moment, looking at his friend. "I thank God that you are well, Lorenz," he said. "I thought we had lost you for certain."

*   *   *

Lorenz recovered his health quickly over the next fortnight. Only two days after he had awakened in his bed at *Auerhaus*, he was able to leave his room and wander in the garden. It was only just past midsummer; it was warm in the sun, but the air was cool in the shade. He basked in the contrasts; to be alive amid such beauty as the rooms and gardens of *Auerhaus* afforded filled him with contentment. For the first time in months, nay, years, he felt a surcease of the inner tensions that had torn at his soul.

419

Was it because he thought little about religion? Pray he did, but he gave no heed to the questions that had stretched his heart on the rack. He rejoiced, rather, in the waxing health of his body and of a mind free from the inner questioning of ineradicable doubt. What had been was past; what would be—well, there was naught he could do about *that*. Best not think about it. There was only the now, freed from past and future and suffused with its own inner meaning. And was not this the very sense of eternity?

When the first day he walked into the family hall, he wondered how he would react to the picture. But as he stood before it, delineating the beauty of the daughter in the mother, he felt no pang, no regret. A twinge of longing came and went; in its wake, the peace of resignation.

To his own surprise, he could wander the garden, sit on the bench by the frog pond, and remember all that had passed between them, but feel no want. It had all, it seemed, become a sweet memory. A brief vision of beauty had been vouchsafed him, for which he now was thankful. Yes, it carried with it a bitter sweetness; but that, too, was a whisper of beauty, a healing balm.

During those days, his mind turned to what he would do, now he was freed of Weissenbrücke. Perhaps he could remain in Nürnberg, for he had learned that the council had declared for the Gospel and instituted Evangelical worship in the churches. Doubtless, much was left to be done. Such work called for laborers; and the conditions for success, he thought, were more promising here than they had been in Weissenbrücke. He could, of course, return to Wittenberg; but (why, he couldn't say) the prospect repelled him.

What he had felt and done in the *Marienkirche* of Weissenbrücke—that, he thought, could await a time of leisure to think on. Today, in this garden, it all seemed so far away in time and place, rather like a churning, nauseous dream but dimly remembered in the daylight.

But could he aid a cause in which he felt he might no longer believe? He shook his head. No, he thought, such a train of thought only confused him now. He had found the Gospel, or so he had thought; should he follow the lead of a passing feeling experienced under the most dire and trying of circumstances? Had he thought too clearly, then? Fear and a morbidity had perhaps addled his brain. He must take care lest, on account of the riot of his feelings, he proved unstable.

Yet, perhaps, he should decline the office of preacher until his mind and feelings settled. He could function as a teacher at the city's *schola*. He could teach any number of subjects—Latin, rhetoric, grammar, poetry, music. By day he could attend to disciplines that would not commit him to the theological ideas of one party or the other. By night, he could struggle with his God . . .

Yes, that perhaps was the path he should choose. He could turn teacher. Once he was well, he would consult with Wenzel Linck on the matter.

* * *

"She and the children of late have spent a good deal of time with her parents. They are at Lenzgrab now."

Veit's mood was not regretful or contented. He spoke as if the whole business were a matter of course.

"Are the Waldhummels not well?"

An ironic look passed over Veit's face. "No, they are quite well—quite as well as ever," he said bemusedly.

Though Veit was normally so transparent, Lorenz could not read him now. His friend seemed to be hiding something. "If he wishes, he will tell me bye and bye," Lorenz thought. "If he doesn't—well, I won't pry."

Yet, Veit needed none of Lorenz's goading. After a short silence, he continued.

"I need not tell you, Lorenz, that Greta and I have never been content with one another. No! That's a lie. I have never been

421

content with her. *She* had been quite content with me—that is, with my position and wealth. Until recently, at least."

"Until recently?"

Veit sighed. "Yes. You see, she and her parents have long been devotees of the reform. The fact that I have stuck with the old Church has vexed them—they cannot understand it at all! They could tolerate it as long as the council wavered; but when it came down on the side of the reform, everything changed. My refusal to go along meant that I would be ostracized from the best society, as would my wife—if she stuck too close to me. She poses now as the aggrieved wife, the victim of her husband's stupidity, lack of piety, or some such thing. In this guise she is accepted into society, while I am excommunicate. It doesn't bother me; I have always found the people of this city profoundly inane. I would much rather be alone, reading, than hobnobbing with tedious tradesmen and their pale offspring."

Despite Veit's nonchalance, Lorenz could see that his friend was troubled. Yes, Veit had ever scorned Nürnberg society—and with the utmost sincerity, too; but he could not brook himself being scorned. "There is a good measure of self-regard in my friend," Lorenz thought, smiling to himself. His absurdity was one of the things that endeared Veit to him.

Lorenz took a sip of his wine. "Well, you will find no censure in me," he said. "In fact, I admire you for not capitulating."

"You, Lorenz?" Veit said, with a look of genuine wonder. "I would have thought that you . . . "

"That I would use the occasion of your wife and Nürnberg's displeasure to wheedle you away from your fidelity? No, Veit. I would never do that. The truth should be embraced only with the utmost freedom."

"Say you so, Lorenz?" Veit's eyes widened. "But you are one of Luther's right-hand men!"

Lorenz smiled. "Are you intimating," he said, "that Luther is perhaps not as committed to gentle suasion as he should be?"

"I don't mean to disparage the man . . ."

"I understand," Lorenz said. "And I am glad that I don't have to answer for Luther, but only for myself. As for myself, I stand by what I said. Follow the course you have set for yourself. God will show you the way."

A silence fell between the two friends. Lorenz dug into his supper—he felt positively wolfish that night. "Yes," he thought as he chewed his food, "I do admire Veit. If I had only the strength of his conviction . . . But I am weak. What if I were wrong?" He swallowed his food and finished off the wine in his glass. When he reached for the bottle, he noticed that Veit was watching him.

"Lorenz," Veit said slowly. "You know, of course, what the council is up to. After proclaiming a reformation of the Church—for the salvation of souls, so they say—they have been relentless in shoving folk into the new church. They leave me alone, of course, because I am a Scheuerl. But others aren't let off so easily. Most of the layfolk have blithely laid aside their old clothes for this year's fashion. The Augustinians and others have easily capitulated. But the Poor Clares have coalesced around that lioness, Caritas Pirkheimer; they won't bend, though the council has assaulted them with preachers and done everything to make their lives miserable. Sankt Katharina's, the Franciscans, and Pillenreuth have stood firm . . ."

At the mention of Pillenreuth, Lorenz shifted in his chair. Veit, he saw, was studying him.

" . . . Some sisters have succumbed, but those that have been forcibly removed from their monasteries are forbidden to return."

Lorenz was troubled by Veit's words, what they portended. What was his friend about to tell him?

Lorenz poured another glass of wine. "Such things should not be," he said slowly. And, he added, "God wants us to be free . . ."

Veit opened his mouth to speak, but hesitated, like one standing at pool side, debating whether to take a plunge into icy water. When finally he did speak, it was not with the words he had intended. That much, at least, was clear to Lorenz. And he felt strangely relieved.

"I am happy to hear you speak thus, Lorenz," Veit said. "Would that every Evangelical thought as you do."

CHAPTER 3

"THE MARIENKIRCHE WAS TURNED OVER to us; for, from that very day, only Evangelical worship was allowed in the city."

His words, he saw, had disturbed her, though she tried to dissemble. "And you, what thought you of this?" she said at last.

What thought he of it? "It was a beautiful church," he said, "even after they had wreaked such havoc on it. We have never countenanced such acts." He knew he had not answered her question; but he did not know how to answer it. He did not know his own thoughts in this.

"I did not lead the worship—Wohlgemut Kraft did. I only preached."

He recalled the day that Peter had summoned him. They met in the *Rathaus*. Peter told him of the council's decision. His smile was dry, ironic. He enjoyed the subtle torture. He knew this was no welcome news to him. "You have triumphed at last," Peter said to him. "The way of the Evangel has been opened—it is for you to take advantage of it. By my cajoling, the council has agreed to make you the chief preacher in the city."

He said little in reply. He merely bowed his acquiescence.

Sunday after Sunday, week after week, he preached Luther's Evangel. Sunday after Sunday, week after week, he played the hypocrite. He had been alone, that day; none had seen what he had done. None, save him who sees all. Sunday after Sunday, he denied before the city what he had wrought in darkness.

Yet, he could at least claim this — that he did not season his speech for the popular palate. Though he could not predict the outcome, his first sermons uttered no justifications for the rebellion and its cruelty. He did not trim his doctrine to the wind; he taught what he had always taught — what was called, at least, the Pure Gospel. He had been certain that this would earn him the disdain of the blood-stained masses of the city; perhaps he would even be driven out by a disgusted council. But, he found, neither the council nor the guilds were hankering for Münzer's radicalism nor the Evangelical order of Rothenberg. They were quite content with his staid Lutheranism, once the peasant hordes had carried their revolution off to Heilbronn.

"No, Lorenz," Peter had said to him one day. "We are all quite happy with your milksop Evangel. We have made enough concessions to the peasants of the neighborhood to keep them more or less content. And, after all, they were nothing without Müller and his gang. The council and the guilds now have what they wanted all along — freedom from the Marshal. That they've got it so completely is owing, in part, to your fine work, both then and now. You keep the rabble thinking on heaven, while their masters attend to the affairs of earth. It serves your purposes and ours."

The words had stung, then when spoken, now when recalled. If he had cooperated, it was incidental to his intention. The Devil will always twist the good to suit himself. Of this he had to assure her.

He could not miss the flicker of uncertainty in her eyes.

"I know," he said to her, "you do not share my faith; but at least do not doubt that I acted according to my convictions. I did what I thought was right and best."

For the first time she turned to look him fully in the eyes. They hesitated in the path. Whatever ambivalence had been there before was gone.

"Of that I am convinced. I do not doubt your truthfulness and honor," she said.

* * *

Peter's arrogant self-assurance was soon punctured. Like so many others, he had reckoned little of the peasants. Those "of the neighborhood," it turned out, were not content. They were vexed with being shoved off to the side. They had not thrown off the Marshal to submit to new masters — especially the burghers, with whom they had long lived in enmity. They no longer would put up with disdain and arrogance.

The council could not long shut the gates of the city against the peasants. They were at last admitted and took their stand in the *Rathaus*. The council were forced to make painful concessions to the peasants, with whom the guilds had made common cause. The lesser tithes and socage dues, which the council had assumed, were forthwith abolished. The forests were opened to the collecting of wood.

The council feared that these were but the beginning of the peasants' demands. Have we, the council asked, overthrown a lord only to submit to slaves? They had been played for fools, that was certain — but of course, they could not admit this of themselves. Someone else had to bear the blame — and that someone was the man to whose plots they had so blithely subscribed. He alone would have to bear the burden of their discomfiture.

Thus was Peter Schwach turned out from the counsels of the city's rulers. From thenceforth, he was a nonentity. He withdrew alone to his rooms in the city.

* * *

But the peasants made few demands in regards to religion. They demanded the right to choose their own ministers. They insisted that only the "Pure Gospel" be preached and all doctrine be drawn from the Bible. Yet, whatever that would mean in the villages, it did not touch the city. The people of Weissenbrücke alone would decide such matters for their city; and they seemed quite content with the preacher, Lorenz List.

Lorenz preached each week in the *Marienkirche;* but the scars of its desecration tore at his heart. He did his best to dissemble, but he feared he could not hide his dismay. But if the crowds detected aught of this, it must have drawn rather than repelled them. It seemed the terror of the time had endowed him with a power of expression he had not before possessed.

"It pained me to see her so ravished—for so it seemed to me," he told her. "*Quam sola sedet civitas,*" he mused and shook his head. "But then, I bestirred myself. I began to organize folk to remove the debris—and this, it seems, stirred the council to action. Soon the church had been cleared. Still, it tore at my heart. The broken windows gaped. Niches were left empty. Side altars stood hacked and damaged, as was the high altar itself."

Again, he shook his head as he remembered. "The council said they would remedy all this," he said. "But, of course, they scarcely had the time to demonstrate the sincerity of their pledge."

CHAPTER 4

WHEN HE HAD LIVED AS A STUDENT in Nürnberg, Lorenz rarely entered the church of his namesake, Sankt Lorenz. For one thing, it lay on the farther side of the River Pegnitz. Nürnberg's other great church, Sankt Sebald's, lay nearer Lorenz's lodgings at *Auerhaus*. Too, the *Schöner Brunnen* stood in the *Hauptmarkt*, hard by Sankt Sebald's. When he visited the fountain, as he often did, he would pay a visit to the church named for his brother's patron.

Today, he passed through the portal of the *Lorenzkirche* with a queer sense of being watched. The saints in heaven, he knew, communicated not at all with the living; God had no need of such intermediaries. It were foolish to think that his patron was looking with displeasure upon him. Or so he told himself.

The church had not suffered from the wave of image breaking that had fallen on Nürnberg in the first heady days of her reformation. Lorenz was glad of that. Sound faith and doctrine need not disdain ancient beauty. The task, he thought, was not to overthrow what had been received, but to cast on it the light of a clearer teaching and purer devotion. That such beauty could at times (as it did with the *Marienkirche*) evoke an imperfect piety only meant that one's faith was not yet strong enough. The answer was not to destroy the beautiful things but to strengthen and embolden one's faith.

It was thus, he told himself, that he had consumed the scattered hosts that day in Weissenbrücke.

As he passed through the nave, Lorenz wondered why he had spent so little time in this church. The wealth of Nürnberg had lavished itself on this temple; the greatest artists of the city had spent their talent on its adornments. How had he forgotten the statues of the Archangel Gabriel and the Virgin, pendant in the choir? And the intricately carved *Sakramenthaus*, with its elaborate stone tracery and saints' images, rising some three-score feet on the Gospel side of the altar? This towering receptacle of the Mystery was in every way as lovely and majestic as the Beautiful Fountain, empty now though it was of what it once enshrined. No wonder the old Church could evoke such fidelity in the hearts of so many!

Today, however, he had no time to study the marvel. He had come to the church for another purpose. The sound of a door opening and shutting with a click and a thud recalled him to it. He turned in the direction of the sound to see a man, clad in a long, black cloak and a scholar's cap, approaching him with a brisk step. And with equal briskness the man, as he drew near, addressed him—"Herr Magister List!" he said.

Lorenz bowed slightly. "Herr Magister Osiander, God's greetings," he replied.

* * *

"The city enjoyed its independence only little over a month. Then, on a day near Pentecost, it was invested."

Not enough time had passed for him not to feel the horror of those days. Many the night he awoke, startled from dreadful dreams of what then befell. Now, he scarcely believed he could relate in speech the tale of those days. But the glance of her eyes, soft with compassion, drew the story from him. The telling of it proved a welcome catharsis.

"We had been told that our lord, the Markgraf Casimir, had secretly embraced the Gospel—and he *had* brought preachers to his domains. Indeed, what is most ironic, the rebels were convinced that he would soon agree to their Twelve

Articles—and well he might have, if the princes had not scored victories against the peasants."

That Bohemian, Casimir—had he not been merely putting his finger to the wind? When it seemed the peasants would prevail, Casimir hesitated in their direction. When the princes gained the upper hand, Casimir discovered he was a good Catholic. Lorenz wondered at such men. How could they live with such scheming vacillation?

"The siege lasted but three days. Then, to quote Peter Schwach, 'someone in the city discovered that the city gates could simply not be kept closed.'"

"That city I deem a bastion of treachery." Her eyes had grown hard, indignant. "It is no wonder, if they could not be true to their faith, they..." Her sentence she left unfinished. She lowered her eyes and blushed. She understood the thrust of her words. Trying to cover her clear sense, "I mean," she said, "if they were not true to their lord, they were capable of betraying anyone."

Lorenz smiled. He understood her true meaning. "You assume, of course," he said, "that it was the insurgents who proved treacherous. But there were prominent burghers and guildsmen who had secretly never gone over to the *Bundschu*. Such men had been hankering for the deliverance they thought Casimir would bring them. Yet, if they knew what would befall, I doubt that even they would have done it. Some of their number paid dearly for their pretense."

Once again, the horrors of that day rose up before his mind's eye, like Samuel, conjured up by the witch of Endor. The *Markgraf's* soldiery, the pillaging, the slaughter of men, women, and children. The cries of terror, of wild, animal fear, cut short by glittering strokes of swords, by the thrusting of spears, the report of guns. He himself sought refuge in the *Marienkirche*—he could not, even then, say why. Why did he not suffer himself to be hacked down in the streets? It all would have been so easy; death would have been simpler than the horror he would soon have to witness.

"When at last the *Markgraf* himself entered the city, he ordered the butchery to stop. It would have been more merciful had he let it continue."

To save their own skin, townsmen turned traitor. They informed on the very men they had once hailed as their deliverers. Members of the council, magistrates, prominent merchants were bound and herded into the *Marktplatz*. Those innocent of the revolution mingled with its ringleaders. The common lot of the city scoured houses for rebels; even the churches provided no sanctuary. "It was in the crypt of the *Marienkirche* that they found me," he said. "They bound me and dragged me into the plaza with the others."

He had been sitting by Heimrad's tomb when they discovered him.

* * *

"I have heard much about you, Herr List. Not only about the trials you suffered for the Gospel in ... in ... what was that town again?"

"Weissenbrücke."

"*Ach!* Yes, Weissenbrücke! A most bitter business it was with those vile peasants, I have heard. Your *able* preaching, alas, could not prevail over their passions."

Though Osiander's face wore a friendly smile, and his tone resonated with regard, the man's demeanor exuded condescension and a hint of censure.

"Though the Fiend prevailed there—for I have heard the peasant tyranny in that place has given way to a Romish one—we have been vouchsafed a most useful worker in the Lord's vineyard of Nürnberg. You are most welcome here, Herr Magister!"

"You are most kind."

"No, not kind, Herr List; not at all!" Osiander grunted a laugh. "Luther has spoken most highly of your intellect and

432

devotion—at least in what he wrote about you *before* the rebellion. And you have most zealous friends here."

"I do?"

"Indeed, you do!" Osiander placed his hands on his knees and leaned forward slightly. "I do not refer, of course, to your *friend*, Herr Scheuerl—a most recalcitrant papist, from what I hear. You really should work on him! No, I refer to the lovely Frau Scheuerlin, his wife, and her honored parents. *Ach!* There are few in Nürnberg more zealous for the Pure Word than Herr Waldhummel and his wife! Frau Scheuerlin has had a reputation for frivolity, but I know nothing of that. To me she has seemed a most righteous and pious wife."

Lorenz smiled to himself. Greta pious? Surely, Osiander was not serious.

Osiander pursed his lips and slowly shook his head. "It is a suffering to that good woman that her husband holds fast to damnable error—as do too many in this city! There is much work to do in this vineyard, I assure you!"

"And it is that, of course, I have come to speak with you about," Lorenz said. "I have sought counsel from respectable men in this city, and they have urged me not to return to Wittenberg."

"So, they have urged you to pitch your tent in this land of promise?" Osiander smiled complacently. "I must say, Herr Magister, that I heartily concur in their judgment. Indeed, Frau Waldhummelin has besought me to urge you to this good resolution!"

"I am gratified to hear of Frau Waldhummelin's good opinion of me," Lorenz said, less than truthfully.

"*Ach!* Yes, remain among us, for there is much work to be done here. Many weeds and tares to be removed. Those pestilent houses *of religion*, as they call them, still remain, though the wise council fathers are doing what they can to show them the True Way. The honorable council members are behaving with the utmost kindness toward them; *perhaps with too much kindness!* Hmm. I myself have been preaching to Caritas Pirkheimer's benighted women, but they have thus far proved recalcitrant to the Clear Word of God! A most cagey she-devil of a papist she is! She has her *sisters* so firmly in her power that we have made little headway there. Some evangelical women have had their charges removed, but only a very few. *Ach!* And then to have Melanchthon take their part! You know, he has urged the council to leave them be? He has even said they do not rely on the righteousness of their own works! He has been deceived by that wily Caritas, I have no doubt of it!"

Osiander obviously expected him to concur in this judgment, and Lorenz would not disabuse him of the error.

"Indeed, we need laborers, many more than we have, to bring in this harvest, Herr List! So, I am most gratified to hear of your resolve to remain with us! But" — and here Osiander cocked his head and rubbed his nose with his forefinger — "I think we understand each other — the best preacher expresses his teaching with the manner of his life. Indeed, to cling to certain modalities of one's former life lived in darkness spreads confusion among the ignorant. Even our great mentor, Doctor Luther, has understood this, and acquiesced, at the urging of his friends."

Osiander's supercilious demeanor irked Lorenz. "Yet," he said at last, "one cannot be faulted for following St. Paul's counsel . . ."

Osiander chuckled. "No, Herr Magister. The Apostle's words retain all their force — how could it be otherwise?

"But, my friend," and here Osiander leaned back in his chair, folding his hands on his belly, "what would Paul say if he were with us today? I think he might give us very different counsel. And can you or I claim that we possess the unction of so illustrious a servant of God? No, no — I daresay, we cannot."

* * *

"From the plaza, I was taken to a dank hole and locked up with some dozen others. The only light we had came from a high, barred window. Much of the day it was only a small square of brightness; only when the sun set did light stream into the cell and spill on the stone floor. At least we could tell the time of day, once a day..."

He would not tell her everything—only just enough.

The durance was a misery, though he had only to endure it for three days—the dried crusts given them for food, the brackish water for drink, the near darkness by day, and the pitch blackness by night. The stench of human sweat, urine, and feces. Though he knew a few of the men with him, he spoke little to them. Nor did they seek to converse with him. Each was doubtless contemplating the cruel torture and death he was surely soon to suffer. Each man isolated himself in his own heart's sorrow.

He did not question why he, who had urged against the rebellion, should be imprisoned. In the darkness of night, he suffered most excruciating terror; at those times, he feared he would have gladly foresworn all, if it could spare his hide. He was not the stuff of martyrs, that was certain! Yet—can one die a martyr for what one no longer believes? Would it not be the honest thing to recant? Even so, he would not utter the words, even if it would save his life. He would not so sin against justice.

No, he could not tell her all this, even though he longed to.

"It was on the third day, late in the day—the sun was shining into the cell—that the little metal opening in the door through which the guards spoke to us screeched open..."

A coarse voice penetrated into their gloom. "Is the preacher, Lorenz List within?" When he heard his own name spoken, he cowered. Had they come for him so soon? And why was he, he alone, being singled out? He hardly dared to answer; he could not at first command his voice.

"Is Lorenz List within?" The voice had grown impatient. "God's body! Why won't any of you say nothin'?"

If only he said nothing—for, though some of his companions knew him, they would not betray him. He was safe, if only he said nothing, nothing at all.

But from what was he safe? From what would he be preserved? Sooner or later, everyone would be taken from that hole. By silence, he would only delay the inevitable. God! How his heart shrank within him! All he would gain would be more days and nights in the vile hole, contemplating what would befall him thereafter. But if he spoke up, all would soon be over and done with, forever.

Still, thinking back on that day, he could not say how at last he had encouraged himself to break the silence. It was as if someone else was articulating the words that his mouth uttered.

"Yes, yes, I am here," he said at last, his words sounding to him queer and muffled in that dank gloom.

"It is I, Lorenz List."

* * *

"Please forgive me, if I sound at all incredulous—but I can scarce believe your words!"

Heretofore, Osiander's tone had been oily and condescending. Now his voice sounded with barely suppressed scorn.

"You would refuse the righteous urging of so pious a woman? No, Herr List, I cannot believe it of you at all!"

"I refuse nothing," he replied. "I only ask for more time to think ..."

"Of what is there to think? I daresay, your course is clear! Would you not snatch this brand from the fire?"

Lorenz hesitated. Then, "I would leave the conscience free."

"No one is urging you toward anything else!" Osiander's tone was of one aggrieved—like that of a weary father chiding his little son. "We are not talking about coercion ... "

"Seduction is a kind of coercion."

"Who has said anything about seduction?" Osiander's frown broadened into a wheedling grin. "Think of it, rather, as gentle suasion."

Lorenz could not say why, now it came to the point, he was resisting. Was it not for this that he had sought this interview with Osiander? To solicit a position in the city so he could undertake what he now was refusing? He felt that, now it came to the point, he could not do this thing.

"Maybe it were best that I returned to Wittenberg..."

"Not at all! What need has Wittenberg of you? The council here has declared for the Gospel. The hearts of most of the people are with us, but not all. Nürnberg needs you, and your friends need you!"

Nürnberg needs me! he thought. *I could do naught in Weissenbrücke — what could I achieve here?* And then he thought of what he might achieve here, and his heart shrank from it.

* * *

The sunlight, after the darkness, was painful to his eyes. The air felt warm after the dank chill of the prison cell. The streets were full of people, but he felt a curious elation and capacity after having been crammed into that crowded hole for so long. The sensation of new-found freedom dispelled for the nonce any angst he might feel for the peril of his situation.

He scarcely noted along what ways they were moving until, having turned the corner of a street, he saw rising before him the *Marienkirche*. The sight of the church was like a sudden drenching with cold water. It recalled him to the menace of the present. Where were they leading him, the three armed guards? Was it to torture and execution? The day was bright; across the sky, white, billowing clouds scudded by with stately grandeur. Would he ever see such a day again?

They passed through a portal, into a large vestibule. There, they stopped and waited. Many other folk were standing about. He wanted to shrink into himself; in the company of such folk,

437

many tripped out in finery, he felt dirty. Didn't the stench of the prison cell cling to him? He noted a dandy of a man standing hard by place a handkerchief over his nose and mouth. Doubtless, it was scented.

The confusion of his thoughts had been like a miasma for his senses; at first he could not tell where he was. But gradually it dawned on him — he was standing in the forecourt of the *Rathaus*. This meant only one thing, he knew: he was being led to judgment.

He could not tell how long he was left waiting, but it seemed an exceeding long time. He was not allowed to sit; but, standing, he lingered, watching one party after another pass through the great inner doors into the council hall. Some of these, after an interval, returned through the doors, their demeanor varying from contentment and pleasure to consternation and dismay.

Then, at long last, his turn came. The doors opened, and his guards pushed him through the portal into the wide space within.

At the far end of the hall, on a raised platform, draped by a canopy, reared two large, throne-like chairs. The chair on his right was empty, but in the other chair sat a man, clad in rich clothing, gold, with a trimming of red. As Lorenz drew near, he noted the man's face; it was ruddy, angular, and clean shaven, except for the fringe of a light brown beard that grew under his chin. His hands, adorned with rings set with jewels, lay folded on his lap. His small, gray eyes were impassive.

Though he had never seen him before, Lorenz knew who this man was: the *Markgraf*, Casimir von Brandenburg-Kulmbach.

Lorenz felt he could expect naught but severity from this man. His very impassivity, suggestive of princely impartiality, savored of a feline cruelty. What mercy could he expect from one who, to gain his power, had driven his own father from the throne?

"Lorenz List, the Evangelical preacher!"

438

A man to Lorenz's right, whom he had not noticed before, spoke the words. The announcement invited the *Markgraf's* attention. In silence, Casimir studied him for some moments. When at last he spoke, in a tired, languid manner, it was not to address Lorenz.

"With what is he charged?"

The man to Lorenz's right replied, "with preaching heresy and incitement to violence and rebellion."

The words smote Lorenz to the quick. Heresy—yes, with that he could be justly charged. But incitement to violence and rebellion? It was utterly absurd!

Casimir now focused his eyes on Lorenz. They were cold and cruel.

"What say you to these charges?"

The *Markgraf's* tone was accusatory. Lorenz thought he could scarce hope for justice or mercy from the man. A cold fear confused and numbed him. He tried to steel himself to answer; his finger nails dug into the palms of his hands.

"Have you naught to say for yourself?" Casimir's little smile suggested pleasure at his victim's fear.

Lorenz at last managed to speak. "My lord," he said (he felt his voice was shaking), "I deem not that I preach heresy. I have preached the Gospel as it is found in Holy Writ; nothing more, nothing less . . ."

"But have you not incited violence against your own proper lord? Speak man! Answer the charge!"

"I have not!"

Casimir leaned forward in his chair. "Do not perjure yourself!" he snarled. "We know well your doctrine! Your Luther and all his mangy followers have incited violence against the lords spiritual and temporal! You cannot deny it!"

The violence of the *Markgraf's* manner angered Lorenz. A sense of indignation wriggled its way through his fear. No, he could not deny the violence of Luther's tirades—but was *he*

439

guilty of it? No, he was certain at least of this, that he had been no rebel to his lord.

When at last he spoke, it was with greater firmness. "I deny that I have ever incited violence against any lord, spiritual or temporal. Our doctrine enjoins obedience to those whom God has anointed our lords and proper masters, save where they contravene divine authority."

Casimir sneered. "Save where they contravene divine authority!" he said with a snort. "And by what authority do you judge the limits of God's authority? You are naught but a scurvy preacher—a renegade monk, no doubt!"

Casimir's words lashed at Lorenz's indignation. The injustice of it! The hypocrisy of the man! Did not this lord himself toy with the reform—until the winds changed course? And now to play the champion of the "rightful authority" of the lords spiritual . . .

"What I am, I cannot say" he said. "I take no refuge in my own righteousness, but in God's Word."

The retort did not seem to annoy Casimir in the least; rather, his eyes gleamed with amusement. He leaned back again in this chair. He laughed. "And you doubtlessly understand God's Word where everyone else has not! God! What presumption!" Casimir shook his head. "Yet I will not banter words with you," he said. "You cannot prove your innocence save by simple assertion of it. What proofs can you offer me that you speak sooth? Have you any to speak for you?"

Lorenz's spirit collapsed at this question. He had, he knew, no one to take his part. He shook his head. "No, I have not," he said.

Casimir yawned. "Well, then, if you have no one to speak on your behalf . . ."

Lorenz steeled himself to hear his sentence. Would it be death alone, or death by torture? The memory of Bruder Thaddeus, burning, the scream of pain, the body engulfed in flames, a black silhouette encompassed by the burning wrath. The Angel Man, mere straw consumed.

Would the man never speak? He feared to hear the words, but he longed for them, like a soul lashed with desire for Hell. But, when at last he heard a voice speaking—to his wonder and disappointment, it was not the *Markgraf's*. It was not Casimir, but the man to Lorenz's right, the one who had accused him of heresy and treachery, who now spoke up.

"My lord, I beg pardon," he said, with a bow. "But there is one who will speak on this man's behalf."

Casimir smiled. "Oh, is there?" he said. He held up his hand and contemplated his finger nails. "Then produce this advocate!" he said with ennui.

* * *

The murmur of the crowd in the council chamber. A shuffling and a movement. And passing through the midst of the throng was one Lorenz had never thought to see—not here, not now. He could scarcely credit the witness of his own eyes—but there she was, in all her beauty and dignity. She appeared as she had that day in the field outside the city: the same nobility of mien, though her lord lay bleeding at her feet.

Countess Mechtilde ascended the dais and lightly took her place on the chair to Casimir's left.

CHAPTER 5

"YOU WOULD SPEAK ON THIS MAN'S behalf?"

"I would."

"Then, I pray, proceed."

She did not so much as glance at Lorenz. She looked out across the crowd, as if she were addressing them all rather than her lord. When at last she spoke, her voice betrayed no pleading. It was if she were giving testimony to facts that touched her not.

"The matter is very simple," she said. "As you well know, my lord, I have plighted my troth to the One, Holy, Catholic Church. I will never swerve, please God, from my fidelity to her. It is thus that I cannot but despise this man as a false prophet and a killer of souls. For this I would gladly seem him burn!"

As she said these last words, she turned her eyes briefly on Lorenz. She was fully in earnest.

"I thank God that my husband turned at the end from his wicked intent to, as they call it, *reform* the Church in his domains. Alas! It was my husband that brought this man here—a man who has, I understand, broken his vows and sullied his consecration. Is this not so?"

She directed the question to Lorenz. He did not answer.

"And would you not have overturned the Church in these domains and instituted your heretical doctrines in its place?"

Her words struck Lorenz to the quick. Indeed, he would

442

have done so; the thought of it, now, dismayed him. He tried to speak, but faltered.

"Answer me!"

"I acted," he said, "in accord with what I deemed was God's word. I acted according to my conscience." But even as he spoke the words, he knew he was deceiving no one.

"Your conscience!" Her tone was disdainful. "You would tempt souls to their destruction, all for the sake of your conscience! You, a mere man, dared to assert *your conscience* as the arbiter of God's truth?"

Her manner was almost savage. It seemed to stir Casimir from the torpor into which he had appeared to have fallen. A smile dimpled his cheeks. "My lady," he said, "if this be advocacy, it is of a most strange kind!"

"I beg no mercy for his heresy!" Her tone was taut and relentless. "If it were merely a matter of this, I would beg you to do away with him at once. But another matter compels me to plead in his regard."

Still Casimir smiled. "To what matter do you refer?" he asked.

She paused before she answered. She fixed her eyes on Lorenz. "One that demands my gratitude," she at last replied.

A murmur stirred the crowd. Casimir looked out across the hall and held up his hand. When the noise ceased, "What," he said, "you feel gratitude toward such a man as this? I can scarcely credit it!"

"I do," she said simply. "You have accused this man of treachery to his lord, but it is not so. To God, yes; but not to my murdered husband."

A murmur again rose from the astonished crowd, but she raised her hand to still it.

"Silence!" she commanded. "Hear me! It tears at my heart that I ask now this boon of you, my lord. But in the days before the vile insurrection, this man came to us to warn us of the impending danger. He revealed the conspiracy at work in the city. Indeed,

I now know he had urged obedience among the very peasants who in the end killed my husband and shed loyal blood in this city. My own loyalty demands that I speak thus in his behalf."

Casimir seemed to enjoy her earnestness. "Loyalty to a heretic?" he purred.

"No," she replied. "Loyalty to a man who, though a heretic, proved himself a faithful retainer to his earthly master and my most beloved consort."

A little smile still played over Casimir's lips, but he rubbed his eyes like one weary. The brief elation he had betrayed in his dialogue with the Countess now relaxed again to torpidity. With a yawn, "My lady," he said, "let it be as you will. This once I shall curb my just indignation against such a man as this preacher. I accede to your authority in this, as the regent for your son in this domain. You may do with this heretic as you think best."

"I thank you my lord," the Countess said with a slight nod of her head. "And fear not—this heretic will not go unpunished. He shall suffer for his crimes."

The Countess turned her eyes on Lorenz. They held a lofty expression, those eyes; and they were beautiful. Justice enfleshed must look so, he thought.

"Herr Magister List," she began, "my son's liege lord has granted to me, my son's regent, the discretion to deal with you. Know that, for your crime of preaching heresy, you deserve naught but death. You have spread the poison of error among my late husband's subjects—and, by doing so, you unwittingly undermined his authority. Yet, you proved your loyalty to your lord—and, I am certain, from a deep sense of duty. Thus, I feel I cannot deliver you over to death—your punishment for heresy I commend to Our Lord. Know this, then—we will spare your life, but you will be banished forever from the March of Weissenbrücke. If you are ever found again within the limits of this my son's domains, you will most certainly die an ignominious death. This is my sentence. I have spoken."

444

Lorenz felt a pang of regret. Still, he bowed his thanks to the Countess.

But the Countess was relentless. "Do not," she said, "rejoice so soon, my dear *magister*, at what you may deem your good fortune. You have heard our mercy, now give heed to our justice. You will remain here in the city, in durance, until such a time as we decree. Then, on that day, you will witness the fruits of your pernicious doctrines. This will be our punishment. You may find death more to your liking."

The Countess said nothing more. She rose, bowed slightly to Casimir, and left the hall.

*　*　*

"Such a resolve does not, I must say, commend you."

Osiander's condescension had irked him. This note of smug censure—as if Osiander were a master and, he, an erring student—affronted him.

"I fail to understand," he retorted, "how my intent is in any way unbecoming to me and my station. I am a scholar, not a preacher!"

Osiander emitted a short, dry laugh

"While it is true," he sniffed, "that your preaching in the hinterlands was ineffectual—for, it seems, you did not suffer yourself to become *all things to all men*—you would not be working among peasants here, but townsmen: indeed, among some of the best of Nürnberg society! Fear not, your pride will not prove such a hindrance among such worthies!"

My pride? Lorenz thought. *It was not my pride but my sympathy . . .*

"And I think," Osiander continued, "that you owe it to Frau Waldhummelin to accede to at least one of her requests. She has evinced a willingness to patronize you. She has taken an active interest in your career!"

But for only one purpose, Lorenz mused. *Never before had she "evinced a willingness" to help me in any way.*

445

"Really," Osiander continued, "you should pity the poor woman! Not only in the matter of which we have spoken, though that has proven a sore trial for her magnanimous heart, but in the matter of her daughter's husband. I can assure you that the sufferings of Frau Scheuerlin . . . but surely you know this!"

Greta's sufferings! Did the man really so misunderstand her?

"You have come to us with high commendations, from Melanchthon and Luther himself! We cannot believe, Herr Magister, that *they* could prove to be so deceived in you! I beg you — hear the Spirit beckoning you. *Noli obdurare cor vestrum!*"

To be preacher of Sankt Aegidius! That such a fat fruit should so fall into his lap was beyond expectation — even if it were a bribe. But did he really need such cajoling? Though his conscience resisted it, had he not desired to do what had been asked of him? And was not *that*, if accomplished, of more moment to him than the cause of reform and the "pure Gospel"? Indeed, he was not as sure of the Gospel as he was of this, his most palpable desire.

*   *   *

He would as lief been buried in the darkness of the dungeon, never to see light of sun or moon again, than to have witnessed it.

Separated from his fellow prisoners, he was led out by himself. Three guards conducted him out of the prison into the street. They led him along the same streets they had the previous day. This time, he knew where he was going.

The day was overcast, and a light rain had begun to fall. The *Marktplatz* opened before him. But something was different about it that day. Large crowds had gathered there — nothing so strange in that. Rather, it was the newly raised scaffold that was different.

With a guard on either side and one behind him, he stood at the base of the scaffold. Glancing up, he saw the executioner and two guards on the platform. Men armed with pikes were lined along the scaffold's sides.

Wailing and lamentation. The sound came from afar but waxed ever louder. To his right, the crowd parted. Through their midst moved a long line of men. The weeping of women and children dogged their steps.

He had not noticed the magistrate before. He stood by the hangman's side. He was declaiming something about treason.

The wailing and lamentation grew ever louder. One by one, the men mounted the scaffold. The hangman, a great, burly fellow, massive strength, a long, black beard, countenance cold and businesslike, took each man and forced him, head and shoulders on the block, to face the sky. Each man struggled but could not resist gigantic strength. The hangman raised his right arm, his hand wielding long silver, dull in the dreary light. He positioned it above one eye and deftly thrust downward. The victim screamed; the women and children wailed; the crowd gasped in horror. Then, a thrust down on the other eye; again the screaming, wailing, and lamentation. When the victim was pulled up from the block, he was forced to stand a moment before the crowd. A bloody ooze dripped from the sockets of the eyes.

One by one they climbed the scaffold. One by one they descended, stumbling in darkness. Some had their right hands cut off; others, both hands. Many of them Lorenz knew; they had been fellow prisoners. The crowds must have known them, too; magistrates, some of them; others, tradesmen and craftsmen, with whom they had carried on custom. But naught elicited pity. The initial shock having passed, the crowds fell to cursing and catcalls.

One by one. One following two, two following three—ten, fifteen, twenty. Lorenz soon lost count. Their number seemed endless. The screams and cries and lamentations clawed his heart—would it never end?

But at last it did end. The last victim stumbled from the

scaffold. The crowd, its blood lust slaked, fell silent. Lorenz felt dizzy and sick. He squatted on his haunches and voided his stomach onto the cobbles.

But his guards would not let him rest. Grabbing him roughly under the armpits, they forced him onto his feet. The crowd was again howling—though some now were laughing wildly. Lorenz saw why—a new victim had ascended the scaffold.

Lorenz could not see the man's features; the magistrate led him along the edges of the scaffold in display before the people, ululating curses and mockery. When Lorenz had gained his feet, the man's back was to him. But Lorenz did not need to see the man's face to know who he was. Peter Schwach.

As in a nauseous dream, Lorenz watched it all unfold. Peter was led to the block. They untied his hands. The hangman grabbed him by the arm; but his grasp must not have been firm, for Peter struggled and tore free. He had made it to the edge of the scaffold before the guards secured him and dragged him back to the block. But for a winking moment, as Peter wavered on the edge of the scaffold, his and Lorenz's eyes met.

More exquisite tortures had been prepared for Herr Sigismund's erstwhile counselor. They tore out his tongue. They cut off his hands. They put out his eyes. The crowd roared as the guards forced him to his feet and, dragging him to the edge of the scaffold, kicked him over the side to the ground below. The mutilated body fell, face downward, only a few feet from where Lorenz stood.

The body twitched and wriggled, like a lizard's severed tail. The handless stumps of the arms moved with mechanical jerks. Then the body jackknifed, knees pulling up to the breast. Peter writhed onto his back, gazing upward with eyeless sockets as if questioning the sky. Then, his mutilated mouth opened wide and bellowed a groaning, animal cry. Pity, fear, and horror overwhelmed Lorenz, and he fell to the ground, convulsed with weeping.

CHAPTER 6

A LITTLE PAST MID-JULY, GRETA returned to *Auerhaus*. While she had been away at Lenzgrab, the house had been almost monastic in its quietness. Now, a carnival spirit accompanied her return. Scarcely anyone had darkened the portal of *Auerhaus* during the month Lorenz had been there. Meals he had eaten often alone; at other times, with only Veit for company. Lorenz did not regret this; he had much think on and much to speak about with his friend. He had had his fill, too, of crowds and agitation. His time at *Auerhaus* had been suffused with the peace of a monastic retreat.

Greta's homecoming banished peace. Supper was dominated by her banter. Callers, who had avoided the house while she was gone, now visited in the hours Greta stirred (from late morning to well past midnight). Many of these visitors were men who, Lorenz mused, had little interest in Greta's conversation. She seemed to relish how their eyes moved over and caressed her shapely body.

Age and the bearing of three children had not diminished Greta's beauty. Indeed, to Lorenz's eyes, it had mellowed and perfected it. Not so willowy, but fuller in figure she was; yet so well-proportioned that nature's artistry could scarce realize a more perfect form. Greta herself was not unconscious of her allure; indeed, though she did not defy the letter of Nürnberg's prim regulations (neckline no more than two fingers below the collar bone), she toyed with the spirit of them. Her gowns revealed as much of her form as they covered.

"Lorenz, it seems such a long time since we saw you last!" she said at supper on the morrow of her arrival.

"Yet, it has been only a few months," he replied.

"Indeed!" she said, cocking her head and laying one beringed hand on the table. "But so much has happened in those months—those *horrid* peasants! And you—*you* were in the midst of it all!"

Lorenz did not answer. He took a sip of his wine.

"It must have been all very *hideous!* However could you stand it?"

Again, he did not answer. She did not seem to expect any answer.

"My husband here has grown so speechless since I've been gone—have you noticed? He scarcely has said a word to me, since I've been back—nor to anyone else, as far as I can see." She pouted prettily. How coaxing she was! Lorenz could only wish she could be silent, even for half a minute; then he could at least suffer the illusion that her beauty penetrated deeper than the soft sheen of her fair skin. "No, he has grown quite morose. I quite wonder if it is you have made him so, Lorenz!"

Lorenz smiled and shook his head. "No, I am afraid I cannot bear the blame, at least for that," he said. "He was quite talkative with me only a day or so ago."

"Then maybe he has been a spendthrift with his words and is all tapped out!" She smiled at her own witticism. Lorenz smiled politely. Veit scowled.

"But, really, Lorenz! I can understand a man talking with his friends; but to act so when his beloved wife returns home after a long absence, and his three lovely children! Husband," she said, for the first time addressing Veit, "husband—are you not happy to have me home again?"

Veit took a sip of wine; then, without looking at her, he said "Yes, of course I am."

"Do you hear him? Do you?" She spoke as with censorious sorrow. "I can't think that he's sincere!"

"But believe him, all the same," Lorenz replied. "You know, we have all been through much."

"Oh, don't I know it! Here in Nürnberg we've lived in constant fear of the peasants. At one point they came within a day's march of the city! We were sure we'd all be murdered in our beds!"

Lorenz smiled to himself.

"But you know," she continued, "my husband, here—he made as if he did not fear a thing! When all the gravest councilors were trembling with alarm—for even my father, who, as you know, is the stoutest of men—even he was uneasy at the tales coming from the south; and my mother took to her bed, so worried she was. She was sick for days on end, constantly calling for my father, who had to attend so many meetings at the *Rathaus*. I had to leave my husband *and* my children to go to her, she needed me so! But he—*he*, it turned out, feared nothing. At least he appeared to fear nothing . . . "

While she spoke, Lorenz glanced at Veit. He sipped his wine, scowling.

Ach! How the woman could talk! And how she could play-act—she was not as addled as she pretended. She was playing coy, in preparation for a sudden spring on her prey.

"But you, you probably are laughing at our fears!"

He smiled and shook his head. "No, I do not laugh," he said.

"Of course you don't!" she said, twisting a ring on her left hand. "For you know firsthand how *terrible* those peasants were. Pray, I do not ask you to tell aught of their goings on. But you can at least assure my husband that there was *much* to fear—that our fears were not groundless!"

Lorenz did not need to answer. He sipped his wine.

She paused. She was watching him out of the corner of her eye. "Here it comes," he thought to himself. When she spoke again, her words were more measured.

"You know," she continued, "he even questioned the wise precautions taken by our councilors. He said they were just a pretense. And what would he have done if the peasants had decided to attack the city? Would they have spared Pillenreuth? I think not."

Greta had pounced. He felt her claws digging into his flesh. Her lips parted; she would not spare him another swipe. She would doubtless have said more had not Veit slammed his wine cup down sharply on the table. An awkward silence followed.

Veit rose from his seat. "Lorenz," he said. "I beg your presence in my study. There is a book there I would show you."

Feeling awkward, Lorenz stood up to follow his friend. But, if Greta had felt any confusion, she hid it with consummate adroitness. She also rose. "I will let you men withdraw to your inner chamber," she said. "And I shall withdraw to mine."

Lorenz bowed and turned to follow Veit. But just when he reached the door of the dining hall, Greta said, "Oh, Lorenz, one more word I pray!"

He turned. Her lips were parted in an enigmatic smile. "My father and mother," she said, "they've heard you are back in town. They would dearly love to see you. Please come and visit them as soon as you can. I think you will find it worth your while."

Lorenz turned and passed from the dining hall. A servant closed the door behind him.

* * *

It was warm that night. The air was still. The casement windows were open to the garden. Frogs chirped and croaked from the pond. Beyond the pond, over the walls, the city streets were quiet, for it was late. Too late, he thought.

Pillenreuth. Why had the mere sound of the name affected him so? Greta had only brought it up to prick him. Prick him it did, deeper than she could know.

Pillenreuth. The nuns there were under pressure to succumb, to embrace the Gospel they did not believe; he recalled Veit telling him so. Some had been forced to leave the cloister. They had been compelled, against their freedom, to abandon the life to which they felt themselves bound. Such things should not be, he thought.

After all, had not Luther himself appealed to his conscience against even the Kaiser's command? To violate his conscience, he had said, is neither right nor proper, or some such thing. But if it were true for him, was it not true for others? And if not, why not?

And where was Luther, now that his followers were doing to others what Cajetan, the pope, and the Kaiser had sought to do to him? He was silent, and silence betokens consent. But if one man's conscience is sacred . . .

Pillenreuth. He recalled the day when, under the embowering arches of the monastery church, he himself had tried to wheedle *her* from her troth. Oh, yes, it was all falsehood—but is not one bound to a falsehood, if his conscience commands it? He had not considered her conscience that day. He had consulted only his own desires.

But he, even he, had at last relented. He had acquiesced to Agnes. He had freed her from Beatrice, and from Else. He had laid aside his claims. She was free from him, free forevermore.

And since his return to Nürnberg, through his convalescence and recovery, he had thought that he himself had been freed. She would henceforth be to him a dream flickering on the verge of consciousness. A spectral image, fading into the recesses of his memory. Desire for her at long last, he felt, had died.

Pillenreuth. The mere cat's purr of that name had confused him. Even now he could not comprehend the feelings it had evoked in him that night. Did he, even now, desire her? No, he did not—he was certain he did not! But if he did not, why this strange contraction of his heart? Why the regret that he did not coax Greta to tell him more?

CHAPTER 7

GRETA HAD NOT BEEN BACK A FORT-night when she announced her intent to host a great fête at *Auerhaus*. "I know you," she said to Veit one evening in the family hall; "you have been living a dreary existence here, all huddled up with your books, while I've been gone. You need some company and merrymaking!"

Veit paused before answering. Then, "I need nothing of the sort," he said shortly.

"Oh, but I think you do," Greta replied with a pretty smile. "But, even if you think you don't, you shouldn't deprive Lorenz here of some diversion. Moreover, he will meet some people that may be of use to him. Some of the *best* people in Nürnberg will doubtless come."

With a gesture of exasperation, Veit stood and then strode across the room. He seemed to be contemplating the painting of Lucretia. "Neither Lorenz nor I care a whit about these *best* people," he said at length.

Greta's lips still smiled. "I hardly think you speak for Lorenz in this," she said, and turned to him. "What say you?" she asked. "Does my *gloomy* husband speak for you, Lorenz?"

Lorenz disliked being the pawn in this chess game of marital strife. Though he found Greta vexing, he thought Veit's manner toward her too severe at times. The husband made it all too clear that he despised his wife.

"I would gladly meet anyone you want to present me to," he

said, trying to steer a middle course between the spouses. "But, I must tell you, I am not certain that I shall remain in Nürnberg."

Greta's smile disappeared in an O of feigned surprise. "Not remain in Nürnberg? Why, wherever would you go?"

"Back to Wittenberg, perhaps."

"Wittenberg? Whatever for?" Greta now addressed him as if he were her absurd child. "But you yourself have said that Wittenberg is so dreary a place . . ."

"I did, but . . ." Lorenz, however, could not finish, for Veit, wheeling around, cut him short.

"Wife, again have done!" he said with apparent exasperation. "Where Lorenz desires to live is his, not our affair! He does not need to stay in Nürnberg."

Greta maintained her composure, despite Veit's peevishness. "No, you are right, husband," she said, nodding her head. "He need not stay here—*but*, he may want to after he has met and spoken to the *right* people. He may learn something that will make Nürnberg seem *very* appealing to him—much more appealing than that old sand heap of a Wittenberg!"

Again, Greta smiled prettily—but this time there was something in her smile that left Lorenz feeling uneasy.

* * *

Greta made sure she invited only the *best* of Nürnberg to her fête; and, as ever, the *best* were more than willing to defer to her. Not only men but women yielded to Greta's beckoning; for if men found her alluring, women seemed devoted to her for her beauty and seemingly perpetual youth. Everyone, it seemed, found her manner and conversation fetching—everyone, that is, but her husband. Indeed, Veit's antipathy for Greta was a matter of universal wonder and the subject of whisperings among the knots of women at the banquet. Sitting on a stone bench near the frog pond that afternoon, hidden by a leafy lilac bush, Lorenz overheard three women sibilate on the subject.

" . . . and so accomplished a woman, too! Why, who else in the city could prepare a party like this in so short a time. You'd think a man would be proud to have such a wife!"

"And so *lovely* as she is, too! It makes no sense!"

"Yes, she is lovely, to be sure—but, you know, she has been putting on some weight lately!"

The women tittered.

"*Ach!* He can't have *too much* disdain for her, then!"

More tittering.

"You think it's that? I thought it was just that she's been catching up with the rest of us!"

"Well, that may be, it may!"

"Well, whatever it is, I must say, if *my* husband treated me so, he would have none of *my* favors."

"Oh, but it is Greta's only way! She could not possibly hold him by her conversation. *We* all love to gossip with Greta, but a man of Veit's learning—we cannot claim much in the way of smarts for her, now can we?"

"No, she gives him what he wants—and she gets what she wants out of him . . . "

Lorenz could not doubt that other knots of woman gossips were saying similar things, though mostly what he heard that afternoon were expressions of wonder at Greta's skill at preparing such a banquet as this, and in so short a time. Lorenz himself was mildly impressed—the food and drink, the decorations, the musicians scattered around the halls of the house and in the garden; one would have thought they were the fruit of long planning. It had been only a week since Greta had said she wanted to hold a banquet.

Lorenz smiled to himself and continued his walk through the garden.

He thought how, that very morning, he had dreaded this banquet. Ever since his return from Weissenbrücke and his illness, he had felt a contempt for the type of society that had flooded *Auerhaus* that afternoon. But now, despite himself, he felt an exhilaration. It was if he had been drawn back into his youth, when Nürnberg had seemed to him a vision of impossible beauty. The women in their rich but modest Nürnberg gowns, the men staid and dignified, the beauty of the garden and the house, decked out in festive finery—was this not the very form and epitome of human society? He thought of Wittenberg, the place to where he had, only this morning, thought to return—could he steel himself to it? The thought of it now repelled him.

He passed through the doors into the family hall. Like the garden, it was filled with knots of people, conversing and laughing. Such merriment! In the far corner, three musicians were now playing. No one paid any heed to him, but that was for the better—for now, at least; he was content merely to observe and think. He glanced over his right shoulder at the painting. His eyes lingered over it longer than had been his wont since his return to the city.

He made his way through the throngs of men and women, into the hall. Guests were still arriving. A servant passed near him, bearing a tray laden with glasses filled with golden wine. He took a glass and sipped the sweet nectar of it. He heard more music, coming from the dining hall; and he followed after its beckon.

Meats of all kinds, breads, sweetmeats, and other viands weighed side tables. The main dining table was set for the banquet, as were several other, smaller tables. He wandered between the tables, taking in the shimmering beauty of it all. He finished his wine just as a servant was passing with a bottle. Golden liquor filled the crystal orb in his hand.

Veit was nowhere to be seen. Of course, he would be holed up somewhere (probably his study) where he would not have to mingle with this crowd. Poor Veit. In other times, it would have been, "those vain Nürnbergers" that he would have avoided; now, it was their poor opinion of him, a hated papist. But then—Lorenz could hardly help smiling. "Now, at least, the feelings are mutual," he thought.

But just then, Veit entered the room through a side door. Those who noticed him, bowed and nodded to him politely, though coldly, Lorenz thought. Veit paid them little heed; he was, rather, glancing about the room. When he saw Lorenz, he made a beeline across the hall to him.

Veit took him by the arm and led him aside.

"Thank God I've found you," he said. "I've come to warn you: Greta has designs on you . . ."

"Yes, she is looking for you—she came to me, asking for you. Her parents are soon to arrive."

Veit's explanation shed little light on his meaning.

"I came to warn you that, if you want to avoid some discomfort, I can take you where she won't find you."

There was something slightly antic in Veit's demeanor. As he spoke, he was glancing from side to side as if afraid of disclosure. But Lorenz felt little concern at Veit's news. His spirits were light. He felt in good humor with the world, even with the thought of having to endure Greta. It could not, after all, be so bitter as all that. "Veit," he said, "whatever is wrong with you?"

Veit gave Lorenz a confused look. His hand dropped from Lorenz's arm.

"If Greta asks for me—I see no need to hide from her."

Veit shot him a questioning look. Then he shrugged his shoulders, as if to say, "well, I warned you." What he did say was, "As you wish, then. If you want to find me, I shall be in my study." Then, without another word, Veit turned and left him.

"How uncanny Veit is," Lorenz thought as he made his way across the dining hall and out through the main doors, into the passageway. He would not seek Greta's company, but he would not shun it either. But as he made his way back into the family hall, he saw Greta, the Waldhummels, and a man he did not recognize standing hard by the picture of Lucretia. They stood in a semicircle around the picture and seemed to be discussing it. Lorenz hesitated, remembering Veit's implied admonition; but then he took another drink of wine. "Well, damn it all," he said to himself.

Lorenz sauntered casually over to where Greta and the others stood. They were facing the picture and did not see him approach.

The stranger was speaking. "The benighted soul!" he said unctuously, shaking his head. "How she clings to her folly!"

"We've done what we could; she will listen to nothing," Frau Waldhummelin said.

"How does she refuse you? With passion or raving?"

Frau Waldhummelin sighed. "With neither," she said. "She's as cold as ice—though if we forced her, she would, I think, turn on us like a snapping cur."

"Oh, mother! I think not. I have never known her to . . ." But Greta did not finish; she had seen Lorenz. Turning to him, she said, with her languid smile, "My dear *magister*, I have been looking everywhere for you!"

Lorenz, feeling pleased with the world, bowed slightly. "You have found me," he said.

The others had now turned to Lorenz. "You, of course, remember mother and father—they have been so eager to see you!"

Lorenz and Herr Waldhummel bowed to one another.

"But I don't think you have met, this our friend—though you doubtless have heard his fame. Magister Andreas Osiander."

The two men bowed to each other.

"*Ach,* Frau Scheuerlin," Osiander said, with a self-regarding grin, "If Herr Magister List has not heard of me—which would come as no surprise to me, I might add—I, at least, have heard of him. Herr Magister, your work and sufferings for the Gospel, not to mention the report of your learning, do you honor." Again, he bowed, but only slightly.

Though he had just met Osiander, there was something about the man Lorenz did not like. "No honor to me, I assure you, Herr Magister," he replied. "All our works are like straw." Lorenz enjoyed the blush that suffused Osiander's cheeks. "Indeed, Herr List," Osiander rejoined, and then added, piously: "Thanks be to God for the grace he has shed on us, by faith and the Holy Ghost!"

Frau Waldhummelin here interposed. "Herr List," she said, "we understand that you intend to remain with us in the city."

"Intent would be too strong a word," he said. "I have not yet made up my mind."

"You have not?" Frau Waldhummelin replied, raising a condescending eyebrow. "Why, where else would you go?"

But Osiander would not let Lorenz reply. "No doubt, my lady," he said, "Herr List would wish to return to that bosom of the Gospel—I mean Wittenberg—where he would again enjoy the favor and confidence of Herr Doctor Luther. But, while I understand your most just desire, Herr Magister," he said, addressing Lorenz, "I would entreat you seriously to consider the good will of these your friends, who have taken an interest in your welfare!"

"Indeed?"

"Indeed, yes! They fairly begged me to accompany them here so as to make your acquaintance. I so jealously cherish any opportunity, outside of my work, for prayer and contemplation, and so like to avoid gatherings of any sort—but, today, I could not in charity refuse the importuning of this lady and her daughter. They have taken great interest in your welfare."

"As you have said."

"As I have said—but so joyous a communication as this deserves repeating, does it not?"

Lorenz nodded his agreement.

"Herr Magister Osiander," Frau Waldhummelin said, "has said he may be able to help you secure a position in the city. The *Aegidienkirche* ... "

But Osiander interposed, "it is uncertain, Herr List. Alas! But, fear not, Herr List, there are other situations that could benefit from your rare talents. I would not speak of them now, of course—but perhaps you could come to me in the next week to discuss the matter? You may find me most days at the *Lorenzkirche.* Shall I expect the pleasure of a visit from you?"

It all had happened so quickly. Just a few hours since, he had thought he would return to Wittenberg; then, the pleasures of the banquet had been working on him; and now, Osiander expressed a desire to meet and discuss "situations" with him. Maybe, a few hours earlier, he would have politely refused; but now he did not. He gladly accepted Osiander's invitation.

* * *

Late that same night, Veit came to Lorenz's room.

Lorenz thought his friend looked worn and weary. And when Veit began to speak, Lorenz saw he had been drinking more than was his wont.

"So, Greta found you," he said thickly. "She told me she had ... "

"Yes, she did."

"She said that she had changed your resolve to leave Nürnberg."

Lorenz shook his head. "If she said that, Veit, she said more than was warranted by anything I said. I said merely that I would speak with Osiander about the possibility. That is all."

"That is all?" Veit said with an ironic grin. "Well, I believe you, as far as your part in this business is concerned. But, I assure you, it is not *what is all* with Greta or her mother."

Lorenz laughed. "You speak as if there were some conspiracy afoot."

461

"You are so sure there is not?"

Veit's manner, at once sodden and admonitory, was irksome. "I am sure," Lorenz said, "that it is nothing more than that, when Osiander arrived, it popped into Greta's head to speak to him about me, and he gave some vague assurances. It will all probably come to nothing. He will meet with me because it pleases Greta . . . "

"It pleases the Waldhummels," Veit interposed.

"Well, if it *did*, it was only for the nonce. I doubt the Wald-hummels give a fig for my welfare, or whether I stay in the city or not. They have probably already forgotten the whole matter."

But Veit slowly shook his head. "I assure you, they have not," he said. "It is very much on their minds. You see, it fits in with their designs."

"Their designs?" Veit's last words discomfited him. His tone hinted at a threat.

"Yes, Lorenz," Veit continued. "Greta and the Waldhum-mels have designs on you. You are right, though; they care little for your personal welfare, except insofar as it serves their purposes."

"Their purposes?"

"Yes," Veit nodded. He began pacing the room.

"I found it out just tonight. My *dear wife* told me that her parents know everything about you — about you and Beatrice . . . " Veit stopped and glanced at him. Lorenz felt himself stiffen, as if awaiting a blow.

Veit again took to pacing the room. "You see, Greta told them everything, just in the past few days. They know about the secret marriage, the correspondence between you. Everything."

Veit stopped and turned as if to see whether his words had hit their mark. They had. The Waldhummels had known *every-thing*, even as he was exchanging pleasantries with them. But why would they offer him assistance to a preferment when they knew that he . . . that he had seduced their niece? Did even Osiander know?

"*Ach*, it was all I could do to keep myself from striking her when she told me she had betrayed our trust," Veit said with heat. "She seemed scarcely ashamed at her part in keeping the matter secret all these years. She told her parents every-thing, absolutely everything! 'Don't you see, Veit,' she said to me, 'that everything is different now?' I answered nothing—I feared what I would say to her."

Veit paused, as if to allow Lorenz to digest this news. Then, he resumed his pacing.

"There is another matter. I have been trying to keep the news from you, at least for as long as you were sick and con-valescing. I was planning to tell you, once you were well—but then when you said you would likely leave the city, I thought, perhaps, I would need say nothing at all. If you returned to Wittenberg, you need never know, and she, too, could be left in peace—whatever peace they would suffer her to enjoy. But now that they know, they have more to torment her with. And when I learned that they had designs on you—I had hoped to keep you from them. You, at least, would not be their means to ruin her utterly."

Lorenz could but dimly surmise the meaning of Veit's words—but even by that light, their sense dismayed him. Was it what he feared—or hoped for? Was it fear or hope—or the fear of losing all hope—that made him reticent to broach the matter, ask the question that could dispel all doubt?

"*Ach*, Lorenz, my poor friend: whatever will you do? They will not let her have what she wants. And you, well, you would involve her in another ruin."

"Veit, for God's sake!" Lorenz exclaimed. "What are you talking about?"

Veit's eyes were downcast. "Surely, you have guessed it," he said. "How could you not? You know of whom I speak, but

463

you do not know all. I do not know if for you this is good tidings or bad—but she is no longer in the cloister, Lorenz. She is no longer Agnes. She dwells again in the city, in the Waldhummels' house, Beatrice once again. But if she is *Beatrice*, she is hardly blessed; no, hardly blessed at all."

CHAPTER 8

IT WAS SEVERAL MOMENTS BEFORE LORENZ could recover from the wonder of Veit's words. *Beatrice was free from the cloister. She was living in the city. She was free.* But what did it all mean, for her, and, yes, for him? But then, the full force of what Veit's words implied hit him, and he recoiled from it. "God, no!" he at last exclaimed. "They did not drag her from the cloister?"

Veit sighed and sadly shook his head. "No, not exactly that," he replied. "But it is all just as bad."

Veit walked to the window and, opening it, looked out into the night.

"It was all so prudent," he began, "oh, so very prudent! Reports had reached the city of the peasant uprisings to the south—of monasteries pillaged, castles torn to the ground, of all the sacrilege and violence and rapine. It was most *prudent* to think that Nürnberg would not be spared what had befallen other cities—at least our lands and villages outside the city. Indeed, the council said it had received reports that the peasants were moving our way. We had heard what befell Rothenberg and your own Weissenbrücke, news that would throw any *prudent* man into consternation. Nürnberg could, perhaps, be defended—but the outlying districts, no."

Veit's tone was bitter. "Just as I said, it was all very *prudent*. The monasteries outside the city, Engelthal and Pillenreuth, were in dire danger. The peasants would certainly not spare

465

them; and as they were made up of nuns, the consequences of inaction on the part of the Council, which is always so protective of women's honor, were unthinkable. Thus, not long into Easter, the Council ordered all the nuns to be brought into the city—for their own safety."

Veit laughed dryly. "Of course, the *Bundschu* provided a convenient pretext for carrying out another of the council's cherished plans. As you know, in March it had proclaimed a reform of the church here. The Mass was abolished, and plans were afoot to break up the remaining monasteries in the city. *That* has not proven so easy, by the way; the council fathers did not reckon on the stubborn and adroit resistance of Caritas Pirkheimer and her nuns, nor of the sisters at Sankt Katarina's. Oh, you can be sure that the council has made life very hard for those women! The Waldhummels' dear friend, Osiander, has seen to that, along with the coterie of his 'preachers of the *Pure Word.*' It seems they can do nothing about these wicked women—even Osiander's golden tongue has failed to nudge them from their 'reliance on human works.' But where the Council has failed with the city monasteries, it could perhaps succeed with those outside the walls."

Veit turned from the window and began pacing the room again. His indignation was palpable. "Once within the city, the nuns discovered they had to deal with a more urbane and refined rapine. They were told that they had to turn their monastery and its lands over to the council! From thenceforth, they were to live in the city—meaning, of course, no longer as nuns." Here Veit stopped and laughed. "Unfortunately," he said, "the council did not reckon on Magdalena Kressin, the Pillenreuth prioress! She was able through her brother, Christoph, to get the Swabian League to take the nuns' part, and the League convinced our august council of the imprudence of their zeal. So, despite their Gospel scruples, once the peasant threat was past, the council had to let the sisters return to their cloisters."

Throughout Veit's recital of the events, Lorenz found himself waxing impatient. He wanted to hear only of one thing; nothing else mattered to him. Veit seemed to divine his friend's mood. He begged pardon for his rambling, "for I doubt, in the circumstances, you care much about the sordid affairs of this city. But these are matters that touch me deeply, and I am afraid I am carried away by my indignation.

"But now I shall tell you of Beatrice.

"She did not return to the cloister with her sisters. Indeed, she was one of three Pillenreuth nuns who, it was said, obtained leave to remain in the city on account of their highly influential relatives. I confess, I wondered at it, for I had heard of her refusals to leave the monastery before. I visited her when she had first entered the city; but since we met in the company of Greta and her parents, nothing was said of the circumstances of her withdrawal. Greta assured me that Beatrice had voluntarily laid aside the habit — and this alone should have given me pause, for my wife is not above lying. But I was willing to believe her tale, though it distressed me deeply."

The recitation of this part of his story seemed to calm Veit; his indignation softened into a cast of sadness. He pulled a chair over to where Lorenz sat. He no longer avoided his friend's eyes.

"But then I began to doubt. If she had willingly abandoned the monastery, why was she holed up in the Waldhummels' house? After paying the dowry to the monastery, Herr Auer had reserved his house and properties to his daughter, in case she should relent. (He never believed in her vocation, you know.) He had died before she made her final vows, so his last dispositions, with the Waldhummels as trustees, remained in force. Now that she was back in the city, supposedly by her choice, I thought I would receive notice that she would take possession of her house; but I did not. Indeed, no one saw her, save the Waldhummels and Greta. I was fobbed off with

467

excuses when I tried to visit her. My doubts became more acute.

"It was her attempt to escape that revealed the Waldhummels' and Greta's lie."

"She tried to escape?"

Veit sighed. "Yes, with the help of a sympathetic servant girl. It seems Beatrice thought that if she just got back to the monastery, that tiger, Magdalena Kresslin, and the Swabian League would protect her; and I daresay, she may have been right about that. But she never got a chance to test it. She and the servant girl were caught near the *Spital Thor* and dragged back to the Waldhummels'. There she was kept under close watch. When the peasant threat at last dissipated, the Waldhummels packed her off to Lenzgrab. Greta and the children went, too, which is why she was not at home when you arrived. At Lenzgrab they remained until their recent return to the city."

Veit again paused and studied Lorenz, as if examining what effect the story had on his friend.

"Greta is now more open—and brazen—about their treatment of Beatrice. They brought her back to the city to see if she would finally behave herself. The fact she did not come tonight betokens that she won't. The Waldhummels now have only two alternatives. The first is to take her back to Lenzgrab, there to wither her life away until she submits. The second..."

"Yes," Lorenz said, "the second . . . "

Veit paused and sighed again. "The second," he said, "is to enlist her husband—you, Lorenz—in their cause. You are to be the means to seduce her back into the world."

* * *

Through the open window came the sound of crickets and the chirping of frogs. A fly buzzed wearily before Lorenz's face. He waved it away.

"You know I cannot do that, Veit."

Veit nodded. "No, I suppose you cannot," he said.

468

Lorenz wondered at his friend's tone. It seemed regretful. "*You* do not urge me to do it?" he said.

Veit smiled weakly. "My wife's mother wants you to," he said. "And she will not let you rest until you do it."

Lorenz contemplated Veit's words, then slammed his hand down on the chair's arm. He stood and walked to the window. Looking out into the darkness, he strove with the warring feelings within. *They* wanted him to; but didn't *he* want to, as well? God, how he wanted to! But yet—how could he join with those *she* deemed her enemies? And more—how could he cozen her against the demands of her conscience? And what was his conscience in the matter? What did the inner voice whisper to him?

"*Ach!* What does it matter to them, Veit? Why not leave her be? Isn't it more in their interest to have her out of the way? The council surely won't let her donate her property to the monastery!"

"No, you are right about that," Veit replied. "But in this, I fear, you are not just to my wife's mother."

Lorenz whirled round. "What?" he said with a biting laugh. "Are *you* defending the Waldhummels?"

"I am merely trying to be just," Veit said calmly. But then he laughed—"*Ach*, Lorenz! Yes, I see—I am so wont to rail against the likes of the Waldhummels that any kind word toward them from me must seem eccentric. But, no; I am not defending them. What they are doing is cruel, and, of course, from where I stand, a sacrilege.

"But, you see, Lorenz, I can say this much, at least, for Frau Waldhummelin—not for her husband, who does only whatever his wife wants, nor for their daughter, who is acting, I am convinced, out of purest spite. Whatever her foolishness and vanity (and she has plenty of both), one thing Frau Waldhummelin takes seriously is the care of her family—in this case, her niece. She has always seen it as her duty to raise her niece

469

up in propriety and to land her in a good marriage. Now, that she is, in her own shallow way, convinced that the new teaching is right, she is determined to drag her niece from that *brothel of Babylon*, as she judges the monastery. And she will use any means, any *cruelty* to achieve her aim."

Veit's words struck Lorenz hard. He felt a sinking inside. "Cruelty?" he whispered.

"Yes, Lorenz." There was anguish in Veit's tone. "Not physical cruelty, no—though I could imagine Frau Waldhummelin striking out in wrath. But she is not used to such displays. Rather than that, a searing coldness, a disdain and condescending despite; the constant reminder, day by day, of her degradation. They will force her back to Lenzgrab, isolate her, and remind her daily of her disgrace. None shall show her the slightest kindness. She shall be cut off from all love and friendship. She will not give in, for she is strong; but she will wither and die within. She will become the lifeless husk of what she is today."

Veit's head had been bowed as he spoke. This was good, Lorenz thought, for he scarcely wanted his friend to notice his confusion. The bitter life to which she would be condemned! He knew she could withstand any coldness and harshness; they would only goad her to resistance. But Veit was right; she would wither and die within. And he—he, perhaps, could save her. She was less proof against love, that he knew; and his love could perhaps melt away her stern refusal. And how he wanted to give in to this desire, this most palpable desire! But something from deep within him forbade it. What he wanted contended with what he ought. How easy it would be to acquiesce—but yet he knew he must not. Had he not promised it in the monastery church at Pillenreuth? And would he have her, even as he was himself, foresworn?

"Veit," he said after a long silence. "You know I cannot. You are not urging me to it . . ."

Veit, who had not changed his position this little while, now raised himself in his chair. All color had left his cheeks. His eyes were sad, but his lips were turned in a slight smile. "No, I know you cannot," he told Lorenz. "But aren't we a confused pair? You who should think it right, refuse to do it. I, who think it wrong, would urge you to it. How to explain it to ourselves? How, to God?"

Veit again leaned forward, resting his head in his hands. He ran his fingers into his hair. "But I can't see her yoked to misery. And as they will never again let her back into the monastery... and you two *are* married, truly married ...

"Can't you see that you alone can save her?"

"I save her?" This time it was Lorenz's turn to smile. "I can save no one," he said. "From me can come no salvation."

471

CHAPTER 9

E AWOKE THE NEXT MORNING, resolved to leave Nürnberg. He could not remain there with her so close to him and free, even if she were at Lenzgrab. The temptation would be too great; and with even Veit urging him, he might well succumb.

And what if she and he should sometime meet?

No, he must leave Nürnberg; on that he was decided. He could not do what they asked of him.

But why couldn't he? On what did he found his scruples? After all, to go to her, to woo her from her error, accorded with everything he had claimed to believe, everything he had taught. It should have been obvious what he should do. But yet he hesitated and then refused. Why?

It was not for the freedom of her conscience; that was a mere pretense. Was it because he knew it would not be for her, for God, for anyone but himself, that he would do it? That he would work on his own behalf, all the while feigning devotion to God and the Gospel? But no, even this was not what troubled him, for he knew men always work for such purposes, for men are depraved. Whatever he felt of the matter, to do it would be good, simply good. God would rectify whatever was crooked in his intent, no benefit accruing to him thereby.

And yet, he would not do it. It was time he left Nürnberg.

* * *

The meeting with Osiander left him confused and angry. How did they dare? They dangled the promise of Sankt Aegidius like a bauble before a child. If he would only be good, do what they wished, he could clasp this little gift in his pudgy hands. Did they really think that what he refused for love, he would do for gain? Yes, Osiander couched the offer in unctuous terms; it was for the *triumph of the Gospel*, the *comfort of souls*—the *salvation of her soul!* But the man spoke with a wink and nod—as if they understood each other!

"The man is a fool, a panderer," he thought as he made his way through the city. "I shall have no more to do with him."

He did not reckon where he went. The streets, the buildings, the people were unsubstantial, like a mist through which he passed. Only his thoughts were substance. He could describe their contours, he could touch them. All else, everyone else, was fantastic.

He felt little wonder, when the mists of his mind dissipated, to find himself in the *Marktplatz*, regarding the pinnacle of the *Schöner Brunnen*. He recalled the far-off day when he had first beheld it. It pained him to think of the innocence of those days. *Then*, he could scarce comprehend the wonder of the city; he could hardly believe that he had been brought within its walls. His future, seen through a golden mist, held only promise of greater wonders. Now, however, the fountain could stir no feeling in his heart. Beautiful it was, but its beauty could not touch him.

Centered on his thoughts, he did not at first notice the man, sitting, hunched over, at the base of the fountain. The man was not one to elicit attention; he was rather commonplace: he was heavyset, with an unkempt, gray beard, soiled clothes, and a soft cap pulled down low over his eyes. But when Lorenz at last noted him, he felt an instant curiosity. He felt he had seen this man before. Though he could not see his face, he felt he knew him. Now he turned to get a better look at him. The man, feeling perhaps the eyes of a stranger on him, glanced up at Lorenz. Then his eyes widened, and his mouth gaped. As for Lorenz—he knew him at last.

"Is it really you?" Lorenz said to him. "Balthas Hecht, what has brought you to Nürnberg?"

* * *

"*Ach*, Lorenz!" The other rose as he spoke; he glanced about, like a cornered dog looking for an avenue of escape. His voice trembled. "I beg ye—do not betray me!"

"Balthas, don't be afraid of me—how would I betray you, and to whom?"

Pulling off his cap, Hecht twisted it in his hands. He laughed nervously. "*Ach*, ye know, I think. Ye knew all along—we were nothin' but a pack of fools! But we've paid—I've paid. I don't need to pay no more. Don't make me pay any more!"

Lorenz felt amusement, but also pity for the man. He really cut a clownish, pitiful pose. "Balthas, fear not," he said. "I know no reason to betray you to anyone—as if I even knew anyone I could betray you to! But even if I knew of a reason to hand you over to whomever, you would need fear nothing from me."

"*Ach*, then just let me be, Lorenz! Let me go my way. I'll leave this city, I swear it!"

"Balthas, all right—I'll let you go your way..."

"Thanks, Lorenz, I'll just be..."

"... But not before I've gotten you something to eat."

Hecht lifted his hand, as if to wave away the suggestion; but let it drop. "Well, I *am* a mite peckish," he muttered.

"Then follow me," Lorenz said with a laugh.

He led the man from the *Markplatz*, turned down a road that led to *Sebaldskirche*, and then down another street that ran by the north wall of the old Augustinian cloister. On the opposite side of the street stood a group of buildings. Lorenz directed Hecht through a small door into a dark tavern. At a table in the far, dim corner of the room they sat down.

"Is this dark enough for you, Balthas?"

"Oh, yes, I feel quite safe here!"

Lorenz called for beer and some cheese, meat, and bread. As he watched Hecht eat, Lorenz thought about his home village, his father, brother, and, most of all, Inge. Ever since returning to Nürnberg, he had thought often of them, of what may have befallen them. He hoped he could get Hecht to tell him something of his family; but, he would not ask him directly. Being an old publican, Hecht had been habituated to telling his customers what he thought they wanted to hear. If it were bad news from home, Lorenz wanted to know it. But he knew he had to steer Hecht inadvertently into blurting out the truth.

He waited until Balthas' supping had begun to abate. Then, "Now that I have bought you food and drink—you *did* find the beer to your liking?"

"*Ach, ja!*" Balthas said, wiping his mouth with his sleeve. "The brewers here do the city honor—indeed they do! And I should know...."

"Well, I'm happy you're pleased—and since you are, you should remember that one good turn deserves another. So, I pray, tell me your story, why you came to Nürnberg."

Hecht grimaced and hesitated; but then, scratching his bald pate, he sighed. "All right, Lorenz, I'll tell ye everything."

Hecht leaned forward in his chair, his forearms on the table. He seemed to be working up his courage.

"*Ach!* I can't deceive ye, so why try?" Hecht said, in a confidential tone. "Ye know that I, like many of the lads, was taken in by the preaching of that whoreson priest, Jäcklein. Ye see, folks around our parts have suffered a long time—and when farmers were suffering, so was my custom. Ye see, I knew what they felt, 'cause I felt it too. The *Bachkrebs* wasn't doing too good, and that's a fact! And then the fellows would come in and talk about their woes. It made me right angry, it did!

475

"Well, the long and short of it is that when Jäcklein led the boys out, I followed them. I thought I was younger than I was, and . . . "

"And they threatened to burn down your inn if you didn't join them—isn't it so, Hecht?"

Hecht blushed. He hemmed and hawed, but then admitted sheepishly that it was so. "But it weren't that I didn't believe in all of it—I did!" he said defensively. "But I was too old to be going out like that, marching over hill and dale, and then sleeping out in the cold. And I knew nothin' about war. They didn't need me, and that's a fact!"

"But you went anyhow."

"Indeed, I did! Ye see, I had no choice. I was about all fagged out when we made our first camp. And was it cold! It was the cold and all that dark that got me to thinkin'. There were a hell of a lot of peasants in that army, but they warn't soldiers, not by a long shot. But with Frau Berthe on their side, I figured they would beat the princes dry. But then, I started thinking about the princes and all their guns and practiced troops; I wasn't so sure anymore that our folks could win.

"I was sitting by a meager fire as I thought these things. I must have looked like I was thinking, for a fellow sitting at fireside by me says to me, 'Are ye thinking what I'm thinking?' I hadn't seen him before, but now that he spoke, I saw it was our old gossip, Thomas Munter, the cobbler. 'I don't know what you're thinking, so I can't say,' I says to him. He then laughs at me and says, 'old Balthas—cagey as ever! Ye know,' he says, 'what I mean—all of this war making business!'

"Well, I says to him I didn't know what he meant (though I sort of did, ye know; I just couldn't let on, for safety's sake). He then begins talking about how the peasants didn't have no chance, once the princes got their forces together. He said he wasn't afraid of Frau Berthe, didn't think she had special powers and all that, and that if we didn't hightail it out of there that night, we were just as good as dead. I ask him if he didn't fear what Jäcklein and the others would do to him, and he says, 'nah! I'll be going back home, and they'll never come back there again. It's not them but the princes we need fear.

"Well, I tell ye—he made a lot of sense, and I didn't want to sleep another night on the hard ground and trudge along muddy roads only to get a bodkin thrust between my ribs or my head knocked off my shoulders. So, that night, he and me ran off in the dark, and a day later, we was back in the village."

Hecht finished off his beer, and Lorenz ordered another stoup for him.

"But I tell ye, I just about cursed Munter and my own stupidity when news came back about how our folk had taken Weissenbrücke and were marching off to new battles. They'd come back, I thought, and burn down my tavern around my ears. But it wasn't more than a month before I heard that the *Markgraf* had beaten our folk and taken back his city. Ye can't know how good I felt about *that!*"

"You felt good about your neighbors' misfortune, Balthas?"

"No, no, no! Ye got me wrong there, Lorenz! It wasn't that! It was just that I didn't need fear their coming back and burning down my tavern—for Jäcklein would've done it for sure! He was just that kind of fellow. No, I was happy because I thought I had nothing more to fear. But I was wrong about that, too. *Ach,* what a fool I was!"

Balthas bit his lower lip. His eyes were moist. He took another drink from his mug. After a few moments of silence, wherein he seemed to be striving for mastery of himself, he continued.

"I figured it was enough for the *Markgraf* to beat the peasants and take Weissenbrücke back again. But it wasn't; he wanted to teach us peasants a lesson, I reckon. Only little more than a fortnight later, he took his army into the countryside and began laying waste to everything in his path. He came as far as our village—I got word just in time that he was coming, God be thanked! I ran off into the woods. But the village—well, he burned every building and house in it to the ground, except the church. What peasants he got his hands on he had tortured and killed. I could see the smoke from where I was in the woods. I could hear screams and crying."

Hecht's words struck Lorenz like a bludgeon. When he sat down to hear Hecht's story, Lorenz figured some misfortune had befallen the man; but he had not expected this tale. "By God," he said; "the entire village destroyed? Every house in it?"

Lorenz's question seemed to confuse Hecht. He looked about the room but then straight at Lorenz. Then understanding kindled in his eyes. He groaned and nodded his head.

"And what of my, of my father's house—the farm?"

"*Ach*, it is gone, all gone!"

"But my father, what happened to him, and . . ."

Another, deeper groan shook Hecht's stout frame. Grasping his bald head with both hands, he swayed from side to side. "*Ach!*" he moaned, "must I answer that? Must I?"

Cold desperation hardened Lorenz. "You must," he gasped in a taut whisper. "I must know!"

"Then I will tell ye. *Ach,* Lorenz! Your father—Johannes List, my old friend—he is dead, Lorenz. He is dead."

CHAPTER 10

ECHT COULD SAY BUT LITTLE OF what had befallen Johannes List that day. He knew that Sebald had not been at home—he had come by the tavern that morning on his way to the neighboring village of Fischbach. He had some business there, it seemed. When Sebald returned in haste and anxious—he had heard in Fischbach of the *Markgraf's* advance—it was too late. The army had come, done its work swiftly, and moved on to the next village.

"At evening, I crept out of the woods when everything seemed safe. *Ach!* The sights that met my eyes! I'll never forget them to my dying day! The houses and buildings was still smoking. My tavern was a smoking heap. There was dead bodies all over the ground—bodies of our friends and neighbors, Lorenz! Some had been tortured, it seemed; some just killed outright. 'Twas then I saw your brother, Sebald. He was standing in the middle of the street like he'd been enchanted by a bogey. He just stood there and stared about him. Then of a sudden he broke into a run. I followed him, though I couldn't keep up with him. When I caught up with him, he was in the courtyard of your house, what was left of it. He was kneeling on the ground by a body.

"It was your father, Lorenz. He lay there, a cudgel still in his right hand. I reckon he had tried to fight them off, and they just struck him down. He had an ugly gash the side of his head.

"I stood just behind Sebald, Then he turned on me, and his face was all screwed up. 'They killed him, Balthas!' he says to me.

479

'God,' he says, 'if only I was here — I could've died along with him.' And then he just bursts out weeping. I never seen no more pitiful sight, a strong man as your brother is, weeping as if he was a maid.

"I wanted to say something, but I didn't know what to say, not at first. But then it hit me — I says, 'don't say so, lad, what would befall your sister, if both of ye was dead?' — for you see, Eitel had never come back . . . "

Horror and dismay, like a swelling nausea, had possessed Lorenz through Hecht's recital. But with the mention of Inge, fear seized hold of him. "Balthas!" he said in a taut whisper, "Inge — she was not, she was . . . " He could not get out the word he feared to say.

"*Ach!* No, Lorenz — don't fear! She was safe, she was well — as well as anyone could be that day. When I said what I said, Sebald grew pale as death. He cries out her name and then leaps up and runs off. I didn't want to leave Johannes alone, but I was afraid for Sebald, what he'd do if he found her — if he found her like everybody else.

"But she was all right. The *Markgraf's* men didn't cross the Tiefer Bach; they went south away, and so they didn't see the Moeller place, hidden away as it is behind the trees. I followed after Sebald, and when I got there, they was clasped in each other's arms, weeping. But she was safe, Lorenz, and most of her children was safe. Her oldest boy had gone off with the father and like him had not returned."

The news that both Sebald and Inge had been spared washed over Lorenz like a refreshing stream. He scarcely listened to the rest of Hecht's recital — how he had stayed with them at *Moellerhaus* for a time; how they had waited in fear — needlessly, it turned out — for the army's return; and how Hecht, at last, left them, "for I feared that I might bring trouble on them, since somebody might know I had gone out. They begged me to stay, but I wouldn't hear nothing of it. I stayed long enough to see Johannes buried, then I lit out.

"He lies in peace now, in the churchyard, next to your mother, Lorenz."

* * *

He left Hecht in the tavern. It was late afternoon. The sun was high, and it was warm. He took his way through the city without aim or destination. He did not want to return to *Auerhaus;* he wanted to be alone—and what better place to be alone than in the city streets?

After wandering about for than an hour, he found himself at the foot of the *Burg.* As if startled from a deep sleep, he gazed up at its height. Large, billowing clouds floated above the castle's spires. Pennants flapped languidly in the gently stirring breeze. With little thought as to where he was, he began the ascent.

As he stood by a wall, looking out over the city, he reflected on the other times he had climbed the *Burg.* The first time was in his youth—his childhood, really—on a cold day, with Veit. The second time was in the struggle of temptation, when he formed the resolve that he would only a short time later break. That, he marveled to think, was not even a year ago.

Today he was full of thoughts, none of which were very clearly defined. He looked out toward the east, where the promised *Aegidienkirche* rose and *Auerhaus* sat nestled among other great houses of the rich and powerful. Much farther east, many leagues to east and north, beyond the walls, beyond the fields and forests, were Erfurt and Wittenberg. His eyes traversed an arc, running from east, to the south, and to the west. They lit lightly on the spires of Sankt Sebald's and those of Sankt Lorenz's a little farther on but did not rest on them. They followed the curvature of the imaginary arc until they collided with the tall tower of the castle palace. He was annoyed. The stern fortifications blocked his sight; he could not look out, over the leagues, to where, far away, his home village once had stood.

Once had stood. Again, the full force of Hecht's tale struck him. The village was no more. His father's house was no more.

481

His father was no more. And his childhood lay buried in the church yard, between his father and his mother.

His thoughts that, before, had been vague and uncertain, now delineated themselves. He had no home anymore, and no family. Since he could return to his village only at the cost of his life, his brother and sister, though alive, must be forever dead to him. He was cut off from his family and his people. He was utterly alone.

He thought of Wittenberg, and the thought of returning there repelled him. To have to act out a pretense of religion, of devotion to a cause he was uncertain he yet adhered to, sickened him. He was not one of them anymore, if he ever truly had been. Luther would see that, and he would be cast out. And the alternative, the invitation whispered to him in the church at Weissenbrücke that Easter Sunday morning; he could not answer it. Even now, even if he wanted to, he could not.

That way was closed off to him, but not by any external bars. And the other path, the path he had trodden now for—what was it? Three, four, five, six years? He had not the heart to follow it longer. He was paralyzed by an aching loneliness, but he would not turn back, return to the old path. Twice apostate he would not be, despised and suspected by all, and thus doubly alone. He would continue along the path he had been following, but with weary step and faltering heart. He would have no soul's companion at his side.

It was not the carrot of Sankt Aegidius that tempted him to do what he had foresworn. He cared not for fame or acclaim, for wealth or preferment. He cared nothing for the city spread out before him in all her beauty. She was now nothing to him but a fair corpse, or a marble statue, lovely to the eye, but pallid and cold to the touch. He wanted nothing more of plastic beauty but, rather, to feel the warmth of another hand in his, fingers entwined with his, a companion along the way, whose heart beat with his heart and whose eyes were alive with love—for him.

CHAPTER 11

THERE WAS A FOUNTAIN AT LENZGRAB, fed by a spring, in a small, enclosed garden, luxuriant, if somewhat rank with growth. Fruit trees—apple, cherry, pear, and plum—ancient but still fecund, grew at random in the garden, as if planted by nature's whim rather than human art. Flowering bushes (rose and lilac) and stands of blossoming cornflowers and lavender accented the cloister.

Four gates placed at the four points of the compass opened into the garden. Stone paths entered through the gates and converged on the fountain, an ornate pillar set amid an octagonal basin, spouting water from its crown. Filling the basin, the water passed through a small aperture, pouring into a brick-lined channel. Along the channel it ran to an opening in the garden's south wall, babbling in a rill into the woods beyond.

He knew he would find her in the garden.

He had arrived at Lenzgrab just the evening before. They were not, he said, to mention his arrival to her. He would choose the time and place. Though he was told she never dined with the family, he wanted to be doubly sure that news of his coming did not reach her. He was thus taken to his room directly. He asked that his meal be brought to him there.

They said she spent most of the daylight hours in the garden. What she did there, they could not say. She brought no book with her nor embroidery.

The north gate to the garden stood open. She did not see him pass through it. She was sitting on the ledge of the fountain's basin, her body angled to the gate where Lorenz stood, but her eyes were turned away. She seemed to be looking south away, over the garden wall, toward the forest. She was clad in a simple brown gown. Her hair, hanging loose now to just below her shoulders, was the rich brown that he remembered. Her shoes cast off, she cooled her feet in the grass. Her hands lay folded in her lap.

For days, he had rehearsed in his mind what he would say when they met; but now that she was there before him, he knew not what to say. He could not decide how to solicit her attention. Should he call out to her? He feared lest he should startle her.

He did not speak. He turned round, took hold of the garden gate, and shut it with a clang.

Startled, she rose up and turned toward the noise. She opened her mouth as if to speak, but made no sound. Her hands that had been clasped she let fall to her sides. Her eyes widened. She seemed like one regarding what she dreads.

Seeing her thus, clothed like a maid, emboldened him. All the longing he had felt for her these many years welled up within him, inundating his uncertainty and fear. Slowly, step by step, he approached her. He came to within a yard of where she stood and halted. She glanced up at him, her eyes alive with apprehension. All color was gone from her cheeks. But she did not turn from him or, as he feared she would, flee.

She, not he, at last broke the silence.

"I knew you would come."

She who spoke was not the young maid from whom he had been parted these many years. The freshness of girlhood was gone from the cheeks. Her face seemed more angular, as if the skin were drawn more tightly to the bone. The light of her eyes shone with the mellowness of twilight, not the brightness of morning. Her voice had a darker timbre. It was a woman, not a girl, who looked up at him—with apprehension, yes, but with the steadiness of self-possession. She was a woman now, though still, to his eyes, fair to look upon.

Yet there was something else he read in her eyes, in her whole demeanor, as she stood before him, not bowed, not shrinking away, but straight, bold, and resolute. She seemed as one buffeted but unbroken, like a tree on cliff's edge that has withstood wind and tempest, but by itself, alone. Her eyes appealed to him, as if she would say, "I will withstand you too, but, I pray, spare me the trial of further assault."

His heart was softened with love, but also pity. He felt he could not harm her, even if he should lose her. He could not hurt her as others had done, as he had done, before. Not again. No, not again.

"Do not fear me," he said. "I come here only as a friend." His voice faltered; he was unsure what to say next. He hunted his mind for the words. Then, at last, they came. They were simple, commonplace. "Will you walk with me, Beatrice?" he said.

She winced, as if he had pressed on a tender bruise. She lowered her eyes, as if irresolute, but then with barely a movement of her head nodded her yes. Without saying more, they two betook their way side by side over the moist greensward, and out of the garden, through the south gate.

* * *

They followed a path, a grassy way that struck into the green twilight of the wood. It was cool under the overhanging boughs and quiet, except for the singing of birds and occasional scurrying of some small animal in the undergrowth. The path more or less followed the course of the garden stream that soon began to run in a deeper, rockier course. The path thrice crossed the stream over small bridges.

The sun hurt their eyes as they emerged out of the wood. The path now made an abrupt left and wound its way, with the forest rising on one side of it and a field extending to the other. The stream cut across this field and ran into the forest beyond. The field this season was lying fallow.

The path followed the edge of the field but then made another abrupt turn to the right, back into the wood. They climbed a thickly wooded saddle of land. The trees here were older and cast deep shadows over the forest floor. A breeze soughed through the leaves, making an ominous sound. Once he thought she had drawn closer to him, but glancing at her he decided it had only a been a trick of the dim, green light

Mounting the summit of the saddle, the path plunged in zig-zags downhill until it emerged again into the sunlight. They had entered a small dell, with a hay field running off to their left. The hay stood tall and green in the summer sun, promising a rich harvest. At the far end of the field, the path wound back on itself so that it skirted the opposite side of the field. It then plunged again into the wood.

At first, the murkiness of the wood seemed darker than before, but it was not long until Lorenz's eyes adjusted to the light. This time, the path did not climb but skirted the knoll on which the garden with the fountain stood. The path then hung to the right, and Lorenz could see, straight ahead of him, the grassy grounds and antique pile of the house at Lenzgrab. He stopped at the verge of the wood and let her go on her way alone.

They said nothing at parting.

* * *

The next day they met again in the garden. Though they had not arranged it thus, it seemed to him as if she had expected him. He merely said to her, "shall we?" And she, slightly nodding, followed him out of the garden and into the forest. That day they followed the same path and, as the day before, walked in silence.

The third day that they met in the garden, he uttered no invitation; she merely joined him. Again, down the path descending the wooded knoll and skirting the edge of the fallow field, not a word passed between them. She walked, sometimes at his side, at others a little behind him. Though she would look about her, she often walked with her head slightly bowed, as if in lost in her thoughts. Once, she stooped to pick some blue flowers that grew at the edge of the field. When she rose, he smiled at the beauty of the flowers and her. "They are lovely," he said.

They passed into the wood where the lofty trees cast deep shadows. She walked slightly ahead of him. Then suddenly, shattering the silence, where a pool of sunlight lay athwart the path, a crash, like a giant clearing his way violently through brush. A large stag with a lordly brace of antlers leaped into the path only a few feet ahead of them. The kingly beast stopped for the briefest moment, glanced them a haughty look, and then vaulted again into the forest; behind him followed four does. At this apparition, Beatrice fell back to where Lorenz stood. He could feel her body pressed close to his and, without knowing it, his arm went round her waist. The bouquet of blue flowers dropped from her hand.

When they came back to themselves, Lorenz felt his arm around her waist. In dismay, he released her; then, catching sight of the flowers scattered at her feet, he knelt down and began gathering them. When he rose and turned to her, he saw her cheeks were suffused with rose. He laughed to hide his own dismay. "We did not expect that, did we?" he said. An awkward silence followed. Remembering the flowers, he held them out to her; but as she took them, he did not loose his hold on them.

"Beatrice," he said, with the shyness of a young boy—but he looked her full in the eyes. "Beatrice, believe me! I want merely to be your friend. But friends," he now smiled, "must sometimes talk to one another."

As he released his hold on the bouquet, she too, though

still blushing, smiled. Then, she too spoke. "I suppose you are right," she said. "But what shall we talk about?"

The ludicrousness of the situation—they two, who had known each other so well, acting like bashful lad and lass—made him laugh again. "I don't know," he said. "But we must talk about something!"

They walked on. For lack of anything else to say, he began talking about the stag—about other such stags that, as a youth, he had seen in the woods near his home. She said little to him except to ask him questions of his childhood and of other commonplace matters. When they at last came to the end of their path together, and he again halted within the eaves of the forest, they lingered for a moment.

"Shall we meet in the garden tomorrow?" he asked

She nodded. "Yes, I would like that, Lorenz."

He smiled playfully. "Then we are friends, Beatrice?"

She mirrored his smile. "Yes, we are friends."

She turned and made her way, alone, toward the great house.

*　*　*

It was she who began the conversation the next day. "They tell me you have but recently returned to the city," she said, hesitantly as if broaching a delicate subject. "They say you were quite ill when you returned."

"Yes, I hardly recall my first week there."

"They say you were near death." It seemed she scarce dared to utter the words.

He smiled. "So they tell me, too," he said.

They walked on, neither speaking to the other for some minutes. He noticed she was pensive. When at last she spoke again, it seemed it was only with some effort. "I have heard that you tried to turn the people of your village from rebellion—and that you came near death in doing so. I must say, that you did an honorable thing."

"But I failed."

She stopped and looked up into his eyes. "Still, you tried," she said. "And you braved death. Success and failure are not the sole measure of a man."

They walked on along the grassy path, under the branches. The light that fell on them was green, and the air was warm as if presaging a storm. Large, billowy clouds rode in the air, at times blocking the light of the sun. And as they walked, he found himself, he knew not how, speaking of what befell him in his home village and in Weissenbrücke. She listened like one who wanted to take in every word—and not just with her ears but with her whole mind and heart. He could sense her compassion, and this drew from him details and events about which he had at first not thought to speak. He did spare her some of the horror of Peter's death.

"He was a despicable man," she said, but without indignation. "Yet, I cannot help pitying him."

"Nor can I."

"Meseems the *Markgraf* was cruel beyond measure"—but even as she spoke the words, she stopped, turned to him. "But your family," she said, "have you heard what befell them?"

Her words were like a swift thrust to his heart. He winced. "Yes, I have," he said. "The *Markgraf* destroyed the village, every single house. My family's house he burned to the ground. My father is dead."

"*Ach*, Lorenz!" She had taken his hands in hers. "But what of your sister and brother?"

"They live, thank God, and are well," he said. "But I shall never see them again."

They stood looking into each other's eyes, but only for a moment. They continued their walk, hand in hand, through the wood where, the day before, they had been startled into speech by the leaping of a stag.

* * *

That night as he lay awake, he wondered if he should broach the question. Would she suspect his motives? Would she withdraw from him for the stirring of memory? Would the cold, hard silence separate them again?

But, the next day, it was not he but she who brought it up. They were sitting by fountain side in the garden. "You are curious, I can feel it," she said, breaking into a shy smile. "As I was about you, yesterday—and you were kind enough to answer my prying questions. It is only fair now that I answer yours."

He shrugged his shoulders. "I hardly know how to begin—or really what to ask."

"Just follow the first suggestion of your mind."

"All right then," he said. "Is all well with you, Beatrice?"

She blushed. "No, but it is better than it has been," she said. "You see, they tore me from the only peace I have known. And they have not been kind. They have thought a goad the fit instrument to prick my resolve. But jab at me as they will, they will not break me!"

"Were you then happy in the monastery?"

"Were you?" He had not expected the riposte. He slowly shook his head. "No," he said.

"No, you were not," she said, and as she said it, her pride seemed to deflate again into sadness. "Happiness is not our lot, it seems."

"But was I happy?" It was as if for the first time she had asked that question of herself. "Not at first, at least. I was very unhappy at first. But as the years passed, I grew content; and from that contentment came peace—peace and resignation. I suppose this is the most of happiness one can expect in life. Even your visit did not long disturb my peace, though I felt sad for you."

"For me?" he said.

"Yes, for I knew you would never know peace. You had cut yourself off from peace."

Her words, were they not true? Had he ever known peace? Would he ever know peace, even if. . . .

They rose from the fountain and passed through the south gate, into the forest. The day was warm with the expectation of rain and close under the trees. Clouds were darkening overhead. She was pensive with memory.

"You see, everything changed this year. We had had no priest for several weeks—our Augustinian brothers refused to say the Mass and the council forbade anyone else. We could have an Evangelical preacher, but no priest. At Easter we had no Mass; we joined only for the singing of the office. That was all. Was I happy, then? No, I was not happy. But I was at peace.

"But then came the summons—the August Council had decreed that we all must leave our monastery—for our own safety, they said. The peasant hordes were at large. I thought little or nothing of this, for the demand seemed reasonable. Yet, it soon became apparent what the Council was up to.

"In my simplicity, I thought they would house us someplace where we could continue our community life. But it was not so. Instead, we were dispersed to private houses belonging to the sisters' kin or their parents' houses. As you know, I was sent to my uncle and aunt, who feigned to welcome me graciously. I feared going there, for my aunt is relentless. I feared her house would become my prison, which indeed it did. I recall vividly the day she gave me the bitter news that I would never return to the monastery. I was henceforth to live, as she put it, 'like a good Christian woman should'—in the world.

"Yet, even then, I was able to cling to peace. I resolved that even if I was forbidden the cloister, I would make a cloister of my heart. They could imprison my body, but not my soul! Oh, it hurt bitterly that I was separated from my sisters; but such, I believed, was God's will. He would give me the strength to withstand whatever suffering was in store for me.

"I could not know how bitter that suffering would be."

491

They walked on, for a while saying nothing. Soon they emerged from the wood, where the path took to the edge of the fallow field. The clouds were darkening overhead. "It seems we will have rain," he said irrelevantly.

She continued with her story, as if he had said nothing.

"At first, they housed me in the city, thinking, probably, that its allurements would make me forget the monastery. But I was determined not to succumb!"

It seemed as if she were talking to herself. Did she even remember that he was there?

"I would not go to the feasts or the dances. I threatened to scar my face, if they forced me! That, of course, restrained my aunt, who could not suffer the shame of it. Imagine what the ladies of Nürnberg would say! She knew I would do it! They forbade me any Catholic prayer book, but I had memorized enough psalms to stay me, and I could make a rosary of my fingers. Most cruelly"—and here she smiled—"they made Greta my companion. I am certain it was not cruelty that moved them in this; they doubtless thought Greta would be a means to draw me into the world. I had to spend long hours with her and her children—who, sadly, have taken more after their mother than their father. It has been a torment!

"It was, I suppose, when they despaired of these measures that they brought me here to Lenzgrab. It's odd—I thought in the city that I longed for solitude; but the isolation here has been bitter. I have had no one to whom I could speak, no friend."

These words he felt gave him an opening. Despite himself, he exploited it. "I hope," he said, "I have been a friend to you, Beatrice."

"You have," she said after a pause, "though I know it is only for a few days. My aunt brought you here, I know, as a lure and snare; but you have not served her purpose. Soon, you will go your way, and I shall carry on my fight. She will tire before I do. She cannot hold out longer than I can."

She spoke as one who clings to a hope that is forlorn or impossible. She spoke bravely, but Lorenz could sense the fear and loneliness that animated her pretense. He knew her—she was not made for solitude. She craved companionship; she craved love. Yet her devotion to duty was strong, though he could sense it was shaken and wavering. Yet her aunt could not overcome it; Beatrice would fight back, like a she-bear defending her cubs. Yet there was one place, he felt, where she was unguarded. Her aunt would never exploit it, for she never would see it. But he saw it. The question was, should he?

The words came to his lips as if unbidden. "Beatrice—pray, believe me that I speak these words only in friendship for you. I would spare you unneeded suffering. You must know your aunt can hold out for as long as you can, for she has all of Nürnberg behind her. The monasteries cannot withstand it. They, too, will succumb. You will never again return to Pillenreuth."

His words were well aimed. She blanched. The resolve that only a few moments before had animated her seemed to collapse. She appeared now a hopeless, forlorn creature. As they passed in silence once again into the forest, he took her hand as if to comfort her. She did not pull away.

The heat that had all that morning pressed in on them seemed heavier in the wood. No creature was stirring; even the birds had fallen silent. Nature was waiting—for what? Lorenz felt the expectation in his flesh. The pity he felt as she told her story was being enkindled into longing. He wanted to hold her and possess her. His love would burn away her loneliness and desolation. She could not, she should not, live thus, alone and friendless, fighting a futile battle against impossible odds! He alone could be her savior.

The dark clouds hanging over the wood were heavy with passion. The sultry air was suffused with longing. Then, what the air, the trees, the very life of the wood seemed to await with trembling expectation sounded forth with a loud crash and boom. A great wind rushed through the forest, bending the trees as if they were stalks of grass. The sudden thunder startled her. She wheeled round, and they stood facing each other. Then a torrent of rain, and more great crashes of thunder. With a groan, he pulled her to himself, and she made no resistance. The warmth of her lips, her body pressed against his were like a sweet balm to an inner aching he had felt for so long. He wanted to melt into her, never to be separated from her again.

The storm passed as quickly as it had come. They parted and stood, looking into each other's eyes with wonder. Then they turned and continued their way, his arm around her waist, hers around his, under the dripping overhang of the forest boughs.

CHAPTER 12

HE PROTESTED—SHE SAW NO REASON for the lie. They had wed 14 years before—she could not see why they must deny before the world what they had not hidden from God. If they needed a public wedding to make them honest, so be it. It was not this but the pretense she objected to.

Frau Waldhummelin tried to maintain her composure, but Lorenz saw she was vexed. With measured tones, she asked her niece if she cared nothing for her name or the family's reputation? The prim fathers of Nürnberg did not look kindly on clandestine marriages; they would probably not punish *this* union, since so much time had passed; but it might sour them on Lorenz. What about his prospects? And what about her father's memory?

Greta voiced her own appeal. "Oh, Beatrice," she said, with a note of genuine distress in her tone. "Just think! If you keep mum, you will be able to wear the loveliest gown on your wedding day. We'll see to it that you are the loveliest bride in Nürnberg!" Beatrice replied that wearing black woolen for so many years had spoiled her taste for finery. Whatever befell, she would be simply clad on her wedding day.

It seemed no reasoning could move her, and Lorenz admired her for it. And he did agree with her, to a point. Now that he had Beatrice again, he felt like thumbing his nose at the world. All the fear and terror he had felt so many years seemed like naught but pantomime shadows on a wall. He was happy, and no one could take that from him. He need fear nothing, not even God. One moment holding Beatrice to his breast was proof, he thought, against the terrors of eternity. Still, the prospect of shameful slinking, of the whisperings of garrulous old women, tsk-tsking about the wanton girl and the boy who took advantage of a father's trust; the servant rutting with his master's daughter in the chambers of his house—a house they now both inherited: this he could not think on with equanimity. Yet, he did not want to oppose her openly in her bold defiance. He could not oppose her, but he could privately, he thought, give such reasons as would convince her. He could appeal to their love.

"You know," he said to her one day when they were alone, "we need not cast our pearls before swine."

She gave him a defiant look. "You are not suggesting that we accede to their opinion of our marriage, that it was shameful?"

No, he assured her, he proposed no such acquiescence. "But I confess that the very fact that the Waldhummels know of our marriage—well, I had hoped that they had never come to hear of it. It was bad enough that Veit and Greta knew. It is our mystery, ours alone. Need we sully it more by making it a matter of general report? You know everyone will only cast dirt on the memory of it."

She did not immediately give in. She argued with him, though in the end she acquiesced.

But the surrender seemed to dampen something of her spirit.

* * *

Still, she refused to wear anything but the simplest brown gown for the wedding. This, of course, distressed Greta, who could not understand why any woman would not want to display herself. It was just unnatural! Frau Waldhummelin was, of course, vexed out of measure. Herr Waldhummel could not, it seemed, care less. He clearly wanted to be shut of the whole business. This niece of his was causing him no end of trouble and annoyance!

The weeks passed. The banns were published. Preparations were made for a grand feast at the Waldhummels'—Beatrice at least could not obstruct that! But then, she took little interest in the preparations and even betrayed no eagerness for the approach of the day. It was if she were utterly indifferent to it. She was not wanting in affection to him; but she seemed to have nothing of a bride's eager expectation of the day. Lorenz had to admit that, given the circumstances, this was little to be wondered at. She was not a bride, after all. But yet . . .

Lorenz himself, of course, was not a bridegroom, but his days were full of expectation and longing. It would not be long before he possessed her again, her whom he had longed for these many years. Like her, he could care nothing for the wedding and the feast; but to hold her flesh to flesh again in his arms, to awake in the morning with her beside him, to live thus, day after day, until death parted them at last; he could scarce await this consummation. If she felt this same longing, she never spoke of it to him. Indeed, when she was not disputing with her aunt, she spoke little at all of their wedding day; not even to him. She did not encourage his forays into the subject. That she loved him, he was certain; but her reticence made him uneasy.

*   *   *

It was on a cool day in September that the wedding party wound its way in a small procession through the streets to Sankt Sebald's church. Andreas Osiander awaited them there, standing before the vaulting sanctuary. (He proffered his services on this occasion in deference to the Waldhummels.) Surrounded by family and friends—even Veit was present as a witness—Lorenz and Beatrice renewed the vows that, 14 years before, they had uttered to one another in an empty church, alone, before God.

Osiander's cheeks were puckered in a benignant smile as he asked them if they freely gave their consent to the union. After each answered yes, Veit handed Lorenz the ring, and he, with a joyful heart, placed it on the fourth finger of her right hand. Her hand was cold to the touch, but he scarce noticed it for the happiness he felt. Then he lifted his eyes to hers. And the fire of his joy collapsed to cinders.

It was as if he were looking into the face of a corpse. No happy but shamefast blush suffused the cheeks. They were pallid as if brushed by sickness or death. No tender light shone from the eyes; they stared out on vacancy. When Osiander bade them join their right hands, he felt no corresponding ardor in the touch. And when she repeated his words, "I am thine, and thou art mine," it was as if she spoke from out of the depths of the earth.

The procession to the Waldhummels' house was for him like a funeral cortege. Throughout the long afternoon and evening of feasting and celebration, she rallied herself; she spoke with guests and laughed at jests. She danced. Yet, the color did not return to her cheeks; and she scarcely spoke to him. Her good spirits were but a pretense. She was keeping up appearances — for the guests. She had no thought for him.

When at last they were alone in their room at *Auerhaus,* she shuddered and then stiffened when he took her in his arms. The wonder, apprehension, pity, and disappointment he had felt that day were kindled into anger. He released her and fairly pushed her from him. Turning from her, he snarled, "if you wish me to leave you alone, I will gladly accommodate you, Beatrice."

She spoke and her tone was bloodless. "Be not wroth with me, Lorenz," she said. "It is not you, it is . . . "

"And what is it?" He was ashamed at the sharpness of his tone. He would master his anger, but he could not. "For these many years I have longed for you; but it is clear you do not

498

want me. I would give you myself, all of myself; but you hold back from me!"

"I have nothing to give. There is naught left of me. You should have wedded another."

Lorenz's heart was smoldering with anger but sick with fear. He thought, "she longs for the bloodless life of the monastery—yes, that is it!" The barren rounds of prayer, the terror, shrinking before the unappeasable wrath of a whimsical God—and the final despair or near despair. The cross.

He felt then that he hated her. She was tearing from him his last hope of a joy that he thought would shelter him, a little while, from dread. But that river of separation that the dead longed to cross was flowing through the room. She stood on one bank and he on the other.

Yes, he felt he hated her. He wheeled round to face her; but when he looked on her countenance, the sharp, cruel words he meant to say died on his tongue. She stood before him, alone, utterly forsaken and forlorn. Wrath gave way before love and desire and pity.

His voice broke. "I want no one but you. There is no one for me but you. You alone are Else."

She shuddered with a soft, soundless weeping. Overwhelmed with pity and desire, he longed to comfort her, but he knew he could never touch with balm the pain that pricked at her innermost heart. That pain could not be healed—no, not for eternity; but perhaps he could make her forget it for a time. He took her by the hands, and she fell, sobbing, into his arms. With his hand he caressed her cheek, and then drew her lips to his.

CHAPTER 13

WHEN HE AWOKE, IT WAS PITCH DARK night. The dream lingered, dancing on the edges of his imagination. But gradually the terror of it subsided. It was, of course, only a dream; yet even now he was not sure it had not all been real. He shifted in the bed and beside him felt her body lying close to his. She was breathing quietly; she was deep in sleep. He ran his hand over the soft skin of her shoulder, down her arm, and over her naked thigh. He sighed and then turned onto his side and, reaching over her back, cupped one breast in his hand. She stirred a little but then sank back into sleep.

But he could not sleep. The dream would not let him sleep. When he closed his eyes, it came back to him in all its vividness.

* * *

They were standing on an ancient bridge, he and Sebastian. They were looking down into a dry moat that encircled a deep well, dark with the void. Everywhere was gray stone, the bridge, the walls of the moat, the heavens above — if, indeed, there were heavens above. No leaf of grass pushed through the cracks in the stone. All was gray and lifeless.

But there was movement. Below them, in the moat moved two lines of men, bent under pain and sprinting swiftly, driven by demonic figures, wielding scourges. The lines moved in opposite directions. From the bridge he could see only the backs of those who ran the outer circuit. They had naught, he knew, to do with him. It was those hastening toward him to whom he must give heed.

"Wait and behold the faces of those other evil-born."

It was Sebastian who spoke, and he turned to look on his friend. With a stern countenance Sebastian shook his head and pointed into the ditch. "See him who comes," he said, "and for his pain seems not to shed a tear."

Reluctantly, he turned and looked down into the pit. At first, he did not know him. Through the gloom he saw only the outline of a man, full formed except for stumps where his hands should have been. As the form moved closer, he recognized it, and was not surprised in the recognition: his face wore the old, impudent smirk.

"What, Peter," he said. "Are you here?"

"You did not expect me?" the other said.

"Not here."

"Where then?"

"Farther down, where the likes of you lie soused in ice."

The smirk disappeared in a glimmer of anger. "Do not play the pious boy with me, Lorenz!" he said. "We know you now. Your fingers played her most skillfully—we saw it all. If I am here instead of there, it is all because of you."

The words dismayed him. He turned for comfort to his teacher, but Sebastian had disappeared. He was alone with Peter Schwach in hell.

He tried to laugh it off. "What do you mean?"

"I mean, it is for your sake."

"My sake, how?"

But Peter did not answer. He began to wave his stumps and dance—and horrible to see, his legs too, lifting high in antic frolic, were bloody stumps. Around him the other spirits and the demons wielding whips took to dancing, and they were laughing! Laughing! All hell was laughing. The laughter rose into the fetid air like a flock of starlings taking flight.

It wheeled round him, round him, obliterating sight; but the buzz of the wings, roaring in his ears, was deafening. He pressed his palms to his ears, but the roar only grew louder and still louder until he felt it would split his skull.

* * *

It was then that he had awakened.

It had been a dream, only a dream. The realization, however, did not entirely still his heart. He nestled more closely to her, but he found no comfort there. He rolled onto his back and lay, staring at the ceiling. What did it mean? Did it mean anything at all?

Slowly he rose from the bed, trying not to wake her. She shifted in her sleep and made a little soughing sound, a sigh, but did not awaken. The air was cool on his naked flesh, and he shivered. The casement window, facing into the garden, was halfway open. He crossed the room to close it. But taking hold of the latch, he hesitated. He opened the window wider. He stared out into the night.

The moon had long since set, but the stars were vivid, preternaturally bright in the early morning sky. Many years before he had looked up into these same heavens, on the night he wrote the letter, bidding her farewell forever. Then, he had thought their only union would be in the heavens, the stars that they, though sundered, together would behold. Now, she lay sleeping within his chamber and he alone gazed up into the wheeling, serried hosts of night.

He did not know how long he stared thus into the night.

He knew he himself would never march in that shining procession. The heavens were closed to him. His lot was to lope with the horsewhipped sinners. Peter was there, holding his place for him. The dream had spoken true.

What, then? Heaven had rejected him, and hell awaited him; only one course was open to him. Neither to look upward nor below but on what lay before him. This life; it alone remained.

He must suck of its fulness, fix his eyes on its fair, caress its softness, inebriate his being with the gorgeous terror of its music. Beauty, only earthly beauty—it would have to suffice for the loss of blessedness. Perhaps he could carry a memory of it with him into hell.

He took one last look at the heavens and then closed the casement window. Groping his way slowly through the dark, he found the bed. He mounted it, pulling the coverlet over him.

"Why were you up?" he heard her ask him. "Only to close the window against the night," he said to her. "It is cold outside." He then pulled her close to him and, wrapping his leg about her legs, lay with his breast against her breast, close entwined. Soon she was breathing softly; and he, thus comforted, too, soon fell into a deep and dreamless sleep.

ABOUT THE AUTHOR

CHRISTOPHER ZEHNDER earned his bachelor of arts degree from Thomas Aquinas College in Santa Paula, California, and his master's in Theology from Holy Apostles College and Seminary in Cromwell, Connecticut. He is the general editor for the Catholic Textbook Project and has written four of the books in its history series, and is currently editing a history of Christendom from the ancient world to the Renaissance. In his native state of California, Mr. Zehnder edited two monthlies serving the Los Angeles region and the Bay Area. He has written for various publications on historical, political, and theological subjects. In 2017, he, with his wife, Katherine, and their children, returned to his ancestral Midwest, making their home in Central Ohio. Mr. and Mrs. Zehnder are lay members of the Order of Preachers (Dominicans).

www.ingramcontent.com/pod-product-compliance
Lightning Source LLC
Chambersburg PA
CBHW011213120626
46545CB00008B/2973